Empire and Nationhood

Empire and Nationhood

THE UNITED STATES, GREAT BRITAIN,
AND IRANIAN OIL, 1950–1954

Mary Ann Heiss

COLUMBIA UNIVERSITY PRESS

NEW YORK

Columbia University Press
Publishers Since 1893
New York   Chichester, West Sussex
Copyright © 1997 Columbia University Press

Library of Congress Cataloging-in-Publication Data
Heiss, Mary Ann, 1961–
    Empire and nationhood : the United States, Great Britain, and
Iranian oil, 1950–1954 / Mary Ann Heiss.
        p.   cm.
    Includes bibliographical references and index.
    ISBN 0–231–10818–4. — ISBN 0–231–10819–2 (pbk.)
    1. Petroleum industry and trade—Government ownership—Iran.
2. Anglo-Iranian Oil Dispute, 1951–1954.   3. Iran—Politics and
government—1941–1979.   I. Title.
HD9576.I62H45   1997
338.2′7282′0955—dc21   97–1146
                                                                    CIP

Casebound editions of Columbia University Press books are printed on
permanent and durable acid-free paper.

Printed in the United States of America
c 10 9 8 7 6 5 4 3 2 1
p 10 9 8 7 6 5 4 3 2 1

TO MY PARENTS

contents

acknowledgments

This book owes its existence to the few pages in Robert Divine's *Eisenhower and the Cold War* that discuss the formation of the Iranian oil consortium. I was intrigued by this topic, especially by the interplay between the public and private sectors that it suggested, and delighted to find no comprehensive account of either the consortium's creation or the Anglo-Iranian oil crisis that preceded it. The oil dispute and its ultimate resolution proved to be more complex subjects than I originally had expected; so did the conclusions I reached after reading the documents. And if this study is not precisely what I had envisioned when I started it almost a decade ago, it is at least one that seeks to address the subject in all its dimensions.

I have been fortunate to have had the support of numerous institutions and individuals during the many years it has taken to complete this study. For generous research support I am grateful to the Department of History, the Center for International Studies, and the Graduate School of The Ohio State University; the Society for Historians of American Foreign Relations; and the Harry S Truman Library Institute. I am especially indebted to the Truman Library, whose Dissertation Year Fellowship was indispensable to the completion of the first version of this project.

Even more important than this institutional support, though, has been the help I have received from individuals too numerous to thank in the limited space I have here. The friendly and competent research staffs at the National Archives, the Library of Congress, the Washington National Records Center, Princeton University, the Harry S Truman Library, the Dwight D. Eisenhower Library, and the Public Record Office made researching this book a less onerous task than it could have been. Martha Garland and Peter Hahn read and commented on the original version, for which I remain deeply grateful. James Goode, Diane B. Kunz, Douglas Little, and Mark Lytle all struggled through the manuscript at various stages, and I hope they will be gratified to see that many of their suggestions made their way into print. Many other people offered moral and intellectual support of various kinds, especially the diplomatic history gang at The Ohio State University and my colleagues and students at Kent State University. They know who they are, and so do I. Heartfelt thanks to each and every one of them.

No one has contributed more to this study than Michael J. Hogan, who saw it through more drafts than I am sure he would have liked. His patience, encouragement, and critical eye made him the best doctoral adviser imaginable, and these same qualities have made him the best of friends now. I am indeed fortunate to count myself among his students.

I am also grateful to Kate Wittenberg of Columbia University Press for believing in this project and expertly shepherding it through the publication process.

My longest-term debt is to my family. My sister, Donna, tolerated many hours of cutting and pasting note cards with all the good humor she could muster. My brother, Glen, generously provided musical and comic relief and a sympathetic ear on more occasions than I can count. And my parents, Edward C. and Mary Ann, supported my educational endeavors, morally as well as financially, without ever asking when I would finish graduate school and get a real job. My debt to them can never fully be repaid, although I hope they will accept this book as a first installment.

Empire and Nationhood

chapter 1

The Anglo-Iranian Oil Crisis:
AN OVERVIEW

This book examines the controversy surrounding the nationalization of the
Anglo-Iranian Oil Company (AIOC). It traces the events leading to Iran's
nationalization of the company in 1951 and details efforts to negotiate a settlement that would reconcile Iranian grievances against the AIOC with
British claims for compensation. Because the British and Iranians sought,
and ultimately received, U.S. aid in resolving their dispute, this book puts
the nationalization crisis in a tripartite framework. It reveals the global as
well as the regional nature of a struggle that historians have misapprehended
and follows that struggle to the autumn of 1954, when the United States took
the lead in organizing an international consortium to replace the AIOC.

No comprehensive history of the nationalization crisis in all its dimensions exists, despite its significance as one of the great recent struggles
between a developing country and a powerful multinational enterprise,
together with its government allies.[1] The episode is usually considered
within larger, more general accounts of Iranian history, the international oil
industry, or Anglo-American relations. The general histories of Iran and its
oil industry provide valuable insights into the range of Iranian political
motives, demands, and policy. Their use of Persian-language sources com-
pensates somewhat for the lack of Iranian government records, which oper-
ates as a limit on this and other studies.[2] Nevertheless, historians must use

these accounts carefully. Some are emotionally inspired and undocumented.[3] Others ignore, distort, or exaggerate the part that British and American leaders played in the nationalization crisis.[4]

Similar problems characterize other studies that treat the Anglo-Iranian oil dispute. Accounts of the international petroleum industry, often based on company records inaccessible to most scholars, tell us something about the inner workings of the major oil companies and their response to Iranian nationalization. But they concentrate on the commercial and financial aspects of the dispute, give short shrift to its geopolitical dimension, and sometimes rely on private conversations or interviews that are difficult to corroborate. The second volume of the official history of the AIOC during this period, based on company records that are now open to outside researchers, provides a generally narrow examination of the oil dispute that is especially weak on its international context.[5] Much the same is true of the literature on Anglo-American diplomacy. Although works in this category yield much useful information, they focus on more than the oil crisis and do not exploit fully the government records of both nations. As a result, they generally fail to detail the often conflicting, often coincident, motives behind British and American policy or to explore the shifting nature of Anglo-American relations during the nationalization dispute.[6] Accounts of the oil crisis itself are similarly deficient. They emphasize either its implications for international law or Britain's case against Iran before the International Court of Justice, instead of placing the crisis in a larger global and historical framework.[7] The only currently available comprehensive account of the crisis that uses primary sources, Mostafa Elm's *Oil, Power, and Principle*, reads in many spots like a memoir and must therefore be used with great caution.[8]

Generally speaking, then, existing accounts of the Iranian crisis are one sided or narrowly focused. For the most part they are grounded in research that is restricted by the authors' primary focus or area of concern. Unmindful that nationalization did not take place in a vacuum, they emphasize specific subjects, ignore others, and present a picture of the crisis that slights its international dimensions.

II

This book covers the nationalization imbroglio from a variety of angles. Drawing on archives in Great Britain and the United States, the book integrates British and U.S. policy to present a coherent analysis and uses similar sources, as well as the literature on Iran, to trace the Iranian side of the triangle, link the nationalization crisis to earlier and subsequent events, and place nationalization within its chronological and geopolitical contexts. After all, nationalization of the AIOC was more than just another episode in the often tenuous Anglo-Iranian relationship. The oil dispute grew out of long-term trends in British, Iranian, and international history and had a tremendous effect on both the world petroleum market and the international economy. Perhaps as important, the Anglo-Iranian controversy prompted the United States to assume a prominent, enduring role in the Persian Gulf region, with effects that are still being played out today. The United States became involved at every stage of the crisis, with public and private elites working incessantly for a solution that would deny the Soviet Union access to Iran and safeguard it for the West.

As this discussion suggests, this book explores the connection between the nationalization crisis and postwar developments in the United States and Great Britain. U.S. policy makers derived from World War II a renewed appreciation of their country's dependence on foreign petroleum resources and a heightened awareness of petroleum's importance to the security of the United States and its Western allies. The nationalization controversy threw both issues into bold relief. It also highlighted Great Britain's dependence on Iranian oil. For the British, Iranian oil was an economic as well as strategic asset. The AIOC's Iranian wells provided British consumers, and especially the British air force and navy, with an inexpensive source of petroleum and the British Exchequer with important foreign exchange at a time when the country's financial position was flagging. For these reasons the British did not believe they could surrender control of the AIOC to the Iranians.

In addition, the nationalization crisis exposed Washington's continuing dependence on the British to defend and guarantee Middle Eastern security. Because the United States could not single-handedly police the globe, it was forced to prop up Britain's position in Iran and elsewhere in order to prevent a potentially devastating loss of the Middle East to the Soviet Union. This U.S. reliance was a blessing for policy makers in London, who saw Anglo-American cooperation as the only way to preserve the informal British empire in the Middle East. Throughout the oil crisis British officials skillfully maneuvered their U.S. counterparts into becoming ever more involved but always on terms that suited Whitehall's purposes. In seeing British policy in the Iranian crisis as much more active and forceful than some scholars have recognized, my study complements the recent revisionist trend that disputes the view that after 1945 a hegemonic United States imposed its will on a helpless Britain.[9]

Eventually, however, U.S. involvement in the Iranian crisis proved to be a double-edged sword for London. Although U.S. aid ultimately preserved for the British some role in the operation of the Iranian oil industry, it also marked a first step toward the reversal of the British and American positions in the Middle East that would culminate in the Suez debacle of 1956. The Iranian nationalization crisis was thus a turning point for Anglo-American relations in the region—and indeed the world over.

The Anglo-Iranian controversy was equally significant as an outgrowth of Iranian nationalism, which erupted in the period after World War II. Nationalism, rather than a simple desire for greater oil revenues, motivated Iranian policy and sustained that policy when its fruits proved bitter. It helped to explain why Iran wanted Britain to abandon its exclusive control of the Iranian oil industry and why the Iranians persisted in the face of tremendous economic hardship. In addition, nationalism links the Anglo-Iranian dispute to earlier incidents in Iranian history, such as Reza Shah's decision in 1932 to cancel the British concession, and to nationalist movements in other parts of the developing world. It also helps to account for the decline of British power in Iran and in other parts of the world where British leaders refused to take nationalism as seriously as they might have.

The role that nationalism played in the oil dispute suggests another important aspect of the story: the clash of cultures that it evidenced between the industrialized West and the developing East. Western cultural prejudices were apparent throughout the oil dispute, because Anglo-American officials consistently used what Edward W. Said has termed *orientalism* when dealing with their Iranian counterparts, especially Prime Minister Mohammed Mossadeq, whom they considered inferior, childlike, and even feminine. They often referred to Mossadeq with gendered language that revealed their conviction that he was neither manly enough for international politics nor fit to hold the office of prime minister. They condemned as personal quirks or eccentricities what were accepted forms of behavior in Iran, failed to see Mossadeq as their equal, and dismissed him as an unworthy adversary whose position did not matter. Anglo-American cables, reports, and other private documents judged Mossadeq and other Iranians by prevailing Western standards of acceptable behavior, instead of measuring them against what was acceptable in Iran.[10] Mossadeq revealed cultural stereotypes of his own, most notably a tendency to demonize the British and blame them for everything bad that happened in Iran. Because he did not completely trust the British or their motives, Mossadeq found it difficult to conduct open and effective negotiations with them. These kinds of attitudes, held by both sides in the dispute, did nothing to contribute to a settlement of the Iranian oil dispute and in fact probably helped to prolong it.

Finally, the Iranian nationalization crisis played a major role in shaping future events in Iran and throughout the Middle East. It occasioned the emergence of the United States as a major regional power and began the transformation of Anglo-American roles in the region that was completed in 1956. It set the stage for twenty-five years of close relations between the United States and the shah of Iran, Mohammad Reza Pahlavi, who emerged after the mid-1950s as the strongest ally of the United States in the Middle East.[11] And it contributed to the anti-Western sentiment that exploded in Iran in the late 1970s, driving the shah into exile and ushering in the Islamic Revolution. Although the leaders of Iran's nationalization drive during the 1950s and those of the revolution during the 1970s differed in many ways, they shared a desire to rid their homeland of foreign influence. Indeed, direct links between the latter movement and the former could be found in the slogans shouted throughout Tehran in 1978 and 1979: "Remember Musaddiq" and "Down with the American Shah."[12]

As this discussion suggests, the nationalization controversy weaves together some of the major themes in recent American, British, and Iranian history. It points to the importance of the Middle East and its oil for the economic and national security policies of the great powers, and it connects this development to the character of the Anglo-American relationship and to the rise of nationalism in underdeveloped countries. Before moving to the oil dispute itself, however, it is essential to establish the historical context for the nationalization crisis, the roots of which were set when the British first became involved in the Iranian oil industry.

III

Britain's exclusive control of Iranian oil began in 1901, when Australian mining entrepreneur William Knox D'Arcy obtained a 480,000-square-mile concession to extract, transport, and refine oil in all but the five northern provinces of what was then known as Persia. With financial backing from the Burmah Oil Company D'Arcy formed the Persian Petroleum Exploration Syndicate. In 1908 D'Arcy's company found substantial quantities of oil, and one year later, with additional assistance from Burmah Oil, it was reconstituted as the Anglo-Iranian Oil Company (then known as the Anglo-Persian Oil Company [APOC]). The company began operations on the eve of World War I, coincident with the British navy's conversion from coal to oil.

To ensure adequate and affordable oil supplies in the event of war First Lord of the Admiralty Winston S. Churchill convinced the British government in 1914 to purchase 51 percent of APOC's stock and to arrange for the Royal Navy to purchase oil from the company at a discount.[13] These two developments, which seemed so harmless in 1914, would pose serious problems for the British during the 1950s. In the short term, however, new capital provided by the British government enabled APOC drastically to expand its operations. Production increased from 273,000 tons in 1914, to 897,000 tons in 1918, to 1,385,000 tons in 1920. Royalties to the Persian government, set by agreement at 16 percent of the company's profits, reached £470,000 in 1920.[14]

Although the Anglo-Persian arrangement appeared to benefit both sides, tensions below the surface threatened the relationship. Royalties fell short of what the Persian government expected. The Persians also complained about the company's refusal to pay royalties on its non-Persian operations, even though they involved the use of Persian oil. In addition, the Persians decried APOC's efforts to hold the government in Tehran responsible for tribal sabotage of the company's operations and lamented its tendency to charge the government excessive rates for the shipment of oil inside Persia. To resolve these differences and thus preserve the concession, which was vital to oil-poor Britain, the two parties signed the Armitage-Smith agreement of 1920. This agreement met most of Persia's demands, notably its call for the inclusion of the company's non-Persian operations in the calculation of royalty payments. In British eyes the agreement constituted a permanent solution to Persia's discontent with APOC. To the Persians, however, it was merely a stopgap until more advantageous terms could be arranged.

Reza Shah's assumption of the peacock throne in 1925 set the stage for Persian redress. An iron-willed military officer with grand plans for Persia's future, Reza Shah initiated discussions with APOC in 1928. His goal was to revise the Armitage-Smith agreement in order to increase Persia's oil revenues. After the onset of the Great Depression, however, the British were reluctant to increase royalties, the talks collapsed, and APOC's royalties to the Persian government followed the downward spiral of Persian production and global prices, dropping from £1,437,000 in 1929 to £307,000 two years later. Frustrated by these developments, Reza Shah canceled the company's concession in November 1932. This did not mean nationalization, because Reza Shah was willing to negotiate a new concession with APOC. But it did signify a new-found Persian awareness of the value of the country's oil and a determination to use that oil for Persian, rather than British, purposes.[15]

The resulting drama foreshadowed in many ways the crisis of the 1950s. The British government laid the case before the League of Nations, decrying the illegality of Persia's unilateral cancellation of the concession. The Persians responded by denouncing the British government for interfering in what they saw as an internal Persian affair. They also pointed out that the Armitage-Smith agreement had not been ratified by the Majlis (or parliament) and therefore disputed its legality. Two decades later both sides would make virtually the same arguments when the British took the Iranians before the International Court of Justice and the United Nations Security Council. In the first episode, moreover, can be discerned the sparks of a smoldering Persian resentment of APOC, sparks that finally ignited the fiery nationalism of the 1950s. Unlike their successors, however, Persian leaders in the 1930s had no desire to run the oil industry. Although loath to admit it, they needed APOC, not to mention the oil royalties that had become an important source of revenue for the Persian government. Practical financial considerations thus defeated nationalist resentment and forced the Persians to sign a new agreement with the company in 1933.

The new agreement, negotiated under the auspices of the League of Nations, appeared to settle all points of contention between the two parties. It provided a more straightforward formula for calculating royalties and guaranteed Persia an annual minimum payment of £975,000. Other provisions gave the Persians more independence from the British company and more control over their oil, reduced by 80 percent the concession area, promised that qualified Persians would receive managerial positions within the company, and pledged to hire only Persians for the company's many unskilled jobs. The only provision that directly benefited APOC was an extension of the concession's expiration date from 1961 to 1993. In hindsight this provision had little significance for the British but fueled Persian discontent that APOC would control the nation's oil resources until almost the end of the century. The agreement, which seemed to resolve a host of outstanding problems between the Persian government and APOC, ushered in a period of peaceful relations between the two parties that lasted until World War II.[16]

Wartime conditions conspired to dash hopes in Iran (as Persia was known after 1935) for greater control over local oil resources. After the German invasion of the Soviet Union in June 1941, Iran became an important artery for the passage of Allied supplies to the Soviet Union. British and Soviet troops thus occupied Iran in August, much to the dismay of Reza Shah, who favored the Axis powers and whose troops resisted the Allied move. When this resistance collapsed, Reza Shah abdicated in favor of his twenty-one-year-old son, Mohammad Reza Pahlavi, who agreed in January 1942 that British and Soviet troops could remain in Iran until six months after the end of the war. Although not covered in the occupation agreement, U.S. troops were also on hand to operate Iran's ports and railways to facilitate the movement of lend-lease goods to the Soviet Union. As the extensive literature on wartime developments underscores, this involvement marked a turning point in U.S. policy.[17] Until then U.S. officials had left the other great powers to their own devices in Iran. With the outbreak of war, however, U.S. officials came to see Iran's strategic importance and value to the Allied war effort and endeavored to shape their policies accordingly.

Indeed, U.S. leaders began looking beyond Iran's wartime value as a corridor to the Soviet Union to its importance as a supplier of petroleum. Wartime consumption convinced them of the finite nature of domestic oil reserves and led to a search for new reserves abroad and for new ways to safeguard existing sources. Although U.S. government officials saw Iran primarily as a buffer between the Soviet Union and the valuable U.S. oil interests in the Persian Gulf, notably in Saudi Arabia, some U.S. companies sought concessions in the area of southern Iran abrogated by the AIOC in 1933. These efforts collapsed, as did Soviet attempts to gain a concession in northern Iran, when the Iranians decided in September 1944 to suspend all concession talks until after the war.[18] Nevertheless, Soviet opposition to this decision and the competition for oil among erstwhile allies signaled differences that would make Iran a diplomatic battleground in the early cold war.

After World War II the Soviets made withdrawal of their troops from Iran contingent upon receipt of an oil concession in the northern part of the country and supported a separatist movement that aimed to liberate the northern province of Azerbaijan from Tehran's control. The resulting dispute was one of the first to go before the nascent United Nations, although Iranian premier Ahmad Qavam ultimately rendered U.N. action unnecessary. By agreeing to Soviet demands for an oil concession he secured the withdrawal of Soviet troops and recognition of the Azerbaijan issue as an internal Iranian problem. In the months that followed, however, Qavam delayed submission of the oil agreement to the Majlis, which was legally charged with affirming foreign concessions. If Qavam thus sought to close the door to a Soviet concession, it was locked forever by a new law sponsored by future prime minister Mohammed Mossadeq and passed by the Majlis in November 1947. The law was both a direct descendant of the 1932 cancellation of APOC's concession and a lineal ancestor of the 1951 nationalization laws. Aside from prohibiting new concessions to foreigners, including the Soviets, it instructed the Iranian government to hammer out a better agreement with the AIOC.[19] In a single stroke the 1947 law thus delivered a deathblow to Soviet designs in northern Iran and set the stage for the Anglo-Iranian dispute of the 1950s.

The United States was not a direct participant in the Irano-Soviet dispute, but it had not been oblivious to the unfolding struggle. On the contrary, along with George Kennan's "long telegram" and the Truman Doctrine, U.S. opposition to Soviet tactics in Iran signaled the development of the containment policy. The State Department worried lest Soviet gains in northern Iran jeopardize the British position in the south and clear a path to Soviet expansion through the Persian Gulf to the oil-rich Middle East, an area of major strategic as well as economic importance to the United States and its allies in Western Europe. Guided by this conclusion, Secretary of State James F. Byrnes defended Iran's sovereignty against Soviet encroachment and sought to mobilize the United Nations against Moscow's policy. The Soviet-American confrontation that resulted highlighted the value that both East and West placed on oil and on Iran's importance in controlling it. It also signaled an increasingly rigid U.S. policy toward the Soviet Union, led to the first U.S. assessments of Iran's importance to Western security, and laid the basis for U.S. intervention in the 1950s.[20]

Once World War II had dramatized the importance of oil as a weapon of both war and peace, planners in Washington had begun to study how best to protect oil-rich areas from Soviet aggrandizement. Their goal was to ensure adequate oil supplies to the West while denying them to the East. In Iran this policy manifested itself in U.S. military missions to the Iranian army and gendarmerie and in the sale of surplus U.S. military equipment to the Iranian government.[21] Through these initiatives the United States hoped to buttress the Iranian government against communist-inspired subversion or Soviet aggression. Washington also hoped to inspire Iranian goodwill toward the United States and thereby boost U.S. prestige in Iran.

Postwar policy makers reiterated the wartime belief that Iran constituted the first line of defense against Soviet penetration of the Persian Gulf. Their thinking encapsulated an early version of what later became known as the domino theory. If the Soviets could dominate Iran, as the Joint Chiefs of Staff explained in 1946, the Soviets could also control the oil-rich areas of Iraq and Saudi Arabia. The United States and its allies would be cut off from a resource deemed essential to victory in a modern war. For this reason alone the Soviets had to be denied even a modicum of influence in Iran, lest they use it to attack Western interests there and throughout the Middle East. Nor was oil the only thing that made Iran important to the

West. Iran lay astride vital channels of communication to parts of the world beyond the Middle East, to India, for example, and to the eastern Mediterranean. If the Western position in Iran gave way to Soviet penetration, or so U.S. policy makers feared, the security of these areas would be imperiled as well. The United States would be forced back to the Atlantic and the western hemisphere, and Great Britain would be isolated and increasingly vulnerable to Soviet pressure.[22] For all these reasons postwar policy makers continued to supply U.S. military advisers and matériel to the government in Tehran.

For other reasons, however, the United States would not provide economic aid on a scale comparable to the assistance going to Greece and Turkey under the Truman Doctrine or to Western Europe under the Marshall Plan. Iran, U.S. policy makers argued, was in better economic shape than Greece, Turkey, and the countries of Western Europe and was thus more capable of containing potential threats to its internal stability and security. The corruption, waste, and inefficiency that plagued most Iranian governments also prompted U.S. analysts to use the China analogy and to limit assistance until the Iranians made greater efforts to help themselves. In addition, policy makers in Washington feared that large-scale aid would be difficult to explain to the U.S. public or would provoke Soviet intervention and thereby lead to the very danger they sought to preclude. Besides, they said, Great Britain was primarily responsible for the defense of the Middle East region as a whole, and Iran in particular. Independent initiatives might undermine Britain's position in the area.[23] Taken together these considerations meant that Iran fell short of top priority in Washington's immediate postwar planning, its strategic location and oil reserves notwithstanding.

Just as U.S. policy makers were wrestling with the postwar importance of the Middle East to Western security, so were the nations of the region redefining their relationship with the great powers. During the immediate postwar period nationalist movements throughout the developing world aimed to expel foreign powers and seize control of their own affairs. Leaders in India and other countries with a colonial heritage sought the overthrow of European imperialist powers, in most cases Great Britain or France. In countries that were not under formal colonial control, Egypt being a case in point, they sought the withdrawal of foreign troops or the nationalization of natural resources or industrial assets long dominated by foreign interests.[24]

This was the case in Iran as well, where nationalist opposition to foreign domination had led to the 1947 law prohibiting new oil concessions and demanding better terms for Iran from the AIOC. In actuality, Iranian nationalism had been evident much earlier, in the struggle against a 1907 plan for Anglo-Russian partition of the country, for example, and in Iranian opposition to a 1919 Anglo-Persian agreement that would have made Iran a virtual protectorate of Great Britain. From its earliest days, then, Iranian nationalism had aimed to eradicate foreign influence from the country. This same aim would be evident in the battle with Britain over nationalization of the oil industry during the 1950s. Instead of creating an effective central government that would attend to the needs of the Iranian people, as Richard Cottam argues, Mossadeq's nationalist movement focused on outside forces by seeking to eliminate British influence from all facets of Iranian life.[25]

For their part, the American and British governments initially tried to accommodate the rising tide of nationalism, especially in countries that were potential allies in the cold war. The United States saw nationalism as preferable to communism. The British agreed. As Wm. Roger Louis has pointed out, "accommodation of moderate nationalism to prevent political extremism" was a principal tenet of the first postwar Labour government.[26] Guided by this tenet, the British hoped to encourage economic and political modernization as a way to preserve their influence and preempt political revolutions in underdeveloped countries. But this strategy was easier to design than to implement. In Iran as elsewhere, nationalist elements viewed British policy with suspicion and would settle for nothing less than complete independence from all vestiges of foreign control. Nor was this the only problem. Despite a U.S. loan in 1945, the British lacked the financial resources to promote economic modernization and development in underdeveloped countries. The sterling crises of 1947 and 1949 made a bad situation worse. Under the weight of these events the British were forced to retrench their overseas commitments, first in Germany and Greece, where they asked the United States to shoulder a larger share of the burden of postwar stabilization, and then in Iran, where the British also sought to bolster their position with economic and diplomatic assistance from the United States.[27]

Although the British were willing to step aside in Germany and Greece, the economic benefits Great Britain derived from its association with Iran made British leaders reluctant to see their position in Iran supplanted by the United States. They resented U.S. efforts to promote political and economic reforms that would make the government in Tehran more efficient and self-supporting. To the British way of thinking these reforms would compromise the British position in Tehran, diminish the financial benefits that London secured from its relations with Iran, weaken British prestige throughout the Middle East, and set a precedent that would encourage similar developments elsewhere. It was better, they thought, to maintain Iran's historic dependence on Great Britain even if U.S. assistance was necessary to do so. The Iranian crisis would ultimately prove the folly of such a strategy, as U.S. involvement in resolving the dispute did not lead to a strengthening of Britain's position so much as a consolidation and expansion of the position of the United States.

As the preceding discussion suggests, the Anglo-Iranian oil controversy provides a good illustration of the early differences between U.S. and British responses to the nationalist aspirations of developing countries, particularly countries with substantial oil resources. On the U.S. side oil companies sought to assuage nationalist sentiment in order to safeguard their concessions and prevent nationalization. They agreed for the first time to give the Venezuelan government an equal share of oil profits and then used this fifty-fifty principle in subsequent negotiations with the oil-producing states of the Middle East. The State Department endorsed this policy. In the case of Saudi Arabia, for example, the State Department encouraged the Arabian-American Oil Company (ARAMCO) to accept Saudi demands for the payment of higher royalties and supported an arrangement whereby the company would deduct the increase from taxes owed the U.S. government.[28] The Saudi agreement, signed in December 1950, profoundly influenced events in Iran, where the British were pursuing a policy markedly different from the one favored in Washington.

British policy makers and AIOC officials alike had historically turned a blind eye to Iranian demands for larger royalties, limitations on the duration of the AIOC's concession, and greater local control over the oil industry. They had also failed to take seriously complaints about the company's interference in Iran's internal affairs and its tendency to act as a sovereign entity, exempt from Iranian law. Some British leaders even went so far as to criticize U.S. companies for seeking to assuage nationalist sentiments, arguing that such a strategy would undermine Britain's position in countries like Iran.

The negotiations prescribed by the 1947 law illustrated the determination of British leaders to maintain their control over the Iranian oil industry, as well as the depth of Iranian opposition to the AIOC. At the start of the negotiations the Iranians submitted a twenty-five–point protest against the company's failure to fulfill the provisions of the 1933 agreement. They complained of the disparity between the oil revenues of the company and of the Iranian government, £250 million and £90 million, respectively, in the years 1945 to 1950. Also featured on the Iranians' list were the company's decision to sell Iranian oil to the British navy and air force at huge discounts, the long-term nature of its concession, and its dilatory and halfhearted efforts to Iranianize its operations. Especially infuriating was the AIOC's use of unskilled Indian workers and its reluctance to give Iranians managerial positions within the company. Well aware of the comparatively generous fifty-fifty principle that now governed U.S. companies in Venezuela, the Iranians demanded a similar arrangement. They also wanted representation on the AIOC's board of directors, elevation of Iranian workers to positions of authority, the right to examine the company's books, and periodic review of the concession itself.[29]

The AIOC seemed willing to pay higher royalties and to speed the pace of Iranianization but was reluctant to consider concessions on other fundamental issues. Iran was Britain's largest single foreign investment and the AIOC's largest operation, providing 76 percent of the company's crude oil in 1949. It thus constituted an asset of enormous, and seemingly irreplaceable, wealth. For this reason the AIOC kept the negotiations of 1948 and 1949 focused on such issues as royalties and Iranianization, where it could afford concessions without losing control of the industry. No doubt concerned about the efficiency and continued profitability of their operations, and blind to the spirit of Iranian nationalism, company officials refused to discuss Tehran's demands for representation on the AIOC's board, access to its books, and periodic review of the concession. In a rare example of self-criticism the AIOC's official historian argued astutely that company officials sealed their fate when they failed to realize that a desire for greater control, not just increased revenue, motivated Iranian policy.[30]

Because of their differences the two sides finally reached what turned out to be an unsatisfactory arrangement, known as the Gass-Golshayan Agreement or, more commonly, the Supplemental Oil Agreement. Signed on 17 July 1949, its main provisions included an increase in Iran's per ton royalty from 4 to 6 shillings and an annual payment of 1 shilling per ton in taxes to the Iranian government. Once the Majlis had ratified the agreement, both provisions would be retroactive to 1948. In addition, the agreement guaranteed a minimum annual payment to Iran of £4 million and a different basis for determining the price of oil sold in Iran.[31] Company officials proudly hailed the supplemental agreement as the best oil pact in the Middle East and said that it would provide Iran with larger royalties than an equal division of profits.

Many Iranians, however, especially some members of the Majlis, thought otherwise. In their eyes the agreement was a fraud perpetrated by traitors who wished to perpetuate British domination of the country. It did not address many of Iran's long-standing grievances against the AIOC, failed to safeguard its national interest, and deserved to be rejected if only because it affirmed the 1933 accord, which critics considered an invalid concession negotiated under duress and signed by an autocratic regime that did not represent the will of the people. Opposition deputies voiced their views when the Majlis debated the new agreement in late July. They monopolized the floor, blocked the government's efforts to make a case for the agreement, and prevented a vote before the Fifteenth Majlis expired on 28 July. A decision on the oil question was thus postponed until early 1950, when the new Majlis would convene.[32]

IV

The reasons for government haste in submitting the supplemental agreement to the Majlis are uncertain, as is whether the Fifteenth Majlis would have rejected the agreement had a vote been taken. What is certain is that the new agreement served as a catalyst for Iranian opposition against the AIOC and that it provided the opportunity for a handful of opponents to consolidate their ranks and turn the elections for the Sixteenth Majlis into a referendum on the oil issue. Because the agreement failed to address important Iranian grievances, it united the Iranian public in unprecedented opposition to both the company and the British government. As this book will show, the failure of British leaders to recognize the strength of this opposition cost them their monopoly on Iranian oil. It also led to a rift in Iran's relations with the West that still runs deep more than four decades later.

chapter 2

Too Little, Too Late
THE STAGE IS SET FOR NATIONALIZATION

The battle lines that characterized the Iranian nationalization crisis were obvious throughout 1950. For Iranian nationalists the goal was control of their nation's oil resources. Such control was a matter of national pride. It was a symbol of their country's independence and one way to its economic and political modernization. For the British the goal was to protect the AIOC's Iranian concession and, by extension, Britain's entire system of overseas investments.

These considerations, not to mention the importance of Iranian oil to Britain's economic prosperity and international prestige, produced a firm and uncompromising reaction against Iranian demands for greater control. For the Americans, at least initially, the goal was a workable compromise that protected legitimate British rights, assuaged Iranian nationalism, and safeguarded U.S. interests in an area of great economic and strategic significance. To the U.S. way of thinking only flexibility and compromise could defuse anti-British sentiment in Iran and avoid nationalization or a potentially disastrous loss of Iranian oil to the Soviets. Guided by this thinking, Washington's policy during this first year of the oil dispute consisted of public displays of neutrality but private criticism of British rigidity. Only after this early approach to the problem had failed did U.S. policy makers become directly involved in seeking a solution to the Anglo-Iranian imbroglio.

II

A satisfactory settlement with the AIOC was one key to Iran's economic development. The severe winter of 1949–50 had hurt that country's agricultural production and added to the economic troubles that had plagued it since the war. More fundamentally, Iran faced the usual problems associated with a peasant, agriculturally oriented economy, including a regressive tax system, serious imbalance of payments, inadequate industrial infrastructure, and poor communication and transportation networks.

To solve its economic problems Iran had embarked on its Seven-Year Plan of "social development through economic improvement." Drawn up by a U.S. firm under the direction of Max W. Thornburg, a former executive of Standard Oil of California, the $650-million plan was a pet project of the young shah, Mohammad Reza Pahlavi, who had spent the closing months of 1949 seeking U.S. economic assistance to finance both the Seven-Year Plan and substantial increases in Iran's military capacity. According to the shah, such expenditures were necessary to guarantee Iran's future. The Seven-Year Plan would bring the country into the twentieth century, and increased military capabilities would allow Iran to defend itself against Soviet expansion. U.S. officials saw things differently. To finance the Seven-Year Plan they recommended more efficient use of Iran's oil revenue and assistance from such institutions as the World Bank. On the subject of military increases Secretary of State Dean Acheson and others reminded the shah of China's Chiang Kai-shek, whose preoccupation with military hardware had contributed to his defeat. With the prospects of substantial U.S. aid thus dashed the Iranian government became increasingly dependent on oil revenue—to be determined by the Supplemental Oil Agreement—to underwrite its military program and economic modernization.[1]

Ratification of the oil agreement would also help to stabilize Iranian politics. The Fifteenth Majlis had adjourned in August 1949 after tabling the supplemental agreement, and parliamentary elections were expected to continue through early 1950. In the meantime Prime Minister Mohammad Sa'ed was hamstrung in his efforts to implement reforms designed to eliminate corruption and centralize Iranian politics. Sa'ed's real forte was foreign affairs. During World War II he had served as ambassador to Moscow and then minister of foreign affairs. Yet despite his lack of experience in domestic politics, the shah had appointed Sa'ed prime minister in 1944 and again in 1948, and Sa'ed had directed the 1949 negotiations with the AIOC that led to the supplemental agreement. Neither Sa'ed nor the shah believed that the oil question would be a major issue in the Majlis elections. Both seemed confident that the oil agreement could be ratified if the AIOC agreed to make minor, but unspecified, alterations before it was submitted to the Majlis, and both privately prodded British diplomats in Tehran to push the company toward such concessions. Despite their common thinking on the oil situation, the relationship between Sa'ed and the shah was troubled. The shah thought Sa'ed weak and indecisive, "incapable of managing the Government," but nevertheless probably the only politician in Iran willing to take the supplemental agreement to the Majlis. And until the agreement had won ratification, the shah was resigned to retaining Sa'ed as prime minister.[2]

Iran's dependence on the oil agreement's ratification raised problems for the pact in Tehran, where critics considered it a symbol of Iran's past, not a route to its economic and political salvation. Leading the opposition was a loose coalition of social, economic, and political groups organized in the National Front. The front was not a political party in the Western sense. It had neither the elaborate platform nor the strict party-line discipline that usually accompany such organizations. Rather, it was an umbrella group that drew its strength from the people and worked through the early months of 1950 to mobilize sentiment against both the oil agreement and the Sa'ed government, which the National Front believed was under British control. The National Front's social and financial support came from members of the urban middle class—students, artisans, shopkeepers, professionals, politicized bazaar merchants, and the intelligentsia—as well as from numerous radical antiforeign religious and clerical elements. Politically, its supporters spanned the spectrum of ideological beliefs. On the left was the anticommunist, labor-dominated Toilers' Party led by Mozaffar Baqai and Khalil Maleki; on the right was the Pan-Iran or National Party, composed of middle- and lower middle-class secondary school students and athletic society toughs; and in the middle was the Iran Party, which drew its primary support from technocrats, professionals, and university students. The front's disparate members were united only by their struggle against "the court-military complex" and "the British-owned oil company." Their immediate goal was rejection of the supplemental agreement; their ultimate aim was the implementation of parliamentary reforms—including limitations on the shah's ability to intervene in politics—that would lead Iran to democracy and real independence.[3]

The National Front's de facto leader was Mohammed Mossadeq, an intensely nationalistic septuagenarian who had dedicated his life to purging foreign influence from Iran. A member of Iran's upper class and a descendant of the Qajar dynasty, Mossadeq had earned a doctorate in law from

Neuchâtel University in Switzerland. His subsequent government posts included stints as governor-general of Fars and Azerbaijan, minister of finance, and minister of foreign affairs. His legislative career began in 1920 when he was elected to the Fifth Majlis as a deputy from Tehran. He was imprisoned in 1940 for criticizing Reza Shah's drift toward dictatorship and gained his freedom the following year only after the Allies forced Reza Shah into exile.[4]

After becoming the leading deputy from Tehran in the Fourteenth Majlis, Mossadeq launched a campaign to end foreign influence in Iran, the most notable component of which was the 1944 law prohibiting new oil concessions without Majlis approval. As we have seen, this law led not only to the denial to the Soviet Union of an oil concession in northern Iran but also to the renegotiation of the AIOC's concession that resulted in the supplemental agreement. As a defender of Iran's national rights Mossadeq enjoyed tremendous support among the Iranian people, who perceived him as a man of honesty, integrity, and true patriotism. During late 1949 and early 1950 he mobilized his supporters in Tehran against the supplemental agreement, which he denounced as a humiliating extension of Britain's control over Iran's oil resources. Upon assuming the leadership of the seven-member National Front faction of the Sixteenth Majlis on 9 February, Mossadeq called for the agreement's rejection and then for the outright nationalization of the AIOC.[5]

Initially, Mossadeq's position had limited appeal. No more than a handful of Majlis deputies favored nationalization, and the idea had no support in the Senate, the elitist upper house provided for in the Constitution of 1906 but not formally established until 1949.[6] As a body drawn from the most conservative elements of the Iranian population, the Senate was bound to oppose Mossadeq's budding campaign for nationalization. After all, such a move would threaten the traditional British interests that had made some senators wealthy and powerful. The shah and other monied groups, including landed aristocrats and merchants with ties to international markets, joined the Senate in denouncing any talk of nationalization.[7]

Also opposed to nationalization was the communist Tudeh Party, which owed its allegiance to Moscow and sought to further Soviet interests in Iran. Although the Tudeh had been forced underground after an assassination attempt on the shah in 1949, it enjoyed substantial support among Iranian workers, especially those in the oil industry, and among university students. For the Tudeh nationalization was a U.S.-inspired plot to supplant the British in Iran to the long-term detriment of the Soviet Union, and its newspaper *Mardum* repeatedly denounced the idea. The party would occa-

sionally change its tune and ally with the National Front, but in 1950 it bit-
terly opposed both nationalization and the nationalist movement, which it
saw as a threat to the Tudeh's position as the best-organized political group
in Iran.[8]

The Senate and Tudeh positions notwithstanding, Mossadeq's campaign
for nationalization encouraged Prime Minister Sa'ed to seek a larger stake
for Iranians in the AIOC's operations and more generous royalty payments
than specified in the supplemental agreement. Success in these efforts
would help assuage nationalist sentiment and add to the funds available for
Iran's modernization. Both Sa'ed and the shah remained convinced that
only these kinds of concessions could ensure Majlis ratification of the oil
agreement. And until they had been obtained, Sa'ed refused to submit the
agreement to the legislature for what seemed certain defeat.[9]

For their part the British adopted what the United States saw as a take-
it-or-leave-it attitude with regard to the supplemental agreement. The
Foreign Office believed that further negotiations would lead to a never-end-
ing spiral of additional demands and further concessions. As Alan Leavett
of the Eastern Department of the Foreign Office reported in January, "The
Persian appetite for concessions 'grows with what it feeds on' and any
weakening of our present attitude at this stage would instantly wreck whatever chances we may have of getting ratification." In addition, Leavett and
his colleagues were convinced that company officials had already gone far
enough in yielding to Iranian demands and that further concessions would
be fruitless. Iranian opposition was "based not on any objective assessment
of the reasonableness of the agreement but on emotion and prejudice,"
Leavett said. He and his colleagues saw "no reason to suppose that any
practicable further concessions" would secure ratification. After all, the
Iranians at this point had merely expressed general dissatisfaction with the
agreement; they had not demanded any specific modifications. Under these
circumstances, Leavett said, neither the AIOC nor the British government
would budge an inch.[10]

This British attitude later prompted Dean Acheson to write that "never
had so few lost so much so stupidly and so fast."[11] What the British saw as
"emotion and prejudice" in Iran, U.S. officials saw as a fervent nationalism
that had to be assuaged if the supplemental agreement were to be approved
and all oil concessions in the Middle East were to be preserved. In addition,
the State Department worried that British inflexibility would undermine the
moderate Sa'ed government, allow revolutionary nationalists like Mossadeq to triumph, and push the Iranians into the Soviet camp, thereby de-
priving the West of Iranian oil. That oil was important for the reconstruc-

tion and rearmament of Western Europe, and replacing it would not be easy. The U.S. ambassador in Tehran, John C. Wiley, chastised his British counterpart for Britain's refusal to consider concessions beyond those already included in the supplemental agreement. To his way of thinking, once the AIOC decided to renegotiate the 1933 accord, it was bound to continue the negotiations until both sides were satisfied.[12] George C. McGhee, the assistant secretary of state for Near Eastern and African affairs, made a similar point in a heated discussion with AIOC representatives in late January. When company officials protested that additional concessions to Iran would leave them with "nothing in the till," McGhee, an oil man himself, responded with angry sarcasm. He had read the AIOC's annual report, McGhee said, and the company's "profits were still far from disappearing." He went on to note the agreements that U.S. oil companies had made with such countries as Venezuela. These agreements included better terms than the AIOC would concede to Iran—terms that were necessary to assuage anti-American and anti-Western sentiment and thus protect U.S. and Western interests. The British company, McGhee implied, should follow the U.S. example. It should "deal with the situation realistically by recognizing the legitimate demands of [the Iranian government]."[13]

To be sure, Acheson and other U.S. policy makers worried that "too much 'take'" on the part of the Iranians was as dangerous as "too little 'give'" on the part of the British. Iranian leaders requested the "good offices and moderate support" of the United States in resolving the dispute with Britain, but U.S. officials refused to become directly involved. Such involvement would be difficult to justify to the British, U.S. officials said, and would run the risk of encouraging Iran's desire to renegotiate the supplemental agreement.[14] Unofficially, however, U.S. policy makers worked closely with the British to resolve the Anglo-Iranian imbroglio. A close working relationship squared with the spirit of cooperation to which both countries aspired and with the leading role that Britain played in Iran and throughout the Middle East. U.S. officials wanted to reinforce Britain's position in the region, both as a prop to stability there and as a barrier to Soviet expansion.[15] At the same time, however, they continued to level strong criticism against British policy and to press the AIOC for additional concessions.

Instead of additional concessions, however, the Foreign Office conceived of a public information campaign that would educate the Iranians to the errors of their ways. By all measures public opinion in Iran ran decidedly against the agreement. The National Front's extensive anti-AIOC campaign played on the nationalistic sentiments of the Iranian people and fomented popular opposition to ratification of the pact. Meanwhile the

Sa'ed government did little to counter the growing impression that the agreement perpetuated foreign control over Iran's national resources at the expense of its economic and political interests. In February 1950 Sir John Le Rougetel, the British ambassador in Tehran, went so far as to privately accuse Iranian officials of waging a propaganda campaign against the supplemental agreement and of inspiring Wiley's pessimism about the prospects for ratification.[16]

Le Rougetel and others argued that the British needed a countercampaign to inform the Iranians of the benefits that would accrue from ratification. "There is still a conspicuous absence of enlightenment," he complained, and "it will not be provided by the Persians themselves." Under these circumstances, Le Rougetel argued, the AIOC should allow its "local representative some degree of freedom in explaining the value of the Agreement."[17] Similar recommendations came from other quarters. Valentine G. Lawford, counselor of the British embassy in Tehran, noted that the general public sentiment regarding the oil agreement was "I do not understand the Supplemental Agreement but I am against it." Alan Leavett urged the AIOC to act before the Majlis met to consider the agreement, thereby countering what he predicted would be a continuing "campaign of abuse and misrepresentation" by Iranian nationalists. The new British ambassador in Tehran, Sir Francis Shepherd, agreed. Shepherd's diplomatic career began in the 1920s and included service in Peru, Haiti, El Salvador, and the Netherlands East Indies. After arriving in Tehran in the spring of 1950, he warned that something had to be done to "familiarize Deputies and Senators with the main points of the [Supplemental] Agreement." Otherwise, he said, it might be rejected.[18]

Despite these and other pleas, AIOC officials were at first dead set against a company-sponsored information campaign. It was up to the Iranian government, they argued, to educate the public and the Majlis to the benefits of the supplemental agreement. Any effort on the company's part to sell the agreement would be construed as interference in Iran's domestic affairs and would undoubtedly backfire. At least one member of the British embassy in Tehran, Valentine Lawford, agreed, telling the shah that it was incumbent on the Iranian government to "do some propaganda." "It must surely be wrong in principle," he later elaborated, "for a large concern like the A.I.O.C. to tout their own cause 'round the Persian bazaars." The result of such an effort, Lawford concluded, "would probably be the reverse of what was intended."[19]

Given the highly charged political situation in Tehran, it was unlikely that a British information campaign would have done much good. The

National Front's attacks on the supplemental agreement had found a receptive audience, both within the Majlis and among the people of Tehran, and
had kept the agreement from coming up for debate in the Majlis. With popular emotion seemingly against the oil agreement the AIOC would sanction
an information campaign only if it was "closely coordinated with the
[Iranian] government" and had its approval. But according to Le Rougetel,
even Iranian officials "who profess[ed] friendship for England" were reluctant to throw their weight behind the agreement.[20] This was true of Prime
Minister Sa'ed, who was widely regarded as pro-British. Sa'ed had been
reappointed to the premiership for the express purpose of securing ratification of the supplemental agreement. But reluctance to "incur the odium" of
the agreement's critics in the Majlis kept him from publicly supporting it,
even in the face of pressure from the shah, who appreciated both the difficulties involved in securing ratification and the importance of increasing
Iran's oil royalties.[21]

Sa'ed's failure on 19 March to win a vote of confidence from the Majlis
gave the shah an excuse to replace him three days later with Ali Mansur, a
staunch conservative from a well-to-do family.[22] Mansur's public career
had begun in 1919 with a term as undersecretary of foreign affairs and
included two terms as minister of the interior as well as other posts. He had
served a short term as premier during World War II and more recently was
director of the Plan Organization established to administer the Seven-Year
Plan. Mansur's appointment as prime minister was not popular in Iran,
where he was widely regarded as corrupt and dishonest. Ambassador Wiley
shared this assessment, referring to Mansur as "the Persian version of Uriah
Heep" and warning the State Department of Mansur's "notoriously sticky
fingers." Nor was the Majlis pleased that the shah made the appointment
without its consultation. But even then the shah failed to fully support the
new prime minister, whom he considered spineless. The shah was especially dismayed when Mansur failed to stand up to the National Front,
which the shah saw as "more dangerous than the Tudeh Party."[23]

Mansur was reluctant from the start to challenge the National Front,
which still sought to reject the supplemental agreement and nationalize the
AIOC's Iranian holdings. He intrigued with Mossadeq to stall submission
of the agreement to the Majlis, pledged to secure passage of the National
Front's electoral reform program before turning his attention to the oil
agreement, and withheld his support for it thereafter. In addition, Mansur
sought to appease the agreement's critics by winning new concessions
from the AIOC. But even when the company agreed in mid-May to an
immediate advance of £3 million and to further installments of £1 million

each at the end of May, June, and July, Mansur could not placate the National Front.

Mansur's decision in June to submit the oil agreement to the Majlis threw opposition deputies into an uproar, and he was forced to try to save the agreement by placing it before a special eighteen-member commission, a move that Ambassador Shepherd deemed "tantamount to shelving [it]." The commission was to examine the agreement, make what Mansur hoped would be a positive recommendation, and thus enable him to overcome critics in the Majlis. But Mansur's hopes could not have been more misplaced. The National Front gained control of the commission and turned it from an instrument for ratification into a vehicle for the supplemental agreement's rejection. When Mansur failed to win ratification, the shah forced him to resign on 26 June.[24]

Meanwhile the British still had trouble squaring their plans regarding the supplemental agreement with thinking in the State Department. Like the British, U.S. policy makers wanted the AIOC to undertake a public relations campaign and were delighted when the company seemed amenable to the idea.[25] But where the Americans would target the "widest possible audience," the British would aim at "key people in [the] Iranian Government."[26] Anglo-American thinking on the proposed publicity campaign reflected the different U.S. and British perceptions of the key players in the Iranian oil dispute. U.S. policy makers recognized the paramount position of everyday Iranians and thus favored a campaign aimed at the masses; British policy makers emphasized Iranian elites and thus envisioned a campaign that would reach only government officials. Given these differences and the lack of Iranian support, the British abandoned the original plan for a vigorous information campaign, limiting their effort instead to a small pamphlet distributed to members of the government. This "Child's Guide" to the supplemental agreement, a joint effort of the AIOC and the British government, was hardly the kind of education effort the State Department had envisioned.[27]

The gap between U.S. and British thinking deepened when the Iranian situation was discussed at a foreign ministers' meeting that opened in May. U.S. delegates arrived in London for the meeting convinced that the "rigid stand [taken] by the [AIOC] and the British Government" had caused Iran's economic problems and the Anglo-Iranian stalemate. Although still convinced that the United States "could not properly inject itself" into the dispute, U.S. officials thought that the London meeting would give them another chance to press their views on the British. They wanted the Foreign Office to "do everything in its power to bring the [oil] matter to a speedy conclusion," specifically to inform Iran of its willingness "to discuss . . . on a frank and equal basis any and all points at issue." Otherwise, U.S. officials feared that Iran's economic difficulties might lead to the expansion of communism in that country.[28]

This position guided the U.S. delegation during the London conference. For the first time in their talks with U.S. officials the British acknowledged that more was at stake in Iran than the supplemental agreement, a commercial transaction whose merits could be calculated on a business ledger that left no room for important political and strategic factors. They agreed with the United States that Iran was "not in good shape" and that it constituted a soft spot in the defense against communist expansion in the Middle East. A workable oil agreement, they conceded, would help to shore up Iran's ailing economy and thereby keep that country out of the Soviet camp. Yet British and U.S. policy makers continued to disagree over whether additional concessions were needed to secure Majlis ratification of the supplemental agreement. The U.S. delegation continued to assert that concessions by the AIOC would facilitate ratification and rescue Iran's economy from the brink of collapse, whereas the British clung to the belief that the supplemental agreement had to be submitted without modification.[29]

Nor could the Anglo-Americans harmonize their differences on the equally important issue of U.S. economic aid to Mansur's government. This was not a new issue for U.S. policy makers, who already had decided that achieving their goals in Iran required an expansion of the modest aid program they had launched earlier.[30] As noted previously, this program provided Iran with military assistance and advice from U.S. missions attached to the Iranian army and the gendarmerie. Both forms of aid were designed to protect the shah against internal threats, but neither included the sort of economic assistance going to Greece, Turkey, and Western Europe. Through 1949 and early 1950 the United States had deemed Iran's monetary reserves adequate and its internal financial situation relatively stable. For these and other reasons the United States had limited its aid and had refused to reverse course in November 1949 when the shah sought more generous assistance.[31]

By the spring of 1950, however, economic conditions in Iran had deteriorated, and Iranian cries for additional assistance were beginning to receive a sympathetic hearing in Washington. Poor harvests during the 1949–50 growing season had sparked a nationwide depression, which if "unchecked might easily result in the political collapse of the country." Although policy makers in the State Department blamed the crisis on the inefficiency of the Iranian government and believed that the Iranians held the power to improve the situation, they were also convinced that increased U.S. aid was "the most effective means of forcing the Iranians . . . to put their house in order." In other words, by mid-1950 U.S. officials were coming to see aid as a tool for pushing the Iranians toward financial and political reforms that would end corruption, increase government efficiency, and so improve the situation as to reduce Iran's need for aid in the future.[32]

This policy reversal was welcome news to Ambassador Wiley, who had lamented in February that the U.S. aid program in Iran had "the dimensions of a bag of peanuts." Iran was the "most vulnerable spot on the [Soviet] periphery," he insisted. The situation there was "bad, deteriorating, and dangerous," yet the country was "crumbling away" and would certainly collapse without immediate economic aid. A similar warning came from William M. Rountree, deputy director of the State Department's Office of Greek, Turkish, and Iranian Affairs, following a fact-finding mission to Iran in March. The Iranian situation was potentially explosive, he reported, and "some form of American financial assistance" was essential.[33] A month later Assistant Secretary McGhee summarized the State Department's new consensus. Iran's economy was disintegrating, he argued, and "might well result in a collapse of the present political structure and [in Iran's] domination by the Soviet Union." McGhee went on to note that the failure of the United States "to extend aid to Iran at a time when substantial assistance [was] being rendered to Western Europe, Greece, Turkey, and certain other Asian countries" had "intensified the feeling of Iranian leaders and the Iranian people that the United States [was] not concerned with their welfare."[34]

To counteract these sentiments and forestall Iran's collapse McGhee recommended an expanded program of U.S. aid. As he and others in Washington saw things, Iran was vitally important to U.S. and Western security. Its geographic position between the Soviet Union and the Persian Gulf made it a valuable territorial prize in the cold war. And its rich oil supplies, which were badly needed to fuel the U.S.-sponsored reconstruction of Western Europe, added to its importance. With so much resting on Iran's continued alliance with the West, U.S. policy makers could not "take the chance of seeing [it] surrender to communism" and should be willing to "take every reasonable step," including increasing U.S. assistance, to ensure that it did not "fall into the Soviet orbit," McGhee said. This recommendation was then embodied in the position papers that the State Department prepared on the eve of the London conference.[35]

At the conference the British were enthusiastic about the prospects of U.S. aid to Iran but not on the terms favored by the United States. The British delegation wanted to link U.S. assistance to ratification of the supplemental agreement. Assistant Undersecretary Wright argued that such a strategy would "bring [the] maximum combined contribution to bear" in Iran. If the Iranians were given U.S. aid without conditions, he worried, they would lose their incentive to ratify the oil agreement.[36] The U.S. delegation, however, considered the British suggestion unwise, contending that it would involve the United States too deeply in the oil dispute and rob the AIOC of any incentive to compromise with the Iranian government. It would also preclude immediate U.S. help for the flagging Iranian economy and prevent U.S. leaders from using their aid to leverage the Iranians into important political and economic reforms, such as an overhaul of the tax system and a campaign against government corruption.[37]

Instead of this linkage, Acheson and the U.S. delegation wanted the British government to force the AIOC to adopt a more flexible posture. They were especially critical of the company's "take it or leave it" attitude, which ruled out even minor modifications to the supplemental agreement. U.S. criticisms were certainly valid. But Iranian leaders had yet to submit official demands, confining themselves to vague and informal requests for higher revenues and stepped-up Iranianization. To the British government's way of thinking, "while individual Persians [had] at various times indicated dissatisfaction with some of [the oil agreement's] provisions, the Persian Government had at no time suggested specific modifications. . . . Failing a concrete approach by the Persian Government we doubted whether we could justifiably ask the Company to consider any modifications," said Ernest Bevin, British foreign secretary.[38] In other words, the Foreign Office was reluctant to ask AIOC officials to modify the agreement when no one knew precisely "what kind of political lubrication might be practicable."[39]

It was only in late June, after General Ali Razmara had succeeded Mansur, that Iranian officials began to articulate specific grievances against the oil agreement and put forward their conditions for accepting it. As the subsequent discussion makes clear, however, even this new-found articulation did not result in satisfactory concessions from the AIOC: the company steadfastly insisted that concessions could come only after ratification.

III

As we have seen, despite the AIOC's promise of £6 million in advance royalties, Mansur had refused to support the supplemental agreement. This prevarication probably stemmed from his fear of antagonizing the National Front, which continued to assail the agreement as an instrument of Britain's traditional control of the Iranian oil industry and the revenue it generated. It deeply angered the shah, who was eager to see the oil issue settled so that Iran could begin to benefit from the new financial arrangements contained in the supplemental agreement and so that the government could get on with the task of political reform. Accordingly, on 28 June the shah replaced Mansur with Ali Razmara, the hero of Azerbaijan who was then chief of the general staff.

Razmara, a career military officer who had long held aspirations to the premiership, was by all accounts honest, hard working, and determined to end corruption and reform Iranian politics. In some ways, though, he was an unlikely choice for the office. He lacked political experience and was unpopular with members of the court establishment, especially the shah's influential twin sister Princess Ashraf. To overcome these difficulties Razmara played the part of a loyal monarchist and ingratiated himself with the shah, going so far as to consult the monarch on even trivial military matters in order to flatter the shah into thinking he was commander in chief in fact as well as in name.[40] Nevertheless, the shah, hesitant to support a powerful general and potential rival but hopeful that Razmara's strong will and determination would successfully resolve the debate over the supplemental agreement and bring order to Iran's otherwise corrupt and inefficient political system, had reluctantly championed Razmara's appointment.[41]

For similar reasons both the Foreign Office and the State Department were initially enthusiastic about the new prime minister, although they were careful to keep their enthusiasm under wraps lest it compromise Razmara's standing with Iranian nationalists. Shepherd predicted that Razmara would make an "efficient, honest, and progressive Prime Minister." Officials at the U.S. embassy in Tehran agreed, adding that "only Razmara [had] the necessary capacity and courage to head [a] positive reform government" and push the supplemental agreement through the Majlis. U.S. officials also believed that a strong prime minister like Razmara would facilitate the distribution of U.S. aid and thereby allow Washington to expand its influence over Iran.[42]

Regarding the oil agreement, in conversations with Wiley before his appointment as prime minister Razmara implied that mere face-saving gestures would secure ratification. Although he paid lip service to the agreement's commercial terms, his primary concern was the issue of Iranianization: the company had to replace its Indian laborers with Iranians and give Iranians a share of managerial positions. With that done, Razmara seemed to say, he could guarantee Majlis ratification.[43]

After assuming office, however, Razmara added other demands. He wanted the AIOC to begin paying royalties on its Iranian production at the new and higher rates stipulated in the supplemental agreement in advance of ratification, and he wanted back payments on all production since the signing of the agreement in July 1949.[44] These payments, he said, were needed to finance the Seven-Year Plan and to underwrite his program of political and economic reform.[45] Razmara's demands seemed reasonable to newly appointed U.S. Ambassador Henry F. Grady, an economist who assumed his post in July fresh from success as ambassador to Athens. In the words of James A. Bill, "Grady was a hard-headed, short, baked-potatolike figure" whose Irish-American heritage and sympathy for the principle of national self-determination made him unpopular in England. Iranian observers saw Grady's appointment as proof that the U.S. government intended to make the same kind of economic commitment to Iran that it had earlier made to Greece and Turkey. President Harry S Truman and Acheson viewed the appointment differently. For them it was a way to quiet Iranian complaints about low levels of U.S. aid while the State Department reevaluated its foreign assistance program. According to the new ambassador, Razmara knew that an oil settlement rather than U.S. aid was the last hope for his development program but that additional concessions by the AIOC were necessary to ensure ratification by what Grady called the "irrational, nationalistic Majlis."[46]

Officials of the British government did not share Grady's belief that Razmara's demands were reasonable. Lancelot F. L. Pyman of the embassy in Tehran cautioned that the AIOC was unlikely to accept the prime minister's proposals for an advance on royalties and back payments on past production, no matter how many times Razmara said that such concessions were essential to Iran's economic stability and reform. Geoffrey W. Furlonge, who headed the Foreign Office's Eastern Department, seconded Pyman's conclusion. It would take "considerable pressure" by the British government to sway the AIOC's opinion, Furlonge explained, and the government would act only if Razmara was "short of money for good purposes" and he could raise the money in no other way. The prime minister did not understand such apparently narrow arguments and, in an effort to make the company act generously, raised the specter of Iran's imminent economic collapse. The Iranian government was woefully short of money, Razmara asserted, and "if something were not done soon to stop [Iran's] disintegration, there would be no oil for the Company anyhow."[47]

With the British government reluctant to act the prime minister took his case directly to the AIOC. In late June Razmara told company officials that unless they granted his request for royalty advances he would be unable to support the oil agreement before the Majlis, a position that almost certainly meant interminable delays and little chance of ratification. If the company adopted "a more reasonable attitude," however, Razmara would back the agreement, along "with [the] necessary face-saving additions, as part [of] his government's 'must' program," Grady reported. The company, Razmara stressed, "should be sufficiently concerned with [the] economic future of Iran as to be more conciliatory and flexible."[48]

The prime minister's proposition presented the British with a dilemma. On the one hand, the AIOC was loath to pay royalties at the new rate, including back payments, "without any guarantee either that the Agreement will be passed or that further concessions will not be demanded when it comes before the Majlis." But on the other hand, some action was necessary "to avoid placing Iran in grave financial difficulties and incidentally seriously endangering Anglo-Iranian relations." Ambassador Shepherd suggested that in exchange for ratification the company agree to negotiate on the two points Razmara found most troubling: Iranianization and either Iranian involvement in the company's management or access to information regarding its operations. So far as the first point was concerned, Shepherd urged the British to play up an AIOC scheme for gradual Iranianization over a period of years. On the second he suggested a "separate subsidiary company" that would oversee the AIOC's operations in Iran and include an Iranian director. Leavett agreed with these suggestions and also questioned the company's hesitation to pay royalties at the new rate in advance of ratification. Iran's financial situation was so desperate, he argued, that withholding assistance "would be difficult to justify both to the Persians, and to the Americans, who [were] going out of their way to provide economic assistance."[49]

Leavett was right about U.S. officials going out of their way to assist Iran financially. They already had opened negotiations for a loan to Iran from the Export-Import Bank and had signed an agreement to provide Iran with funds from the Mutual Defense Assistance Program.[50] Both initiatives squared with the earlier recommendations coming from the State Department, and both reflected the growing U.S. concern for the situation in Iran. U.S. policy makers feared that unless the supplemental agreement or a similar arrangement with Britain was signed, control of Iranian oil might fall to the Soviets. Such a development would have far-reaching implications for Western security, especially for America's Western European allies, who received a substantial portion of their oil from Iran and the other countries of the Middle East. This concern only intensified after the outbreak of the Korean War, at which point U.S. officials began to worry not only about the loss of Iran's oil to the West but also about its vulnerability to a Soviet assault from the north. To prevent these eventualities Truman proposed an expansion of U.S. economic and military assistance to Iran (and other countries). This assistance would not materialize before 1951. But the administration had at least signaled its support for an expanded aid program and would renew this pledge in October, when the United States and Iran signed a technical assistance agreement under Truman's Point IV program—the first such agreement in the Middle East.[51]

Mounting U.S. concern for the situation in Iran and that country's place in the global framework of U.S. policy led to new Anglo-American tensions. To be sure, U.S. policy makers still assigned the British primary responsibility for the defense of Iran. U.S. resources and attention, which already had been committed to financing Western European reconstruction, were now being diverted to the war in Korea as well, which meant that the United States could ill afford to become embroiled in a crisis in Iran. The war in Korea also heightened Iran's importance for the Western alliance. Losing access to Iranian supplies would hamper the war effort, spur fears of civilian rationing in the United States and Western Europe, and compromise the West's general military capabilities vis-à-vis those of the Soviet bloc.[52] To alleviate the rising tensions in Iran, U.S. policy makers were more determined than ever to secure ratification of the supplemental agreement, which made them more critical of what they saw as the AIOC's obstructionism. In July Grady chided the British for treating the supplemental agreement as little more than "an oil question, whereas [the] Iranians have come to regard it as [a] political issue." AIOC officials, he believed, were "counting heavily on financial necessities" to force the Iranians to capitulate; the AIOC hoped, in other words, that budgetary requirements would force the Iranian government to abandon its demands and accept the supplemental agreement without modification. Such an "unduly optimistic" attitude was not founded in reality, the ambassador proclaimed. On the contrary, the inflexible British policy risked "the overthrow of the present government" and the triumph of Mossadeq, who wanted to nationalize Iran's oil resources. Joseph J. Wagner, second secretary of the U.S. embassy in Tehran, concurred. British officials, he argued, had to recognize that "they [were] no longer merely in the oil business in Iran" but were "involved in a play of social forces" that required "unselfish action and long-range vision." Unfortunately, he lamented, the company and the British government seemed to lack both characteristics.[53]

Secretary of State Acheson's position was even firmer. In his view Razmara's government represented Iran's best hope of stability; its survival required fresh British initiatives that would allow Iran to save face and secure the supplemental agreement. British intransigence, Acheson asserted, was "inappropriate to current internal Iran[ian] and world conditions." Britain was no longer in a position to dictate the terms of a concession to the Iranian government. Nationalist sentiment in Iran had to be taken into account, and London's failure to do so could lead only to Iran's collapse, expansion of Soviet influence, and a dangerous setback for the West. The best course, Acheson asserted, was for "positive action" by the British government to stem the AIOC's intransigence. The company may traditionally have acted "as a law unto itself" in Iran, but such behavior was out of step in the changing world of 1950, and the company would have to be brought into line by firm government action.[54]

The British and U.S. governments also took different views of how Anglo-American cooperation should work and for what purposes. Ernest Bevin and his colleagues saw it as the antidote to an Iranian strategy that would "play us one against the other." If successful, Bevin worried, this strategy would spell disaster for the British position in Iran and throughout the Middle East.[55] Indeed, it was obvious to Bevin and others that Britain could not maintain its position without U.S. assistance. The search for this assistance had been evident throughout the Anglo-Iranian crisis. But the negligible results had led to British complaints about Washington's "one-sided" policy of encouraging Iranian aspirations while urging British moderation. U.S. officials also appreciated the value of close Anglo-American cooperation but on terms different from those favored in Britain. Where policy makers in London wanted the United States to buttress Britain's position in Iran, those in Washington looked to British concessions that would stabilize Iran and protect the Middle East against Soviet advances. "The stakes are too high in Iran," Acheson asserted, to "permit [the oil] matter [to] drag [on] any longer." If the British did not make additional concessions, he and other U.S. officials feared, Iran might collapse and its oil might be lost to the West forever.[56]

These differences, apparent from the start, deepened in proportion to the AIOC's refusal to approach the Iranian crisis with greater flexibility. The British had repeatedly lamented the Iranians' "bazaar method of negotiation," which meant their constant bidding up of unrealistic and ever-changing demands.[57] By late August, in fact, Razmara had added a long list of new demands to those he had made soon after taking office. In addition to royalties due under the new rates set forth in the supplemental agreement, Razmara wanted guarantees that Iran would pay no more for the oil it consumed than did the AIOC's most favored customers (the British navy and air force), that Iranianization would be completed within ten years, and that Iranian officials could audit the company's records pertaining to its business in Iran and to its exports.[58] Because these demands were not onerous, or so the prime minister insisted, he expected the company to approach them with a "responsible attitude." When AIOC officials were less than receptive, Razmara reminded them that "while Iran needed oil revenues, the oil company was just as much in need of Iranian Government cooperation and protection." In a veiled reference to the 1932 cancellation of the company's concession he went on to say that Iran could give the British "plenty of trouble if they [did] not cooperate."[59]

Threats like this made Acheson nervous because they pointed to a deepening crisis in an area deemed vital to Western security and economic well-being. Through Ambassador Grady, Acheson urged Razmara to put his concerns about the supplemental agreement in a geopolitical context that included economic and political stability in Iran and throughout the Middle East. Nationalization of the oil industry, Acheson reminded the prime minister, would be a financial and economic disaster for Iran and could open the country up to Soviet expansion. It was better to continue negotiations with the British than to take rash and unconsidered action that could result in Iran's collapse to communism and the subsequent denial of its vast oil resources to the Western alliance, especially at a time when the war in Korea was straining free world supplies to the limit.[60] The British also received a share of the secretary's criticism. Acheson excoriated the AIOC for approaching the supplemental agreement "as [a] commercial proposition without economic, political and strategic considerations important to [the] outside world." The British government seemed to understand the larger importance of the agreement, or so Acheson believed, but it was not doing enough to control the AIOC, which he saw as the "last remaining obstacle" to ratification.[61]

Acheson's praise for Whitehall's open-mindedness was premature. To be sure, Shepherd and others recognized Iran's precarious economic state and the need for greater flexibility by the AIOC. As the ambassador noted in September, Razmara's government was "short of money," and funding for the Seven-Year Plan was virtually gone.[62] But most officials in the Foreign Office remained opposed to any concessions, portraying the supplemental agreement as fair by any standard and repeating their conviction that concessions would do more harm than good. According to Furlonge, additional concessions would merely encourage the Iranians "to open their mouths wider and might decrease, rather than increase, the Prime Minister's will to push [the oil agreement] through the Majlis."[63] Bevin was of the same opinion. In his view, moreover, pressure from Washington only encouraged Iranian efforts to play the United States against Great Britain, thereby prolonging the dispute and contributing to Britain's declining prestige in Iran and throughout the world. It would be better, he and other British officials agreed, if the State Department advised Grady "to disabuse the Persians of any idea that they [could] obtain further concessions."[64]

Better still in the minds of British policy makers was a joint Anglo-American loan to Iran conditional on ratification of the supplemental agreement. Bevin resurrected this idea, which Wright had suggested in May, in late summer as part of his ongoing effort to put U.S. power behind Britain's flagging position in Iran. Because the British treasury lacked the resources to float a loan on its own, the scheme's success depended on U.S. cooperation. Although Lewis A. Douglas, U.S. ambassador to England, believed that the proposed loan would assure the most efficient use of Anglo-American funds and prevent the Iranians from playing the two countries against each other, several factors prevented the scheme's implementation.[65] Some British officials feared that the loan might be used in part to balance Iran's budget, whereas others wondered if it could be justified when the British treasury was strapped and when the Iranians could get sufficient funds in the form of oil royalties simply by ratifying the supplemental agreement. But the coup de grâce to the idea came when Acheson rejected the scheme, no doubt for the same reasons he and others had earlier refused to link U.S. aid to Iran's ratification of the supplemental agreement. An Anglo-American loan, he told Douglas in August, would not serve the "best interest of any of [the] countries involved."[66]

Spurned by Acheson, the Foreign Office turned to the AIOC. It urged the company to float a loan to Iran, which the British treasury would guarantee and which would be used to keep the Iranian economy afloat and smooth the road to ratification of the supplemental agreement.[67] In talks at the Foreign Office, however, company officials continued to exhibit what Razmara called a "negative attitude." Sir William Fraser, who headed the AIOC's board of directors, seemed to believe that any additional concessions "would be fatal." Fraser had been intimately involved in the 1933 renegotiation of the company's contract and had helped to shape the supplemental agreement.

Undeniably a shrewd financier, Fraser was out of his element in dealing with international conditions in the postwar period. As one Foreign Office official observed, Fraser "did not think politics concern[ed] him at all," had "all the contempt of a Glasgow accountant for anything which [could] not be shown on a balance sheet," and steadfastly refused to make any concessions to the Iranians. He maintained that such issues as oil prices and Iranianization had been settled in the supplemental agreement. Razmara had raised them again merely to delay ratification, Fraser believed, and the company would reopen negotiations on these and other issues only if Iran ratified the agreement. Fraser eventually conceded that a company loan, guaranteed by the British government, might help to solve Iran's short-term economic problems until ratification of the oil agreement provided a more permanent solution. But his general reluctance to make concessions or to undertake the loan did not please British government officials, especially Wright, who was convinced that the AIOC failed fully to appreciate the larger implications of the Iranian situation or the political nature of the oil dispute.[68]

While the British were discussing whether to provide a loan to Iran, the State Department was sharpening its critique of British policy. A briefing paper drafted for an Anglo-American conference on the Middle East scheduled to convene in London in September 1950 described as sophistry the AIOC's claim that it could not afford additional royalties or other assistance to Iran.[69] The company's operations were *exceptionally profitable*," the paper asserted. Its offers of assistance thus far were "a small concession" by comparison and would do little to stabilize Razmara's government, advance the Seven-Year Plan, or assure ratification of the supplemental agreement. The paper recommended that Assistant Secretary McGhee and the other delegates to the London conference adopt a hard line with the British, urging them to accept Razmara's demands and to take Iranian threats of nationalization more seriously.[70]

Representatives of the major U.S. oil companies echoed these views. At an 11 September meeting at the State Department the assembled executives supported the department's belief that Iran's position was reasonable, that "compliance with it would be a sound commercial proposition," and that the British government was not as eager as it should be "to effect [a] settlement on reasonable terms." The executives were especially critical of the British government, arguing that the AIOC could not have held so firmly to its position against strong official pressure for concessions. In reporting the results of this conversation John A. Loftus of the State Department's Office of Near Eastern Affairs argued that footdragging by the Foreign Office was "perhaps the most important point for Mr. McGhee to have in mind in his London discussions."[71]

Sir Oliver Franks, the British ambassador in Washington, alerted the Foreign Office to the likelihood that McGhee and company would repeat the State Department's standard criticism in the London meetings. U.S.

policy makers, he said, believed that oil companies could "be made powerful instruments" in an Anglo-American "policy to develop the economic resources" of the Middle East. They wanted the companies to heed the rising tide of nationalist sentiment and to ensure that their conduct was "beyond reproach," for once they had "become a subject of criticism," as the AIOC had in Iran, it was "extremely difficult . . . to recover the initiative." Franks also reported the U.S. belief that the British government's majority ownership of the AIOC gave it more control over the company than the U.S. government had over U.S. oil companies and that it should therefore be able to ensure AIOC compliance with Iranian demands.[72]

This was an accurate forecast of the U.S. position in the London talks, which opened on 21 September. After stressing the seriousness with which his government viewed the Iranian situation, McGhee expressed disappointment that the AIOC "had not shown the same sense of urgency." He conveyed the views of the U.S. oil companies, whose representatives he had recently met, especially their belief that "so long as [the AIOC] did not lose control of its board of directors there was little it could not afford to agree to." The company had to accommodate Iranian demands, McGhee argued, if it wanted to protect its investment in Iran. "The advantage in negotiations today lay with the country where [the] oil properties [are] located," he asserted, "and about the best [the] companies could do was to fight a graceful rearguard action." McGhee pointed to the Arabian-American Oil Company (ARAMCO) to illustrate the type of policy he had in mind. ARAMCO was negotiating a new agreement with Saudi Arabia that was sure to be generous to the Saudis. McGhee thought that the AIOC would be advised to meet current Iranian demands before the Saudi Arabian terms became known, because at that point Iranian expectations would surely escalate. Although the British listened to McGhee's assessment of the situation, they refused to make any commitments and merely reiterated the importance of Anglo-American accord. They did, however, express doubts that the AIOC would meet Razmara's demands for price guarantees, more rapid Iranianization, and the right to audit the AIOC's books.[73]

McGhee was not alone in believing that only positive intervention by the British government could save the supplemental agreement. According to Wagner, second secretary of the U.S. embassy in Tehran, the AIOC's "stupid arrogance" and the cavalier manner in which it dismissed Razmara's threat to cancel the company's concession might well force the prime minister's hand. Indeed, Wagner asserted that the best way for Razmara to endear himself to the Iranian people would be to follow Reza Shah's example and cancel the AIOC's concession. Much more was at stake in Iran than a commercial arrangement, he asserted, and unless the British adopted a more open-minded attitude they would lose even that. Grady also thought the company's position "quite incomprehensible," whereas Rountree was dumbfounded that the British government had not changed its policy "one iota despite the present world situation." The Foreign Office, he lamented, seemed willing "to let [the] AIOC come first and to permit the Iranian internal situation to remain in a constant state of turmoil." Although past efforts to achieve an Anglo-American understanding had failed, Rountree urged the State Department to keep trying to "introduce a note of realism" into British policy and "induce the British Government to escape from its bondage" to the AIOC.[74]

U.S. criticism of British, and especially AIOC, policy stemmed from the belief that inaction on the oil question would lead only to economic disaster in Iran and to that country's fall to communism. Razmara's government was having trouble meeting day-to-day expenses and had halted implementation of what Iranian Trade Union leaders had derisively dubbed the "70-Year Plan." U.S. policy makers blamed these developments on what they saw as an AIOC campaign to "force the Iranians to their knees." This was a dangerous strategy of economic warfare that threatened the entire Middle Eastern policy of the United States. Unless something was done soon to stop Iran's economic decline, Razmara's government might collapse, communist interests might gain control, and the country's oil might be lost to the Western alliance. To prevent these disasters U.S. officials wanted the British government to take an active role in forcing the AIOC to make concessions to the Iranians. Barring such action, officials in Washington could only conclude that Whitehall was deliberately "sabotaging [American] efforts to strengthen Iran in order to preserve [Britain's] dubious supremacy and control [there]."[75]

By late 1950 U.S. pressure had modified thinking within the Foreign Office. Interdepartmental discussions on the Iranian crisis already had elicited a view that "His Majesty's Government . . . should play a more active part" in inducing the AIOC to reach a settlement with Iran. The "minor palliatives" offered by the company's "hard-boiled business brains" were insufficient; they would have to negotiate a new agreement with Iran or accept "fundamental modifications in the Supplemental Oil Agreement."[76]

R. J. Bowker and Eric A. Berthoud of the Foreign Office explained the new thinking in December, saying that too much was at stake for the British government to pursue "a policy of complete inaction." Bevin already had said much the same thing to Sir William Fraser. He advised Fraser to be as forthcoming as possible with the Iranians, give Razmara's demands close and careful consideration, and "find something to offer, even if it were somewhat painful, provided always it was not disastrous." Bevin advised Fraser to make concessions to Iranian sentiment, not only in the AIOC's interest but in the general interest of Britain itself. The country was strategically and financially dependent on Iranian oil and could not run the risk of losing such a valuable resource. But that was exactly what would happen if the AIOC continued to take a hard line with Razmara.[77]

The AIOC had given no signs that it would respond to this change in government policy. In reply to Bevin's plea to make an offer to Razmara, "even if it were somewhat painful," Fraser repeated the company's usual line that it was difficult to find something the Iranians would accept. This was partially true. Razmara's demands did change over time. To the list noted earlier he added such things as renegotiation of the supplemental agreement in five to ten years, company agreement to provide to the Iranian government an amount of oil equivalent to the amount it used in Iran, and company financing of the construction of cement plants and a gas piping project.[78] Razmara repeatedly emphasized his support for the agreement and his willingness to endorse it publicly, provided the company made concessions to placate his more radical opponents at home. Razmara's plan was for his government and the company to secretly agree in advance on certain concessions, for the two parties to debate these concessions in public, and for him to convince the Majlis to accept the supplemental agreement so long as the AIOC promised to make the already agreed-upon concessions. As Shepherd explained the prime minister's strategy, "There would be a sort of bogus cock-fight in the course of which one feather would be lost . . . and this the Prime Minister would stick triumphantly in his cap." If the company went along, Razmara proclaimed, he was confident of a favorable outcome in the Majlis.[79]

The AIOC was not as generous as Razmara hoped. It did agree to provide free oil in the field, investigate the feasibility of the cement and pipeline projects, and make a contribution to Tehran University. It was also prepared to reconsider some of the supplemental agreement's provisions after ratification and make additional early royalty payments, including a payment of £3 million in September and another £1 million at the end of each of the next five months.[80] But the company refused to make any changes in the agreement itself, which meant that it would not accede to Razmara's demand, announced in November, for a fifty-fifty sharing of profits from its oil operations in Iran. This arrangement would bolster Iran's deteriorating financial condition and bring its oil revenues into line with those received by Venezuela and then being demanded by Saudi Arabia.

AIOC officials, however, dismissed Razmara's demand as little more than an effort to disarm Iranian nationalists, who thought the British government got more from the Anglo-Iranian relationship than did the Iranian government, particularly in the taxes that the AIOC contributed to the British treasury and in the secret discount price that the British admiralty and air force paid for Iranian oil. Taken together, company officials told the Foreign Office, Razmara's demands were too costly. Having reached "the end of their tether," AIOC executives in November again ruled out further concessions.[81] This did not bode well for the future of the supplemental agreement, which had been before the Majlis Oil Commission since 26 June.

IV

Iranian nationalists had never been enamored of the supplemental agreement, but it was not until the fall of 1950 that its rejection and nationalization of the AIOC's Iranian holdings became real possibilities.[82] Razmara was bluffing when he warned that he would "cause trouble" for the British if they did not meet his demands. He thought that Iran stood to lose as much from cancellation of the oil concession as the British and that it could not manage its oil operations without considerable outside assistance. The shah thought likewise, arguing that Iran lacked the technical know-how and international marketing and distribution facilities to export large quantities of oil. The points the shah raised were certainly valid, but his opposition to nationalization was probably also a function of his position as a member of the Iranian upper class, which had traditionally been closely allied with British interests.[83]

Razmara was bitter at the AIOC's failure to appreciate the seriousness of the situation. Unemployment in Iran was rising, prices for such staples as meat, bread, and sugar were high, and the government was practically bankrupt. Given the country's deteriorating economy, Razmara could not understand the AIOC's failure to be more generous. This compounded his consternation at his political position—not all Iranians shared his beliefs about the dangers of nationalization. Indeed, as Wagner of the U.S. embassy in Tehran noted, the feelings of literate Iranians regarding the oil question would "only be assuaged on that day, if it ever comes, when they take over the oil operation themselves through nationalization or some other similar move." The British embassy in Tehran had concluded much the same thing. It asserted that the British saw the oil agreement as merely a device for increasing the financial return of the Iranian government, whereas the Iranians viewed it as a referendum on the desirability of having a foreign corporation control the oil industry. This explained the widespread Iranian opposition to the supplemental agreement and the mounting public support for nationalization.[84]

As mentioned earlier, the National Front led the drive for nationalization of Iran's oil operations and for expulsion of all foreign influence from the country. The party's influence in the Majlis was not substantial—it held only 7 of 131 seats. But its members acted as a bloc and used their status as popularly elected deputies to win the cooperation of their colleagues.[85] The front also acquired a disproportionate representation on the eighteen-member Majlis Oil Commission that Mansur had appointed to study the supplemental agreement just days before his June resignation. The commission had originally contained three front members, but political maneuvering had brought the number to five, including Mossadeq, who was elected chairman, and Hossein Makki, one of Mossadeq's staunchest supporters, who served as recording secretary. The front's influence became even stronger than these numbers would suggest, in large part because many other commissioners also opposed the oil agreement. Some did so out of personal inclination, others for fear of being branded British stooges by the National Front, still others because they worried that ratification would lead the Soviets to renew their demand for an oil concession in the north, thereby reconstituting the historic Anglo-Russian domination of Iran.[86]

The National Front representatives on the oil commission dominated its proceedings from the start. They spent the initial meetings examining the government's records pertaining to the supplemental agreement, particularly the twenty-five–point protest prepared during the 1949 negotiations with the AIOC. After considerable study they found the agreement deficient in several respects. It did not grant the Iranians the right to inspect the AIOC's books, nor did it sufficiently provide for Iranianization of the company's workforce, give the Iranians information about the company's sales to the British admiralty and air force, or invest them with control over the price of oil sold in Iran. In addition, they complained, the agreement's financial provisions failed to provide Iran with sufficient revenue.[87]

As the commission's discussions continued, the oil question took on political as well as economic significance, especially for Mossadeq and the other National Front commissioners. It was bad enough, they argued, that the supplemental agreement's financial terms were unfairly slanted toward Britain. Worse yet, the pact perpetuated Britain's domination of Iran's oil industry, an indignity created by the D'Arcy Agreement of 1901 and furthered by the AIOC's 1933 concession. Such domination was no longer acceptable. Iran's aroused national consciousness prevented silent acquiescence in this domination, and the emergence of the United Nations as the guarantor of the rights of small nations meant that Iran did not have to go along. Instead, Mossadeq proclaimed, Iran should nationalize its oil industry, produce enough oil to satisfy domestic requirements, and leave the remainder "in the ground until the future generation could better benefit from it." Although nationalization was not universally popular among the commissioners, the fervor with which Mossadeq presented it kept the commission from dismissing the idea out of hand.[88]

Already leaning against the supplemental agreement, the commission called on Finance Minister Golam-Hossein Foruhar and Prime Minister Razmara to justify the government's support of such an obviously deficient pact. Their arguments were not convincing; the commission was unmoved even by Razmara's revelation that he was conducting secret negotiations with the AIOC.[89] In mid-October the commission exercised its legal right of interpellation, asking the government publicly to explain its views on the oil agreement. On 18 October Razmara announced to the Senate that he would not have sent the agreement to the oil commission had he not supported it. He was deliberately vague about his support, however, and did not repeat his declaration in a later appearance before the Majlis. It is likely that he saw his statement as a means of mollifying critics on the oil commission and thereby moving the agreement to the Majlis, where he was more confident of his ability to secure ratification so long as the AIOC made some real concessions. Whatever the statement meant, it was enough to convince the Majlis to end the interpellation but not to ensure a vote of confidence in the government.[90]

In the oil commission the outcome was even more unfavorable. On 25 November the commissioners voted unanimously to reject the Supplemental Oil Agreement as detrimental to Iran's national interest. It is not clear whether the commission saw its vote as the last word or as a spur to further concessions by the AIOC. It is significant, though, that Mossadeq was unable to mobilize the commission behind his demand for nationalization. The commission adhered to its instructions to report on the acceptability of the supplemental agreement and refrained from considering any other proposals. Undeterred, Mossadeq touted nationalization as the only way to secure "the rights of the Iranian people." Although the commission did not recommend nationalization, the decision to reject the oil agreement was a blow to the British. As Richards reported, however, "it was generally anticipated."[91]

U.S. and British officials interpreted the commission's decision differently. U.S. policy makers were more pessimistic than ever about the supplemental agreement's chances of ratification. The AIOC's failure to make concessions jeopardized Razmara's government, to which U.S. officials had "necessarily . . . tied [their] hopes," and imperiled U.S. strategy in Iran and throughout the Middle East. This strategy focused on appeasing local peoples "by bringing them greater benefits through development" and depended on ratification of the supplemental agreement to provide Iran with substantial oil revenues. To protect Western interests in Iran as the United States defined them the AIOC would have to renegotiate the supplemental agreement with a view to Iran's original demands and the principle of fifty-fifty profit sharing that ARAMCO had just granted to Saudi Arabia. According to officials in the State Department, fifty-fifty agreements were sure to become the norm throughout the Middle East.[92]

Although the British preferred to blame Razmara for failing to maneuver the supplemental agreement through the oil commission, they still entertained hopes that it could be salvaged. ARAMCO's new agreement with Saudi Arabia was another matter. The British "could not understand why ARAMCO apparently felt itself compelled" to accept the Saudis' demands without a fight and refused to strike a similar arrangement with Iran. But they also recognized that news of the ARAMCO settlement would make ratification of the supplemental agreement far more difficult and at one point considered asking the State Department to delay announcing it. By mid-December, Holmes reported, the British were "simply marking time" while awaiting the Majlis decision on the oil agreement. Confident that the agreement could somehow be pushed through, the AIOC refused to consider additional concessions. Instead, John Stutesman of the U.S. embassy in Tehran reported that it saw political action as the "way out of [its] difficulties." Specifically, Stutesman suspected that the company might try to replace Razmara with a new prime minister "who could push through an oil agreement."[93]

Nor were the British swayed when Ayatollah Abol-Qassem Kashani, an outspoken nationalist and close ally of Mossadeq, denounced the oil agreement. Kashani's opposition to foreign influence in Iran dated to Reza Shah's reign, when Kashani had opposed the 1933 oil agreement as an unfair infringement on Iran's sovereignty. His subsequent criticism of what he saw as Mohammad Reza Shah's pro-British tendencies implicated Kashani in the February 1949 attempt on the monarch's life and resulted in his banishment to Lebanon—which neither prevented him from being elected in absentia to the Sixteenth Majlis nor silenced his criticism of Britain's apparent domination of Iran's affairs. In early June 1950 Mansur had allowed Kashani to return to Tehran, where the ayatollah received a hero's welcome and was greeted by Mossadeq.[94] Almost immediately upon his return Kashani condemned Britain's "plundering" of Iran's oil wealth and urged "all deputies who hold the interests of the country more important than foreign influence" to support nationalization of the oil industry, thereby ending "the enslavement of the nation." U.S. officials believed that Kashani's views "reflect[ed] or [led] the opinions of a large number of Iranians," but the British refused to take him seriously. At best, in an early indication of the orientalism that would guide British thinking throughout the oil dispute, they saw his statement as just another example of "the emotional approach of most Iranians to the oil issue." At worst they suspected a clumsy effort "to blackmail the [AIOC] into further concessions." Although "other foreign observers [were] not so certain," Richards told the State Department, "few officers of the British Embassy or of the Oil Company in Tehran show[ed] concern that the Iranian Government might cancel their concession."[95]

Razmara's thinking paralleled the British point of view. He was not initially fazed by the oil commission's resolution, because he had known for some time that most of its members were opposed to what he saw as an "unintelligible" agreement.[96] He still planned to submit the pact to the Majlis and was sure that cooler heads would prevail there. Razmara's confidence did not dim when legislative debate opened in the face of growing public support for nationalization. He expected the deputies to do little more than return the supplemental agreement to him with instructions to seek new concessions through further negotiations with the AIOC. In fact, so sure was he that the Majlis would follow this course that he began circulating among the deputies a petition that would empower him to commence negotiations with the company without waiting for a final vote. He also continued to press E. G. D. Northcroft, the company's chief officer in Iran, for additional concessions.[97]

Nothing Razmara did had the desired effect. His petition, which according to parliamentary rules required seventy signatures, secured only forty-five when private pledges of support evaporated in the face of rising public clamor for nationalization. His discussions with Northcroft revealed that Iran and the AIOC remained "poles apart" and convinced him that the company was unlikely to make concessions even if he could initiate further talks.[98] Finally, as U.S. officials had predicted, the ARAMCO negotiations so fueled the flames of public opposition to the supplemental agreement as to virtually guarantee its rejection. In the face of such overwhelming obstacles Razmara thought his only option was to withdraw the agreement from the Majlis. On 27 December Finance Minister Foruhar stated the government's case, thereby earning the distinction of being the first, and only, Iranian cabinet minister to come out publicly for the supplemental agreement. Foruhar reiterated the government's support for the pact, lamented that it had to be withdrawn without a favorable vote, and went on to criticize nationalization as unworkable and impractical. "Governments and Parliaments are only temporary things," he said, "but we must think here of the future of our country. Would it not be preferable for us to put aside our personal animosities and instead of sowing discord in public opinion to draw together in unity so that we may preserve the best interest of our Country?"[99] It is likely that the government withdrew the agreement to prevent the Majlis from sending it back to the oil commission or, worse, voting for nationalization. What was not at all clear was the wisdom of this move.

U.S. and British officials wondered about Razmara's next step, particularly when so much of the population seemed to support nationalization. Opposition deputies in the Majlis had staged a "disorderly demonstration" during Foruhar's speech and later joined National Front supporters in public demonstrations for nationalization. Given widespread Majlis opposition to the government, the prime minister suggested dissolving that body and holding elections for a more malleable assembly. The shah opposed this course, ostensibly because it would circumvent the Iranian constitution. But his real reasons were probably much more self-serving. The shah no doubt feared that dissolving the Majlis would strengthen Razmara's power by freeing him from having to answer to the assembly. It would also anger Iranian nationalists, who would see such a move as an act of treachery designed to benefit the AIOC. Razmara was thus forced to ask the AIOC for additional advances to tide the Iranian government over until a satisfactory permanent arrangement could be worked out. When Ambassador Shepherd apprised him of the company's likely refusal to make such advances, Razmara suggested some other alternative, perhaps a loan from the British government to keep Iran's economy going until a new oil agreement could be negotiated. Under no circumstances, the prime minister assured Richards, would his government attempt to nationalize the oil industry, no matter how intense the public clamor for such action.[100]

V

Razmara's promises were not enough to calm U.S. fears about Iran's security. The supplemental agreement's apparent demise left the country's economic future uncertain and renewed the possibility that it would "drift . . . toward the Russians." This was distressing news to U.S. officials, who had recently reaffirmed the strategic importance of Iranian and Middle Eastern oil generally for the Western alliance. Six months into the Korean War, it now seemed doubtful that the Soviet Union would directly invade Iran. Instead, Soviet policy seemed designed to wean Iran away from the West by playing up local dissatisfaction with the paltry level of Western aid and promising a better return for alliance with Moscow.[101] To counteract this strategy Washington already had increased its aid to Tehran. But given its ongoing commitments to Western Europe and the war in Korea, the U.S. contribution to Iran's economic stability was limited. This made it all the more important that the British seek a rapid resolution to the burgeoning Anglo-Iranian oil dispute. Their failure to recognize that nationalist sentiment had fostered Iran's opposition to the supplemental agreement could lead to disaster, not only for Iran and Britain but for the West as a whole. With these considerations in mind U.S. officials would spend the coming months acting as honest brokers in the Anglo-Iranian imbroglio. The goal was a compromise settlement that served the interests of all concerned, but the outcome, as we will see, was a miserable failure.

chapter 3

Washington in the Middle
THE NATIONALIZATION OF IRANIAN OIL

The Iranian oil crisis came to a head during the first half of 1951. After a four-month effort to win government support for nationalization the National Front attained one of its goals when Mohammed Mossadeq became prime minister in late April. Thereafter the front's leaders hoped to use oil profits to finance the Seven-Year Plan for economic development and improve the standard of living for all Iranians. Their plans, however, met with strong opposition from the British government, which was determined to protect the AIOC, even if this required military force.

Iranian oil contributed heavily to Britain's balance of payments, which in early 1951 had taken a turn for the worse. Iran was also strategically important for Britain and the Western alliance in general. In addition, and perhaps most important, British officials feared losing influence in Iran so soon after withdrawing from India and Palestine and worried that successful Iranian nationalization would spur similar actions in other parts of the world, notably in Egypt where the British were concerned about the safety of the Suez Canal. For all these reasons the British would not acquiesce in Iran's unilateral cancellation of the AIOC's contract, especially when the Iranians had abrogated the right to do so in the 1933 concession agreement.

The U.S. government appreciated Britain's distress at the potential loss of Iranian oil, but U.S. leaders, preoccupied with the escalating war in

Korea and the ongoing reconstruction of Western Europe, would not openly support the British position. State Department officials were primarily concerned about the cold war implications of the crisis. They feared that strong British opposition to nationalization would result in political chaos in Iran and ultimately push that country, and its plentiful oil supplies, into the Soviet camp. But because U.S. policy makers also feared the consequences of nationalization for other international investments, they tried to moderate Iranian policy as well. The best course, they counseled both sides, was a negotiated settlement that paid lip service to the idea of nationalization but also recognized the contractual rights of the AIOC. Such a settlement, they maintained, would safeguard the interests of both Britain and Iran while preserving world peace and the global balance of power.

As we will see, these arguments swayed neither Britain nor Iran. Foreign Office declarations about the rule of law and the sanctity of contracts collided with Iranian assertions that nationalization was a duty as well as a right. Resolution of the oil crisis was also hampered by serious cultural differences between policy makers in the West and their Iranian counterparts. Anglo-American officials, who remained wedded to the orientalism that had dominated Western thinking on the Middle East for generations, had difficulty dealing with what Sir Francis Shepherd, the British ambassador in Tehran, termed "characteristic defects in the Persian mode of conducting business."[1] U.S. and British officials found Prime Minister Mossadeq particularly difficult to handle; they came to consider him inferior, childlike, and feminine, not manly enough for international politics and unfit to hold the office of premier. Although U.S. policy makers tried at first to steer a middle course as honest brokers of the Anglo-Iranian imbroglio, as time went on they found themselves assuming a more pro-British position that would use Whitehall to protect Iran and its oil from communist expansion at a time when U.S. resources were committed elsewhere.

II

Continuing talks between the AIOC and the British government in early January 1951 gave little evidence that the company's position was softening. Although the company's managing director reported that the AIOC had "never closed the door" to the principle of fifty-fifty profit sharing, he expressed doubt that Iran would accept such an arrangement, particularly if it meant surrendering claims to profits from the AIOC's non-Iranian operations. Besides, he said, the AIOC's original concession had been based on profit sharing between the company and the government and had been changed at Iran's request. Under these circumstances company officials remained steadfast in their support of the supplemental agreement, saying that it was "not possible . . . to produce an oil agreement in simpler terms" and blaming Razmara for not doing enough to support it.[2]

British policy makers applauded the AIOC's apparent readiness to consider an equal division of profits with the Iranian government but did not share the company's admiration for the supplemental agreement. B. A. B. Burrows of the British embassy in Washington thought the agreement "unintelligible to the ordinary person" and called for "some really new approach" to the Iranian problem. Ambassador Shepherd in Tehran agreed. The "time for waiting" and for temporary "palliatives" had passed, he asserted. Needed was a "fairly long term and imaginative solution," achieved, if necessary, by "pressure brought on the company . . . at the highest level." Similar expressions came from Geoffrey W. Furlonge and Eric A. Berthoud in the Foreign Office and from at least one member of the AIOC's staff, Sir Frederick Leggett, the company's labor adviser. All three considered the supplemental agreement a dead letter and believed that only a fresh and imaginative approach to the oil question would satisfy Iranian aspirations and avert a potential disaster for the AIOC's position in Iran.[3]

Specifically, in a scheme that resembles the settlement ultimately worked out in 1954 Furlonge, Berthoud, and their colleagues called for the creation of a new oil company that would deal only with Iranian operations. The Iranians would receive 50 percent of the company's profits as well as the right to appoint one member of its board of directors. Although the advocates of this arrangement recognized the difficulties associated with organizing a new company, they nonetheless saw it as the best way to settle the oil dispute "in the face of ever more vociferous [Iranian] nationalism." As Ambassador Shepherd put it, "The risk of not [going along] may in the long run be greater." And to ensure that the AIOC went along, he and other officials were prepared to "exert such [governmental] pressure, as may seem called for."[4]

Indeed, the Foreign Office had decided by mid-January that "there might be advantage[s]" to departing from the traditional policy of government noninterference in the AIOC's operations and instead working to push the company toward greater flexibility. After all, the company's methods had now been discredited; the oil question could no longer be "treated on a basis of finance or normal commercial practice." In addition, the Foreign Office considered Iran's precarious economic situation "politically frightening." Some kind of financial assistance was clearly necessary to stabilize the country's economy and forestall a takeover of the Iranian government by extremists in the Tudeh Party or the National Front. With the British treasury preoccupied with the balance-of-payments crisis the AIOC would have to shoulder the burden of such assistance, even if it had to be coerced into action. A passive government policy risked other dangers as well, including the loss of "American sympathy" in Iran and the prospects of Anglo-American cooperation in the Middle East as a whole.[5]

All these dangers were real enough, especially the possibility of Anglo-American discord. U.S. officials believed that the British government was pursuing a mistaken policy that left the AIOC with too much power. Ambassador Grady in Tehran, for example, asserted that despite "their frequent expressions of a common purpose with us . . . the deeds of the British Government and AIOC are producing exactly the opposite effect." British failure to reach a settlement with Razmara during the fall of 1950 had allowed the oil question to reach a point of hysteria, Grady said, and he feared that Iran was on the brink of "becoming another satellite of Russia." Secretary Acheson concurred. He did not understand how the British could show so "little concern . . . over developments in Iran," or how they could continue to follow such a "dangerous course." Because the Iranian situation had important worldwide ramifications Acheson was prepared, if need be, to step up U.S. pressure on the British government.[6]

In the meantime Prime Minister Razmara urged the Majlis to appoint a new commission to study the oil problem. This commission, to be composed of three deputies, three senators, and three distinguished private citizens, would consult with the prime minister, draw up amendments to the supplemental agreement, and submit a new proposal to the AIOC. The new terms, or so Razmara hoped, "would be so eminently fair" as to "be acceptable to the AIOC, especially when [they] became known to the public." Through the proposed commission, in other words, the prime minister apparently intended to mobilize public opinion in Iran and abroad on behalf of an oil settlement that would isolate both the AIOC and his critics in the National Front.[7]

Once again, however, Razmara was swimming against a swelling current of Iranian enmity toward the AIOC. The National Front had stirred up considerable public opposition to the supplemental agreement and had kept the oil issue at center stage in the Majlis, where Mossadeq and his allies continued to press for nationalization. On 11 January their anti-AIOC campaign pushed the Majlis to reject Razmara's proposed commission. Instead, that body gave the original commission, headed by Mossadeq, exclusive jurisdiction over the oil question and two months to formulate a new oil policy.[8]

The Majlis's decision did not bode well for the AIOC's position in Iran. At best the commission would push for a fifty-fifty sharing of profits, an arrangement that the company was willing to discuss; at worst it would demand immediate nationalization, an option that the company still considered more threat than substance.

"Nobody, including the National Front, had thought out what it meant," the AIOC's chief officer in Tehran told representatives of the Treasury, Foreign Office, and Ministry of Fuel and Power at a mid-January meeting in London. The idea was nothing more than a stick that the National Front was using "to beat the [Iranian] Government and frighten the British and the Company." Ambassador Shepherd thought along similar lines. As he saw things, only the "feebleness of successive [Iranian] Governments" had allowed the "demagogues" of the National Front to popularize the idea of nationalization. All that was needed to remedy the situation, at least according to the ambassador, was a strong statement from Razmara's government explaining the impracticality of nationalization and recommending a settlement with the AIOC.[9]

But as both Grady and Shepherd subsequently reported, the reversion of the oil dispute to the original commission called into question the government's ability to retain control of the situation. After all, that commission was headed by Mossadeq, contained a number of National Front supporters, and backed the ever more popular idea of nationalization. In Grady's opinion it had not "distinguished itself through constructive unemotional consideration of [the] oil question" and was unlikely to take an objective view of the situation. Shepherd too found it "difficult to have any confidence in a commission which produced so lamentable a document" as the November 1950 report rejecting the supplemental agreement. Nor did the ambassadors believe that Razmara's government, which was running a monthly budget deficit of £1.5 million, could remain afloat in the months required to implement the new plan or that Razmara was strong enough to resist the increasing public clamor for nationalization.[10]

Even Razmara, who was usually optimistic, viewed the new developments with trepidation. He acknowledged that nationalization had won the support of "an important group in the Majlis." That group had wrested control of the oil issue from the government and placed it before a commission that was controlled by Mossadeq and his allies. This commission would be "more difficult to deal with" than the one Razmara had proposed, although the prime minister still thought that "something concrete" could be accomplished if the AIOC acted in good faith.[11]

With this goal in mind Razmara renewed his earlier efforts to win additional financial support from the AIOC for the ailing Iranian economy. Lack of funds had already forced the government to delay the payment of municipal salaries and curtail implementation of the Seven-Year Plan. It had also been a contributing factor in the dismissal of Overseas Consultants, Inc., the U.S. firm that had drafted the plan.[12] To help meet current government expenses Razmara asked the AIOC to deposit £10 million of fully convertible sterling in the Bank Melli, the national bank of Iran. This deposit would be treated not as an advance against oil royalties but as a loan to be used by the Bank Melli to support a new issue of Iranian currency. But these provisions raised concern among officials in the Bank Melli. Fearing the inflationary results of a new currency issue and worried that Iran could not afford to increase its foreign debt, they ultimately blocked Razmara's proposal.[13]

The AIOC had been willing to negotiate the loan, no doubt hoping to bolster Razmara's government against more radical alternatives and buy more time for the prime minister and the company to outmaneuver their opponents in the National Front. The company was also willing to consider additional financial advances, in lieu of a loan, to the Iranian government. The AIOC would "not pay out money under the Supplemental Oil Agreement in the absence of ratification," said Sir William Fraser, but it would make advances against its accumulated reserves, "even if this meant advancing more than was due on oil already extracted." Although these advances would not be "tied to any [particular] concession or agreement," the company clearly believed that redressing "Iran's precarious financial situation" would contribute to "a more favorable climate for negotiation of an oil settlement."[14]

In early February 1951 Razmara and the AIOC agreed on a timetable for company advances to the Iranian government, but the prime minister prohibited public announcement of the agreement for fear it would lead critics to portray his government as a British stooge. For the same reason the exchange of letters formalizing the agreement made it appear as if the company had initiated the transaction, which began with a secret payment of £5 million on 8 February. This was the first installment of what company officials and the British government hoped would be a yearlong program to stave off economic and political collapse in Iran and provide Razmara with time to plan his next move.[15]

The next initiative, though, came not from Razmara but from the oil commission, which in early February asked the government to assess the feasibility of nationalization. The request seemed to signal the commission's preferred course of action and confirmed the shah's fears that Mos-

sadeq and his colleagues would vote for nationalization without considering other alternatives.[16] Razmara shared these fears, especially the shah's
belief that Iran lacked the technical know-how to manage the complex oil
industry. The prime minister's initial strategy was therefore to delay the
government's response to the commission's request and instead initiate
studies on various aspects of nationalization by the ministries of finance,
justice, national economy, and foreign affairs. These studies, he believed,
would prove that nationalization was unworkable and allow him to steer the
oil commission in a more moderate direction. While these studies were
under way, moreover, Razmara laid plans to consult with members of the
oil commission not clearly identified with the National Front and seek their
support for a policy that stopped short of nationalization.[17]

Razmara needed all the support he could muster. The Foreign Office's
earlier assertion that only "a small if vociferous minority" of Iranians supported nationalization had by mid-February been roundly discredited. By
that time, in fact, nationalization had become a cause célèbre for the Iranian
people, who increasingly backed the National Front's assault against
Razmara's apparent refusal to heed the popular will. Support for nationalization was especially high on the National Front–controlled oil commission. In Shepherd's estimation seven or eight of the commission's eighteen
members "would definitely vote for nationalisation . . . and their influence
would be quite likely to secure them a majority." This was bad news for
Razmara as well as for the AIOC.[18]

To avert disaster in Iran the AIOC resumed talks with Razmara that
looked toward a profit-sharing arrangement similar to ARAMCO's agreement with Saudi Arabia. E. G. D. Northcroft, the AIOC's chief officer in
Iran, reaffirmed the company's willingness to consider such an arrangement but was quick to point out that it would take at least a year to implement and would require the Iranians to abrogate their claim to profits from
the AIOC's worldwide operations. After Razmara dismissed these qualifi-
cations as unimportant, he and Northcroft agreed on 10 February to a proposal whereby the AIOC would establish a new subsidiary to manage its
Iranian operations. Profits generated by the new subsidiary would be
divided equally between the AIOC and the Iranian government, and Iran's
claims against the company would be satisfied through a lump-sum payment. Curiously, this proposal made no mention of Iranian representation
on the new company's board of directors, a key Iranian demand throughout
1950. Nevertheless, initial company reaction was jubilant, as it appeared
that resolution of the oil dispute was imminent.[19]

This optimism was shattered when Razmara presented the proposal informally to moderates on the oil commission in terms that left the door open to nationalization. To be sure, Razmara told the commissioners that "nationalisation at [the] present stage might prove a national disaster." But he refused to "rule out nationalisation as [a] long term solution," suggesting instead that his government continue "to study its practicability and report back to the Majlis" at a later date.[20] The prime minister's strategy was clear enough. Although endorsing the new proposal, he sought to present it in a fashion that would appease nationalist sentiment in Iran, disarm Mossadeq and the other supporters of nationalization on the oil commission, and win support from the moderates. Once the commissioners understood the depth of British opposition to nationalization, as well as the legal, technical, and financial difficulties of such a course, Razmara expected them to pass a resolution that paid lip service to the idea of nationalization while authorizing him to negotiate on the basis of the AIOC's new proposal.[21]

If this was Razmara's strategy, it was one that the British found hard to accept. Ambassador Shepherd asserted that the British government "could not be indifferent" to threats of nationalization, however vague or imprecise. He also pointed out that the AIOC's contract was valid until 1993 and that Articles 21 and 26 of the 1933 concession agreement specifically forbade nationalization. In addition, Shepherd seemed to blame Razmara for allowing the nationalization movement to gain so much ground: had the prime minister taken a stronger stand on the supplemental agreement and worked more actively for ratification, he reasoned, it would not be necessary to appease public sentiment by hinting that nationalization offered a viable long-term solution. Nor was Shepherd the only one who thought Razmara had failed to "give a strong enough lead" in the right direction. Some members of the oil commission were confused by his waffling on the issue of nationalization and did not know where he stood. The National Front—which had now emerged as the only organized political force in Iran, albeit through what the British saw as intimidation and threats of violence—was calling for his resignation. The British government was pressing Razmara to present the new proposal he had worked out with the AIOC, or something similar, to the oil commission. And the AIOC had decided to release a long report that would outline its position on nationalization, explain why Iran was unable to run its oil industry, and thereby persuade the oil commission that nationalization was impracticable.[22]

Razmara bowed to British pressure—thereby confirming the prevailing, culturally motivated belief within the Foreign Office that it was "Iranian nature to respond favorable [sic] to stiff talk"—and on 4 March informed the commission of Britain's strong opposition to nationalization. Although he did report the AIOC's willingness to arrange a more equitable sharing of profits with the Iranian government, he remained silent on the company's willingness to discuss a fifty-fifty arrangement, probably in hopes of garnering all the credit for such a scheme when the time came. He also made public the reports of his ministers, which showed nationalization to be impracticable, and repeated his conviction that such a course would be disastrous. These initiatives, Razmara hoped, would secure either the oil commission's outright rejection of nationalization or, barring that verdict, an examination of the question by foreign experts that would delay final action until a better arrangement could be worked out with the AIOC.[23]

The prime minister's newfound resolve, in Shepherd's prejudiced view, showed that he was "responding to treatment." Razmara's strong stand before the oil commission thwarted National Front plans for immediate nationalization. It also seemed to portend a political shift in Iran toward a more moderate policy and renewed hope of an oil settlement among British and U.S. officials, who believed that Razmara had finally found the courage to stand up to Mossadeq and the pronationalization faction on the oil commission. And although Anglo-American officials were reluctant to declare victory, most agreed that Razmara's long-awaited public opposition to all-out nationalization had greatly improved the chances of a satisfactory settlement.[24]

Anglo-American hopes were dashed, however, when Razmara was assassinated on 7 March by a member of the radical Fedayan Islam, a religious terrorist group that favored nationalization. Razmara's death was a direct result of his antinationalization stance before the oil commission. It resulted in widespread rejoicing throughout Iran and generated veiled warnings that others who opposed nationalization would meet the same fate. Ayatollah Kashani, whose Society of Moslem Warriors was allied with Mossadeq's National Front, was especially threatening, calling Razmara's assassination a "brilliant stroke of great courage and virtue" and proclaiming that "other traitors" to Iran would be "similarly struck down." Political murder, for Kashani and his followers, at least, was apparently a morally defensible means to a greater end. For the Anglo-Americans Razmara's death meant the loss of an important, if often ineffectual, ally in Iran. To be sure, Razmara had only recently adopted a strong stance vis-à-vis the National Front and was certainly not all that the British and U.S. governments would have wanted in an Iranian prime minister. But at least he was someone the Anglo-Americans could trust. The same would probably not be true of his successor. As far as the Anglo-Americans were concerned,

Razmara's assassination, and the threat of further violence that it engendered, showed how politically charged the oil question had become. It also marked a turning point in the Anglo-Iranian dispute and set the stage for a deepening crisis in the months ahead.[25]

III

Razmara left no designated successor. Potential prime ministers abounded, such as former prime minister Ahmad Qavam and perennial hopeful Seyid Zia, but none seemed likely to win the support of the shah, who was now considered the key to the oil situation, or of the British and the Americans, for that matter. Officially, the Foreign Office and the State Department refrained from expressing their preferences for fear of exposing themselves to charges of interfering in Iran's domestic affairs or of compromising the credibility of any future prime minister by making him appear to be an Anglo-American puppet. Behind the scenes, however, they sought to influence the shah's selection by encouraging him to take "forceful action" and reminding him of the importance of appointing someone he could trust. These entreaties did seem to have some effect on the shah, who appointed Hossein Ala as Iran's new prime minister on 11 March.

Ala was a British-educated aristocrat whose career in public service spanned more than three decades and was marked most notably by stints as minister or ambassador to Madrid, Paris, London, and Washington. He was unquestionably loyal to the shah and had his complete confidence. But Ala's relations with the National Front were strained at best, and it was the National Front that had taken control of the oil issue.[26]

Even before Ala had assumed office it was obvious that he would have difficultly controlling the National Front, which, according to Shepherd, was in a position to bully the oil commission. At a meeting on 9 March, in fact, the commission had bowed to National Front pressure by unanimously supporting the principle of nationalization and beginning work on a plan for putting nationalization into place. Neither Shepherd nor the Foreign Office was initially dismayed by this development. Because the commission's plan was not due for two months, the ambassador thought that the delay left "the way open for negotiation." His colleagues in London agreed. Now the AIOC would have time to publicize its recent advances to Iran and reiterate its willingness to negotiate on a fifty-fifty basis, both of which might soften opinion in Iran. But officials in the Foreign Office and the AIOC also thought that immediate action by the British government would be necessary to guard against a change in the status of nationalization from "'whether' to 'when.'" Revising an idea discussed earlier, they proposed that a diplomatic note be sent to the Iranian government and published shortly thereafter. The note would reiterate Britain's opposition to nationalization and warn Iran that any step in this direction would lead to a dangerous confrontation between the two countries. The hope was that by warning the Iranians of the consequences of nationalization the British could thus forestall "the tendency of the oil question to slip down hill."[27]

On 13 March Shepherd implemented this strategy by delivering a note to Ala that summarized Britain's position on the oil question. It recounted the history of the supplemental agreement, listed the legal and practical obstacles to nationalization, revealed the AIOC's recent advances to Razmara, and repeated the company's willingness to negotiate on a fifty-fifty basis. In polite but pointed language the note also emphasized that the British government could not "be indifferent to the affairs of the Anglo-Iranian Oil Company, an important British, and indeed, international interest." Although expressing the hope that future discussions would "take place on a fair and reasonable basis," the note clearly implied that such a basis left no room for nationalization.[28]

If Ala transmitted Shepherd's note to the Majlis, no evidence exists that British warnings influenced that body when it reconvened on 15 March. On the contrary, the National Front dominated the session, turning it into what Grady called a "complete emotional display." Although only a handful of Majlis deputies actually belonged to the National Front, strong pronationalization sentiment among nearly all quarters of Iranian society, "from religious reactionaries of the far right to Tudeh members of the far left," guaranteed their support.[29] Whereas the shah and the British had hoped to delay the session by preventing a quorum, the National Front coerced attendance by threatening to brand all absentee deputies as traitors. It then succeeded in unanimously pushing through the oil commission's resolution endorsing the principle of nationalization and giving the commission two months to draft a plan for putting nationalization into place.[30]

The absence of debate on the resolution, and its unanimous acceptance by the Majlis, portended grave difficulties for the AIOC's position in Iran. Ambassador Grady termed passage of the resolution a "most serious" development. The principle of nationalization was now widely accepted in Iran, he said, and the Ala government had revealed a "complete absence of [the] courage needed to oppose [it]." Grady blamed the British failure to adopt a "statesmanlike approach" to the oil question for allowing the situation to get out of hand. Had the British made a "good offer" several weeks earlier, the United States might have backed them publicly. Instead, they had pursued a hard-line policy that the State Department had been unable to support. Nor did Grady believe that U.S. action was appropriate now. "The problem must be considered [a] British one," he asserted, in which the United States was "in no way involved."[31]

In Washington Acheson had reached a similar conclusion. As always he was concerned with the economic and strategic implications of the Iranian crisis, implications that he thought the British failed fully to grasp. He wanted to keep Iran outside the Soviet orbit and Iranian oil "flowing to world markets." He also wanted to protect U.S. prestige around the world, which would suffer if the oil dispute precipitated economic unrest that led to Iran's collapse to communism. But despite the gravity of the situation Acheson agreed with Grady that direct U.S. intervention in Tehran was out of the question. After all, he proclaimed, the United States recognized the "right of sovereign states to nationalize," provided they made "just compensation"; U.S. intervention could alienate the Iranians and "result in [the] loss of Iran to [the] Soviets." Like Grady, moreover, Acheson blamed the British for the deepening crisis. The latest in what Acheson saw as a series of British errors was Shepherd's note to Ala of 13 March, which the secretary thought had precipitated the Majlis's resolution in favor of nationalization. It was his belief that a change in the "policies and/or management" of the AIOC was long overdue, and he hoped that the two-month delay while the oil commission prepared its report would allow British leaders time to formulate a "skillful, fresh" approach to their problem in Iran.[32]

The British response was less skillful than Acheson had demanded, but signs existed that U.S. opinion was making a difference. Despite concerns in Washington that the "growing xenophobia" and "hatred of [the] AIOC [then prevalent] in Iran" would make such a course provocative and might undermine Ala's government, the Foreign Office decided to publicize Shepherd's recent note to the prime minister in hopes that "baring [the] lion's teeth" would forestall a rush toward nationalization. For similar reasons the British also resumed their propaganda campaign in Tehran, warning of the difficulties that nationalization would entail, especially because British officials believed the Iranians incapable of running the oil industry on their own, and of the danger of a potential confrontation with Great Britain.[33] At the same time, however, officials in the Foreign Office conceded that any government in Tehran that ignored the "principle of nationalization" could not hope to survive. They were still unwilling to accept nationalization as a fait accompli. But they did acknowledge that further

British concessions would be needed if the AIOC hoped to assuage nationalist sentiment and retain a semblance of its former control over Iranian oil. Although AIOC officials remained reluctant to make additional concessions, the Foreign Office had concluded that some sort of "friendly partnership" that gave Iran "something more than a fifty-fifty" share in the company's profits but still ensured AIOC control of the industry might stop the drift toward all-out nationalization. Working "hand in glove" with the AIOC the British government set about preparing a new proposal along these lines for presentation to the government in Tehran.[34] In the interval, moreover, they sought to mend fences with their colleagues in Washington, where imminent Anglo-American talks on the Iranian problem would soon highlight again the different strategies of the two allies.

Both the Americans and the British had called for these discussions in the wake of recent events in Iran. For the United States consultation might prevent the British from continuing the tough stand that had characterized their recent note to Ala. Such a strategy, the State Department feared, might undermine Ala's government and push Iran into the Soviet camp, thereby destroying Western strategy for the Middle East. To prevent such a calamity, the State Department argued, immediate bilateral discussions and the formulation of a joint policy regarding the Iranian situation were essential.[35] The British agreed to the talks but for narrower reasons. As the situation in Iran deteriorated, U.S. officials had begun saying, "We told you so." They had stepped up their complaints against the AIOC's "anachronistic policies" and "colonial attitude," criticized the Foreign Office for failing to push the company toward a more flexible and realistic policy, and cautioned the British against using "financial or other pressures" to achieve their objectives in Iran. Given these and other criticisms, the British worried that U.S. leaders would declare their support for Iran, which would jeopardize the Middle Eastern interests of both countries, undermine Anglo-American relations in general, and "play into the hands of the Russians." It was thus important that the Iranians be disabused of any ideas about Anglo-American discord. The United States must lend its full support to British efforts in Iran.[36]

The continuing differences between British and U.S. thinking became clear when the Washington talks opened on 9 April. The U.S. delegates, led by George McGhee, stressed the importance of maintaining political stability in Iran if that country was to be denied to the Soviet Union. Their arguments echoed U.S. intelligence estimates, which had also emphasized the importance of Iranian oil for the Western alliance, especially during the Korean War. Demand for aviation gasoline and other fuels needed for military transport had increased so substantially since the outbreak of the war that U.S. policy makers considered rationing civilian supplies. To forestall such a development Iran had to remain firmly within the Western bloc. If Iran was lost to the Soviets, McGhee and his colleagues warned the British, its oil would be lost as well. The British must therefore accept nationalization in principle if they hoped to retain control of the Iranian oil industry in practice. In other words, the assistant secretary asserted, the British had to find some way of accepting the term *nationalization* while ensuring that they retained effective control of a nationalized Iranian industry. To this end McGhee pressed the British to arrange some sort of partnership or management contract that did not involve "real equity ownership" but gave the Iranians significant financial profits. The British, for example, might offer to operate the oil industry for Iran and split its profits equally between the AIOC and the Iranian government. McGhee was especially enamored of the fifty-fifty principle, which had worked so well to ameliorate nationalist sentiment in Venezuela. Such an arrangement, he believed, "had an aura of fairness understandable to the ordinary man" and therefore offered the best hope for success in Iran.[37]

The British conceded Iran's strategic and economic importance to the West, yet they were unwilling to make the AIOC a casualty of the cold war. The company's position in Iran was important as a "bargaining weapon" and because of the "power it gave [the British government] to control the movement of raw materials." It also made an important contribution to Britain's balance of payments and to "total Anglo-Dutch oil production," contributions that grew in importance during the balance-of-payments crisis that gripped Britain during 1951. The AIOC's Iranian operations provided Britain with £100 million annually in foreign exchange, as well as twenty-two million tons of oil products and seven million tons of crude oil each year, with the latter especially important during the continuing war in Korea. In addition, the British admiralty received 85 percent of its fuel needs from the AIOC's Abadan refinery at secret—but generally assumed to be favorable—prices and did not relish the prospect of having to seek alternative sources of supply.[38]

Under these circumstances the British felt that they could not allow Iran to gain control of the company, nor would they consider reducing the duration of the AIOC's concession, which was valid until 1993. Still doubtful of the depth and strength of the nationalization movement in Iran, which in their minds "had no solid grievances to feed on," the British rebuffed U.S. entreaties for a plan that contained "some flavour or facade of nationalisation while retaining [the] substance of control." To them the AIOC's concession was more than a mere commercial contract. It was a moral agreement that Iran could not abrogate unilaterally.[39]

With each side so firmly wedded to a contrary position it is not surprising that the Washington talks failed to produce a common posture on Iran. U.S. officials categorically refused to support a British policy that would not recognize, at least in principle, Iran's legal right to nationalize its oil industry. The British refused to concede this right, pinning their hopes instead on a slightly improved version of the plan earlier offered to Razmara, which they called "Persianisation and partnership." The most important features of this plan, worked out in conjunction with the AIOC, would create a new U.K.-registered company to handle the AIOC's Iranian concession and assets and divide that company's profits equally between the Iranian government and the AIOC. The Foreign Office saw this proposal as likely to appease the Iranians and allow for a resolution of the oil dispute. The United States disagreed. Although McGhee thought the new proposal an improvement over previous British initiatives, he was dismayed that the British still refused to recognize Iran's legal right to nationalize the AIOC's property. This meant that Iran was bound to reject the new proposal, he said, and that the United States was bound to maintain its position of "benevolent neutrality" until the British made further concessions.[40]

Just as British and U.S. officials held different positions going into the Washington talks, so did they assess the meeting's results differently. U.S. promises of benevolent neutrality and hints at further support boosted British spirits. British Ambassador Oliver Franks thought that U.S. officials had "moved very considerably from their earlier disapproval and were now anxious to help." McGhee and his colleagues, however, found the talks "unsatisfactory and disappointing." The British, they lamented, had allowed the AIOC crisis "to take precedence over the more important question of keeping Iran free and independent." Nor were U.S. officials optimistic about Britain's ability to manage the Iranian crisis in the future. Because the proposal that the British unveiled in Washington stood little chance of winning Iranian support, it would lead to disaster for the British and might ultimately push Iran into the Soviet camp.[41]

Developments in Iran during the Washington talks seemed to confirm U.S. pessimism. On 9 April the Iranian government had replied to Shepherd's note of 13 March, saying that its "business [was] with the A.I.O.C.," not the British government, and condemning the company's rigid defense of the supplemental agreement, which did not square with nationalist aspirations in Iran or with "the rights of the Iranian people." Despite the threatening tone of Shepherd's note, the Iranian government refused to bow to pressure from London or take any action until the Majlis Oil Commission had made its recommendation. British policy makers, who characterized Iran's reply as offensive, were even more alarmed when Mossadeq publicly affirmed the inevitability of nationalization, stating that the matter had "passed from the stage of decision to that of action." He rejected arbitration, denounced as unlawful the British government's interference in the oil dispute, and labeled Shepherd's note an exercise in intimidation. He also blasted the Washington talks as intolerable Anglo-American interference in Iran's internal affairs and noted angrily that Iran had not even been invited to participate in discussing its future.[42]

By this time, in fact, support for nationalization was running so high in Iran that Ambassador Grady warned of "outright confiscation." Almost nothing that the AIOC could offer would be acceptable to the Iranians, who were motivated more by their hatred of the company's "Victorian paternalism" than by any practical considerations. Iranian opposition to the company, he said, was evident in a strike that had broken out in the southwestern oil fields and spread, with Tudeh assistance, throughout the country. The strike, a direct response to the AIOC's decision to discontinue a hardship allowance for workers in the outlying oil area of Bandar Mashur, was fueled by promises of higher wages and more comprehensive benefits under nationalization. It halted oil production and prompted Ala to declare martial law for two months. Yet even in the face of such obvious Iranian opposition to the AIOC, the Foreign Office and the company continued to believe that they knew how to deal with the Iranians. In Grady's opinion such claims flew in the face of reality. Clearly, the ambassador reported, the British were badly misinformed about what was happening in Iran and were operating "on the assumption that the Iranians would not cut off their noses to spite their faces." In truth, he said, in a display of the same sort of cultural superiority that led the British to think they knew best how to handle the Iranians, "there is nothing they love better to do." The task, he concluded, was to find a formula that would satisfy both "Iranian emotions" and British demands for an "efficient operation of AIOC properties" and the "cash income" those properties generated.[43]

This task, difficult under the best of circumstances, was made more difficult by the lack of "any constructive thinking" in Iran, Grady reported. Although Ala received a vote of confidence on 17 April, there was widespread feeling in Tehran that he was inadequate to "the present difficult position," Shepherd said. According to Grady, who was increasingly convinced that the AIOC and the British government must "take the initiative," neither Ala nor any of his advisers had concrete ideas about how to resolve the situation. Instead, the prime minister seemed content to let things drift. Unable to marshal substantial support in the Majlis or from the shah, he could neither disarm the National Front nor stem the rising tide in support of nationalization. By late April, in fact, the prime minister had apparently abandoned hope of remaining in office for any appreciable length of time.[44]

In the absence of firm leadership in Tehran the Foreign Office moved to implement the plan it had unveiled in Washington. The first stage called for informal exploratory talks between Ambassador Shepherd and Prime Minister Ala to "determine an appropriate basis for opening negotiations" with the AIOC. Shepherd outlined the British proposal to the prime minister on 26 April and signaled his hope that Ala would use it as a basis for negotiations with the AIOC. The ambassador found this meeting disheartening. Ala completely rejected his assertion that nationalization, although perhaps an option "in due course," when the Iranians could really operate the oil installations, was impractical and out of the question now. Instead, the prime minister insisted that, unless the British accepted the principle of nationalization and the right of the Iranians to "run the [oil] industry," they would lose everything. Although Ala promised to give the proposal further study, it fell far short in his mind of what members of the "National Front were demanding" and what the oil commission would accept and was therefore unlikely to win the commission's acceptance.[45]

Ala's predictions were borne out when the oil commission met later that same day to consider a resolution that would build on the Majlis's earlier endorsement of nationalization in principle by establishing an Iranian company to replace the AIOC and exploit its holdings. This nine-article resolution called for the creation of a thirteen-member committee that would take control of the company's assets, arrange for the continued sale of Iranian oil to previous customers, and make provision for the payment of the company's claims against Iran out of current receipts. The commission's hastily called meeting surprised the prime minister, who unsuccessfully tried to reason with Mossadeq. On 27 April the commission presented Ala with a fait accompli by passing the Nine-Point Resolution, thereby nationalizing the oil industry and establishing an Iranian board to take over the AIOC's operations. Grady called the commission's action "ill-considered and un-thought-out" but conceded that the Nine-Point Resolution would "probably become [the] law of Iran within a few days." "Nothing that anyone might do at this date," he lamented, "can forestall such action."[46]

Indeed, events moved with even more speed and finality than Grady had anticipated. In what McGhee and other U.S. officials termed "a most serious development," Ala suddenly resigned in protest over the commission's decision, thereby removing from power the only Iranian politician who might have been able to keep the National Front at bay and negotiate an oil settlement that the AIOC could accept. But Ala's resignation was not the only blow to the Anglo-American position in Iran. Making matters worse was the Majlis's appointment of Mossadeq as Ala's successor rather than Seyid Zia, the expected appointee. Seyid Zia, who had co-led the 1921 coup that brought the shah's father to power, was widely considered pro-British, and if appointed prime minister he had promised to dissolve the Majlis, which would greatly improve the AIOC's position in Iran.[47]

Although Zia's appointment at one point appeared certain, maneuvering in the Majlis led instead to the surprise selection of Mossadeq, who received 79 of the 100 votes cast. Ambassador Shepherd informed the shah that officials in London "would have no confidence" in the new prime minister. But given the strength of Mossadeq's support in the Majlis, the shah felt compelled to acquiesce in his appointment. As a precondition for accepting the office Mossadeq demanded ratification of the oil commission's decision in favor of nationalization. Without approval of the measure before his acceptance of the premiership he feared an opposition filibuster regarding the confirmation of his cabinet that might derail his government and cripple the nationalist movement. The prime minister–designate got his wish when ratification received unanimous support from all deputies present; the absence of prolonged debate signaled both the widespread support for nationalization within the Majlis and the seriousness of the situation for the British.[48]

With passage of the measure likely by the Iranian Senate the British mounted a desperate eleventh-hour campaign to rescue their position in Iran. In a protest statement approved by the Foreign Office the AIOC asserted that the 1933 agreement specifically prevented Iran from unilaterally abrogating the oil concession.[49] The Foreign Office reaffirmed this view when Shepherd issued a statement that reviewed the history of AIOC-Iranian relations and proclaimed London's belief that Iran had surrendered its right to nationalize the company's holdings when it signed the 1933 agreement. Shepherd's release also quoted an earlier statement by the new foreign secretary, Herbert Morrison, who had replaced the ailing Ernest Bevin on 9 March. Morrison assumed office at a critical point in the oil dispute, and it is possible that he could have done nothing to avert the coming crisis. But given his inexperience in foreign affairs and the stark contrast the bombastic and confrontational Morrison made to his calm and moderate predecessor, the chances for an amicable resolution of the oil dispute under Morrison's direction were slim. Indeed, his first public pronouncement regarding the situation was a bellicose warning to Tehran that "uni-lateral or precipitate action" would "have very serious and far-reaching consequences."[50]

These British initiatives, together with the rapidly deteriorating situation in Iran, greatly complicated efforts to achieve a common Anglo-American strategy. Secretary of State Acheson feared that "events might now be mov-ing so quickly . . . that there would be no time to deal with them sensibly." He lamented Britain's stubborn refusal to concede Iran's right to national-ize the oil industry. He also still believed that British leaders could at least "offer the shadow of nationalisation so long as [they] retained a few vital practical points," by which he undoubtedly meant that the British should propose an arrangement that would allow them to manage the oil industry on behalf of Iran and split the industry's profits equally between the AIOC and the Iranian government. McGhee made much the same argument, albeit with more passion and spirit. He blamed the halfhearted British pro-posals for contributing to Ala's resignation, stressed the importance of acceding to Iranian demands, and adopted what the British called a "hec-toring attitude" that amounted to "unhelpful needling" and advocated "appeasement" of the Iranians. From the U.S. point of view, however, it was the British who were being unhelpful and wrecking the chances for Anglo-American cooperation in a constructive solution to the oil imbroglio. The British were dead set against any concession to the princi-ple of nationalization, determined to "fight it out on this line if it [took] all summer," and unable to see that such a policy had not succeeded in the past and would not succeed in the future. On the contrary, U.S. officials argued again, it would play into the hands of Iranian extremists and push the coun-try into the waiting arms of the Soviet Union.[51]

The situation worsened on 1 May, when the shah signed into law the nationalization resolution that the Majlis had voted earlier and the Senate had subsequently approved. Under the Nine-Point Law Iran officially nationalized the AIOC's holdings, laid plans to assume its operations, and promised to pay compensation to the company—but only if the AIOC set-tled all of Iran's outstanding counterclaims. To initiate the takeover of the AIOC's operations the new law created the Mixed Oil Commission, con-sisting of members of the Senate and Majlis and representatives chosen by the new prime minister, whom Shepherd described as "extremely difficult" to negotiate with, not "easily amenable to reason," and possibly "tempera-mentally incapable" of getting "down to realities." British officials feared they would have their hands full "trying to get some of the facts of life into the head of Dr. Musaddiq, who seemed to be singularly ill-informed on many questions of demonstrable fact." He had, they said, spent the last forty years doing "nothing but listen to the sound of his own voice" and was "entirely impervious" to reason; the chances of "ever being able to negotiate with him [were] nil."[52] By drawing such conclusions about Mossadeq so soon after he assumed office British officials revealed their unwillingness right from the start to take him seriously or treat him as an equal. Instead, they wrote him off almost from day one—and ultimately convinced their U.S. counterparts to do the same.

Clearly, Mossadeq's appointment did little to brighten the chances for a satisfactory Anglo-Iranian settlement. In fact, as subsequent developments revealed, it marked a turning point in the oil dispute and significantly dimmed the chances of a successful resolution of the oil dispute. Nor was the situation helped by the continuing intransigence of the AIOC, the Foreign Office's stubborn adherence to the rule of law, or the reluctance of U.S. leaders to get more deeply involved in the ongoing crisis. Under the circumstances, as the following discussion reveals, the two months after passage of the Nine-Point Law saw little progress toward a constructive solution.

IV

The initial British reaction to the Nine-Point Law and Mossadeq's premiership did not bode well for a solution to the oil dispute that satisfied both British and Iranian demands. Officials in the Foreign Office attributed Mossadeq's rise to power to the success of "a small band of extremists" in "impos[ing] their will on the Majlis" and "silenc[ing] the voices of reason" in Iran, of which they believed "there may well be many." Given the circumstances, British officials believed that their task was to convince "intelligent Persians" that Mossadeq was a reactionary and a mad man on the lunatic fringe whose nationalization scheme was absurd and impracticable. Meanwhile Shepherd stressed the danger of communist advances, detailed the practical obstacles to Iranian operation of the oil industry, and reiterated Britain's legal objections to cancellation of the AIOC's concession. As Shepherd's last point suggests, no signs were evident of a more flexible British approach to the Iranian crisis; even the interdepartmental Persian Oil Working Party failed to produce an acceptable proposal.[53] Although British policy makers were willing to resume discussions with the government in Tehran, they continued to insist on preserving "the oil company as such even if a separate Persian branch is created." In other words, even passage of the Nine-Point Law could not induce them to accept the principle of nationalization. Prime Minister Clement Attlee summarized the British view in a stern message to Mossadeq on 2 May. Likening Iranian actions against the AIOC to those of communist countries, he warned that nationalization "would seriously affect the social and economic well-being of the Persian people, and might lead to an unhappy and most difficult situation" between Britain and Iran.[54]

Attlee's message produced an acrimonious exchange between Mossadeq and the Foreign Office. Where Attlee saw danger in Iran's apparent emulation of communist regimes, Mossadeq blamed the current crisis on the AIOC. Iran, he said, was prepared to compensate the British company and sell Iranian oil to its former customers at fair rates. But it would never forsake the new plan to control its oil industry, which was the best way to "strengthen the economic structure of the country," provide for the "general welfare of its people," and "put an end to [the country's] general poverty and dissatisfaction." Moreover, the prime minister argued, Iran was only doing what Britain had already done: using "social reforms" to prevent communism.[55] For these reasons Iran was duty bound to proceed with nationalization, even if this course led to a confrontation with the British government, which seemed likely. But as Sir Francis Shepherd made clear, "the British could not stand aside with folded arms while the Iranians pursued a course leading to inevitable disaster." Indeed, as a majority stockholder in the AIOC, the British government was determined "to protect its interests in every way [it] properly [could]." The British would take the AIOC's case to the International Court of Justice (ICJ) at The Hague, and they warned again that unilateral action by Iran would have "serious consequences."[56]

If relations between the British and Iranian governments had reached a nadir, so had those between Iran and the AIOC. On 8 May the company formally requested arbitration by the ICJ under Articles 22 and 26 of the 1933 concession, appointed an arbitrator, and invited the Iranians to appoint one of their own. Mossadeq expressed astonishment at the company's request, which he quickly rejected. He reiterated that Iran had a sovereign right to nationalize its oil and that this right could neither be surrendered nor arbitrated by an international authority.

Mossadeq was especially vocal in denouncing the validity of the 1933 concession agreement's prohibition against nationalization. Because that agreement had been signed by an autocratic regime that did not truly represent the Iranian people, it was null and void and could not be used to limit Iran's national rights. The Majlis would not retreat from the Nine-Point

Law: it represented the will of the Iranian people and had been duly passed by the Iranian legislature and signed into law by the shah. To Mossadeq's way of thinking nationalization of the oil industry constituted not only the realization of Iranian national aspirations but also the rebirth of Iranian morality. For almost fifty years, he proclaimed, the AIOC had intruded into Iran's internal affairs and contributed to the corruption and moral decay of the Iranian people. Mossadeq also blamed the company for the pathetic condition of Iran's urban slums, saying that the AIOC forced people in Tehran to "live like prehistoric man" while it grew rich on Iran's oil. The time had arrived for the Iranians to retake control of their lives. The AIOC, he said, was welcome to send a representative to Tehran but only to hammer out arrangements for the smooth transfer of its former holdings to the Iranian government. As one observer explained, the company was invited to join in "digging its own grave," or the Iranians would proceed on their own.[57]

As Anglo-Iranian discussions were reaching a deadlock, the United States was busy formulating its policy for dealing with the crisis. U.S. leaders reaffirmed Iran's right to nationalize the AIOC, but they would sanction neither nationalization without compensation nor abrogation of the company's contract against its will. In other words, they believed that any settlement of the oil question had to take account of both Iranian and British rights. Above all else, U.S. policy makers were concerned about Iran's position in the global balance of power. As a crucial bulwark against Soviet expansion in the Middle East and as an important supplier of petroleum Iran was a vital link in the Western security chain, especially while the Korean War was diverting both Western resources and attention from the Middle East. Therefore avoiding steps that might compromise Iran's position or push it into the Soviet bloc was essential. Such an eventuality, Acheson explained, might require "extraordinary political measures," presumably including action to remove Mossadeq from power. But his real goal remained a negotiated settlement that assuaged Iranian demands and thus made such measures unnecessary.[58]

With this goal in mind Ambassador Grady sought to persuade Mossadeq to resume negotiations with the British. He was not sanguine about the prospects. Like the British, he and other U.S. officials considered the prime minister to be little more than a demagogue who was "ludicrously misinformed" regarding the AIOC's operations, greatly overestimated Iran's ability to run the AIOC's operations, and incorrectly assumed that U.S. and other foreign oil companies would come to Iran's assistance. Grady tried to disabuse Mossadeq of these notions and moderate his position but to no avail.[59]

In fact, Grady and other U.S. officials—and their British counterparts as well—found it terribly difficult to comprehend Mossadeq, who seemed to them unwilling to face realities and negotiate reasonably. On the contrary, because the Iranian government rejected their view of the situation, U.S. and British officials were increasingly inclined to dismiss it as "lunatic" and "almost farcical." Cultural differences reinforced the prejudices of British and U.S. officials and hampered their ability to deal effectively with the situation. To Anglo-American officials, who were used to formal diplomatic negotiations conducted under controlled circumstances, dealing with the Iranian prime minister was an altogether novel and somewhat unsettling experience.[60]

Because of his age and poor health Mossadeq usually worked from his bed while dressed in pajamas, the color of which became a standard feature of reports from Anglo-American diplomats in Tehran. Some days, in fact, they considered worthy of note that the prime minister wore two sets of pajamas on top of each other—khaki and green one day, blue and khaki another. He was also prone to fainting spells and apt to weep and become emotional during his meetings with British and U.S. officials, particularly when speaking of the suffering the Iranian people had endured at the hands of the evil AIOC. It was clear that Anglo-American officials were not quite sure how to deal with Mossadeq, whom Shepherd variously described, with more than a hint of sarcasm, as "the educated Doctor" and "our friend Musaddiq." Their consternation only increased in mid-May when, for security and health reasons, Mossadeq moved into what Shepherd dubbed a lair on the second floor of the Majlis building. Protected by blockaded doors and bodyguards Shepherd referred to as "thugs," the prime minister remained ensconced in the parliament for several weeks. Shepherd found the arrangements bizarre and apparently had difficulty taking the prime minister seriously.[61]

So did policy makers in London and Washington, whose search for a way to avoid the total and complete nationalization of the AIOC was becoming increasingly difficult. Mossadeq's anti-British sentiment had reached a level that Grady described as "white heat," and he insisted that nationalization of the AIOC was Iran's "indisputable right." The company and the British in general had preyed upon Iran for decades, the prime minister asserted, and it was finally time for the nation to take control of its oil. He was also firmly opposed to compensating the AIOC unless it first addressed Iranian claims against the company, which in Grady's calculation were far greater than anything the AIOC might receive for the property it would lose as a result of nationalization. Even arguments that unilateral

Iranian action would jeopardize future foreign investment in Iran and that Iranian oil was not irreplaceable did little to move the prime minister, forcing Grady to conclude that a negotiated settlement was probably next to impossible.[62] U.S. officials got no further with the shah. Although unhappy about Mossadeq's assumption of the premiership, the monarch was convinced that any action to remove the new prime minister from power would probably backfire by turning him into a martyr. Instead, the shah preferred to wait the situation out, convinced that once the failure of Mossadeq's nationalization became clear, the Iranian people would turn against him.[63]

Nor were the Iranians the only annoyance to U.S. officials. In a display of what Walter S. Gifford, U.S. ambassador to England, characterized as "natural [British] stubbornness," the Foreign Office still insisted that the AIOC retain its holdings in Iran, even in the face of the State Department's assertion that "nothing short of a low bow to nationalisation" would satisfy the Iranians. Ambassador Grady was particularly critical of the British position, blasting what he sarcastically termed their "brilliant and effective" handling of the oil question, especially their continued refusal to accept the principle of nationalization. Such an attitude, he said, placed the United States in the position of having once again "to bail [the British] out as we have so often before." This was clearly not a task that the ambassador relished.[64]

The two sides also were unable to agree on the potential use of British force in Iran. As early as March 1951 the British had begun to reinforce their naval and ground forces in the Middle East.[65] But as the Iranian situation deteriorated throughout the spring, the chance of more resolute action to protect the AIOC's position and keep Iranian oil flowing became increasingly likely. Policy makers on the defense and chiefs of staff committees and within the Foreign Office began to consider the use of force to hold the Iranian oil fields and safeguard the AIOC's refinery at Abadan, as well as to protect British citizens from hostile Iranian action. Defense Minister Emmanuel Shinwell made a strong case for such a course but was eventually overruled by more practical colleagues, who noted the difficulties involved. Britain's balance-of-payments crisis, they said, would prevent it from financing what was sure to be a long drawn-out struggle to control the oil installations; nor were British military reserves or public opinion likely to sustain such an operation. In addition, holding the oil fields and the Abadan refinery would not ensure the continued flow of oil, because essential local labor would be unavailable in the event of a British invasion.[66]

More important than the economic and political obstacles to a military operation, however, was U.S. opposition to such a move. After discussions with President Truman and the National Security Council, Secretary Acheson enumerated the circumstances in which the United States could sanction the use of British force: at the invitation of the Iranian government, in the event of Soviet military intervention, to counter a communist coup d'état in Tehran, or to evacuate British nationals in danger of attack. The use of force in any other instance, he argued, particularly against the Mossadeq regime, would be a prescription for disaster because it might invite Soviet countermeasures.[67] Although Acheson's position temporarily halted British plans for a military operation against Iran, it did not quash them entirely. As the next chapter reveals, the possibility of a British invasion remained alive until the AIOC withdrew from Iran in October.

Another area of Anglo-American discord concerned U.S. assistance to Iran, which in 1951 would amount to approximately $30 million. The State Department saw this aid as a way to bolster the shah against internal threats, increase U.S. influence in Iran, and keep that country firmly in the Western camp. This assistance had become even more important after the failure of a proposed Export-Import Bank loan and the halt in oil revenues threatened to push Iran into a financial abyss. But in the Foreign Office's estimation U.S. assistance only stiffened Iran's opposition to an oil settlement and further weakened the British position in Iran. Accordingly, the British tried without success to convince Washington to cancel, delay, or drastically curtail future aid to Iran.[68]

The British failure in this regard combined with persistent U.S. criticism and the general decline of British power in the Middle East to produce a bitter reaction in London. Foreign Secretary Herbert Morrison was "rather annoyed" at the lack of U.S. support regarding the Iranian situation and at what he regarded as U.S. efforts to "order me about." Ambassador Gifford saw Morrison's lament as a sign of frustration with the "growing Near East practice of twisting the lion's tail" when Britain's diminished power kept it from taking "preventive or retaliatory action." The situation, he said, struck at the foundations of British pride and "efforts to re-establish themselves as equal partner[s]" with the United States around the world. The British Cabinet had said as much earlier when it bewailed Britain's declining influence not only in Iran but in Iraq, Egypt, and Israel as well. This sorry state of affairs increased the need for U.S. assistance in bringing the Iranians to their knees, but also made the British all the more frustrated to be so dependent on an ally that would not support what it considered an unwise policy.

It was perfectly fine, British officials asserted, for U.S. officials "to say exactly what they thought about [the AIOC]" to the Foreign Office. But "in a country [such as Iran] where a wink was as good as a nod," public criticism, including that delivered with some regularity by Ambassador Grady in Tehran, "was equivalent to withdrawal of support" and struck the British as conduct unbecoming of an ally.[69]

If the U.S. government was reluctant to make a full-scale commitment to its British ally, neither would the government or the major U.S. oil companies take advantage of the AIOC's predicament or throw their full support behind Iran. To be sure, the U.S. majors were unrestrained in their criticism of the AIOC's past policies in Iran. But they also refused to profit from the AIOC's distress. In discussions with the State Department in mid-May oil company executives said that no responsible firm would consider supplanting the AIOC in Iran. This kind of "concession jumping," they argued, would threaten concessions in other parts of the world by inducing countries to forfeit contracts with one company in favor of more lucrative arrangements with another and would thus amount to "cutting the industry's own throat." They also acknowledged that Iran's campaign against the AIOC called into question the country's likelihood of honoring any future oil agreement. Such sentiments pleased Assistant Secretary McGhee, who worried about the consequences for Anglo-American relations should U.S. companies appear to be moving in on the AIOC's territory. Besides, he reasoned, the Iranians might be more inclined to compromise with the British once they understood that U.S. firms would not market nationalized oil or operate a nationalized industry.[70]

U.S. hopes seemed to be realized in the weeks after the State Department's 18 May announcement, as first the British and then the Iranians responded with what appeared to be more flexible and conciliatory policies. In a statement to the House of Commons on 29 May Prime Minister Attlee announced that although his government could not allow Iran unilaterally to cancel the AIOC's contract, it was prepared to accept "some form of nationalisation, provided . . . it were satisfactory in other respects"—presumably the payment of adequate compensation to the company and British retention of control of Iranian oil. As Attlee had explained earlier, it was "the title and all that was implicit in it" that was important. The British would accept the word nationalization because it would allow the Iranians to save face. But the nationalization that the British had in mind would not allow the Iranians to gain control of the oil industry.[71]

U.S. policy makers applauded this step, believing that it would strengthen the hand of Iranian moderates, including the shah's, and weaken that of Mossadeq and the extremists. Two days later Mossadeq invited the AIOC to send a delegation to Iran, an invitation that the company was prepared to accept. President Truman urged Attlee to push the company to send a delegation to Tehran with instructions to negotiate a settlement that recognized Iran's right to nationalize its oil resources. Attlee seemed amenable to this suggestion, telling Truman on 6 June that the British government could not accept a "breach of contract" by Iran but would authorize a delegation of AIOC officials to initiate discussions with Iran that looked toward a settlement that would involve nationalization in principle. Ambassador Shepherd thought that AIOC officials would now have a chance to explain to Mossadeq "the difference between [the] Anglo-Iranian Oil Company and a small garage." His sarcasm notwithstanding, both British and U.S. policy makers were cautiously optimistic about the coming negotiations.[72]

The reasons to be cautious were good ones, and British officials were not at all certain that they could "bring the Prime Minister down to earth." Mossadeq still insisted that discussions be conducted within the framework of the Nationalization Law, which left no room for alternatives to all-out nationalization and would therefore prevent the AIOC from retaining control of Iranian oil. Although officials in the Foreign Office continued to search for a way to deal with the prime minister, they believed that "if [Mossadeq] is as mad as he seems," their effort was sure to fail. Such sentiments, commonplace within the Foreign Office, were evidence of a prevailing British tendency to see Mossadeq as an irrational, unworthy adversary whose position could be dismissed out of hand. Centuries of imperialism had convinced them of their superiority when dealing with peoples in underdeveloped countries, and the British found it easy to condemn Mossadeq as incapable, naive, and even feminine when he refused to yield to their point of view.[73]

British officials were especially incredulous at what they considered Mossadeq's "almost fanatic" disregard for the economic consequences of nationalization. "Tant pis pour nous. Too bad for us," was his usual response when reminded that Iran's oil industry might shut down as a result of the Anglo-Iranian confrontation. "It would be better for Iran to be rid of all foreign influence," Mossadeq asserted, "even if disorder and communism follow." Mossadeq's long-standing opposition to the Tudeh Party, however, called into question his willingness to see communism triumph, as did his subsequent efforts to maintain the flow of oil. Seen in this light, his dire warning of a communist Iran was probably a negotiating ploy designed to exact more concessions from the British and greater support from the United States. Torn between his desire to expel the British and his practical responsibility to ensure that Iranian oil continued to flow, Mossadeq believed that by flirting with communism he could have both.[74]

At the same time the prime minister proceeded as if the outcome of the talks was foreordained. He had an Iranian flag placed atop AIOC headquarters in Tehran and publicly proclaimed that the company's property now belonged to the Iranian government. He also ordered the Temporary Managing Board, which the Mixed Oil Commission had set up to run the oil industry until the National Iranian Oil Company (NIOC) had been organized, to sever all the AIOC's previous contracts and announced that its workers would henceforth work for the Iranian government. These and other actions, taken over the objections of ambassadors Grady and Shepherd, did not bode well for the coming talks.[75]

When the AIOC delegation, led by Basil Jackson, vice chairman of the company's board of directors, arrived in Tehran on 10 June, it thus found the company's operations already under siege. The situation deteriorated as negotiations got under way. The Iranians refused to begin discussions until the company had surrendered its bank deposits and turned over all its receipts, less 25 percent that would be set aside for payment of the AIOC's legitimate claims against the Iranian government. The AIOC steadfastly refused to meet these demands and received support from the State Department and the Foreign Office, both of which considered Iran's demands completely unreasonable and totally unacceptable.[76] In an effort to get the talks off to a better start and guarantee the continued flow of Iranian oil, the AIOC delegation offered Iran an immediate advance of £10 million. The company was also willing to make additional payments of £3 million per month until the dispute was settled and to organize a subsidiary company that would run the AIOC's operations on behalf of the NIOC, which at that point existed only on paper. To Grady, whom the British were careful to keep informed, these proposals constituted a generous basis for the negotiation of a satisfactory settlement. But after only thirty minutes of deliberation the Iranians rejected the proposals as contradictory to the Nationalization Law because they did not allow for full Iranian control of the oil industry. As far as the Iranians were concerned, the negotiations were terminated; the British delegation was advised to prepare for its departure.[77]

Anglo-American discussions yielded U.S. agreement that Iran's conduct had been "demented" and "completely unjustified" as well as much-coveted promises of U.S. support for the recent proposals advanced by the British but rejected by the Iranians. Ambassadors Grady and Shepherd urged Mossadeq to moderate his position, warning again of the economic hardship that would result from a shutdown of the oil industry. Already, Grady observed, Iranian consumers were surprised to learn that they had to pay for gasoline pumped from nationalized wells. Public distress and disillusionment would only grow, he told Mossadeq, if Iran maintained its course.[78]

But Mossadeq continued to insist that the AIOC would be "dispossessed," even if this meant completely stopping oil operations. Nor did he seem concerned about a hostile public reaction. Instead, in a display of how circumscribed his political position had become, he said that "public feeling against the Anglo-Iranian Oil Company [was] so intense" that no government "would ever dare" to be associated with it. Under the circumstances Mossadeq surely felt politically unable to make the kinds of concessions that British and U.S. officials sought. On the contrary, he had no choice but to demand that the company cease its operations. Any other course would place him at risk of attack by the same nationalist forces that had destroyed his predecessors.[79]

When appeals to Mossadeq were ineffectual, Grady and Shepherd once again implored the shah to take action against the government. He could demand Mossadeq's resignation, they suggested, or call for the dissolution of the Majlis; either action might lead to a government more amenable to reason. The shah appreciated the potential dangers of Mossadeq's policies but remained reluctant to openly oppose the popular prime minister. He was also afraid of exceeding his constitutional powers by directly acting to remove Mossadeq from office and of incurring the public opprobrium that was sure to stem from such a move. If Mossadeq was to fall, the shah said, it would have to be under his own weight. With little chance of an immediate improvement in the situation the British delegation decided to return to London. U.S. officials lamented that this decision might doom all chances of a negotiated settlement. But even they agreed that Iranian action made further discussions unlikely.[80]

Following the collapse of Anglo-Iranian negotiations Mossadeq's government moved to consolidate its control over the AIOC's operations, with some unexpected results. It proposed an antisabotage bill that would prevent the British from interfering with oil production, only to withdraw the bill from the Majlis when Mossadeq realized that it would drive British workers from their jobs, halt oil production, and further weaken the Iranian economy.[81] Similar consequences were threatened by a government decree that required tankers calling at Abadan to recognize the NIOC as the legitimate owner of Iranian oil and pay it, rather than the AIOC, for the oil the tankers loaded. The AIOC and other international oil companies bristled at the regulation and refused to cooperate, which meant that oil exports ground almost to a halt in late June; after storage tanks at Abadan filled to capacity, refinery officials began preparing to suspend operations. By that time, in fact, the AIOC seemed resigned to withdrawing from Iran.[82]

The British government had also written off the chances of a negotiated settlement with Mossadeq.[83] In additional examples of their tendency to see Mossadeq in the worst possible light, officials in the Foreign Office described him as an "elderly lunatic" whose "crazy policy" was bent on wrecking Iran and handing it over to the Soviet Union. His recent conduct of the oil negotiations, they believed, proved his intention to implement nationalization without a thought to either the AIOC's rights or Iran's well-being. Nevertheless, the British government was not yet ready to accept Berthoud's assertion that the prime minister's removal was "now objective number one." Instead, it mounted an anti-Mossadeq propaganda campaign in Tehran and stepped up efforts to encourage Iranian opposition to the prime minister, which Shepherd believed, however incorrectly, to be mounting by the day. In addition, London began readying plans for replacing Iranian oil with other supplies and for evacuating the AIOC's British employees from Iran.[84]

Mossadeq had not expected this kind of British opposition. He knew that closing down Iran's oil industry would have serious consequences, not only for his country but also for Great Britain and "all other countries which use Iranian oil." His repeated assertions that Iran valued "independence more than economics" thus appeared as hollow bluffs designed to push the British into negotiations and win U.S. support. It was apparently the prime minister's hope that Anglo-American fears of a communist Iran would moderate their opposition to nationalization and allow him to take control of the AIOC's assets. When these plays to the balcony failed, however, Mossadeq adopted what Grady termed a "more conciliatory attitude," making an oblique appeal for U.S. mediation of the dispute. Perhaps, as Ambassador Shepherd jokingly reported from Tehran, a transfusion of U.S. blood that Mossadeq had recently received helped to account for his "more reasonable" posture.[85]

Mossadeq's appeal came just as U.S. policy was hardening against his "demented" policy and the "threat and fear" tactics he was employing against the British, the most recent examples of which had been his rejection of the British proposals and his government's continued moves to confiscate the AIOC's property. It was also coincident with the U.S. decision, in a paper from the National Security Council, to "bring its influence to bear" in finding a settlement to the oil crisis that preserved both Iranian and British rights. To keep the door to a future solution open in the interim the United States proposed a sixty-day moratorium on Iran's efforts to take control of the AIOC's property. During this period oil operations would continue unhampered while the British and Iranians tried to reach a permanent arrangement. Although the British were prepared to accept this proposal, Mossadeq rejected it on the ground that nothing could be done to halt the implementation of the Nationalization Law.[86]

Britain's acceptance of the U.S.-sponsored moratorium signaled its desire to solve the oil crisis amicably. It also revealed the Labour government's desperation at its continued inability to attain such a solution and perhaps a desire to mend fences with the U.S. government. On 21 June Conservatives in the House of Commons had mounted a protracted assault against the government's handling of the Iranian situation, blaming the Labour Party for inspiring the current crisis by advocating nationalization at home, criticizing its plans for evacuating the AIOC's staff, and urging strong action to protect the oil fields and the Abadan refinery. Although Morrison later acknowledged privately to Ambassador Gifford that he was sometimes tempted "to tell Mossadeq that 'either he stops or we'll come after him,'" his public attitude was much more restrained. Indeed, the foreign secretary's parliamentary rebuttal to the opposition's charges was less a defense of the government or a plea for parliamentary unity than a biting counterblast against the Conservatives, whom, he argued, had yet to accept that "the imperialism on which they were brought up is dead." Sounding much like Acheson and other U.S. policy makers, Morrison asserted that drastic or forceful action in Iran would only exacerbate the situation, lead to Soviet intervention, and run the risk of further U.S. criticism. Needed instead was some kind of peaceful solution.[87]

In an effort to defuse the mounting partisanship that had come to characterize the oil crisis the government conferred with Winston Churchill, Anthony Eden, and other Conservative leaders a week later. This extraordinary meeting, which came at Churchill's request, produced little in the way of new suggestions. It did, however, convince the assembled leaders of the necessity for U.S. cooperation in the Iranian crisis and might have prompted Churchill's plea that Truman accept Mossadeq's request for mediation. The Iranian situation was much more important than the war in Korea, Churchill proclaimed, and he decried the U.S. government's apparent failure to appreciate its seriousness.[88]

V

U.S. leaders would have disputed the assertion that they failed to comprehend the seriousness of the Iranian crisis. On the contrary, they knew well what the crisis could mean for the economic and strategic positions of the Western alliance. For this reason they began a reformulation of their policy toward the Iranian crisis that led ultimately to acceptance of Mossadeq's appeal for U.S. mediation. But with Britain and Iran pursuing such dramatically polarized positions and with cultural differences increasing the gap that separated them, it remained to be seen whether U.S. intervention could harness the tide of Iranian nationalism to a constructive settlement.

chapter 4

From Honest Broker to British Partner

U.S. POLICY IN TRANSITION

The Iranian and British positions in the AIOC dispute grew further apart during the last half of 1951. Events made it clear that Mossadeq's idea of nationalization meant the AIOC's total expulsion from Iran. Throughout the summer he intensified his efforts to gain control of the AIOC's installations and then to sell nationalized oil on the open market, all in hope of raising revenue that would free the Iranian people from the chains of poverty.

These efforts ran headlong into a wall of British opposition. Worried that Iran's confiscation of the AIOC might lead Egypt and other nations to take similar action against British assets, policy makers in London adopted what one official described as a campaign "aimed at bring[ing] down the Mossadeq government by a combination of economic sanctions, international pressure, intimidation, and propaganda."[1] This campaign intensified after Anglo-Iranian discussions in August failed to resolve the dispute and the United Nations refused to intervene in October. The AIOC formalized an informal boycott of Iranian oil that had begun in July, enlisting the aid of the other international petroleum companies, including the U.S. majors. The other companies were deterred from purchasing Iranian oil by both the AIOC's threat of legal action and their reluctance to assist in Iran's assault against the company. In addition, the British government mounted a propaganda campaign in Iran that sought to discredit Mossadeq's government and arouse his domestic opponents.

As Anglo-Iranian tension escalated, U.S. policy shifted dramatically. U.S. officials, who had grown increasingly disillusioned with Prime Minister Mossadeq, abandoned benevolent neutrality in favor of outright backing of the British position. Mossadeq, the United States joined the British in concluding, did not understand the realities of the international oil industry or the dangers his policies posed to Western interests and to Iran's long-term security. Like their British counterparts, U.S. policy makers believed that those policies set a dangerous precedent that could undermine the sanctity of private contracts and encourage nationalization in other parts of the world. They could also wreck Iran's economy, push that country toward communism, and open the door to Soviet expansion into the Middle East. But despite these dangers, U.S. leaders were not yet convinced that Mossadeq should be removed. That conviction would come later, after the crisis had dragged on for another year. At the end of 1951, however, U.S. policy makers had gone so far as to side with the British, thereby transforming what had begun as an Anglo-Iranian dispute into a trilateral conflict in which Great Britain and the United States were allied against Iran.

II

In the immediate aftermath of the failed Jackson mission of June continued Anglo-Iranian discord on a number of important issues threatened to halt Iranian oil production entirely. One point of contention concerned the kind of receipt to be signed by tanker captains who took on Iranian oil. The Iranians wanted the receipts to pledge payment for that oil to the National Iranian Oil Company (NIOC), whereas the British argued that pledges of payment to the NIOC would prejudice the AIOC's position in any permanent settlement of the oil dispute.

As the two sides fruitlessly debated the issue throughout the early part of July, the AIOC, with the backing of the British government, threatened legal action against any company that purchased Iranian oil. The international petroleum companies, which were loath to abet the unfair treatment of one of their brethren or to encourage nationalization in other countries, took these warnings to heart. Beginning in late July they acquiesced in a British-led boycott of Iranian oil, which they saw as a legitimate defense of the AIOC's rights. As a result, tankers bypassed Abadan for other producers. Iranian oil exports declined so substantially that production seemed likely to stop by the middle of August.[2]

The British and Iranian governments also disagreed over the legitimacy of an interim ruling regarding the oil dispute issued by the International Court of Justice (ICJ). In response to a British request for adjudication of the conflict the court on 5 July issued a temporary injunction that would freeze the oil situation while the court debated its jurisdiction in the case. The British welcomed the injunction. Because it recognized the British government as a legitimate party in the oil dispute and ordered the Iranians to cease their takeover of the AIOC's operations, Ambassador Gifford believed the injunction might have a "useful psychological impact" on Mossadeq, encourage Iranian moderates, and line up world opinion on Britain's side. The Iranians were less enthusiastic. They condemned the injunction as unlawful interference in their internal affairs and as evidence that the ICJ was subservient to British interests. Insisting that the oil dispute was a matter between Iran and the AIOC, Mossadeq refused to be bound by the court's instructions.[3]

On the contrary, the Iranian government continued its takeover of the AIOC. Amid much fanfare in Tehran, it published documents seized from the AIOC's Information Office that purported to prove the company's "sinister" interference in Iranian politics. U.S. officials downplayed the incident by claiming that much of what the documents revealed "would normally be within the scope" of an information office's activities. But Iranian officials took the revelations seriously and no doubt used them as an excuse to confiscate the company's property, take control of its day-to-day management, and order its workers to sign contracts with the NIOC. As the Iranians gained control of the AIOC's operations, the company's British personnel at the Abadan refinery and its field workers began complaining about the "undignified and intolerable" way their new Iranian supervisors were treating them. In a sign of how cultural differences exacerbated the oil controversy British workers were especially vociferous concerning the "indignities of having Iranians 'push them around.'" They blamed U.S. policy for encouraging Iranian excesses and criticized the British government for not doing enough to resolve the crisis. Under the circumstances Ambassador Shepherd wondered how long the British workers could persevere, especially as decreasing exports from Abadan rendered their jobs superfluous and left them idle in the scorching summer sun. A mass exodus, he thought, was probably inevitable.[4]

Indeed, the idea of withdrawing from Iran had begun to gain currency with some elements of the British government. The embassy in Tehran, along with the AIOC's on-site managers, advocated complete and immediate withdrawal as the best way to bring the Iranians to their senses and hasten the fall of Mossadeq, whom the British government was now determined to remove. According to these officials, once the Iranian government discovered that it could not operate the oil industry without British assistance, it would welcome the AIOC back on terms the company could accept. Even the threat of a British withdrawal, this group argued, might make the Iranians more malleable. Cabinet members, company officials in London, and leaders of the Conservative opposition disagreed. To them withdrawal was an unacceptable admission of defeat that would spell the end of Britain's involvement in Iran: once out, the British could never return. As Winston Churchill argued, the AIOC should not allow its personnel to be "hustled and bullied out of Abadan." It should hold its position for as long as possible in hope that a show of British resolve would convince the Iranians to abandon the idea of nationalization. This option conformed to the ICJ's ruling, which prohibited any action that hampered the continued production of Iranian oil. It was also the option that prevailed; the Cabinet and the AIOC decided in mid-July to hang on in Iran until conditions there became truly unbearable.[5]

Concurrent with this decision was renewed discussion in London of the use of force to topple Mossadeq and protect Britain's position in Iran. Government officials in London shared Ambassador Shepherd's belief that Mossadeq lacked "the reasoned support of influential political opinion" in Iran and was instead backed only by a "few fanatical individuals." As they saw things, the prime minister's failure to stabilize the situation in Iran could lead only to economic and political disaster for his country, which meant that covert action to remove him from office might become necessary. Although Foreign Secretary Morrison had ruled out this option in a parliamentary debate of late June, Mossadeq's continued refusal to reach a negotiated settlement convinced some British policy makers that military force was the only way to guarantee the safety of the AIOC's employees and secure Britain's hold over the Abadan refinery. Defense Minister Shinwell and his allies continued to believe that a show of force would shore up British prestige in the Middle East, bring the Iranians to their senses, and drive Mossadeq from office. Churchill and many Conservatives agreed. Despite such bipartisan support, however, the government made no final plans for military action at this time. As noted in chapter 3, economic and strategic problems continued to discourage military intervention, as did U.S. insistence that force could be used only in limited circumstances.[6]

For their part the Iranians apparently discounted threats of British intervention or withdrawal. Nor did the empty tanker berths at Abadan convince them of the serious economic consequences that would result from seizure of the AIOC's operations. Instead, Mossadeq and his advisers clung to the belief that the British were bluffing: surely the AIOC would rather accept Iran's definition of nationalization than risk losing everything. Accordingly, the prime minister made little attempt to curtail efforts to seize the AIOC's facilities. It was only a matter of time, he maintained, before the British became resigned to Iran's takeover of the AIOC. Years of accumulated Iranian grievances regarding British exploitation of Iran's natural resources had finally come to the surface, and the British would simply have to adjust to new realities. Mossadeq also seemed convinced that even if the British did withdraw from Iran, the Americans would come in to replace them in order to avert a collapse of the Iranian economy. Either way, it seemed, the Iranian government would get what it wanted.[7]

So far as the United States was concerned, both Britain and Iran were "pressing their luck to the point of suicide in [a] game of Russian roulette," Acheson said.[8] From Tehran Grady excoriated Britain's "legal hairsplitting" and its periodic threats to shut down the oil industry. These tactics, he and other U.S. officials argued, were parts of a British strategy that relied on economic pressure to destabilize a regime that the United States believed to be immensely popular with the Iranian people and that was unlikely to be replaced by a government more amenable to British influence. Rather than replacing Mossadeq, officials in the State Department had begun to think about replacing the AIOC.[9]

Convinced that the company overestimated its chances of retaining a dominant position in Iranian oil, State Department officials were considering a multinational managing organization to take its place and thus ensure both the continued availability of oil revenues to the Iranian government and the continued presence of Iranian oil on world markets. But this did not mean that U.S. leaders were uncritical of the Iranians. On the contrary, they still thought that Mossadeq had nationalized the AIOC without adequately planning for the continued production of Iranian oil. He had refused the recent offer of the Jackson mission, which the United States considered fair, and was now proceeding with apparent disregard for how his actions might imperil Iran's security.[10]

The security question was uppermost in the minds of U.S. leaders and would set the stage for their decision to intervene more directly in the oil crisis. At an Independence Day meeting with British Ambassador Oliver Franks, W. Averell Harriman (special assistant to the president), and officials from the State Department Acheson reiterated the dangers of a protracted Anglo-Iranian struggle. If an immediate solution to the dispute was not found, Acheson warned, the British might be forced either to withdraw from Iran or to undertake military operations to protect their position there. The first course would leave Iran's oil fields vulnerable to Soviet expansion; the second might trigger Soviet military intervention in the north. Neither would achieve Britain's objectives. Nor were these the only routes to disaster. A long-term crisis could also lead to Iran's economic collapse, foster the spread of communism in that country, and pose a real danger to U.S. allies in Western Europe. After all, the nations of Western Europe received much of their oil from Iran, and with the Korean War straining supplies to the limit, alternate sources would be difficult to find. To avert these potential disasters Anglo-Iranian negotiations had to be resumed. But because the two parties were unlikely to call for such a resumption on their own, Acheson proposed that Harriman initiate "quiet talks" with both the Iranians and the British to seek "some common denominator" on which renewed talks might be based. Such a mission would also buy time for what Acheson described as "more sensible" Iranians to influence Mossadeq.[11]

Winning British and Iranian support for Harriman's mission was not easy. To be sure, the British saw U.S. intervention as a key to resolving the crisis, especially because they had developed no viable solutions. But mediation was not the sort of intervention the British had in mind. Morrison and others wanted Anglo-American solidarity behind the ICJ's recent injunction, seeing this as the best way to force Iran into line with a ruling that served British interests. With this kind of thinking in the background the British agreed to support Acheson's proposal only after the secretary instructed Harriman to emphasize the legitimacy of the court's ruling as the basis for a modus vivendi between the disputing parties.[12]

Thereafter Truman formally proposed the mission in a personal message to Mossadeq. He stressed U.S. support for the ICJ's ruling and offered the services of Harriman, one of his "closest advisers" and one of America's "most eminent citizens," to help Iran implement it. Mossadeq's initial reaction was cool. He could not accept a mission designed to implement a court ruling that Iran had rejected, but he would welcome Harriman if Iran's Nine-Point Law of 1 May 1951 served as the framework for further talks between his government and the AIOC. This law, it will be recalled, put the nationalization principle into action: it called for the transfer of the AIOC's assets and revenue to the nascent NIOC and required a complete British withdrawal from all facets of the Iranian oil industry.[13]

Mossadeq's insistence on the Nine-Point Law got to the heart of the differing British and Iranian conceptions of the Harriman mission and cast doubt on its prospects for success. According to British policy makers, Mossadeq saw Harriman's mission as a way to split the Anglo-Americans apart, not as a vehicle for renewed Anglo-Iranian discussions. They worried in particular that Mossadeq would try to use Harriman's visit to win U.S. support for additional British concessions, especially regarding the Nine-Point Law, which they categorically rejected. The British considered it crucial for U.S. officials to disabuse the prime minister of these delusions, stand by the ICJ's recent ruling, and do nothing to enhance Mossadeq's political standing. Unless Harriman took this tack in his talks with the Iranians, Morrison asserted, Britain's position in Iran would be seriously compromised. But even if the United States did take a firmly pro-British stance, British officials were "not sanguine" about Harriman's chances of success. On the basis of their past experience in negotiating with the Iranian prime minister, especially the disastrous Jackson mission that Mossadeq had derailed without even a fair hearing, they thought it highly unlikely that Mossadeq would conduct what they would consider fair and rational discussions. In the end the British probably saw Harriman's mission less as a means of settling the dispute than as a means of educating U.S. officials to what the British saw as Mossadeq's "intransigence and unreasonableness."[14]

Whitehall's concerns were uppermost in Harriman's mind when he left Washington on 13 July. Accompanied by oil expert Walter Levy, State Department petroleum adviser William Rountree, and President Truman's air force aide Robert Landry, Harriman stopped first in Paris, ostensibly to collect his interpreter Vernon Walters but also for secret consultations with British officials who were then attending a meeting of NATO principals.

During discussions with his old friend Hugh Gaitskell, chancellor of the exchequer, Harriman promised to maintain close contact with Ambassador Shepherd in Tehran. He also ruled out Iran's Nine-Point Law as the basis of a settlement. The United States supported Iran's right to nationalize the AIOC, Harriman repeated, but it could not sanction the Nine-Point Law, which was vague, did not take account of the AIOC's legal rights, and might encourage other countries to expropriate foreign-owned companies without proper regard for their rights. U.S. officials, Harriman promised, would not push the British to go beyond the Jackson proposal, which had provided for British control of the production, distribution, and marketing of Iranian oil. This proposal, he said, was fair to both Britain and Iran. It also had the advantage of preventing the dangerous precedent of awarding Iran better financial terms than those that prevailed in other oil-producing countries. In return for U.S. support on this score Harriman asked the British not to jeopardize his efforts by announcing the withdrawal of the AIOC's employees or the closure of the Abadan refinery or by taking their dispute with Iran before the United Nations Security Council. Other U.S. officials made similar entreaties, the British agreed, and Anglo-American harmony had been restored by the time Harriman arrived in Tehran on 15 July.[15]

Having mollified the British, Harriman then set about reaching an agreement with the Iranians. Despite Mossadeq's "cordial attitude," Harriman's initial discussions with the prime minister were "completely unfruitful." Mossadeq, reported Harriman, seemed to demonize the British, at whose feet he laid all of Iran's troubles. The British were, the prime minister maintained, crafty and evil. They "sull[ied] everything they touch[ed]," and they had to be driven from Iran without delay. This passionate opposition to the British stemmed from Mossadeq's conviction that they, and especially the AIOC, had ruthlessly exploited Iran for decades, and it was a constant element in his discussions with Harriman. By describing the British in universally negative terms Mossadeq used cultural stereotyping in much the same way that the Anglo-Americans did when they challenged Mossadeq's fitness to hold office. He castigated the Anglo-Americans as a group and revealed an unwillingness to revise his thinking even when Harriman pointed out its shortcomings. Also hampering the negotiations was what Harriman saw as the prime minister's inability to comprehend the consequences of an AIOC withdrawal. Mossadeq wrongly believed, for example, that British technicians would be willing to work for the NIOC and that U.S. oil companies would purchase nationalized Iranian oil. Nor was this the half of it. Even if Mossadeq could be disabused of such ideas, Harriman feared that public sentiment would prevent him from accepting any arrangement that allowed the British to retain effective control over Iran's oil industry. Popular opinion, he believed, was too wedded to the idea of nationalization to accept anything less than total Iranian control. The challenge for Harriman thus lay in formulating a settlement that satisfied Iranian sentiment while preserving British rights, that accepted the principle of nationalization but skirted the specifics of the nationalization laws.[16]

To win Iranian support for such a settlement Harriman first worked to convince Iranian cabinet officials, members of the Mixed Oil Commission, and important senators and Majlis deputies of "the dangers of the [Mossadeq] Government's policy." The hope was that they might sway the prime minister. After a week of such discussions Harriman and Levy had convinced at least some Iranian leaders that a continued shutdown of the oil industry amounted to "cutting their own throats," because other oil-producing countries would expand production to meet the Iranian shortfall. The Iranians had realized their political objectives through nationalization, Harriman asserted. Now they had to "combine reason with enthusiasm" if they were going to safeguard their oil revenues and harness them for economic development. They had to forgo any attempt to secure a financial return greater than that of other Middle Eastern oil producers, which meant accepting a fifty-fifty profit-sharing arrangement. They would also have to accept what Harriman proposed as modified conditions for proceeding with Anglo-Iranian negotiations.[17]

According to Harriman's proposal, the British would have only to reaffirm their earlier acceptance of the Iranian law of 20 March, which endorsed the principle of nationalization, rather than acquiesce in the Nine-Point Law of 1 May, which applied that principle to the AIOC's assets. This modification would allow the British to negotiate with the Iranians over how the principle of nationalization would be applied. It was a modification the Iranian politicians agreed to accept and was only one sign of renewed progress after Harriman's arrival in Tehran. At the same time Ayatollah Kashani and other members of the National Front agreed that discussions with the British should resume, as did the shah, who displayed unusual resolve in ordering Mossadeq to settle the oil crisis immediately. Although their motives for pushing to resolve the oil crisis are not clear, it is probable that both Kashani and the shah believed that the United States would guide the British toward a settlement that assured Iran's rights.[18]

The prime minister appeared to be coming around as well. The prospects of a permanent halt in Iran's petroleum exports highlighted the importance of resolving the dispute as soon as possible. Already, production at Abadan had fallen from eighteen million gallons per day before nationalization to about five million gallons, the refinery was producing at only 12 percent of capacity, and the last tanker had left Abadan on 3 July. These facts, and the importance that the shah and Mossadeq's advisers placed on an early settlement, convinced the prime minister to resume discussions with a mission led by a British Cabinet minister.[19]

Harriman, who proved to be quite perceptive regarding the political plight facing Mossadeq, had played a major role in leading the prime minister back to the negotiating table. He dismissed British assertions of Mossadeq's waning domestic popularity, arguing instead that nationalization was the most popular political idea in Iranian history. But this popularity had proved to be double edged, as it prevented the prime minister from accepting anything less than the total nationalization he had promised the Iranian people. Thus, in Harriman's assessment, Mossadeq's "rigidity" was as much the result of "practical political factors" as "his own emotionalism." This realization set Harriman apart from his British counterparts, who attributed Mossadeq's rigidity to an irrational state of mind, dismissed and denigrated him as an unworthy adversary, and set their sights on driving him from office.[20]

Having worked hard to convince Mossadeq to negotiate with the British government, Harriman was sorely disappointed when Whitehall raised reservations.[21] Officials in London did not want a repetition of what had happened to the Jackson mission, which had been confronted with what they considered outlandish Iranian demands that had doomed the chances for a settlement even before negotiations had gotten under way. Ambassador Shepherd was especially pessimistic about the chances of satisfactory negotiations with Mossadeq, who seemed completely unwilling to accept "the facts of life in the oil business" despite "repeated testimony" by British and U.S. officials. The British would not dispatch another mission to Tehran unless the Iranians proved their intention to negotiate in good faith. The British government would authorize a mission, the Cabinet decided on 26 July, only if the Iranians ceased harassing the AIOC's personnel and interfering in its operations. In exchange for the resumption of bilateral discussions, in other words, the British government expected Iran to comply with the ICJ's injunction by formally suspending the Nine-Point Law and restoring the status quo ante, which meant a return to British control of Iranian oil.[22]

It was clear to Harriman and other U.S. officials that the Iranian government would never accept the British position. Nor did they believe it should. In their minds the British government still failed to recognize how deeply the Iranian people resented the AIOC, and the British in general, and remained blind to the "disastrous consequences" that would result from a failure to take advantage of Mossadeq's agreement that negotiations could be based on the law of 20 March, rather than the statute of 1 May. Conditions in the oil fields, they argued, should be the subject of direct Anglo-Iranian negotiations, not a precondition for them. Public opinion in Iran, U.S. officials believed, would prevent Mossadeq from acquiescing to the British demand to curtail the Temporary Managing Board's efforts to implement the Nine-Point Law until negotiations had resumed. Moreover, the prime minister was unlikely to accept sole responsibility for the situation in the oil fields. After all, he might argue, had Britain complied with the terms of the Nine-Point Law, the oil industry would already be peacefully under Iranian control. Thus, although both the British and Iranian governments seemed amenable to renewed discussions, progress stalled over the conditions under which those discussions could begin.[23]

To resolve the dispute Harriman shuttled between London and Tehran in search of language that would satisfy both parties, finally producing a compromise that allowed the talks to proceed by papering over the serious differences that still separated the two sides.[24] These differences, however, were temporarily overshadowed by Morrison's announcement that a British delegation, led by Sir Richard Stokes, a British Cabinet minister, would arrive in Tehran on 4 August.[25] The results at that point seemed to vindicate Truman's decision to broaden U.S. involvement in the oil controversy by sending Harriman to Tehran, and Harriman, having brought the two parties to the conference table, had agreed to remain in Tehran to facilitate their discussions.[26]

III

Despite the high hopes surrounding the Stokes mission, it seemed doomed from the start. The nationalization issue had aroused emotions in both Iran and Britain, becoming a rallying point for Iranian independence and a symbol of British prestige. The campaign for nationalization had achieved Mossadeq's goal of uniting the Iranian people, giving them hope of one day gaining "independence from British domination" and transforming the prime minister into Iran's Gandhi in the process. But it had also limited his options by subjecting his every action to the close scrutiny of a public that would no longer permit British domination of Iran's oil industry. As Ambassador Grady put it, Mossadeq had "bunked" the Iranian people into believing that nothing less than total Iranian control of the oil industry was acceptable, and he was now unable to "debunk them even if he wished to." He had become a prisoner of a public frenzy for nationalization that he had helped to create, and any concession to the British ran the risk of alienating the public and toppling his government.[27]

Britain's Labour government faced a similar problem. Churchill and other Conservatives continued to assert that the government's inept handling of the Iranian crisis had damaged British interests in Iran and was imperiling the nation's position throughout the Middle East as well. The latest attack had come in parliamentary debates on 30 July, when Churchill blasted government policy makers as "unequal to the enormous and complicated" Iranian problem. They were, he said, "only liv[ing] from hand to hand and week to week" in Iran without any long-range policy. Only Harold Macmillan among the opposition appeared to deplore the use or threat of force in Iran, but his pleas for moderation failed to quell public cries for stronger action against the Iranians. Nor did Acheson's continued reminders that the United States would sanction the use of force only if needed to evacuate British citizens from Iran.[28] For members of the British public, as for the Conservative opposition, Iran's action against the AIOC was an assault on British pride and prestige that could not be allowed to continue. Inflamed Iranian and British popular sentiment prevented both Mossadeq and Stokes from risking potentially unpopular concessions, which practically guaranteed the failure of the Stokes mission before it had even begun.

Another factor that boded ill for the mission's chances was the selection of Richard Stokes as the British negotiator. Stokes's background as a successful businessman did not prepare him for talks with Mossadeq, whose negotiating tactics had already frustrated U.S. and British diplomats alike. As Wm. Roger Louis has noted, the lord privy seal sought to make Mossadeq a "'jolly good' business offer," which Mossadeq proved unable or unwilling to accept. Nor could Stokes cast off traditional British perceptions of the Iranians as inefficient, corrupt, and dishonest. According to Franks, Stokes was incapable of "dealing with the Iranian mentality," a mentality that was apparently characterized by an inability to grasp details, a refusal to face unpleasant realities, and a stubborn determination to pursue a chosen course of action no matter what the consequences. With such prejudices guiding his talks with Mossadeq it should not be surprising that Stokes made little headway with the prime minister. Nor should it be surprising that U.S. officials found his selection altogether unsatisfactory; Harriman was especially disappointed, having thought Hugh Gaitskell, chancellor of the exchequer, a much better choice.[29]

Making matters worse, in discussions before Stokes's departure British officials had revealed their determination to retain effective control of Iran's oil operations—preferably through a "suitably camouflaged" AIOC but if necessary through some other means, such as an international consortium with substantial British participation. U.S. officials had earlier suggested such an arrangement as a means of assuaging Iranian fears that the AIOC would continue to dominate Iran's oil operations. Although the proposal had gone no further than a few general discussions, the British now resurrected it as a way of retaining some vestige of their former control of Iranian oil. In fact, the British appeared to rest their hopes for a settlement on a revised version of the Jackson proposal, which Mossadeq had rejected in June and denounced again to Harriman in July. The British were not foolish enough to resubmit Jackson's plan in toto. But they did think it possible to dress it up with appropriate "trimmings or sweetenings." In theory this would make the old proposal more palatable to the Iranians; in practice it helped to doom the Stokes negotiations from the start.[30]

Mossadeq also entered the negotiations with an agenda that presaged failure. Contrary to the concession he had apparently made in agreeing to the Harriman formula, he was determined to base the discussions on the law of 1 May, which provided for the actual disfranchisement of the AIOC. Because he accepted the company's disfranchisement as a fait accompli, in other words, Mossadeq would discuss only how the British might adjust to that reality. For him the only topics for discussion were Iran's continued employment of British technicians, compensation to the AIOC, and oil sales to Britain. Although the British were no doubt willing to discuss these issues, their primary concern was guaranteeing that the AIOC be allowed to remain in Iran even though the oil industry had been nationalized. But that was an idea that Mossadeq refused even to consider. By taking such a determined position regarding the scope of the coming negotiations Mossadeq helped to guarantee the Stokes mission's failure.[31]

In the discussions themselves Stokes began with a series of veiled threats that were hardly calculated to assuage Iranian nationalism and smooth the way to an amicable settlement of the oil dispute. Without a resolution of the controversy, he warned Mossadeq, the AIOC and other international oil companies would seek alternate sources of petroleum, and Iran would be left to collapse economically and politically. Stokes was even blunter in discussions with the shah, stressing the "rather frightening" power of the international oil companies, which, he said, "could kill the Persian oil business stone dead" if necessary. In subsequent meetings with other Iranian officials Stokes repeated that stalemate at the negotiating table meant stagnation of the oil industry, "economic suicide" for Iran, and eventual revolution. The West could do without Iranian oil, he said, but the Iranians could not do without Western markets. Unless the oil crisis was solved, the economic decline that would accompany Iran's loss of oil revenues would lead to revolution, perhaps even to communism. Although Mossadeq countered these warnings with what Stokes described as "long harangues about the [AIOC's] wickedness," the lord privy seal still hoped that repeating them would help to make Mossadeq and his colleagues more amenable to British views.[32]

Harriman supported Stokes's efforts by continuing his campaign to educate the Iranians to the complex realities of running the oil industry. In fact, while touring the Abadan refinery, Harriman was said by Stokes to have exclaimed, "The lunacy of these people thinking they could run this themselves!," a remark certainly not meant for Iranian ears and one that revealed Harriman's latent anti-Iranian prejudices. After several discussions dominated by warnings of impending disaster if the Iranians proceeded with their takeover, Stokes detected what he described as a "definite improvement in the atmosphere." It was clear, he reported, that the Iranians were coming to see the consequences of their actions against the AIOC and becoming more inclined to the idea of compromise with the British position.[33]

Given this improved atmosphere, Stokes was optimistic on 13 August when he revealed the British government's so-called Eight-Point Proposal, which was little more than a reworked version of the ill-fated Jackson proposal.[34] Like that proposal it called for continued British control over Iranian oil. Stokes's proposal provided for transfer of the AIOC's "installations, machinery, plant and stores" to the NIOC, with compensation to be included in the operating costs of the oil industry. A British-controlled purchasing organization—basically the AIOC under a different name—would purchase and market "very large quantities" of Iranian oil and designate an operating agency to discover, produce, and refine that oil. Although the NIOC would be the owner of Iran's oil operations, it would not actually run the industry because, according to Stokes, "prudent businessmen" would not sign long-term contracts with an operation "run by the Persians." Under Stokes's plan British interests would receive what amounted to a monopoly over the marketing of Iranian oil, a reality not concealed by terms that put the operating agency under the AIOC and required the purchasing company to share its profits equally with the Iranian government. Other provisions would reinforce the British monopoly. The Iranians, for example, would control only domestic oil operations. And though represented on the board of directors of the operating organization, representation would be arranged on terms that would not enable them to control the organization's day-to-day operations. Despite these limitations, the Foreign Office pronounced the terms equitable and consistent with the law of 20 March.[35]

Mossadeq's reaction was decidedly unfavorable. He bristled at the suggestion that compensation should come from operating costs, as this would place an unfair financial burden on Iran and limit its share of oil profits. He also objected to provisions that would give a British purchasing organization what amounted to a monopoly over the marketing of Iranian oil and would allow British managers to dominate Iranian oil operations. Such provisions, he told Harriman, amounted to a "concession in disguise," something "he could never sell . . . to [the] Iranian people."[36] Rather than reject the proposals outright and thereby end the chances for a negotiated settlement, however, Mossadeq offered counterproposals that would dilute the purchasing organization's monopoly, settle the questions of profit sharing and compensation in a more pro-Iranian fashion, and eliminate exclusive British control over the operating agency.[37]

Stokes found these countermeasures unacceptable. National pride, Britain's balance-of-payments needs, and the best interest of the AIOC, he said, all demanded that Britain control the worldwide distribution of Iranian oil. Fairness dictated that the AIOC receive just compensation for its lost assets. And practicality necessitated British control over day-to-day operations, because the AIOC's British staff in Iran almost certainly would refuse to work for any company that was not British controlled. In Stokes's opinion Mossadeq was caught in a dilemma: if he accepted anything less than the Nine-Point Law, he risked an immediate loss of office. But he faced the same prospect if the British severed negotiations and withdrew from Iran, because the economic collapse that would result could lead only to a popular uprising against his failed government. Unwilling to choose between two equally unattractive alternatives Mossadeq, in Stokes's view, had introduced his counterproposals to buy his government time with the Iranian people while keeping discussions with the British going in hopes of attaining some additional concessions.[38]

Further discussions belied that hope. Stokes and his delegation grew increasingly frustrated with what Peter Ramsbotham of the British embassy in Tehran denounced as the prime minister's "negative and feminine tactics"—perhaps the starkest sign yet of how British cultural assumptions shaped thinking about Mossadeq. Like most women, they believed, Mossadeq apparently had trouble making up his mind, sought to avoid a final decision, and always wanted something better. Stokes was clearly put off by Mossadeq's effort and held firmly to his proposals, which, he said, conformed to both the law of 20 March and the Harriman formula. They represented Britain's best offer, and if the Iranians were not prepared to accept them, the AIOC would look elsewhere for its oil; this was "not politics," he said, but "simple arithmetic."[39]

Mossadeq, meanwhile, resigned himself to British domination of the marketing of Iranian oil but adamantly opposed British control over the oil industry's operations, even after Walter Levy explained that efficiency dictated such control. A British-controlled operating agency would merely revive the AIOC in a new form, said Mossadeq. The Iranian people would never accept an arrangement in which the "servant (meaning the British) would be bigger than the master." It was clear to Mossadeq and other Iranian nationalists that, as a former official in the Foreign Office recalled years later, "in return for recognising the principle of nationalisation," the British government believed that "the Persian government should forego [sic] its insistence on that principle."[40]

Harriman had privately endorsed Stokes's proposals but had avoided a public affirmation, lest it appear that Great Britain and the United States were ganging up on Iran.[41] In an effort to salvage the negotiations and avoid Iran's inevitable collapse to communism, however, Harriman now decided to throw his influence squarely behind the British, resorting to the same threats and economic leverage that they had used earlier. In a meeting with Stokes and Mossadeq on 19 August Harriman endorsed Stokes's proposals as a "good basis" for a settlement. The provisions for the purchasing and operating organizations, Harriman said, aimed not to revive the AIOC in disguise but to provide the necessary infrastructure for the production and marketing of Iranian oil on the world market. Rejection of the proposals, he warned, would lead to misery for the Iranian people and have an adverse effect on world opinion, especially in the United States, where policy makers were reluctant to increase economic assistance to Iran unless it first showed a willingness to help itself. If Iran was not to be left to its own devices, Harriman explained, it had to accept the Stokes proposals.[42]

Harriman's position delighted the British, who had long been calling for Anglo-American solidarity in Iran, but failed to have any effect on the negotiations. Mossadeq still opposed British control of the oil industry's operations and now proposed that some twenty British section heads, responsible to the NIOC's board of directors, be given day-to-day control of the industry. However far such a proposal went toward assuaging Mossadeq's nationalist sensibilities, it would be almost impossible to implement. Stokes complained that "no responsible person" would work under the system Mossadeq proposed, formally withdrew his proposals on 22 August, and announced his intention to suspend the negotiations unless the Iranian government gave in. Mossadeq, he lamented, was not prepared to accept conditions that would allow British managers and technicians to remain on the job and was instead determined to proceed with the AIOC's complete and total disfranchisement, no matter what the consequences. Harriman joined Stokes in laying the mission's failure at Mossadeq's feet. The prime minister, Harriman asserted, was living in a "dream world" where "the simple passage of legislation nationalizing [the] oil industry creates [a] profitable business and everyone is expected to help Iran on terms that he lays down." Mossadeq, Harriman asserted, did not understand the realities of the international oil industry or the dangers his policies posed to Iran's long-term security. His hopes that U.S. companies would step in to produce or sell nationalized Iranian oil were misplaced, as was his belief that Iranian oil was irreplaceable. If Mossadeq did not confront reality, Harriman repeated, the Iranian people would face certain misery and Iran would lose international support, especially in the United States. After eleventh-hour appeals to Mossadeq proved ineffectual Stokes suspended the negotiations and left Tehran on 23 August. Harriman departed the following day.[43]

Despite their failure to mediate a settlement, Harriman believed that he and Stokes had made some progress in educating Mossadeq to the realities of the global petroleum trade. Future progress might therefore be possible. In hindsight, however, what seems most important about his mission was the emergence of a common British and U.S. approach to the Iranian problem. Made possible to some extent by British willingness to accept nationalization in principle, Anglo-American unity was encouraged by other factors as well. Both nations agreed on the importance of keeping Iran allied to the West, in part because of its plentiful oil supplies, in part because of its strategic location as gateway to the Persian Gulf. They were also united in believing that the implications of any Iranian settlement would extend beyond the borders of Iran and affect international agreements everywhere. They were even moving toward a common assessment of Mossadeq as a destabilizing influence in Iran, with whom a negotiated settlement to the oil crisis was all but impossible. For the British these conclusions were welcome developments that signaled Washington's greater involvement in the Iranian crisis and gave hope of closer Anglo-American cooperation in the future.[44]

IV

In the meantime the British escalated the campaign of economic and political pressure they had earlier launched against Mossadeq in an effort to "let the Persians stew" while the implications of Stokes's withdrawal sunk in.[45] The AIOC withdrew its remaining British field personnel and reduced the refinery staff to about 350. It also halted payments to most of its Iranian workers as of 30 September and renewed its threats of legal action against would-be purchasers of Iranian oil.

The major U.S. oil companies were eager to go along with the boycott because they understood the importance of maintaining solidarity with the AIOC. The State Department also acquiesced, no doubt in an effort to avoid costly and potentially damaging lawsuits against U.S. companies and preserve a united front with the British. In addition, the British government imposed a ban on the export to Iran of such scarce commodities as sugar and steel and denied Iran its former right to freely convert sterling into dollars.[46] It also stepped up its anti-Mossadeq propaganda in Iran in hope that opposition elements would see the folly of the prime minister's policies and come out publicly against the government. Now that a "reasonable agreement" with Mossadeq seemed impossible, asserted Ambassador Shepherd, "the moment has come for us to try and get him out" and replace him with a prime minister who was "reasonable and friendly" rather than "rigid and impractical." Finally, the British government beefed up naval operations in the Persian Gulf in an effort to intimidate the Iranian government.[47] Taken together, these measures were part of a British strategy designed to force Mossadeq's compliance with British demands or to replace his regime with one that would.

At the same time U.S. policy makers began laying plans to cope with the collapse of the Iranian oil industry. In July the U.S. Petroleum Administration for Defense (PAD), the agency responsible for managing U.S. oil supplies during the Korean War, had formed the Foreign Petroleum Supply Committee consisting of nineteen of the nation's oil companies. The committee quickly formulated what became known as Plan of Action No. 1, the heart of which was a call for cooperation by the nineteen companies in an effort to replace the 660,000 barrels of oil per day formerly supplied by Iran. This amounted to one-third of total Middle Eastern production and one-quarter of all refined products outside the western hemisphere. To offset the loss of this oil the parties to Plan of Action No. 1 increased production and refining in other countries, realigned imports and exports, and allocated markets. Under other circumstances these activities might have been construed as a restraint of trade. But because industry cooperation was deemed necessary for national security, the companies involved were granted immunity from antitrust prosecution under Section 708 of the Defense Production Act of 1950.[48] Plan of Action No. 1 remained in effect until early July 1952. According to PAD head Oscar L. Chapman, the plan helped to avoid "desperate supply dislocations" and increase free world petroleum production by 750,000 barrels per day.[49]

The PAD and its Foreign Petroleum Supply Committee demonstrated the pattern of corporate collaboration that had developed between the U.S. government and the U.S. oil companies. Industry officials provided the State Department and other agencies with invaluable assistance in dealing with the worldwide shortages caused by the Korean War. They were also instrumental in advising the government on how best to deal with the concurrent loss of Iranian oil that resulted from the AIOC's boycott. And by finding alternatives to Iranian oil they assisted Anglo-American efforts to convince Mossadeq that his country's resources were not irreplaceable. In this way the U.S. oil companies were accomplices in what amounted to

Anglo-American sanctions against Iran: by ensuring that the consequences of the Iranian shutdown ran only one way, against Iran, the British and Americans were trying to induce Mossadeq to adopt what they would consider a more reasonable posture.[50]

If the Anglo-Americans had hoped to use the boycott to coerce Mossadeq into making concessions, they succeeded only in forcing his hand. Driven to the point of desperation, Mossadeq rallied the Iranian public to his side by blaming the breakdown of the Stokes talks on the AIOC's attempt to repackage an old proposal. Stokes's proposals, he asserted on 5 September, contradicted the nationalization laws and were unacceptable; if the British did not submit others within two weeks, he would cancel the residence permits of the AIOC's remaining British employees. This was necessary, Mossadeq said, because as long as British workers remained, other companies would doubt the authenticity of Iran's nationalization and refuse to purchase its oil, further damaging its failing economy.

Mossadeq also sought to silence his critics by warning that if they dared to speak "the people of Persia will smash their heads." Such statements further convinced British officials that Mossadeq suffered from a "hysterical state of mind," failed to grasp the seriousness of the situation, and represented a real danger to his country. They also appeared to vindicate the decision of 6 September to break off the Anglo-Iranian negotiations, which earlier had been simply suspended.[51]

Mossadeq's new offensive against the British was designed to do more than rejuvenate Iran's ailing economy. It was also an effort to protect his political position because public criticism of his government seemed to be mounting. The prime minister's opponents did not constitute an organized force. Nor did they have specific goals, other than publicizing their dissatisfaction with Mossadeq's conduct. Some senators and Majlis deputies, along with a portion of the more educated populace, denounced the failure of the nationalization campaign and decried the hardships ahead if that campaign were continued. Others chastised the government for neglecting such issues as administrative and land reform while single-mindedly pursuing nationalization. Anglophiles expressed outrage at Iran's worsening relations with the British government. By late August opposition deputies had repeatedly denied Mossadeq a quorum in the Majlis. And by early September, as Ambassador Shepherd reported optimistically, their movement was "not only gaining ground" but "also gaining respectability." It was only a matter of time, Shepherd implied, before Mossadeq's opponents forced him from office.[52]

To counter the opposition's charges that he was making no progress on the oil question Mossadeq seemed to retreat from his earlier insistence on the immediate withdrawal of the AIOC's British staff. He first temporized on the expulsion order, saying that he would give the British additional time to formulate new proposals. Then he introduced his own program in an unsigned memorandum delivered to Ambassador Shepherd on 19 September. Far from being a new advance, however, the prime minister's scheme was a retread of what he had already proposed to Stokes, which explains why the British rejected it three days later, convinced that Mossadeq meant the proposal not as a basis for renewed discussions but as a device for disarming his critics in the Majlis. With no other alternative apparent Mossadeq ordered all the AIOC employees to leave Iran by 4 October.[53]

Mossadeq's order shocked policy makers in London, who immediately sought U.S. intervention. It was one thing, they said, for the AIOC willingly to scale back its Iranian operations by withdrawing its personnel; it was quite another for Mossadeq to order the staff out of the country. If enforced, Attlee explained in a personal message to Truman, the order would be an affront to the ICJ ruling, a serious defeat for Britain, and a blow to Western prestige throughout the Middle East. By making a negotiated settlement of the oil crisis all but impossible it would also endanger Western access to Iranian oil, lead to economic chaos in Iran, and hamper efforts to contain communism in that country and throughout the Middle East.

None of these arguments was new to U.S. officials, who had been making them for some time. What was new was Britain's plan for averting disaster in Iran: decisive action by the shah to remove what they termed the "thoroughly undesirable," "incapable and disastrous" Mossadeq from office. Although the culturally motivated British maintained that it was "impossible to hurry the East" and that the shah personally "clutch[ed] at every straw to postpone or avoid action," they believed that the shah would move against Mossadeq if assured of U.S. support, and in late September they launched a campaign to win that support.[54]

These efforts came to naught. Although U.S. officials doubted the likelihood of a negotiated settlement with Mossadeq, they were not yet ready to work for his removal, even alongside the shah and the British. Officials in the State Department disputed the British contention that the shah was ready to dismiss Mossadeq. On the contrary, they argued, the former appreciated the constitutional limits on his power and Mossadeq's enormous popular support. They also contested the British assumption that Mossadeq's removal would kill the Iranian nationalist movement, saying instead that any move against him would probably only stimulate nationalist sentiment. Under these circumstances, they concluded, Anglo-American efforts were better channeled into propping up the shah as a viable political force that could ensure Iranian stability.[55]

In addition to nixing British plans to overthrow Mossadeq, U.S. policy makers refused to sanction Britain's use of force in Iran, either to destabilize Mossadeq or to safeguard the AIOC's position. In mid-September Acheson reiterated the U.S. prohibition against military action except to protect British lives. President Truman later made the same point in a personal message to Attlee. At a meeting on 27 September the British Cabinet also ruled out the use of force to maintain the British position at Abadan, in part because the odds against success were staggering, in part because the British "could not afford to break with the United States on an issue of this kind."[56]

The Cabinet's decision involved political risks to the Labour Party, which expected a stiff Conservative challenge in the general election scheduled for 25 October. As the government recognized, its handling of the crisis in Iran threatened to become a major issue in the campaign. Conservative criticism of Labour's Iranian policy, muted while hope of a favorable settlement still existed, was sure to intensify once it became known that Labour had abandoned force as an option. Churchill and others would certainly claim that Labour had reneged on its parliamentary promises to defend Abadan, accuse the government of being weak and indecisive, and promise to do a better job of protecting Britain's interests worldwide.[57]

To meet these charges, and to show other nations that Britain could not be kicked around, the Labour government announced on 29 September that it would take the Anglo-Iranian controversy to the United Nations Security Council. The goal was an order that would force Iran's compliance with the ICJ's interim injunction and forestall the expulsion of the AIOC's technicians. The British announcement did not please U.S. policy makers. Appealing to the Security Council, they feared, was a serious blunder that would strengthen Mossadeq's domestic position, win Iran international support, and doom all remaining chances for a negotiated settlement. In addition, it was unlikely that Iran would comply with a resolution on Britain's behalf or that a majority of the Security Council would support one. Furthermore, the Soviet Union would surely veto any resolution aimed against Iran in order to enhance its standing among underdeveloped countries as the defender of small nations against Western imperialism. For these and other reasons the United States considered Britain's appeal to the Security Council a major mistake that called into question the Labour government's understanding of the larger ramifications of the Iranian crisis.[58] U.S. officials grew even more apprehensive when Mossadeq—in a brilliant move that temporarily halted opposition activities in Iran, signaled the depth of his personal involvement in the oil dispute, and ultimately hurt the British case before the Security Council—announced he would journey to New York to plead Iran's case himself.[59]

For their part the British discounted U.S. concerns. They saw an appeal to the Security Council as a last-ditch effort to salvage their position in Iran, as well as their global reputation. Having abandoned the use of force, they said, the Labour government had no choice but to appeal to the rule of law even in the face of tremendous odds.[60] The British cleared the first hurdle when the council voted on 1 October to place the case on its agenda. The next challenge would come when floor debate began in mid-October.[61] In the meantime the AIOC decided to withdraw from Abadan on 3 October in what was then described as Britain's "M[iddle] E[ast] Dunkirk" and "the blackest day" in British foreign relations. This decision, which was announced with "funeral headlines" in the British press, dashed hopes that speedy Security Council action would counteract Mossadeq's expulsion order.[62] But it did not lead the British government to reconsider its recourse to the council. After extended discussions with the United States, the British decided to seek a resolution that would declare the Anglo-Iranian dispute a threat to international peace and call for renewed discussions between the two countries.

Lingering U.S. doubts about the wisdom of appealing to the Security Council made acceptance of even this course doubtful. But more important were worries that a row with Great Britain on this issue would seriously affect the Anglo-American relationship. In what Ambassador Gifford called a tirade Foreign Secretary Morrison complained of "being lectured by the United States" and of receiving only 20 percent cooperation from the Americans when he expected 100 percent; in another he denounced the State Department's apparent proclivity to blame both the British and the Iranians for the continuing dispute by objecting to "being put into the dock together with Dr. Musaddiq." Ambassador Shepherd was also upset at what he saw as the lack of U.S. support for Britain's position, so upset, in fact, that he was "hopping up and down in [his] chair." The British, he said, had "been the saints" in the oil dispute, whereas Mossadeq had "been the naughty boy."

The lack of U.S. support was especially troubling in light of the upcoming British general election, which had, after all, prompted Morrison's appeal to the Security Council in the first place. Morrison even mused that perhaps the United States was trying to sabotage Labour's chances for reelection by allowing Mossadeq "to ma[k]e a fool" of him before the

British people. Eager to dispel these suspicions U.S. policy makers agreed that the British should call the shots in the Security Council, while they provided loyal support. Privately, however, they expected the worst.[63]

The Security Council debate on the Iranian case was everything the United States had feared it would be. In a stirring and highly effective two-day speech that showcased his training and talents as a lawyer Mossadeq eloquently elaborated Iran's long-standing grievances against the AIOC. He painted the dispute as one between a helpless nation and a great imperial power, a dispute that amounted to a pairing between David and Goliath, and denounced the Security Council's interference in what he said was an internal Iranian affair. On Britain's behalf Sir Gladwyn Jebb made a hollow plea to the rule of law and the sanctity of contracts. Even though U.S. officials believed in Jebb's arguments, they considered them ineffectual. Indeed, only Brazil and the United States supported Britain's contention that the oil crisis threatened world peace. China, Ecuador, Yugoslavia, and the Soviet Union disagreed, whereas France, Turkey, India, and the Netherlands were uncommitted. Clearly, the British could not secure the seven votes needed to pass the resolution they had in mind. As a result, they decided instead to table their resolution until the ICJ had ruled on its competence in the oil dispute.[64]

The outcome in the Security Council was a defeat for Britain in the eyes of the world and embarrassed the Labour government at home. In the general election held on 25 October Churchill and the Conservatives defeated the Labour Party by a margin of 26 parliamentary seats, securing 321 seats to Labour's 295. Anthony Eden became the new foreign secretary, "a great and signal improvement [over Morrison], except on Iran," as Dean Acheson recalled years later. So far as Iran was concerned, Acheson eventually came to believe that Eden and his colleagues were "out of touch with the world of 1951." They were taking advice from the same individuals who had poisoned the judgment of the Labour Party and had "allowed the [British] government to follow the AIOC meekly into disaster," Acheson believed. Acheson may also have been concerned about the jingoism that had characterized the Conservative Party's election platform and the "truculent braggadocio" that seemed to characterize the new government's rhetoric once it took office. The secretary, as we know, had repeatedly warned the Labour government of the dangers of a bellicose policy in Iran, and he was no doubt worried that Churchill's government would be harder to convince.[65]

Initially, however, Acheson hoped that the Conservatives would launch a new initiative in the Iranian crisis. He urged them to take advantage of

Mossadeq's presence in Washington, where the prime minister had traveled following the Security Council debate, in order to reopen negotiations with the Iranians. The British did allow the United States to sound out Mossadeq on the possibility of renewing discussions, not in hopes of negotiating a settlement, however, but because the British saw the Washington talks as an opportunity to involve the United States more deeply in the crisis.

V

Mossadeq's visit to Washington followed a series of discussions that the State Department had initiated with him even before the Security Council had convened to debate Britain's resolution. Conducted by George McGhee, these fact-finding talks were not intended to produce concrete proposals. Instead, the department merely sought some sense of where the prime minister stood on the three issues he had earlier been willing to discuss with Stokes—arrangements for the sale of oil to the British, the NIOC's employment of British technicians, and compensation to the AIOC. The goal was to change Mossadeq's mind about refusing to "come to any agreement with either the British government or the AIOC." McGhee also tried to educate Mossadeq to the realities of the international petroleum industry, to convince him that no oil settlement was possible that flew in the face of normal commercial principles or that gave Iran better terms than those in force elsewhere.[66]

By the time Mossadeq appeared before the Security Council on 15 October, McGhee had made some progress. Mossadeq would permit a purchasing organization to act as a broker for the AIOC's former customers if they so chose but only for a period of ten years. He would also allow British technicians to work in Iran and would exempt the Abadan refinery from nationalization if it was operated by a neutral agency. To McGhee these were significant concessions that gave hope of Mossadeq's eventual agreement to some kind of direct British involvement in the oil industry. They also suggested that Mossadeq might finally be willing to accept a commercially sound settlement.[67]

McGhee had less luck regarding compensation. Mossadeq refused to discuss specific arrangements for determining the amount of compensation or accept the idea that compensation might involve more than the stated book value of the AIOC's Iranian assets. In fact, he wondered at times why Iran should have to pay compensation at all; its oil-producing neighbors, he argued, had not done so. McGhee's assertions that other countries had not seized foreign-owned installations failed to shake Mossadeq's resolve. Nor did reminders that other nations were replacing Iran in world oil markets.[68]

Much of what McGhee told Mossadeq echoed the sentiments of U.S. oil executives. The State Department had held regular meetings with representatives of the major U.S. oil companies throughout the Iranian crisis, relying on industry experts for guidance and advice and enlisting their cooperation with government policy. Initially, oil company executives had supported Iran's case against the AIOC and had urged the State Department to push the British toward a more flexible posture.

But as the crisis dragged on, their position did a 180-degree turnaround. In discussions held during September and October representatives of the U.S. majors now warned of the dangerous precedent that would be set if Mossadeq received terms better than those prevailing in other oil-producing countries. U.S. investments worldwide, not only in oil but in other commodities as well, might be threatened. U.S. prestige throughout the Middle East might also be damaged by creating the impression that the United States could be blackmailed and manipulated. It was better to lose Iran entirely, the executives believed, than to run such risks, and for this reason they were 100 percent behind the British position on limiting concessions to Mossadeq.

McGhee and other officials conceded the importance of preserving the sanctity of international contracts. But they hoped to do so without driving Iran into the arms of the Soviet Union. Iran's proximity to the Soviet Union and its "strategic location with respect to the Middle East as a whole," Harriman explained, dictated special treatment that would not be necessary if Iran was located at the tip of South America. In other words, preserving Iran's Western orientation required an accommodation of its aspirations and desires, even if British oil interests had to suffer in the process. Guided by this hierarchy of objectives, the State Department had therefore declined to throw its weight totally behind the British for fear of alienating the Iranians.[69]

In an effort to reach a settlement that went some distance toward protecting both British and Iranian interests, McGhee, Acheson, and other U.S. officials continued discussions with Mossadeq after the Security Council closed debate on the Iranian case. Mossadeq reaffirmed the agreements he and McGhee had reached regarding the brokerage powers of the purchasing organization and the arrangements for efficient management of the oil industry. The prime minister also confirmed his belief that a neutral company should own and operate the Abadan refinery after paying appropriate compensation to the AIOC. All the company's other properties would be transferred to the NIOC. With regard to compensation Mossadeq believed that in the end Iran's claims against the AIOC would offset the claims of the company itself. As a result, neither side would need to make any direct payments. The prime minister's tentative agreement on these questions gave the State Department hope that a negotiated settlement might be possible.[70]

Mossadeq's stand on other issues, however, indicated otherwise. For one thing he withdrew his earlier promise that British technicians could return to Iran. Consultation with his advisers, he said, had convinced him that the Iranian people would see the return of even one British technician as a defeat.

More problematic was his stand on the price of Iranian oil. Although Mossadeq apparently agreed that Iran would use an outside agency to market and distribute its oil, he did not seem to accept that the distributing company would buy Iranian oil at a low price and sell it for more on the open market. Walters, Harriman's interpreter, reported that Mossadeq "could not understand why an oil-producing country could not get the same price for its oil as an oil-producing company." Unwilling to be bound by the two-market system under which the international petroleum industry operated, the prime minister wanted the price at which Iran sold oil to the distributing agency to equal the price that that agency charged retailers. This was about $1.75 per barrel, whereas Saudi Arabian oil sold for 88 cents per barrel and Kuwaiti oil for about $1.09 per barrel. At $1.75 per barrel, as McGhee and other U.S. officials tried to point out in a futile effort to get the prime minister "down to earth" on the question of price, Iranian oil would not be competitive in world markets; distributors would seek less expensive oil elsewhere.[71]

Mossadeq's insistence that Iran would leave its oil in the ground before it would accept less than $1.75 per barrel was probably a bargaining ploy. The prime minister surely understood that a distributing organization would not work for free and must have known that Iran would never receive $1.75 per barrel for its oil. But he must also have known that insisting upon such a price gave Iran a better chance of improving upon the $1.10 per barrel suggested by the United States. Unwilling to tip his hand in discussions with McGhee, Mossadeq argued instead that it was "not the amount of revenue but the price that counted." To the United States this statement was another example of the twisted logic that the U.S. officials believed governed Mossadeq's approach to the oil controversy. He had supposedly nationalized the oil industry to improve the lot of the Iranian people but was pursuing a course that could only end in failure. In truth, however, Mossadeq's position signified his conviction that more was at stake than a commercial settlement. Involved was Iran's right to control its resources. Unless the British and the Americans grasped this point, the chances for a negotiated settlement were slim indeed.[72]

U.S. officials presented the scheme they had hammered out with Mossadeq to their British counterparts at a NATO meeting in Paris. At the heart of the U.S. proposal was the sale of the Abadan refinery to a neutral, preferably Dutch, concern, which was assumed to mean Royal Dutch/Shell. All the AIOC's other properties would be transferred to Iranian ownership, but Iran's claims against the company would render direct compensation unnecessary. The refinery operator would guarantee the NIOC access to the latest technology and would employ foreign non-British technicians on an individual basis but only until trained Iranians could take their places. A purchasing organization, to be established by the AIOC, would "buy, ship and market" at least thirty tons of Iranian oil for a period of fifteen years.[73]

The State Department was sorely disappointed when Eden initially dismissed the proposals as "totally unacceptable" from a commercial standpoint. Shell would not run the Abadan refinery unless it could purchase some of the oil it refined, especially if this task drew staff from its operations elsewhere. Nor would the AIOC yield production control to another company or contract with an outside refiner that could charge what it wished for its services. In addition, the British government resisted efforts to surrender control of the oil operations to the Iranians, as this would rob the exchequer of much needed tax revenues. It also considered the compensation arrangements totally inadequate: it was unthinkable that the AIOC would sell Abadan, which alone was worth at least £250 million, for what was sure to be a nominal sum, or that it would allow Iran "to make fictitious counter-claims to justify what was virtually a confiscation."[74]

Perhaps more important, the British raised political and diplomatic objections to the U.S. proposals. As Acheson saw it, the new Conservative government could hardly expect to win domestic support for a settlement that smacked of appeasement after it had lambasted its predecessor for weakness in Iran. Nor could it allow such a settlement to challenge Britain's international prestige. Eden and others feared a domino effect: if Iran appeared to prosper at Britain's expense, other nations would follow its lead, with catastrophic results for Britain's "credit and standing throughout the world." British officials were particularly worried lest Iran's assault on the AIOC inspire Egypt to take similar action against the Suez Canal or the British base astride it. "Oil is important," the British implied, "but [our] position in the Middle East is vital." For this reason both the British government and the AIOC preferred to sacrifice Iranian oil rather than accept an agreement based on the U.S. proposals.[75]

In rejecting the U.S. proposals the British revealed their desiderata for an acceptable settlement. Iran had fairly to compensate the AIOC for the loss of its assets and operate the oil industry efficiently enough to ensure the payment of compensation. Iran could not, as a result of its "unilateral expropriation" of the AIOC, expect to receive better terms than nations that "respected their contracts." Nor could Iran exclude British firms from its oil industry, because this would set a dangerous precedent that other countries might follow. The first three requirements, according to the State Department, could easily be met. The last was next to impossible, given the anti-British hysteria in Iran, but it was also the most important to the British. More than anything else, Acheson explained to his colleagues on 10 November, the British feared the loss of their earnings on investments around the world, the security of which depended on "confidence in British power and in the pound." If the government in London acquiesced in a settlement that rewarded Mossadeq for expropriating British property or discriminated against British interests, other nations would follow Iran's lead and Britain would soon have no international properties whatsoever. To prevent such an eventuality the British had adopted a hard-line stance that excluded renewed bilateral discussions. Acheson seemed sympathetic to British thinking on this score, saying that asking them to accept total exclusion from Iran "would be like asking [the United States] to step aside in favor Guatemala."[76]

Rather than resume talks with the Iranians, the British believed that the best solution to the crisis was direct U.S. entry into the Iranian oil industry. In other words, it seems that Eden and his colleagues believed that they could purchase U.S. support in Iran by offering U.S. oil companies a share of Iranian oil. Specifically, they envisioned a multinational consortium, presumably an Anglo-Dutch-American group, that would take over the AIOC's Iranian operations.[77] U.S. participation would dilute the power of the AIOC, they believed, and thus assuage Iranian fears of British domination. It would also satisfy requirements for efficient operations, allow the AIOC to remain in Iran, if only as a member of the consortium, and convince the Iranians of the inviolability of the Anglo-American alliance. After all, Eden and others argued, Great Britain and the United States "were partners in the whole of the Middle East and [Iran] should be no exception." The Americans, however, demurred. Among the practical and political problems with the idea were the unfavorable press it would generate and the unlikelihood that U.S. oil companies, which had access to adequate reserves elsewhere, would be inclined to participate. Although the State Department would change its mind within a few years, in 1951 it did not yet see the need for U.S. participation in the Iranian oil industry. With the United States thus opposed to Eden's only firm proposal Acheson sadly acknowledged that Mossadeq would have to return to Tehran empty handed.[78]

Although McGhee and Mossadeq had continued their discussions while the British government debated the merits of the U.S. proposals, their talks yielded no solutions. Mossadeq rejected a number of options that would have provided for international operation of the Iranian oil industry. Nor would he allow British technicians to return to Iran or accept less than $1.75 per barrel for Iranian oil, the two provisions that McGhee described as most sought after by the British. Iran would do without oil revenues, Mossadeq said, rather than substitute one foreign master for another or accept an agreement he deemed unfair. As Vernon Walters explained in another example of how politically constrained the prime minister had become, Mossadeq thought he would be better off returning to Iran without a settlement than returning with one he had to "sell to [his] fanatics." To be sure, such a course might result in the complete collapse of the Iranian economy. But this was a calamity Mossadeq still hoped to avoid through additional loans from the United States. He discussed the possibility of such assistance with U.S. policy makers before his departure for Iran on 17 November. He also discussed with officials of the International Bank for Reconstruction and Development (IBRD) a scheme whereby that institution would run the Iranian oil industry while Britain and Iran worked out a permanent settlement.[79]

VI

The Iranian oil crisis was no closer to a solution in late 1951 than it had been at the beginning. If anything, Britain and Iran seemed further apart, with neither side willing to abandon its interests. By October the AIOC had withdrawn from Abadan and was replacing Iranian oil by increasing production elsewhere and purchasing crude from U.S. companies. It was also continuing its boycott of Iranian oil sales, which received widespread support from other international oil companies, including the five U.S. majors.

The Iranians were less successful in dealing with the crisis. They tried in vain to generate revenues by selling oil on the open market, only to be stymied by the British-led boycott. In the meantime growing budget deficits and other financial problems portended an imminent collapse of the Iranian economy and, or so U.S. officials worried, a communist takeover of the government in Tehran. To the U.S. way of thinking this would have disastrous consequences for the Western position in the Middle East. Not only would it alter the global balance in strategic materials, it would provide the Soviet Union with a valuable gateway to the Persian Gulf. Without either an immediate resolution of the oil crisis or a massive infusion of U.S. aid, Iran was likely to go the way of China.

To prevent the "loss" of Iran U.S. policy makers had become increasingly involved in the Anglo-Iranian dispute. Initially, their role as an honest broker had involved mediating between the two disputants without openly favoring either side. This strategy had dominated U.S. policy through the Harriman mission in mid-1951 and was characterized by appeals to both the British and the Iranians for moderation. By late 1951, however, U.S. policy makers had grown decidedly more sympathetic toward the British, in part because the British had accepted nationalization in principle, in part because U.S. officials had experienced firsthand how "emotional, impractical, and unrealistic" Mossadeq could be,[80] in part because the U.S. oil companies had now come down firmly in the AIOC's camp. To be sure, important Anglo-American differences remained over the wisdom of using economic pressures to weaken Mossadeq's domestic position and the authenticity of Iran's nationalist movement. But these were minor matters compared to the general transatlantic agreement, which stemmed at least partly from Western cultural prejudices about Mossadeq's personal quirks and perceived unfitness for office, on the prime minister's culpability for the continuing crisis.

chapter 5

Stalemate

AN ANGLO-IRANIAN TEST OF WILLS

The eight months after Mossadeq's visit to the United States brought what Dean Acheson described as "static trench warfare" on the Iranian front: both Iran and Britain sought to win a war of attrition against the other.[1] Mossadeq rejected an interim settlement proposed by the International Bank for Reconstruction and Development, whereas the British continued to lead an international boycott of Iranian oil exports. The British also managed to replace Iranian oil with petroleum from other sources, including U.S. companies, which made it easier for the British to wait until economic pressures forced Iran to capitulate. Mossadeq gave no sign that he would abandon the goal of nationalization, however, even though the loss of oil revenue contributed to a steady deterioration of the Iranian economy.

As the oil crisis persisted, U.S. determination to reach a settlement intensified. Because the U.S. Petroleum Administration for Defense had replaced Iranian oil with other sources of supply, officials in the State Department agreed with their British counterparts that an Iranian settlement had become less important for meeting the West's supply requirements. But resolving the crisis was still necessary if the West was to safeguard the Middle East against Soviet encroachment and internal subversion. For these reasons, the Americans argued, Iran's deteriorating economy needed rapid attention, as did the country's precarious political situation. With these factors in mind

U.S. policy makers continued to seek a settlement that would assure Iran's allegiance to the West without sacrificing Britain's position in the Middle East and throughout the world.

Yet international realities prevented the United States from pushing the British too hard toward such a settlement. U.S. officials feared that pressing the British might alienate them just when their support in Korea was crucial. U.S. officials also knew that their commitment to the recovery of Western Europe and preoccupation with the Korean War made them dependent on the British to protect Iran and the entire Middle East from communist expansion. This dependence prevented the United States from criticizing British policy as loudly as might otherwise have been the case and probably helped to string out the oil crisis a little longer. More important, it tied the United States to hard-line British policies in Iran that were not always wise or farsighted.

II

Deprived of oil revenues that once provided 40 percent of its income, the Iranian government was fast approaching financial ruin by the fall of 1951. Facing a monthly budget deficit of 150 million rials, it was unable to meet its payroll, not to mention the salaries of seventy thousand idle oil workers, which amounted to another 140 million rials. Nor could the government sustain the monthly expenditures of more than 100 million rials required to support the Seven-Year Plan. As the U.S. embassy noted in October and November, Mossadeq's administration had not been able to ease these financial pressures through a program of government economies or by drawing on sterling balances that previously had been used to support Iran's currency. Without an immediate resolution of the oil crisis, new U.S. ambassador Loy Henderson feared, the Iranian economy would collapse.[2]

As Iran's economy deteriorated, political conditions grew worse. Opposition forces abandoned the truce they had declared when Mossadeq left for the United States, launching an antigovernment campaign that threatened to destabilize the country. The shrinking prospects for a negotiated settlement with the British, made less likely by Churchill's victory in the British elections, spurred opposition elements who decried Mossadeq's lack of leadership and sought his removal in elections for the Seventeenth Majlis that were scheduled for the fall. The opposition's reemergence heartened the British embassy in Tehran, of course, where analysts argued that Mossadeq's downfall was imminent and that the British would be able to negotiate a favorable settlement with his successor. To help move events in this direction the British continued their antigovernment propaganda campaign. They also tried once again to convince the shah to move against Mossadeq.[3]

U.S. policy makers were less sanguine. They worried most of all that mounting political instability and worsening economic conditions in Iran would pave the way to victory for the Tudeh Party, which in turn would open the door to Soviet expansion into the Middle East. Instead of following the British lead and waiting for an economic crisis to topple Mossadeq, they thought the United States should provide Iran with economic assistance. Although the State Department still hoped that a negotiated oil settlement would render such aid unnecessary, it was prepared to offer financial assistance if Iran began drifting toward communism. As Acheson was careful to assure the British, however, such aid would bolster the Iranian economy, not Mossadeq's regime. It would be limited, he said, and would be given directly to the shah and the Iranian people, rather than to the prime minister.[4]

Iran was in economic and political turmoil when Mossadeq returned from the United States on 23 November after a stop in Cairo for a meeting with Egyptian Prime Minister Mohammed Nahas. In a move that must have fed British and U.S. fears of a Middle Eastern alliance against the West, the two pledged to support each other's struggles against a common enemy. But Mossadeq's first order of business was regaining the upper hand in his struggle against political opponents at home. The failure of his talks with McGhee, he proclaimed, stemmed from British efforts to "drag out" the oil crisis until Iran collapsed. This was a misplaced hope, the prime minister asserted, because Iran's struggle against British imperialism was a matter of national pride that would continue at all costs. Iran's struggle was supported throughout the Middle East and had won plaudits from former Mexican president Lazaro Cárdenas, who had spearheaded his country's oil nationalization drive during the 1930s. The Iranians had a duty to persevere in their struggle and could do so, Mossadeq seemed to promise, with economic assistance from the U.S. Treasury, the Export-Import Bank, and the International Bank for Reconstruction and Development (IBRD). This promise, together with the prime minister's fiery rhetoric, seemed to shore up his domestic support, at least temporarily.[5]

The IBRD's offer to run Iran's oil industry pending an Anglo-Iranian settlement held attractions for British officials as well. In their minds the bank's involvement was a means to reintroduce "efficient Western management" into the Iranian oil industry until arrangements could be made for

Britain's return. Accordingly, the British government had joined the AIOC in initiating discussions with IBRD officials just as Mossadeq was leaving the United States. These talks were later transferred to London, where they eventually produced an agreement under which the bank would engage a neutral agency to manage the AIOC's operations in Iran, purchase Iranian oil at an unspecified but competitive price, and market that oil through established British distribution channels. The proceeds would be divided three ways, one-third to Iran, one-third to the managing agency, and one-third to an escrow account to be used to compensate the AIOC. Although the proposed arrangement left unsettled the question of price, which the McGhee-Mossadeq discussions had shown to be a sticking point, it offered the "glimmer of a solution" to the oil problem and therefore won the support of U.S. officials, who hoped that the IBRD arrangement would restart the Iranian oil industry and obviate the need for U.S. aid to Iran.[6]

U.S. officials placed even more hope in the IBRD proposals after Mossadeq announced his intention to break the British boycott by selling oil to all potential buyers, even those from communist bloc nations. The AIOC's former customers had been given a chance to purchase Iranian oil from the NIOC, he asserted, but had acquiesced in the boycott of Iranian oil instead. Unless these firms signed purchase agreements with Iran by 24 December, he would find other buyers. If implemented, Mossadeq's plan could endanger the strategic balance in the Middle East, or so U.S. officials worried. It could also trigger the Battle Act of October 1951, which prohibited recipients of U.S. aid from shipping strategic raw materials, including oil, to countries behind the iron curtain. If Mossadeq carried out his plan, the United States might be forced to curtail all assistance to Iran, including the U.S. military missions then attached to the Iranian army and gendarmerie and the $23 million in assistance from Truman's Point IV program, scheduled for 1952. Ambassador Henderson futilely warned Mossadeq about the effects of a withdrawal of U.S. assistance. The prime minister refused to allow U.S. law to restrict his freedom to sell oil to whomever he wished. With Mossadeq's position thus likely to halt U.S. assistance the State Department increasingly saw the IBRD plan as the last hope for saving the Iranian economy.[7]

Mossadeq's offer to sell oil to the communist bloc was probably more bluff than substance. Few, if any, iron curtain countries had the wherewithal to purchase and ship large quantities of Iranian oil, let alone the need to do so. Still, Mossadeq must have thought that he had something to gain by at least offering them the oil. As noted earlier, the prime minister was well aware that U.S. leaders thought it essential to maintain Iran's Western orientation, and he seemed particularly adept at raising the specter of communism to get what he wanted. The British considered it unlikely that Iran would fall to communism, telling the Americans that Mossadeq was playing them for fools. But these warnings had no effect at the State Department, where policy makers continued to steer by cold war landmarks.

On a local level Mossadeq's open-ended oil sales offer was undoubtedly designed to quash criticism that nationalization had failed. This was especially true after violent confrontations erupted between students and police at Tehran University on 6 December. The brutality with which the government subdued the protesters inspired angry press attacks and antigovernment outbursts. On one occasion hecklers in the spectators' gallery of the Majlis shouted down the prime minister as he attempted to speak; on another, opposition and government deputies engaged in fisticuffs on the floor of the Majlis. With elections looming Mossadeq may have hoped that a few signed contracts would quell the rising discontent, demonstrate the uselessness of the British-led boycott, and protect his political position against his domestic critics.[8]

As further proof that he was making progress on the oil question, Mossadeq agreed, however halfheartedly, to receive a mission consisting of Hector Prud'homme, the IBRD's loan officer for Iranian affairs, and Torkild Rieber, a former chairman of Texaco. The mission was to present the proposals hammered out earlier with the British, including Iran's rehiring of British technicians and the sale of Iranian oil at prices that would not disrupt petroleum agreements with other countries. The prime minister had refused to consider either eventuality during his earlier negotiations with Stokes and McGhee. On 24 December a U.S. news agency reported that Mossadeq had vowed to reject the IBRD proposals as well, and the prime minister's firmness on these questions filtered down to his supporters, who demonstrated against the bank's involvement on 29 December.[9]

If the Iranian people were not agreed on the wisdom of having the IBRD intervene in the oil dispute, they were united about the havoc the ongoing dispute, and the accompanying loss of oil revenues, was wreaking on the country's economy. Mossadeq's austerity program had not yet significantly reduced government expenditures, nor had an inaugural offering of government bonds or new taxes on luxury goods and nonessential imports generated much income. The prime minister also tried to decrease Iran's dependence on oil revenues by instituting a strategy of "non-oil economics." But this strategy, which sought to increase such other exports as carpets and agricultural products, had yet to show significant results. By mid-January Mossadeq was warning Ambassador Henderson that a communist revolution was imminent unless the United States provided Iran with immediate financial assistance.[10]

Mounting political instability seemed to confirm Mossadeq's warnings. General opposition to the government, fueled by the prime minister's failure to solve the oil crisis, continued to grow. Many Iranians rejected the government's call for a nonoil economy, resisted Mossadeq's efforts to collect new taxes, and called for an immediate oil settlement with Great Britain. Violence broke out in some areas of the country during the national election campaign for the Seventeenth Majlis, which had gotten under way in late December and was expected to continue through March. With Iran's future resting on the results of these elections both Mossadeq and his opponents waged vigorous campaigns that turned the elections into a referendum on the government. Although early returns from Tehran and other districts produced victories for Mossadeq and the National Front, many critics attributed the results to government fraud—a charge that Mossadeq denied but that independent observers seemed to confirm. Opposition elements in the Majlis also added to Mossadeq's woes by scheduling an interpellation of the government for 22 January, apparently in hopes of generating antigovernment publicity that might influence the elections in areas where voting had not yet been completed. As the only organized opposition to Mossadeq the Tudeh Party was sure to profit from the prime minister's political troubles.[11]

Despite the potentially destabilizing effects of Iran's economic and political problems, the Truman administration was reluctant to provide Iran with assistance that would be used to meet normal government expenses. Officials in the State Department, although not discounting the seriousness of the situation, believed that Mossadeq was exaggerating the danger in order to strengthen his political position, especially in the upcoming Majlis interpellation. It was probable, they asserted, that Mossadeq wanted to use promises of U.S. aid to silence criticism that he was leading Iran toward economic disaster. These officials also feared that U.S. aid would decrease Mossadeq's need to negotiate an oil settlement, encourage other national leaders to follow his example, and anger the British. After considerable discussion, and against the advice of Ambassador Henderson, who warned of an imminent Iranian collapse, the State Department in mid-January had affirmed its earlier decision that budgetary aid should "be associated in some way with [the] oil situation." Until an oil settlement had been reached, in other words, the United States added to the economic pressure on Mossadeq by deciding to provide the Iranian government with assistance only for development or military purposes.[12]

With little prospect of bolstering his sagging political position with U.S. aid Mossadeq sought instead to rally public opinion against the British. On 9 January, in what was widely regarded as a bid for popular support, the prime minister accused the British government of intriguing with everyone from Majlis deputies to students and journalists in an effort to "ruin Iran economically [and] politically." Although vague about Britain's crimes, Mossadeq was probably referring to the AIOC's boycott of Iranian oil and to alleged interference by British consular officials in Iran's internal affairs. When the British dismissed Mossadeq's use of what they called the "well-worn theme" of political intrigue and refused to acknowledge his unsubstantiated charges—charges that recent scholarship seems to confirm—the prime minister ordered all British consulates in Iran closed by 21 January, one day before the scheduled Majlis interpellation. The Iranian government also announced that British diplomats who had served in Iran would not be allowed to return. This policy generated a firestorm of British protest. In the short term it threatened the proposed appointment of Sir Robert Hankey to succeed the departing Sir Francis Shepherd as ambassador in Tehran. In the long term it would seriously hamper the British embassy's operations by keeping Persian-speaking diplomats from returning to Iran for service. These protests, however, failed to move the prime minister, who believed that novice diplomats who lacked contacts with Iranian Anglophiles would be less likely to interfere in the country's domestic affairs.[13]

Mossadeq's anti-British actions were an astute political move. By skillfully diverting the focus of the Majlis interpellation from condemnation of his failure to solve the oil crisis to endorsement of his efforts to end British interference in Iran, the prime minister guaranteed the interpellation's failure. In fact, it had to be canceled when Mossadeq's threats to publicly brand his opponents as traitors kept so many deputies from attending the session that a quorum was not possible. From this point on the Sixteenth Majlis ceased to function, and the Senate became Iran's only legislative body.[14]

III

If Mossadeq's action against the British boosted his political position, it also contributed to a worsening of Anglo-Iranian relations by further jeopardizing the chances of settling the oil crisis and causing new alarm in Washington. U.S. policy makers hoped to take advantage of an impending visit by British Prime Minister Winston Churchill to promote an oil settlement. Churchill had proposed the visit in November as a way of establishing the kind of close personal relationship with President Truman and other U.S. officials that he had earlier developed with President Franklin D. Roosevelt. In addition, Churchill and other British leaders saw the talks as part of a continuing strategy to "make the US-UK relationship more obvious to the world" and to win U.S. support for British policy not only in Iran but also in Egypt, where the government of Mohammed Nahas had recently abrogated Britain's treaty right to station troops in the Suez Canal area.

Churchill, Eden, and their colleagues in London were convinced that an Anglo-American partnership in the Middle East "would divide [Britain's] difficulties by ten." Had the United States made a greater effort to cooperate with Britain in the past, the prime minister believed, neither "the Iranian troubles" nor "the Egyptian problem, which he called 'a bastard child of the Iranian situation,'" would have developed. Instead, things had happened precisely as the British had feared: Iran's assault on the AIOC had now inspired similar action in Egypt and might set a dangerous precedent for other countries as well. A "unified [Anglo-American] front," Churchill believed, not only would have prevented these unfortunate developments but also would serve to reconcile Britain's declining resources with its worldwide responsibilities and preserve some remnant of its former position throughout the Middle East, especially in Iran.[15]

Officials in Washington doubted Churchill's ability to duplicate his wartime relationship with Roosevelt. But they did see the talks as a means of squaring Anglo-American differences on a number of important issues. One was the question of the European Defense Community, which London was not supporting as strongly as Washington would have liked. Another was Britain's lack of support for the U.S. position in Asia, notably its recognition of the communist government in China and its somewhat restrained support of the U.S.-led police action in Korea. A third area of concern, and one closer to our purposes, involved the hopes of officials in Washington to coordinate Anglo-American policy toward the Middle East. To this end briefing papers and intelligence reports prepared for Churchill's visit reiterated the interrelated goals of the United States in Iran: to maintain that country's alignment with the West and to preserve Western access to its oil. Because Iran was the key to a noncommunist Middle East, U.S. leaders urged immediate resolution of the oil dispute, even if this meant sacrificing "legitimate British interests" to the larger goal of preventing a "tragedy . . . to the entire West." Although they acknowledged Britain's traditional dominance in the Middle East, U.S. planners went on to assert that the "increasing stake" of the United States in the area must be accompanied by a "commensurate role in the development of [regional] plans and policies," especially in light of Britain's declining ability "to maintain and defend Western interests." This did not mean that U.S. leaders were prepared to play a more active role in *implementing* Anglo-American plans. With its resources severely limited by its commitments to Western Europe and by the war in Korea the United States needed Britain to carry Middle Eastern defense. All U.S. policy makers seemed to be saying was that the time had come for the United States to join Britain in *formulating* Western strategy for the region, and especially for Iran.[16]

Secretary Acheson made all these points when the Washington talks opened on 5 January. He also sought to spur the British to action. Because the situation in Iran and throughout the Middle East "might have been devised by Karl Marx himself," Acheson argued, it warranted immediate attention. By "sitting tight" and allowing Iran to drift toward communism the British and the Americans "would be like two people locked in loving embrace in a rowboat which was about to go over Niagara Falls." To avert disaster, Acheson concluded, the two nations "should break the embrace and take to the oars." They should launch new initiatives immediately or the collapse of Iran was imminent.[17]

The British delegation to the Washington talks disagreed. As had been their wont throughout the oil crisis, these officials emphasized that underdeveloped agricultural countries like Iran were always hardier than they appeared. Because it had no industrial infrastructure or financial apparatus, Iran could remain afloat for some time; as British ambassador Franks put it, "[we] often encounter serious threats" in Iran but "seem never to go over the cliff." In addition, the delegation believed that Mossadeq was raising the specter of collapse to frighten the United States into loosening restrictions on economic aid or forcing Britain to make further oil concessions. The delegation also doubted that the Soviet Union would jump to Mossadeq's assistance, either by providing financial assistance or by purchasing Iranian oil.[18]

These arguments failed to sway U.S. policy makers. To their way of thinking the Iranian situation was rapidly degenerating into a dangerous game of chicken in which each side, Britain and Iran, sought to outlast the other. The dangers inherent in such a course fueled U.S. fears for Iran's safety. By virtue of its position astride the Soviet Union Iran was crucial to Western security in the Middle East, and U.S. officials were determined to maintain its stability. They placed their primary hopes for an oil settlement on discussions that were then under way between Iran and the IBRD, even though, as we will see, these discussions had not gotten off to an auspicious start. But U.S. policy makers believed that the British should be ready with a new proposal in case these talks failed. Such a proposal, they asserted, should abandon "general principles" for a "practical solution" to the Iranian problem. Because Mossadeq's primary goal was to compensate the AIOC so that nationalization could be said to have been accomplished, the State Department suggested a specific amount of compensation—the equivalent of $400 million in free oil. After making compensation in this amount, Iran would continue to provide Britain with oil at a discount of 25 or 30 percent—an amount, according to U.S. calculations, that would give Iran approximately 60 percent of the oil industry's profits. This proposal left many questions unanswered, yet it clearly revealed the State Department's determination to resolve the crisis. "The situation in Iran cannot go on indefinitely without incurring the very real danger that a solution will come too late," Secretary Acheson cautioned. "It is [therefore] best to have alternatives."[19]

British officials denounced the U.S. proposal as unrealistic and unacceptable. The compensation figure was far too low, even as part of a settlement that canceled Iran's claims against the AIOC. Nor was a sixty-forty division of profits acceptable, not only because it was unfair to the AIOC but also because it would jeopardize Britain's other international contracts, which were its "life blood" and an essential element of its balance of payments. To British policy makers the proposal stemmed from the State Department's "fidgety and theoretical" approach to the Iranian problem and epitomized the kind of "bad" settlement they feared most. It sacrificed legitimate British concerns to Iranian demands, "put a premium on confiscation," and was motivated by an "exaggerated" U.S. fear of communist expansion in Iran rather than an objective assessment of the situation.[20]

This last point constituted the real stumbling block to Anglo-American agreement on the terms of an Iranian settlement. Despite the State Department's acknowledgment that Mossadeq was "reckless and dangerous" and that his government was "undesirable," it continued to see him as the only alternative to the Tudeh Party and to push the British toward a settlement of the oil crisis before Iran's economy collapsed and Mossadeq was forced to turn to the Soviet bloc for assistance. British policy makers accused U.S. policy makers of allowing their obsession with communism "to shade any possible [oil] solution in favor of Iran." Although not downplaying the dangers of a communist coup in Iran, the British remained more sanguine about that country's economic resiliency. Its "feeble primitive economy" may have deteriorated, they said, but Iran was a long way from collapse. The Foreign Office also continued to doubt that the Soviet Union would assist Mossadeq. In its estimation the real danger of communism in Iran came not from the oil crisis but from Mossadeq's continued tenure as prime minister. By failing to curb the rising power of the Tudeh Party and by wedding Iran to a nationalization policy that could lead only to economic chaos, Mossadeq was leading the country straight into Moscow's arms.[21]

If the Washington talks, which formally adjourned on 18 January, failed to resolve the Iranian crisis, they did provide for a complete airing of Anglo-American differences. They also led to continued discussions of the Iranian question in London, where Paul Nitze and Harold Linder of the State Department held numerous meetings with representatives of the Treasury, Foreign Office, Ministry of Fuel and Power, and AIOC in mid-February. Initial talks revealed agreement on several key points: Mossadeq's political position would probably improve after the Majlis elections, Iran's economy was deteriorating but not as rapidly as the State Department had originally believed, and the shah was unlikely to move against Mossadeq. The talks also revealed that the State Department now shared British doubts about Mossadeq's chances of receiving aid from the Soviet Union, either as direct financial assistance or through oil purchases. As Nitze reported, the State Department, along with the CIA and the Defense Department, believed "that the Soviets probably estimate that their best chance of gaining control of all or parts of Iran is by allowing the situation to continue to deteriorate rather than by bolstering any Iranian Government."[22]

These agreements notwithstanding, U.S. and British leaders continued to differ over the importance of finding an immediate settlement to the oil crisis. The United States, Nitze and Linder repeated, still feared that a protracted dispute would adversely affect the Iranian treasury and discourage domestic moderates who might otherwise oppose Mossadeq. It was therefore advisable, they argued, to be prepared to continue discussions with Mossadeq if the IBRD proved unable to arrange a settlement. The British, though, bristled at the thought of giving Mossadeq another chance. If his blatant attempts to blackmail the West succeeded, and he was continually offered proposal after proposal until all his demands had been met, other nations would follow Iran's lead, with disastrous results for Britain's international position. It was far better "to let time do its work," the British maintained, by which they meant allowing the economic consequences of the oil crisis to force an Iranian capitulation. If the United States still insisted on keeping Iran afloat, British officials much preferred direct assistance to either an "unsatisfactory oil agreement" or a break in their boycott of Iranian oil.[23]

Increasing U.S. economic or financial assistance to Mossadeq, however, was not really a viable option. Neither Congress nor the U.S. public would acquiesce to aid to balance Iran's budget when it could obtain "revenues of a very great magnitude" merely by settling the oil dispute. Such assistance could be no more than a temporary palliative. It would not permanently solve Iran's economic crisis, which stemmed from the loss of oil revenues, and would actually prolong that crisis by delaying Iran's need to reach a settlement with Britain. For these reasons U.S. leaders continued to believe that assistance should go hand in hand with an acceptable oil settlement and should be used as leverage to induce Mossadeq to reach an accord with the AIOC.[24]

In the meantime Nitze reported that the Truman administration was willing to resume strictly military aid to Iran, which had been halted on 8 January 1952 because Mossadeq refused to comply with provisions in the Mutual Security Act that required recipients of U.S. military aid to declare their allegiance to the West. Renewed military aid to Iran, U.S. officials argued, was necessary primarily to enable Iran to fend off an internal communist coup. It would also preserve U.S. prestige; augment U.S. influence over Iranian officials, especially the shah; and keep Mossadeq from using the termination of U.S. aid to bolster his political position. With so much riding on continued military assistance to Iran, by mid-January U.S. policy makers were even willing to make "considerable concessions in the form and wording" of Mossadeq's promise to ally Iran with the West in order to ensure a resumption of aid.[25]

Like the preceding Anglo-American discussions in Washington, the London talks failed to result in bilateral agreement on a solution to the Iranian crisis. U.S. policy makers still stressed the greater international danger inherent in the crisis, whereas the British took a more "empirical" approach designed to protect their economic interests. Yet the talks did lead the British and U.S. embassies in Tehran to produce a joint assessment of the situation that owed more to British than American thinking. It predicted Mossadeq's continued ability to forestall economic collapse, at least in the short run, questioned the Tudeh's chances of assuming power, and doubted that Mossadeq could woo the army from its traditional loyalty to the shah. Iran's failure to obtain aid from the Soviet Union and Mossadeq's continued intransigence on the oil question had pushed U.S. thinking on Iran more into line with Britain's. In the coming months the two nations' policies, although falling short of total unanimity, would become closer still, eventually resulting in a joint Anglo-American approach to Mossadeq in late summer. Meanwhile British and U.S. leaders looked to the IBRD for resolution of the oil crisis.[26]

IV

The IBRD's negotiations with Mossadeq, conducted at first by Hector Prud'homme and Torkild Rieber and then by IBRD vice president Robert L. Garner as well, lasted from early January to mid-March 1952. Throughout these discussions the bank sought the prime minister's acceptance of a plan whereby it would engage a neutral agency to operate the Iranian oil industry, purchase Iranian oil at an undetermined yet competitive price, and market the oil through British channels. This arrangement, which was to last for two years, called for an equal division of oil proceeds among Iran, the neutral managing agency, and an escrow account to cover compensation to the AIOC. Although the IBRD realized that British control of the managing agency was impossible, it was convinced that the technicians needed to run the Iranian industry, especially the Abadan refinery, could be obtained only from the AIOC.[27]

Despite the bank's concerted efforts, the talks ultimately proved unsuccessful. Iranian and British thinking on the key issues of the return of British technicians and the selling price of Iranian oil were irreconcilable. Nor was it possible to arrange a satisfactory conception of who the bank was working for. On 13 March the IBRD conceded its failure to resolve the oil dispute and left the Iranians and the British to once again seek a settlement on their own.

Problems over the return of British technicians to Iran and the price at which Iranian oil would be sold on world markets, which had been sticking points in the earlier McGhee-Mossadeq discussions, did not surprise the bank's negotiators. From their first meeting with the prime minister these questions seriously threatened chances of a final settlement. Mossadeq vowed to "step aside and let someone else take responsibility [for] Iran's future" rather than allow any British nationals or former employees of the AIOC to work in the Iranian oil industry.[28] With regard to the selling price of Iranian oil the prime minister rejected the bank's plan for large discounts over prevailing prices because this would deprive Iran of much needed and much deserved revenues. He also came to insist that the price Iran received for its oil should be based not on the market price for crude but on the higher price paid for refined products. Because the Iranians had a refinery, he seemed to be saying, they should be entitled to profit from its operation. Mossadeq's position might also have represented what one Iranian called "oriental bargaining" and might have been his way of ensuring that the price Iran received was somewhere between the low crude price and the higher product price.[29]

British officials had different ideas on both scores. They could not allow the prime minister to exclude British nationals from the Iranian oil industry, as this would jeopardize Britain's international standing by encouraging other nations to adopt similarly discriminatory policies. But if Whitehall was unable to accept "specific discrimination" against British nationals, it was willing to consider a gradual return of British technicians in order to smooth the road to an agreement.[30] Although the British government disagreed with Mossadeq over the question of prices as well, this was not really a sticking point for them, as they believed that it was useless to discuss how an oil settlement would operate before the exact terms of such a settlement had been decided.[31]

The questions of technicians and price also posed problems for the IBRD. With regard to the first, bank officials tried to convince Mossadeq of the impossibility of finding enough non-British personnel to run the Iranian oil industry at even a fraction of its former capacity. And even if non-British technicians could be found, the bank as an international agency could not be told whom to hire or be party to a settlement that discriminated against British technicians. Concerning price, the bank believed that Mossadeq's hope of selling large quantities of undiscounted oil was unrealistic. Trying to do so would make it uncompetitive on world markets and encourage purchasers to seek lower-priced oil from other sources. In addition, the bank dismissed as impractical Mossadeq's idea of using refined products rather than crude as the basis for the selling price of Iranian oil.[32] Ultimately, the bank's firmness on these questions combined with Iranian and British intractability to doom the IBRD's attempt to reach a settlement.

Aside from highlighting long-standing differences over technicians and price, the IBRD's involvement added a new wrinkle to the quest for a settlement—the issue of who it represented and on whose authority it would operate the Iranian oil industry. Throughout his discussions with Prud'homme and Rieber Mossadeq insisted that the bank operate "on behalf of the Iranian Government" alone. By refusing to purchase nationalized Iranian oil, he maintained, the British had forfeited any interest in the Iranian oil industry and could not therefore be a party to any settlement that the IBRD might arrange. In other words, the IBRD must abandon all pretense of playing the role of intermediary and act purely as Iran's agent. Only then, maintained the prime minister, could the bank guarantee Iran's nationalization of the AIOC.[33]

Like technicians and price, this demand posed problems for both the British and the IBRD. According to British officials, accepting the idea that the bank was acting solely on Iran's behalf would threaten Britain's legal rights and might prejudice its case against Iran before the International Court of Justice (ICJ) that was, after all, based on the contention that the British government was a legitimate party to the oil dispute.[34] The IBRD objected as well, reiterating that its position as an international agency prevented it from taking sides in the dispute.[35]

The possibility that disagreement on these points might jeopardize the chances for a settlement concerned U.S. officials, who feared the consequences of a breakdown of the IBRD's negotiations. Because they believed that Iran's economic collapse would likely follow such a development, U.S. officials would grant the IBRD wide flexibility in negotiating with Mossadeq and introduced plan after plan in hopes of finding something that the British would accept. In fact, the Americans even went so far as to propose that the IBRD purchase the oil stocks stored at Abadan at 50 percent below prevailing prices. This would resolve several problems at once, or so the State Department argued: it would keep the oil out of Soviet hands, provide Mossadeq with much needed revenues, contribute to economic and political stability in Iran, and buy time for discussion of a permanent settlement.[36]

British policy makers, though, would have nothing of the stock-buying plan, which Roger Makins, British deputy undersecretary of state for foreign affairs, sarcastically called "another bright [American] idea." From the British point of view the proposal had numerous drawbacks. It would involve a costly rerouting of tankers, challenge the AIOC's boycott of Iranian oil, and encourage the Iranians to constantly refill the storage tanks. That the State Department had even considered such a "preposterous proposal" aroused British fears about the real goals of U.S. policy. Continued insistence on British concessions to Mossadeq suggested that the United States valued Iran's position over Britain's and that the United States might go "off on a tangent of [its] own." Certain that U.S. officials were pursuing a misguided policy in Iran, Whitehall offered the State Department a simple choice: an effective British ally the world over or a collapse in Iran, which it thought unlikely. According to the British, U.S. policy in Iran was rapidly undermining the chances of achieving the first alternative.[37]

Officials in Washington quickly took the defensive. Reiterating the points they had made during the recent Washington and London talks, U.S. leaders sought to reassure the British that the United States valued Britain more than Iran, that it depended on a "strong and viable Britain" for the achievement of Western aims throughout the Middle East, and that it was not trying to placate Mossadeq at Britain's expense. Nor could there be any doubt that U.S. leaders placed as much importance on the development of a common Anglo-American policy toward Iran as their British counterparts. Unwilling to permit differences over the IBRD mission to disrupt overall Anglo-American harmony, U.S. officials allowed Whitehall to determine the mission's final terms—which in effect guaranteed its failure.[38]

The unsuccessful U.S. efforts to push the British toward greater flexibility paralleled efforts by several influential Iranian senators to pressure Mossadeq to resolve the oil dispute. From its creation in 1949 Iran's Senate had opposed movements such as Mossadeq's National Front, because they challenged the position of the ruling elite that dominated the upper house. This opposition intensified as early election results for the Seventeenth Majlis showed gains for the National Front and suggested that Mossadeq might eventually become strong enough to actually dissolve the Senate. To save their political positions and to stave off a full-scale social revolution leading senators for the first time condemned Mossadeq's reluctance to reach an oil settlement. The prime minister, these senators said, was more interested in protecting his "personal prestige" than in doing what was best for Iran. In meetings with Garner and Henderson they pledged to support any "reasonable [oil] proposals . . . even though they might be disappointing to [the Iranian] public." The Senate's intervention, which, according to the Foreign Office, constituted the first time that any "responsible political body" had opposed Mossadeq, assumed even more significance, given the effective dissolution of the Majlis in January.[39]

By early March the prime minister faced opposition from a number of sources. The bazaar, once a Mossadeq stronghold, had become indifferent toward the prime minister, and the army had become downright hostile, according to observers in the Foreign Office. The Senate continued to condemn Mossadeq's refusal to sign an agreement with the IBRD, as did the government's economic ministers, who feared Iran's imminent collapse. Even the shah spoke against Mossadeq, proclaiming to acting British chargé d'affaires George H. Middleton that he would give Mossadeq "one last chance to come to an agreement with the [IBRD]." If he failed to do so, the shah would have no choice but to make a change in prime ministers. Predictably, British and U.S. officials hailed these developments, especially the "first glimmer of hope" that the shah would "intervene in a positive manner," as signs that an oil settlement might actually be possible.[40]

These hopes for an imminent settlement, like previous ones, proved to be unfounded. Mossadeq not only refused to make concessions on the questions of technicians, price, and the bank's authority but also now insisted that the IBRD retain all existing Iranian oil employees, "whether or not they were actually required by [the] scale of operations." His reasons for such a demand are obvious: he wanted to prevent widespread layoffs and unemployment. But as Prud'homme and British officials argued, whatever the merits of such a policy for Iran, it would hamper efficient oil operations and doom all prospects of running the Iranian oil industry on a profitable basis. Middleton, in fact, tried to convince the shah that it was simply "not within [Britain's] power" to redress Mossadeq's concerns. The United Kingdom, he said, "could not change conditions in the world oil industry" to suit Mossadeq's whims, and the prime minister's insistence that it do so would doom the IBRD's proposals. When subsequent discussions revealed no Iranian movement on "management, technicians, or prices," Prud'homme concluded on 13 March that there was "no possibility of reaching an agreement" with Mossadeq. Three days later the IBRD mission left Tehran, saying that it would return only if further progress toward a settlement seemed possible.[41]

In his postmission discussions with British leaders in London Prud'homme hinted at the fundamental obstacle to a satisfactory settlement: the differing backgrounds from which the IBRD and Iran approached the oil crisis. Because officials of the IBRD saw the dispute "as an industrial and business matter," they sought to reach a commercially acceptable solution. Their approach was much the same as that initially taken by the AIOC, which had tried to placate the Iranians with financial inducements, such as higher royalties, and was ultimately just as fruitless. The Iranians wanted more than just higher revenues; they wanted their national sovereignty. For them the oil crisis was "90 percent political and only 10 percent . . . operational and business." Iranian accounts of the mission said much the same thing, asserting that "the World Bank delegates were more concerned with the economic aspect of the problem whereas we attached greater importance to the political aspect"—preserving the nation's independence and freeing it from "British bondage." This emphasis explained Mossadeq's insistence that the IBRD act exclusively on behalf of Iran, which was the only way to guarantee the inviolability of its dispossession of the AIOC. With both sides seeking such incompatible ends the IBRD mission was bound to fail. Subsequent efforts to resolve the dispute were doomed as well.[42]

It is also likely that the bank delegation's cultural prejudices shaped the outcome of its negotiations with Mossadeq. Like U.S. and British officials who had found discussions with Mossadeq to be something of a challenge, bank officials often succumbed to condescension and sarcasm. In describing the best strategy for dealing with the Iranians, for example, Prud'homme stated that a settlement could be achieved only if the bank convinced them to "come off their high horse" by "suggest[ing] that this might be a nice place to stop, then talk for a while about the scenery, then suggest dismounting, then mention Omar Khayam, then bring a step ladder so that the rider can get off the saddle without appearing to dismount etc. etc." Like other Anglo-American officials Prud'homme and his colleagues called the Iranians "those people," spoke of the "twists and warps in the Iranian mind," seemed surprised to find the prime minister alert and "on his feet," and felt it significant to relate how, on one occasion, "Dr. Mossadegh got out of bed, put on his slippers, and escorted us to the hall." The cultural prejudices and assumptions that motivated such statements could not help but have influenced the outcome of the bank's negotiations.[43]

V

In the period immediately following the failure of the IBRD mission the parties to the Iranian dispute weighed their options. Policy makers in London had not been "unduly disappointed" by the mission's failure, assuming that the lack of a settlement had weakened Mossadeq's position, perhaps fatally.

Opposition to the prime minister now came from a number of sources, and the possibility existed that he might lose power after the opening of the new Majlis. The Tudeh Party press called the IBRD's recent mission an unwelcome interference in Iran's internal affairs that revealed Mossadeq's subservience to Western interests. The prime minister also faced continuing opposition from the Senate, which saw the growing popularity of the National Front as a threat to its very existence. Even more important from the British point of view, the IBRD negotiations had improved Anglo-American understanding on the Iranian question. Both nations agreed that negotiating with Mossadeq was impossible and that imminent economic collapse in Iran was not likely. On the contrary, they estimated that the Iranian government would be able to finance itself through June "and probably a good deal longer." Anglo-American agreement on these points had resulted from the IBRD's failure and from the recent discussions on Iran in Washington and London. Whitehall now had reason to expect even closer Anglo-American cooperation.[44]

British thinking in the wake of the IBRD mission did not portend that kind of cooperation, however. Officials in the Foreign Office refused to make additional approaches to Mossadeq but proclaimed their willingness to negotiate with a "more flexible" prime minister. The terms of future negotiations remained uncertain.[45] Although most points, such as management arrangements, selling price, and the length of a new contract, would depend on the attitude of Mossadeq's successor, the Foreign Office continued to insist that no agreement was possible that gave Iran better terms than existed in other countries or than it would have had without nationalization. This point became increasingly important as the AIOC replaced Iranian oil by increasing production in other areas, purchasing oil from U.S. firms, and constructing additional refineries to replace Abadan. Having thus softened the blow of the Iranian shutdown, the British were increasingly determined not to reward what they saw as Iran's lawlessness by acceding to Mossadeq's demands.[46]

Although British officials were concerned with how the situation in Iran affected their national interests, U.S. policy makers were pessimistically assessing the broader implications of the oil crisis. Continuation of the dispute, they argued, made "the probability of losing Iran to the Soviets . . . increasingly imminent." But the danger did not stop there, because the Soviets could be expected in short order to use their newly won Iranian position to move through "the Middle East corridor into India and Africa" and thereby alter the East-West balance of power. In addition to gaining control of valuable territories the Soviets would acquire the Middle East's substantial oil resources, which would then be denied to the Western European rearmament and economic recovery efforts. Oil shortages, rationing, and a weakening of Western Europe would surely result; threats to "the pro-Western alignment" of countries like Italy and France might even be possible.[47]

To U.S. policy makers these dangers dictated a reassessment of the role of the United States in Iran and the entire Middle East. The Near Eastern Affairs Division of the State Department asserted that although Britain had traditionally borne the brunt of Middle Eastern defense, its declining global position had now forced the United States to bear "an increasing share" of that burden and to take "more initiative . . . in the determination of [regional] policies." The department's Policy Planning Staff (PPS) echoed these sentiments, saying that America's NATO commitment to Turkey, which was "geographically, strategically, and militarily a part of the Middle East," made the United States "directly concerned" with the defense of the region. But because its commitments in Western Europe and preoccupation with the war in Korea prevented the United States from committing forces to the defense of the Middle East, it could still do little more in the region than play an advisory role. In the future, though, U.S. policy makers hoped for closer Anglo-American cooperation in the determination of Middle Eastern policy, particularly with regard to Iran. In this sense the latest U.S.

reassessments confirmed long-standing beliefs but did not produce any real changes in policy.[48]

Meanwhile Mossadeq was using the lull in the negotiations with the IBRD to regain the political offensive by renewing his attack on the British. Britain's greed and its desire to dominate Iran, he maintained, had doomed the IBRD's efforts to solve the oil crisis. Although he professed his will-ingness to resume discussions at any time—provided the IBRD accepted his conditions on the exclusion of British technicians, the nature of IBRD involvement, and the selling price of Iranian oil—the British, he said, were not so open minded. Instead of pursuing negotiations Britain was "forc[ing] other countries to join it in suppressing Iran." Foremost among these col-laborators, he told a group of newly elected Majlis deputies on 14 April, was the United States, which had supported the AIOC's boycott of Iranian oil and had helped it to locate other petroleum supplies. Despite such for-midable opposition, the prime minister implored the Iranian people to stand firm. If they caved in to international pressures, they would be following "the road to hell," which analysts at the U.S. embassy assumed meant capitulation to communism.[49]

To prevent economic collapse Mossadeq renewed his vow to finance the Iranian government without oil revenues, although such a course, as the U.S. embassy reported in early April, was unlikely to succeed. Iran's prospective budget deficit of more than 5 billion rials was so substantial that it could probably be met only by "substituting the out-put of [the] print-ing presses for oil revenue," an option Mossadeq refused to consider. Instead, he repeated his pleas for U.S. financial assistance, without which, he feared, "Iran would not exist much longer as [a] country." These gloom-and-doom predictions notwithstanding, U.S. policy makers steadfastly refused to provide Iran with budgetary assistance; it was clearly their inten-tion to use financial assistance as leverage to force Mossadeq into an oil set-tlement with the British.[50]

In late April, however, the Truman administration did agree to resume the military aid to Iran that had been suspended on 8 January. Retreating from his earlier stance that Iran could not be "governed by US legislation," Mossadeq now agreed to satisfy the spirit of the Mutual Security Act. He declared that Iran would "support and defend the principles of the charter of the UN," "defend its freedom and independence" from an outside attack, and welcome U.S. military assistance. This was a far cry from the outright declaration of allegiance to the West required by the Mutual Security Act, but U.S. fears of the consequences of a prolonged denial of military assis-tance led the State Department to accept it anyway. Nor did it signal a genuine change of heart on the part of the prime minister, who still objected to aligning Iran with either the West or the East. In actuality the prime minister's compliance with U.S. requirements stemmed from "direct pressure" by the shah, Henderson reported to Washington. Although the military missions remained in Iran on essentially Mossadeq's terms, his being forced to accept them at all gave U.S. policy makers cause to rejoice—the resumption of military aid had simultaneously guaranteed Iran's security and weakened Mossadeq's position, however minimally.[51]

Mossadeq fared no better in the political than the economic realms. Of the seventy-nine deputies eventually elected to the Seventeenth Majlis, only thirty staunchly supported him. Slightly more than one-third were political opportunists who would sell their votes to the highest bidder, about a dozen were unconditionally committed to the shah, and the remainder defied easy categorization. Mossadeq's supporters came primarily from Tehran and other urban centers, such as Tabriz in Azerbaijan. Deputies from the provinces, who oftentimes were elected only because powerful landlords instructed the peasants on how to vote, may have paid lip service to Mossadeq's program but were dedicated to its collapse. The presence of so many opposition deputies called into question Mossadeq's continued domination of the Majlis; these new developments in the Majlis, coupled with the prime minister's already shaky relationship with the Senate, made his position even more tenuous. Although Mossadeq's opponents lacked both a coherent political platform and a definite legislative agenda, they did damage the prime minister's position. So did the press, the Tudeh Party, and some mullahs and other religious figures who now criticized both Mossadeq's failure to solve the oil crisis and his acceptance of U.S. military aid. Even some of Mossadeq's strongest supporters, among them Ayatollah Kashani and Hossein Makki, allowed personal rivalries to distract them from the National Front's crusade against Britain. As these individuals sought to increase their personal influence in the front, they broke the coalition into numerous contending wings that would eventually split from Mossadeq's centrist faction and contributed to the movement's destruction. Unable to quell rising public violence, the government in late March had declared martial law in Tehran. As Ambassador Henderson reported in early April, even this unjustified step was unlikely to restrain Mossadeq's opponents.[52]

Public displays of opposition to Mossadeq convinced the shah that "steps must be taken in [the] near future to have [Mossdeq] replaced." This was not the first time that the shah had declared his opposition to the prime minister, only later to change his mind. Policy makers in Washington, worried that the monarch might again lose his nerve, sought to reinforce his belief that Mossadeq had to be replaced. This was as far as U.S. officials would go, however. They refused to become involved in concrete plans for Mossadeq's removal, suggest replacements for him, or guarantee specific amounts of U.S. aid to prop up a new government that might replace his. Although U.S. officials seemed convinced of the undesirability of Mossadeq's government, they were not yet ready to actively engage in planning a coup.[53] Despite their profound conviction that Mossadeq had to be replaced, British policy makers were similarly restrained. Although they welcomed the shah's anti-Mossadeq posture, they doubted his ability to support his words with action. Recent scholarship suggests that British agents were already working to undermine Mossadeq's government, and Whitehall may have feared that encouraging the shah too early in the planning process would unduly jeopardize British plans against the prime minister.[54]

For their part British policy makers continued to pursue a settlement that fell considerably short of what the Iranians were demanding. The only concession to Iranian nationalism they were willing to make was the acknowledgment that the AIOC as such could not regain control of Iranian oil. In the AIOC's place the British envisioned a multinational managing agency that would operate the oil industry on Iran's behalf. Although British thinking was not fully developed, it obviously built on earlier proposals for such an organization. But even with multinational operation of the Iranian oil industry, the AIOC was to receive the bulk of Iran's oil to sell on the open market. Moreover, British policy makers still refused to accept either "open discrimination" against British nationals or violation of the fifty-fifty profit-sharing principle. These were crucial points, asserted Sir Donald Fergusson of the Foreign Office, the importance of which the State Department's "backroom boys" simply did not understand.[55]

Fergusson's criticism notwithstanding, the State Department continued to voice concern that "the British seemed more interested in getting rid of Mossadegh than they [did] in getting a settlement of the oil dispute." Although recognition that the AIOC could not return to Iran "greatly enhanced the prospects of a settlement," U.S. officials thought it only the first of what should be many British concessions. In the State Department's estimation the consequences of a continued impasse, which might lead to the collapse of Iran and the entire Middle East, dictated that the British consider further concessions. But no amount of U.S. pleading could elicit from the British either the substance of an acceptable oil agreement or the tactics by which they hoped to reach one. These were questions that would depend on the nature of the new Iranian government, the British reported. In the meantime the best they could offer the United States were promises to remain flexible and to "keep the US fully informed" of their plans.[56]

VI

As British and U.S. officials debated the terms of the oil settlement to be proposed to Mossadeq's successor, the prime minister was preoccupied with the case Britain had lodged against Iran in the International Court of Justice at The Hague. As noted earlier, Britain had officially protested Iran's nationalization of the AIOC in May 1951, and two months later the ICJ had ordered a return to the status quo ante until it could rule on its competence in the matter. In June 1952 the court finally began hearings. To demonstrate the importance that Iran attached to nationalization and its respect for the international organization Mossadeq represented Iran personally before the court.

Like his earlier appearance before the U.N. Security Council, Mossadeq's speech before the ICJ was less an argument about the question at hand—the court's competence—than an attack on Britain and the AIOC. A standing-room-only crowd gathered on 9 June to hear the prime minister denounce British imperialism, intimidation, and threats. Mossadeq justified nationalization as Iran's only recourse against the AIOC, which had become a "state within a state . . . running an espionage system . . . treating its Iranian employees . . . like animals," and keeping them "out of technical posts." Surely, he asserted, the court could not "reproach a small nation" like Iran for defending its "financial, economic and industrial life" against Britain's "crafty attack." Mossadeq was confident that the court would decide that it had no jurisdiction over the nationalization case. Such a decision would then remove the obstacles to the sale of Iranian oil on the open market and hasten a negotiated settlement with the British.[57]

Mossadeq did not attend the subsequent sessions of the proceedings, when Iranian counsel Henri Rolin and British lawyers Sir Eric Beckett and Sir Lionel Heald actually addressed the question of the ICJ's competence, and public interest in these more technical statements was low. Rolin argued that the court had no jurisdiction in the case because the Anglo-Iranian oil dispute stemmed from a commercial agreement between a government and a private company and because the D'Arcy concession agreement of 1901, which established the AIOC's position in Iran, predated Iran's acceptance of the ICJ's convention in 1932. Beckett and Heald disagreed, asserting that the AIOC's contract was both a commercial agreement and a treaty and that the court's competence extended to all disputes that arose after Iran had signed the declaration, no matter when the treaty or convention in question had been negotiated. After both sides had presented their cases, the court adjourned for deliberations, and Mossadeq returned to Tehran—but only after restating his belief that an ICJ ruling in Iran's favor would end Britain's boycott of Iranian oil and allow the nation to enjoy the fruits of nationalization.[58]

Even while the ICJ hearing was in progress, Iran moved to break the boycott. In mid-June the *Rose Mary*, a 632-ton Panamanian freighter, had loaded one thousand tons of Iranian oil at the Persian Gulf port of Bandar Mashur on behalf of the Ente Petrolifero Italia Medio-oriente (EPIM), a private Italian oil company. This "experimental voyage" was designed to test the strength of the AIOC's boycott. If it succeeded, the EPIM planned to send larger tankers to Iran to purchase twenty million tons of Iranian oil over the next ten years. The *Rose Mary*, Mossadeq proclaimed, was only the first of many ships that would soon transport Iranian oil, and the British could do nothing to stop them.[59]

Mossadeq was wrong. On 17 June British naval vessels forced the *Rose Mary* into British Aden, where local authorities promptly impounded its cargo. The AIOC then instituted legal proceedings against everyone associated with the tanker's activities—its owners, captain, charterer, and the EPIM. Although the dispute over the true ownership of the *Rose Mary*'s cargo dragged on for months, the stopping of the ship in a British territory foretold the outcome. The *Rose Mary* case ended in triumph for the British by upholding the legality of the AIOC's claims to Iranian oil. It also contributed to the deterioration of Anglo-Iranian relations, further widening the gap between the two nations and delaying settlement of the oil question.[60]

When Mossadeq returned from The Hague on 24 June, however, the *Rose Mary* episode still looked like an Iranian victory, and the prime minister sought to use it, and his brilliant appearance before the ICJ, to line up public support for his government. Ostensibly to thwart those "foreign agents" who sought to destroy his government but actually to prevent his opponents from winning election, Mossadeq exercised his legal right as prime minister to halt elections for the Seventeenth Majlis once a majority of deputies had been elected. As a result, only 79 of a projected total of 136 deputies were selected. As per usual procedure, Mossadeq then submitted his resignation to the shah but agreed to remain in office if the Senate and Majlis pledged "in advance to adopt all emergency [financial] measures" he might propose. Such a move, the prime minister maintained, would allow him to move quickly to meet the country's mounting economic problems and to prevent his opponents from blocking his legislative program. When the shah balked at Mossadeq's request, it appeared that the latter would at last go down to defeat. But the shah again vacillated by leaving the responsibility for instituting a change in governments with the Senate and Majlis, indicating only that if they decided to replace Mossadeq he would not oppose them.[61]

The shah's failure to stand firm against Mossadeq virtually guaranteed the prime minister's reinstatement. Even the election of one of Mossadeq's staunchest critics, Hasan Imami, as speaker of the Majlis, could not prevent Mossadeq from receiving a vote of inclination from that body on 6 July. Of the 63 deputies present, 52 voted for the prime minister, whereas 10 abstained. The vote surprised both the shah and Anglo-American officials, who had anticipated the prime minister's defeat, and was widely interpreted as stemming from the shah's lack of leadership and the opposition's reluctance to come out against Mossadeq, especially while the ICJ was debating its jurisdiction over the oil dispute. The Senate first refused to reappoint Mossadeq until it had examined his program and then decided to vote on his reappointment without actually giving him a vote of confidence. Accordingly, 14 of 36 senators present voted to reconfirm Mossadeq's appointment; 19 others abstained. The Senate's fears that Mossadeq would call for its dissolution, coupled with its anger at the government's suspension of the Majlis elections, accounted for the weak show of support for Mossadeq. Indeed, had the shah not ordered his senatorial appointees to vote for Mossadeq, the outcome likely would have been different. On 10 July the shah asked Mossadeq to form a new government.[62]

Mossadeq agreed to remain prime minister only if his earlier demand for unlimited plenary powers in "financial, economic and banking affairs" for a period of six months was met. In the four days of frantic political discussion that followed, however, it became clear that Mossadeq also wished to become minister of war in his own cabinet. Mossadeq justified this demand by saying that granting him such power would prove the shah's faith in his ability to govern. But this argument was only partially true. Far more important was that control of the army, along with extraordinary economic powers, would have enhanced Mossadeq's authority at the expense of the shah—a fact that grew in importance as the prime minister's domestic opponents continued to multiply. When the shah, who could not accept a prime minister stronger than he was, rejected Mossadeq's demands, the prime minister resigned on 17 July. Such a course presented Mossadeq with the best of all possible worlds: it prevented him from becoming an ineffective and powerless prime minister while preserving his chance to return triumphantly to office at a later date.[63]

As Mossadeq's successor the shah immediately appointed Ahmad Qavam, whose two previous terms as prime minister had included service during the tumultuous confrontations with the Soviet Union in 1946 and 1947. Speaker of the Majlis Imami and members of the royal family considered Qavam Iran's only hope, as did Ambassador Henderson and Chargé d'Affaires Middleton. A hastily called session of the Majlis, which lacked a quorum when only forty-two of the seventy-nine deputies showed up, nevertheless gave Qavam a vote of inclination, and Iran embarked on its first post-Mossadeq government. Anglo-American leaders were quick to offer the new prime minister verbal and financial support. The British, whom recent scholarship credits with Qavam's selection, immediately signaled their readiness to reopen direct discussions on the oil question, and U.S. officials announced plans for a substantial grant of financial assistance.[64]

This support notwithstanding, several factors immediately combined to threaten the new government's existence. First, the presence of at least thirty pro-Mossadeq deputies in the Majlis hampered Qavam's ability to accomplish his legislative agenda. Indeed, the government would have difficulty getting anything done, as Mossadeq's supporters vowed to boycott the Majlis until his reinstatement. Second, Qavam aroused popular indignation by supporting concessions on the nationalization issue and calling for the separation of religion and politics. His intentions with regard to the latter matter were especially unwise, considering the increasing influence of mullahs and other religious figures in all facets of Iranian life. Finally, the shah publicly refused to support the new prime minister. The fearful monarch even refused to invoke his constitutional right to dissolve the Majlis, despite warnings from Qavam and his supporters that only dissolution of the obstructionist and pro-Mossadeq Majlis would enable the new prime minister to govern effectively.

In the shah's mind dissolution of the Majlis would involve him too deeply in politics, pit him against the nationalist movement, and undermine his position. The shah also rejected Qavam's call for the imposition of martial law, which meant that the prime minister could not arrest the National Front's leaders, whose interference in political affairs was already challenging his regime. The shah did not think the situation sufficiently dire to merit martial law, nor did he wish to be accused of assisting opposition assaults on Mossadeq and other members of the nationalist movement. As a result, Qavam held an untenable position: he could not win the shah's support unless he demonstrated his ability to govern and contained the National Front. But he could do neither without the prior support of the shah.[65]

Qavam did not have long to ponder his dilemma. On 21 July Tehran erupted in massive antigovernment demonstrations instigated by Mossadeq's supporters in the Majlis and fueled by Ayatollah Kashani's exhortations that the struggle against Qavam constituted a holy war. The prime minister, Kashani declared, was a "traitor and a gangster" whose policies did not represent the interests of the Iranian people. If he continued to block the popular will, the ayatollah asserted in what many took to be a veiled reference to the assassination of Razmara, it might be necessary to "eliminate" him. The National Front saw the fight to remove Qavam as a struggle for its existence and stopped at nothing to win, even resorting to a tacit alliance with the Tudeh Party. This temporary truce between the two groups did not mean that they had permanently settled their differences. On the contrary, it amounted to a marriage of convenience against a common enemy, Qavam. After a day of bloody fighting that resulted in numerous casualties Qavam unceremoniously resigned. With no other option the shah asked Mossadeq to return to office, virtually on his own terms. This was a significant victory for the National Front, which had now defeated the shah and his supporters in a head-on confrontation. The 30th Tir Episode, as the uprising was popularly called in Iran, stemmed from both the shah's refusal to support Qavam and the National Front's skillfulness in portraying Qavam's weakness as likely to lead to foreign domination of Iran. Because both the British and the Americans had supported Qavam, the episode steeled Mossadeq's position on the oil question and further delayed a settlement.[66]

The prime minister's uncompromising attitude was further strengthened just one day after his triumphant return to office, when the ICJ ruled 9 to 5 in Iran's favor. The ruling affirmed Rolin's arguments against the ICJ's competence to resolve the nationalization case and withdrew its July 1951 injunction. Iran, it seemed, was now free from the court's earlier exhortation against interfering in the production of oil and entitled to seek purchasers on the open market.[67]

VII

The Iranian people generally considered the ICJ decision a victory for Mossadeq, especially coming as it did on the heels of his reappointment as prime minister. It was popularly perceived as a vindication of Iran's sovereign right to nationalize the AIOC and as a legal deathblow to the British boycott. Indeed, the decision prompted a number of prospective purchasers to follow the EPIM's lead in sending tankers to Abadan to pick up previously purchased oil. Overjoyed, the Iranian people sent telegrams and letters to Tehran and declared a public holiday to celebrate Mossadeq's victory.

But like Iran's apparent victory before the Security Council the ICJ decision rang hollow for Mossadeq and his supporters. Britain did not drop its boycott of Iranian oil, nor did it seem any more willing to make concessions to Mossadeq's demands on the oil front. In truth, the court's decision, along with Mossadeq's return to office, inaugurated an increasingly acrimonious phase of the oil dispute. Buoyed by recent developments, Mossadeq became even more convinced of the righteousness and popularity of his campaign against the AIOC and more determined to see that campaign completed. And the British became more determined to protect what they saw as their rightful dominance of the Iranian oil industry, even if they had to do so without the help of international bodies like the Security Council and the ICJ. As subsequent events made clear, however, the British would find increasing U.S. support for their position in Iran as the United States moved ever closer to a position of true partner to Great Britain in the oil dispute.

chapter 6

Washington Takes the Lead
THE LAST-DITCH SEARCH FOR A SETTLEMENT

No real progress toward an Iranian settlement was made in the six months following Mossadeq's return to office. In fact, an acceptable settlement was less likely in January 1953 than at almost any time since nationalization.

The British continued to insist on retaining some interest in Iran's future oil operations, and the Iranians steadfastly refused to consider such a possibility. By the end of 1952 both sides seemed resigned to leaving the oil dispute unresolved. The AIOC had totally replaced Iranian oil with other sources and had thus lost its economic incentive to reach a settlement. And Mossadeq had embarked on a full-scale effort to create an oil-less economy that would terminate Iran's dependence on oil revenues and ensure the country's economic and political independence.

Officials in Washington, however, were not willing to abandon the quest for a settlement. As before, the Truman administration warned of the dangers of a protracted Iranian crisis. It was true that quick action by the U.S. majors had prevented the Iranian shutdown from creating oil shortages in the West. But also true was that the longer the Iranian crisis dragged on, the more likely it was to create economic chaos in Iran and lead other oil-producing countries to nationalize their resources. This second possibility, U.S. officials argued, would create additional oil shortages that the Western world could probably not absorb and would provide the Soviets with access to oil reserves that the free world could ill afford to lose. So concerned was the Truman administration about the situation that it was willing to sanction a plan to involve the U.S. majors in the production and marketing of Iranian oil by subordinating traditional U.S. concerns about trusts to the national security considerations inherent in achieving a settlement.[1]

Given the dangers of a protracted Iranian crisis, the Truman administration worked tirelessly during its last six months in office to reach a settlement that both Britain and Iran could accept. These efforts constituted the culmination of the U.S. shift toward a partnership with Britain against Iran and set the stage for even closer Anglo-American cooperation during the Eisenhower administration. Ultimately, these new efforts fell prey to the mutual Anglo-Iranian antipathy toward any settlement that did not guarantee each side its maximum goals, and Truman therefore left office in January 1953 with the crisis still unresolved but with U.S. policy set on a course from which it would not deviate in the years ahead.

II

Mossadeq's dramatic return to office and the ICJ's decision not to intervene in the Anglo-Iranian dispute appeared to put the prime minister in a stronger political position than ever before. Assumption of the defense portfolio also strengthened Mossadeq's position vis-à-vis the shah, whose support for Qavam's ill-fated government had eroded his credibility with the Iranian population and reduced him "to impotence," according to the British embassy in Tehran. Given the monarch's declining popularity, Anglo-American policy makers became convinced that he was likely to be a "negligible political factor," if not "a mere figurehead," for the foreseeable future. The same seemed to be true of the Senate and the Majlis. In early August Mossadeq cajoled both bodies into renewing his plenary powers for another six months. Under this arrangement he could govern virtually by decree. Perhaps most important, Mossadeq's position with the Iranian population seemed unassailable. The riots that had restored him to office suggested that he was not so much "a freak in Persian politics" as "the only element of power," according to the British.[2]

Appearances were deceiving, however. Mossadeq actually confronted serious problems. Ayatollah Kashani, who had played a vital role in the prime minister's return to office, wanted compensation for his efforts. He demanded Mossadeq's ear on such significant issues as the oil crisis, which the ayatollah was adamantly opposed to settling, and sought the speakership of the Majlis, a position he secured on 7 August in a development that "obviously shocked" the prime minister, causing him so much "distress and agitation" that Ambassador Henderson thought "he might lose consciousness." From that point on the relationship between Kashani and Mossadeq deteriorated as each struggled to become the most powerful figure in Iranian politics. The Tudeh also threatened the prime minister. In the immediate aftermath of Mossadeq's return the party fomented public opposition to any oil settlement with Western interests. Although Mossadeq was not a Tudeh sympathizer, after the 30th Tir Episode he did nothing to quell its rising power and visibility. Richard Cottam has attributed Mossadeq's lackadaisical attitude to his conviction that communism could not be destroyed through government repression and his belief that the Tudeh, as the party of the Soviet Union, provided a useful counterweight to the British-oriented feudal right. Mossadeq's reluctance to subdue the party gave U.S. policy makers cause to fear a communist takeover of his government.[3]

Analysts in the State Department were also concerned about Iran's economic situation. With the Iranian government adhering to Mossadeq's "mad and suicidal" policies U.S. officials feared that a crisis was just around the corner, particularly after the Truman administration withdrew the offer of $26 million in aid that it had made to Qavam. An insignificant increase in nonoil exports had done nothing to alleviate the government's monthly budget deficit of 300 million rials. Other parts of Mossadeq's economic program also failed, including his efforts to raise tax revenues by imposing stiffer duties on luxury goods and assessing wealthy landlords at higher rates. Nor did Mossadeq believe that the answer lay in printing more currency, as this would fuel inflation, further weaken the economy, and ultimately benefit the communists. Under these circumstances the prime minister was forced to pin his hopes on an oil settlement, which alone seemed capable of reviving Iran's sagging economy.[4]

On 25 July Mossadeq made what Anglo-American officials considered his first positive suggestion for a resolution of the eighteen-month dispute. In a meeting with British chargé d'affaires Middleton Mossadeq proposed outside arbitration on the compensation question, which he called "the only outstanding point to be settled." Once that issue had been settled, the NIOC would allow the AIOC to distribute ten million tons of oil annually, an amount that Mossadeq thought likely to generate sufficient income "to balance the budget" and stop "the drift towards [communist] revolution." To avert an economic crisis in the meantime the prime minister needed financial assistance from the AIOC and the British government. From the former he wanted the £50 million that its recently released 1951 balance sheet had shown Iran was owed under the unratified supplemental agreement. From the latter he demanded immediate release of Iran's frozen sterling balances, which amounted to £10 million.[5]

Mossadeq's proposal had serious drawbacks. It would not provide for large-scale oil production or efficient operation of the oil industry. Nor would it supply Britain with significant quantities of sterling oil or Iran with substantial revenues. But it would strengthen Mossadeq's government by resolving its most pressing problem, the oil crisis, and allowing the prime minister to stifle mounting charges that nationalization had failed. Still, British and U.S. officials thought that there would "never [be] a better opportunity of reaching a settlement of some kind" and immediately set about assessing the proposal's feasibility.[6]

Their discussions had not gotten far when Mossadeq abruptly withdrew the offer of arbitration, claiming that only the Iranian courts could decide the matter of compensation. The prime minister's sudden change of heart probably resulted from pressure by Kashani and other extremists whose "avowed object [was] to drive all foreigners and foreign influence from Persia," the British embassy reported. They may have convinced Mossadeq that popular outrage at the thought of outside arbitration would end his premiership. Or they may have argued that arbitration was a compromise on the Nationalization Law and might result in the return of the British—a dubious proposition, to be sure, but one likely to sway Mossadeq away from arbitration. Whatever its cause, Mossadeq's withdrawal represented a setback for the Anglo-Americans and a hardening of their criticism of his government. One example of the British and American tendency to practice pop psychology on the prime minister was that Mossadeq's withdrawal of the arbitration offer confirmed their "doubts about [his] mental stability" and made it less likely that they would treat him with respect or take him seriously in the future. Both Henderson and Middleton believed that Mossadeq's mental position had "seriously deteriorated." Convinced that the prime minister was "not quite sane," the British government appeared to abandon any hope of reaching an agreement with him.[7]

With no faith in Mossadeq British and U.S. officials sought other solutions to the Iranian crisis. One they considered was a coup d'état to replace Mossadeq with what they would consider a more reasonable prime minister. Policy makers in Whitehall had long believed that this was perhaps the only way to secure an acceptable oil settlement. And by late July certain U.S. officials, including Henry A. Byroade, assistant secretary of state for Near Eastern, South Asian, and African affairs, had conceded that the "most unorthodox methods," including a coup, might be necessary to stop Iran from "going down the drain." The lack of qualified Iranian leadership and the shah's likely vacillation, however, forced the National Security Council (NSC) to conclude in early August that a successful coup would be "practically impossible," at least for the time being.[8]

Instead, U.S. policy makers based their hopes on a new approach to the oil problem itself. Formulated by Secretary of State Dean Acheson and transmitted to the British in an aide-mémoire of 31 July 1952, the U.S. plan consisted of four points: the United States would provide Iran with an immediate grant of $10 million; the AIOC would purchase the oil stored at Abadan at commercial prices, "less an appropriate discount"; compensation would be settled by an independent commission; and discussions would begin immediately on permanent arrangements for the sale of Iranian oil. Acheson's plan was a stop-gap measure designed to shore up the ailing Iranian economy and thus "prevent [the] loss [of] Iran to [the] West" until a final settlement of the oil controversy could be negotiated. Mossadeq, whom Ambassador Henderson—in yet another example of the Anglo-American tendency to label Mossadeq with psychological maladies—described as "neurotic and periodically unstable," might be a weak reed against communism. But he was "the least bad of several undesirable alternatives," and the State Department was resigned to bolstering his government. Indeed, the situation in Iran was so critical as to prompt the department to call for a joint presentation of the new proposals to Mossadeq, a course that constituted a sharp departure from the Truman administration's previous reluctance to join with the British and thus signaled a real change in its thinking. The need to stave off Iran's collapse to communism, and the desire to escape the public opprobrium that would stem from such a development (especially in an election year), left the administration, in Acheson's estimation, with no other choice.[9]

Initial British reaction to Acheson's proposals was unfavorable. It appeared to the British that in its "anxiety to ward off communism in Persia," the State Department had unfairly slanted the proposals toward Iran. As the U.S. plan stood, they said, the AIOC would be forced to purchase Iranian oil before arbitration, Mossadeq would receive U.S. aid virtually unconditionally, and the British blockade on Iranian oil sales would be scuttled with no guarantee of an acceptable settlement.

To redress these shortcomings the British wanted to link the provisions of the proposal more closely together. U.S. aid would be contingent on the opening of discussions toward a permanent sales agreement, oil purchases would be delayed until the arrangement of satisfactory terms of reference regarding compensation, and the boycott of Iranian oil would be preserved until "conclusion of a final settlement." These measures, Eden implied, would ensure that Iran followed through with permanent arrangements for the sale and distribution of its oil. In addition, he suggested that arbitration should address not only the amount and terms of compensation but also "the amount of wrong the [AIOC] had suffered and [the] means of providing redress," which was another way of saying that the AIOC should be compensated for the loss of its concession as well as for its physical installations in Iran.[10]

Eden's "very rigid position" dismayed U.S. policy makers and raised the specter of an Anglo-American break over Iran. "The only resemblance I could see between the aide memoire we had given to the British Government and Mr. Eden's reply," Secretary Acheson railed, "was that they were both written on paper with a typewriter." In a 12 August message to Eden Acheson declared that the "stringent" British proposals could not be "accepted either by Mossadegh or by any government that we can expect as a successor." President Truman concurred in a later message to Prime Minister Churchill. Unless the British accepted the nationalization laws, which had "become as sacred in Iranian eyes as [the] Koran," he asserted, Iran would go "down [the] communist drain." If Britain would not work with the United States to prevent this calamity, Truman implied that he would act unilaterally.[11]

Such talk both angered and worried British policy makers. On the first score, Churchill spoke for many when he reminded Truman that the British "were helping all [they could] in Korea," implying in the process that U.S. aid in Iran was nothing less than a fair quid pro quo. With regard to the second, British officials believed to a man that an Anglo-American break "might well mean the end of [British] influence in [Iran] for a long period and have serious repercussions elsewhere." Among the potential consequences of unilateral U.S. action were unconditional U.S. aid to Iran and the eventual erosion of the oil blockade, perhaps with Washington's acquiescence. To forestall such unpleasant eventualities Ambassador Franks advised the Foreign Office to work hard "to convince the Americans that our views on the handling of the oil problem are compatible with our common objective of preventing Communist rule in Persia."[12]

Prime Minister Churchill did just that in late August, when he assumed control of foreign affairs while Foreign Secretary Eden recovered from abdominal surgery. A firm believer in the virtues of transatlantic unity, Churchill thought that he and Truman should send a joint telegram to Mossadeq that said simply, "If you Musaddiq will do (A), (B) and (C), we two will do (X), (Y) and (Z)." Although the prime minister was not specific about just what these points might be, Acheson termed the proposal "the first . . . real break in the British position." To be sure, some U.S. officials worried that Churchill's proposal would tie the United States "to the umbilical cord of the British Empire" and give the Iranians the impression that the Anglo-Americans were ganging up on them. Others, led by Secretary of Defense Robert Lovett, were dismayed by the overly complex wording of the British proposals, at one point exclaiming in frustration that "English is their language initially and they ought to be able to write it." These problems notwithstanding, on 24 August Truman agreed to join with Churchill in new proposals to Mossadeq.[13]

III

Having taken the plunge toward Anglo-American cooperation, U.S. officials, in the words of Ambassador Franks, became "agog for action" and lost no time in agreeing to what became the Truman-Churchill proposals. Informally presented to Mossadeq on 28 August by Chargé d'Affaires Middleton and Ambassador Henderson, the proposals repeated Acheson's plan of 31 July but tied the individual provisions more tightly together, as per British demands. Once Mossadeq had submitted the question of compensation to the ICJ and commenced discussions with the AIOC for the distribution of Iranian oil, the AIOC would dispose of the oil already in storage at Abadan, the British government would relax restrictions on exports to Iran and on Iran's use of sterling, and the United States would provide Iran with $10 million in economic assistance.

Ambassador Henderson and other U.S. officials sorely hoped that the Iranians would accept these terms, particularly because they offered Iran much-needed assistance at a time when economic pressures threatened to push Mossadeq toward such "radical measures" as the dismissal of government employees and a reduction of the armed forces.[14]

According to Henderson, however, Mossadeq's initial reaction to the proposals "was not only negative but to an extent hostile." He saw the Anglo-American plan as a "nefarious snare" to reimpose the 1933 concession agreement on Iran, transform a purely internal dispute into an international one, and negate the nationalization laws. Especially galling were the provisions regarding arbitration and U.S. assistance. If the British insisted on the first point, Mossadeq said, the Iranian government would have to review the AIOC's claims before they could be presented to the ICJ, presumably for the purpose of squelching any attempt to claim compensation for the loss of future profits. Iran, though, would be free to make unlimited claims against the company, including assessments for the losses it had sustained because of the AIOC's boycott. As to the second point, Mossadeq thought it "smacked of charity" and was totally unacceptable. Iran wanted only what it deserved, he proclaimed, and had no intention of "going around with a beggar bowl in hand."

This explained his demand for the £50 million, which he saw as a legitimate claim against the AIOC. The Majlis may never have ratified the supplemental agreement, Mossadeq maintained, but that agreement "had superseded the 'de facto' 1933 Agreement" and "there could therefore be no question of the legitimacy of [his] claim." Given Mossadeq's opposition to the proposals, Henderson and Middleton decided to postpone official submission until they had consulted with policy makers in Washington and London and Mossadeq had had a chance to cool down. In the meantime Mossadeq threatened to sever diplomatic relations with Britain unless he received immediate financial assistance.[15]

After extended discussions Anglo-American officials concluded that additional concessions to Mossadeq "would merely be submitting to [his] blackmail" and create the impression "that he had only to make a further scene in order to get everything he wanted." The British were especially adamant about the importance of holding firm on the Truman-Churchill proposals and more generally about the necessity of preserving a joint Anglo-American front against Mossadeq. Officials in the Truman administration shared these concerns and agreed that they would make no alterations to the joint proposals, which both the British and the Americans considered fair and reasonable. Mossadeq, though, continued to believe otherwise and rejected the proposals in an exhausting meeting with Henderson and Middleton on 30 August. He also renewed his threat to break diplomatic relations with Great Britain.[16]

Still, British and U.S. leaders did not abandon hope of using the Truman-Churchill proposals as the basis for a settlement. Both the Senate and the Majlis were scheduled to discuss the proposals in mid-September, and in the interim the Anglo-Americans mounted a propaganda campaign to sway Iranian legislators toward a favorable judgment. The AIOC, the cousins said, had made substantial concessions in agreeing to the Truman-Churchill plan: the company had recognized nationalization as a fact and had abandoned its exclusive claim to all oil produced in Iran since the promulgation of the nationalization laws. British officials also recruited such friendly states as India, Iraq, Egypt, France, Belgium, Italy, and the Netherlands to talk up the proposals with Iranian officials. As it turned out, however, these efforts had little effect, as most Majlis deputies remained unwilling to defy Mossadeq. Nor did the international effort move the prime minister, who called the Truman-Churchill proposals "not only altogether inequitable, but more severe and impracticable than earlier proposals." On 16 September the Majlis supported his rejection of the Anglo-American démarche; the Senate followed suit one day later.[17]

Although categorically rejecting the Truman-Churchill proposals in a speech to the Majlis, Mossadeq offered his own terms for a settlement, which for the most part merely repeated his earlier demands. Compensation, he said, should be referred to the Iranian courts, where both the AIOC and the Iranian government could submit whatever claims they wished. The ICJ could decide the matter should the AIOC reject the jurisdiction of the Iranian courts, but only if both sides stated their claims in advance and only if the company limited its claims to the value of its physical properties in Iran and of the oil in storage at Abadan at the time of nationalization. The latter stipulation would prevent the company from claiming compensation for the loss of future profits. Mossadeq also continued to demand £50 million from the AIOC, which he now insisted be paid in dollars to meet his government's need for convertible currency. The demand for payment from the AIOC, British officials reported, was the cornerstone of the ever "more intransigent" Mossadeq's plan, and it was clear that Mossadeq was "not prepared to talk business until he [got] his £50,000,000."[18]

The British government found these terms "quite unacceptable." It was nonsense, the Foreign Office said, for Mossadeq to speak of "his £50 million." Iran had forfeited its claim to this money by rejecting the supplemental agreement, and the government would under no circumstances ask the company to pay up. Besides, the AIOC had already used that money to defray the cost of replacing Iranian oil. No more realistic was Mossadeq's expectation that the AIOC would surrender its right to claim compensation for losses stemming from the cancellation of its concession, which was valid until 1993. To do so would not only deny the company its rights but also threaten concession agreements everywhere. What Mossadeq offered, Whitehall fumed, were "not so much counter-proposals" as "terms for complete capitulation." Far from demonstrating a desire to settle the oil dispute, Mossadeq's speech to the Majlis proved his intransigence and steeled British opposition to making any further concessions to his demands.[19]

As British leaders awaited Iran's formal response to the joint proposals, they sought Washington's support for their hard-line stance. In discussions with U.S. officials the British highlighted the unfairness of Mossadeq's demands on the AIOC, emphasizing the importance that Iran not profit from its expropriation of the company. They argued that giving Mossadeq money would not halt the spread of communism in Iran because the recent rise of the Tudeh Party stemmed not from the government's financial problems but from Mossadeq's lenience. Most of all they stressed the necessity of Anglo-American unity. The United States, the British asserted, had already affirmed the fairness of the Truman-Churchill proposals; to urge additional British concessions now would damage Britain's position in Iran, lead Mossadeq to ever greater demands, and gravely damage Anglo-American relations. These arguments worked. U.S. officials promised to stand firm with the British until Mossadeq had formally replied to the Truman-Churchill proposals. After that point U.S. policy would depend on the course of events.[20]

The British became even more determined to preserve a joint Anglo-American front after Mossadeq's 24 September reply to the joint proposals proved his intention to split the allies apart. By addressing the British government almost exclusively the prime minister's message ignored the joint nature of the Truman-Churchill proposals. It also failed to mention the U.S. offer of financial assistance, probably because Mossadeq had already rejected it.[21] Instead, Mossadeq provided what the British termed a "highly partisan" account of the oil dispute, a restatement of the imperfections of the Truman-Churchill proposals, and a reiteration of the counterproposals he had previously presented to the Majlis. To the British, the response was so "unconciliatory" and "insolent" as to belie Mossadeq's professed desire to settle the oil dispute. Even worse, it was essentially an ultimatum that gave the British ten days—until 4 October—to accept. Although Mossadeq did not spell out the consequences of failing to do so or of replying unfavorably, Middleton feared that a rupture of diplomatic relations would probably result.[22]

Despite the seriousness of such a course, British leaders decided immediately to reject Mossadeq's counterproposals. Financially, they said, Britain could not afford to accept the Iranian conditions. Already engaged in a "critical . . . struggle for solvency," the nation could ill afford to absorb the £60 million in annual losses caused by "Persian degradations" against the AIOC, let alone the repercussions for its worldwide economic interests from Great Britain's acknowledgment that Iran need not compensate the AIOC for its lost concession. Nor were the British psychologically inclined to meet Mossadeq's demands even had the money been available. Caving in would have set a dangerous precedent and fatally weakened Britain's prestige when it was struggling to come to grips with its diminished global position. These factors dictated that Whitehall immediately and categorically reject Mossadeq's counterproposals—preferably in a detailed statement that refuted his claims, highlighted the ludicrousness of his demands, and left no room for misinterpretation.[23]

Next, British policy makers sought U.S. consent to make this a joint endeavor. Anglo-American cooperation in the Truman-Churchill proposals, they said, had already had a positive effect in Tehran, where Mossadeq was seeing for the first time that he could not play Britain off against the United States. Breaking ranks and submitting to Mossadeq now, Churchill said, would be disastrous for Britain's prestige and economic position. It would also do irreparable damage in the United States, for it would mean large-scale U.S. assistance "to bribe [the] Persians . . . not to become Communists." In order to prevent these eventualities, Churchill implored, they had to preserve a joint front against Iran.[24]

U.S. officials were less sure about the merits of a concerted hard-line stance against Mossadeq. Instead of contributing to a settlement, they feared that U.S. association with such a policy would further erode the U.S. position in Iran, which Henderson thought had theretofore "survived the [v]icissitudes of [the] oil problem." They also worried that a peremptory reply to Mossadeq might "close the doors to further discussion" and result in a revolution in which more extreme elements like Kashani could come to power. Given these concerns, U.S. policy makers decided that under no circumstances could the United States join Britain in a line-by-line rebuttal of Mossadeq's recent treatise. The State Department, however, would not object if Whitehall decided to send such a communiqué, in which case the U.S. government would merely acknowledge receipt of Mossadeq's message with a press release.[25]

Churchill, Eden, and other British officials were "most disappointed" with what they termed an "unhelpful American attitude." It "would not do" for U.S. officials to abandon the British now, as this would only embolden Mossadeq to stiffen his demands. The British, Eden reminded Acheson, had already made significant concessions at Washington's urging; the United States could not fairly expect them to yield anything else. If Truman would not sign a joint message with Churchill, the Foreign Office suggested "parallel messages maintaining the common position." This was the minimum necessary to show Mossadeq that he could not split the Anglo-Americans apart, or so the British argued. To secure Washington's agreement the British were willing to scuttle plans for a detailed refutation of the Iranian counterproposals.[26]

Although Acheson feared that even collaboration of this kind would tar the United States and risk the further loss of U.S. prestige in Iran, Truman overruled him. The importance of the Anglo-American alliance led the president to agree to join Churchill in sending similar but not identical messages to Mossadeq. These messages would seek merely to clarify the joint proposals and make no mention of Iran's counterproposals. In Truman's eyes this option seemed the best alternative. It would prevent the British from sending what U.S. officials termed an "unnecessarily provocative" point-by-point refutation of Mossadeq's counterproposals, it would refocus attention on the joint proposals, and it would preserve the united Anglo-American front.[27]

In separate meetings with Mossadeq on 4 October Middleton and Henderson presented similar notes to the Iranian government that sought to dispel Mossadeq's fears about the joint proposals. The notes emphasized Anglo-American recognition of "the fact of nationalization," eschewed any intention "to revive the 1933 Concession, or any concession," and ruled out forcing the Iranian government to accept either "foreign management of the oil industry" or a "monopoly purchase of oil." Both messages expressed hope that Mossadeq might accept the Truman-Churchill proposals now that they had been more fully explained, as they were perhaps the last chance to settle the oil controversy.[28]

Mossadeq's initial reaction said otherwise. "It was now too late," the prime minister tearfully told Middleton, for him to reconsider the proposals. Without the £50 million he had requested "Persia would soon be dead," and "it was no good negotiating with a dead man." "Events must take their course," he regretfully concluded, and in an oblique reference to his earlier threat to sever diplomatic relations with Britain he wished Middleton "success in [his] future career." In a subsequent meeting with Henderson Mossadeq lamented that the United States had sanctioned Britain's "economic and political" attack on Iran by failing to persuade the British to meet his demand for the £50 million. "The original bad impression made by the joint message," he said, "could not be effaced"; in the prime minister's eyes the United States had now been linked inextricably with Great Britain in a campaign of economic warfare designed to bring down his government.[29]

The prime minister's official responses to the British and U.S. governments reiterated his 24 September counterproposals. Mossadeq gave the AIOC one week to send a delegation to Tehran to discuss the implementation of his terms. As a show of good faith, and as a means of solving Iran's pressing economic problems, he wanted the company to make available £20 million of the £50 million before the talks began; the remainder was to be paid upon completion of the negotiations, which were expected to take three weeks. In still another veiled reference to his earlier threat to break diplomatic relations with Britain Mossadeq stressed the "impossibility of the continuation of [the current] state of affairs" and denied responsibility for "any eventuality resulting from" his policies. He also asserted that "the prompt and immediate settlement of this matter would be a great and important contribution towards insuring the peace and prosperity of one of the sensitive areas of the world."[30]

Acheson needed no reminder of the seriousness of the situation. The possibility of a protracted oil crisis was bad enough, for it threatened the economic and political stability of Iran and opened the door to communist expansion throughout the Middle East. But now the secretary had to deal with the potential severance of Anglo-Iranian diplomatic relations, which, he declared, "would not make further negotiations easier." In a desperate effort to keep Mossadeq from taking precipitous action Acheson sought a new approach to the oil problem that abandoned broad principles regarding each side's claims for compensation in favor of "a simple and arbitrary" lump sum of oil payable over a number of years. This way, the AIOC might receive compensation for the value of its lost concession without making specific mention of this fact in the settlement. To solve Iran's economic problems in the meantime the country would receive advances against future oil sales, which would be made to some unnamed distributing agency "in which British interests might indirectly be satisfied." The State Department had yet to hammer out the fine points of such a proposal. But Acheson told the British that unless something along these lines was offered to Mossadeq soon, the prime minister would break diplomatic relations with Britain and destroy all chances of ever settling the dispute. It was therefore important that when the British rejected Mossadeq's counterproposals, as Acheson agreed they must, they also stress that "there were further ideas to discuss."[31]

British officials remained much less pessimistic about the Iranian situation than their U.S. counterparts and thus less inclined to placate Mossadeq in order to achieve a settlement. Although they acknowledged that a severance of relations would be "unhelpful," they doubted that Mossadeq would take this step and preferred to risk it rather than accept the latest U.S. plan, which they considered "a non-starter" and "not likely to bring about a settlement." U.S. officials had supported the Truman-Churchill proposals, and they were wrong to expect the British to move beyond them. The British government and the AIOC, the Foreign Office argued, already had made "substantial concessions" to Mossadeq, only to be met by ever stiffening demands that the United States now seemed to sanction. The AIOC was not likely to abandon outside arbitration for an arbitrary lump sum of oil, nor did the British government think it should. An award determined by an outside arbitrator would have more authority than an agreement between governments and would thus stand less chance of being repudiated or watered down by one party. It was also more likely to be acceptable to the British public and to contain the domestic political damage of an Iranian settlement. For these reasons the Foreign Office seemed inclined to reject the U.S. proposals, which it doubted Mossadeq would accept. In its view, a firm stand against Mossadeq still held the best chance of encouraging "more realistic Persian elements to counsel moderation."[32]

Whitehall's adherence to the Truman-Churchill proposals, even in the face of certain Iranian rejection, prompted the State Department to issue renewed threats of unilateral U.S. action. If nothing else, the department thought that it might have to prop up the Iranian government with financial assistance. But because this was really not the department's preferred course of action, Acheson sought to forestall it by sending Paul Nitze, director of the State Department's Policy Planning Staff, to London for another round of direct negotiations with the British.[33]

On 14 October, meanwhile, the British government told Mossadeq that his counterproposals were "unreasonable and unacceptable." The prime minister, Eden said, could not unilaterally limit the scope of the AIOC's claims for compensation to only the value of its physical facilities in Iran. Nor could he claim compensation for losses incurred as a result of the AIOC's boycott. The company was merely exercising its legal rights in defending the oil, which it regarded as its property. Eden also totally dismissed Mossadeq's "fictitious" claim to the £50 million that Iran would have received at the end of 1951 had it ratified the supplemental agreement. The British government, he said, was not prepared to even "entertain this request," particularly when Mossadeq sought at the same time to limit the AIOC's right to claim just compensation for its losses. Finally, the foreign secretary reiterated the points he had made in his message of 4 October, especially that the British recognized Iranian nationalization and still hoped to use the Truman-Churchill proposals as the basis for future discussions.[34]

Political forces within Iran would not have allowed Mossadeq to accept the Anglo-American proposals even had he been so inclined, which was far from the case. As the Iranian ambassador to the United States had earlier told officials in Washington, Mossadeq was "a prisoner of the situation" in Iran, where he "was constantly under pressure to take some 'desperate' action." His internal political position had "weakened considerably" since his return to office in July. According to Eden, it was "becoming clear, even to the ignorant people, that Musaddiq [was] incapable of constructive action."

His decline was coupled with the rising power of Ayatollah Kashani and other more radical elements in the National Front, who consistently opposed all efforts to solve the oil crisis. In the wake of Eden's note of 14 October these elements pressed Mossadeq to make good on his threat to sever diplomatic relations with Britain, and there seemed little chance that he could renege on his pledge. On the contrary, the prime minister became increasingly preoccupied with what he believed, quite correctly as it turned out, was a "British conspiracy to overthrow his government." And in a radio address to the nation on 16 October he announced that in light of Britain's unfriendly attitude, relations between it and Iran would be broken off.[35]

Because Mossadeq outlined no specific timetable for severing diplomatic relations, Ambassador Henderson made one last pitch to avert what U.S. officials saw as an impending disaster. On 18 October Henderson told the prime minister that the United States was considering new but unspecified solutions to the oil dispute. Would Mossadeq be willing to postpone the severance of relations until these ideas had been finalized? As a gesture of friendship toward the United States Mossadeq agreed to delay a formal announcement until 22 October, thus giving U.S. officials four days in which to formulate a new plan.[36]

Mossadeq's deadline gave added importance to Nitze's mission to London. Originally intended to more closely align Anglo-American policy, the talks now became an eleventh-hour search for a new approach to the oil problem. Despite extensive discussions with both government officials and representatives of the AIOC, however, Nitze was unable to secure agreement on a new proposal. The British clung steadfastly to the idea of arbitration and refused to accept a lump-sum settlement. They denounced Nitze's estimate of compensation on the order of thirty to fifty million tons of oil, saying that the AIOC was entitled to much more. They also questioned the soundness of restarting Iran's oil industry at the expense of countries like Iraq and Kuwait. These countries had honored their concessionary contracts and had helped the AIOC to replace its lost Iranian production, and it would not be fair to penalize their good behavior.[37]

Because the British were so determined that Iran not profit at the expense of other nations, they could not accept the newest U.S. proposals. "Mossadegh has slapped our faces (ours and America's)" by rejecting the Truman-Churchill proposals, they intoned; to so quickly replace those proposals with others would merely encourage him to commit further depredations and fatally weaken the British position throughout the Middle East. As the British saw it, the new U.S. plan stemmed from "internal political considerations," namely the Truman administration's desire to settle the oil crisis before the 4 November presidential election. It was "bad in principle, dangerous in its repercussions and impracticable," and should not even be mentioned to the Iranians. In its place the British proposed a two-phase settlement that resembled the Truman-Churchill proposals. Under this proposal Iran would agree to outside arbitration on compensation, which would be followed by talks on the distribution of Iranian oil. Nitze doubted the likelihood that Mossadeq would accept such a proposal. But in the interest of Anglo-American unity he promised to present the scheme to his colleagues in Washington.[38]

IV

As British and U.S. officials debated the terms of an oil settlement, Mossadeq escalated the Anglo-Iranian crisis by severing diplomatic relations with Great Britain on 22 October.[39] According to Hossein Ala, Iran's minister of court, Mossadeq's primary motivation for breaking relations was "to justify [the] severe measures of economy which would shortly be forced upon the country." In other words, the prime minister apparently believed that the Iranian people would more willingly accept the strict austerity measures that would be necessary to help the country deal with its mounting economic problems if they were accompanied by the expulsion of Britain's diplomats.

If the severance of diplomatic relations with Britain was designed to strengthen Mossadeq's popular position, however, it did not have the same effect with members of the Senate, many of whom feared that expelling the British would imperil Iran's traditional diplomatic strategy of playing the great powers against one another. In the senators' eyes no good was likely to come from this latest "twist to [the] lion's tail," and they therefore sought to moderate the prime minister's harsh anti-British stand.[40]

Mossadeq's animosity toward the British government was patently clear in a radio address he delivered upon the expulsion of the British. The contents of the address held few surprises, although its tone was more strident and defiant than Mossadeq's previous communications. The "covetous" AIOC, he asserted, had "not acted for a single day as a commercial enterprise free from politics." It "had a finger in every pie of corruption" in Iran during the last fifty years and had no wish to reform now. On the contrary, whereas the Iranian government had "spared no effort" to reach an oil settlement, the British government and the AIOC had "deliberately caused the failure of the various oil missions," brought "financial and economic pressure on the people of Iran," and seemed determined to turn back Iran's nationalization. The British government, which monitored the broadcast through the BBC, gave the message little publicity. "We want to let the Persian situation 'stew' for a time," A. K. Rothnie of the Foreign Office declared. "The less the polemics the better."[41]

U.S. officials thought differently, especially about the volatility of the situation. On 30 October Henderson reported that a "real political and social revolution" was in progress in Iran. The traditional ruling elite had been totally disempowered, the shah had come "under [the] complete control" of Mossadeq, and the Tudeh Party had solidified its position as the National Front's only "organized challenge." Because Mossadeq's government was continuing "along [the] same road as [the] Tudeh," Henderson believed that a sudden communist coup was unlikely. Instead, the government would probably drift toward communism, with "no dramatic moment or precise date" when it had "reached [the] point of no return."[42]

On this much U.S. policy makers agreed. On how best to prevent an Iranian disaster they did not. Officials at the U.S. embassy in Tehran and in the Department of Defense called for unilateral action either through the provision of economic aid or the purchase of Iranian oil. Now that events had forced primary responsibility for Iran onto the United States, they argued, it might become necessary to scuttle close collaboration with the British in order to save Iran. By contrast, officials in the State Department continued to advocate close Anglo-American cooperation. The United States, Acheson said, may have inherited primary responsibility for Iran; in time it might even "assume responsibility in the wider areas of the Middle East." But in no sense could the United States act with wanton disregard for legitimate British interests in the region. As he had done throughout the crisis, Acheson argued that "it is only by correlating our efforts with the British that the limited resources available to us for the area can be employed with any lasting effectiveness in developing stability and a capability of defense in the Middle East." Acheson was correct in seeing Anglo-American cooperation as the best use of limited U.S. resources. Yet this close reliance on the British in Iran and elsewhere robbed U.S. policy makers of the chance to push Whitehall toward more flexible policies. This had been the case throughout the Iranian dispute, as U.S. policy makers had tempered their criticism of British policies that Washington had not always considered wise. And it was even more evident now that the U.S. government had been inextricably linked to the British through the Truman-Churchill proposals.[43]

Despite the potential drawbacks to close ties between London and

Washington, Acheson saw no other alternative. The seriousness of the Iranian crisis, he believed, dictated even closer Anglo-American cooperation in Iran than had been the case in the past, as well as greater U.S. involvement not only in the search for an oil settlement but also in that settlement's implementation. For one thing, the secretary said, the United States would have to provide Iran with significant financial assistance, probably through the U.S. government's purchase of Iranian oil. For another, private U.S. companies would probably have to play a substantial role in marketing and distributing Iranian oil but only with British approval. This role, he said, could be filled in one of two ways: either one or more U.S. oil companies already operating in the Middle East could step in or a new corporation of companies that lacked a regional presence could be formed.[44]

In fact, Acheson had already presented a preliminary scheme for involving the U.S. oil companies in Iran at an interdepartmental meeting on 8 October, where representatives of the Treasury Department had given their support. He had more trouble selling the idea to officials in the Justice Department, who were then waging an antitrust suit against the U.S. majors. According to Attorney General James P. McGranery, "It would be most difficult to work out a program involving the majors and at the same time maintain the present anti-trust action." Although saving Iran from economic and political collapse was certainly a noble goal, McGranery was not at all certain that doing so necessitated the kind of action Acheson outlined. The heart of the matter, he observed, lay in determining "whether the national interest in finding a solution to [the Iranian] problem was more important than the principles involved in the [antitrust] suit."[45]

This conundrum had already revealed itself in the controversy surrounding publication of a Federal Trade Commission (FTC) report of mid-1951 titled "The International Petroleum Cartel." Based almost entirely on documents subpoenaed from the oil companies, the report was a damning exposé of past industry efforts to limit production, allocate markets, and otherwise control world oil supplies. It detailed the various intercompany agreements that had prevailed in the industry and implied that oil-producing nations would have received higher revenues had these agreements not existed. Confident that the report would force the major petroleum companies to reform, the FTC had lobbied President Truman for its immediate release.[46]

Support for the report's release was not unanimous. According to the departments of State and Defense and the NSC, the report "would do the national interest irreparable damage." It would undermine the confidence of foreign governments in U.S. companies and "greatly assist Soviet propaganda," which sought to portray the United States and other Western nations as imperialist and colonial powers. With particular reference to Iran, officials feared that the report would jeopardize chances for an oil settlement "by damaging, perhaps irreparably, the status of the US as mediator." The major U.S. oil companies also opposed publication, arguing that it might threaten U.S. national security by endangering continued access to Middle Eastern oil. Siding with the report's opponents, President Truman agreed on 6 June 1952 to suppress the document temporarily. To dispel any impression that he condoned the practices it described, though, he also said he intended to "speak to the Attorney General about the possibility of presenting the facts in this matter to a grand jury."[47]

In this way the FTC report had led directly to the antitrust proceedings McGranery mentioned at the 8 October meeting. After several months of investigation the Justice Department on 1 August 1952 had issued subpoenas to "all oil companies in the United States having an interest in the production, purchase, sale, refining, [and] transportation . . . of crude oil outside the United States." The subpoenas were sweeping in their coverage, calling "for literally millions of papers and documents" from the oil companies in the United States and "many millions more in foreign countries." The aim of the grand jury investigation was a criminal indictment of the major oil companies for violation of the Sherman Anti-Trust Act, which prohibited industrial and commercial combinations that restrained trade. Conviction under the Sherman Act could result in a fine or imprisonment and might lead to parallel civil suits and a breakup of intercompany agreements. Even acquittal could jeopardize the major oil companies' concession agreements and imperil Western oil supplies.[48]

The potentially damaging effects of the grand jury investigation were not lost on either the state and defense departments or the British government. Acheson and Secretary of Defense Lovett opposed the proceedings. Although both publicly obeyed the president's request to cooperate with the inquiry, they argued privately that a federal investigation of the oil companies would damage their prestige in oil-producing countries around the world and lead those countries ultimately to conduct similar inquiries. It might also fuel nationalism throughout the Middle East at a time when the U.S. government was trying to contain nationalization to Iran.[49] Officials in the British government also objected to the grand jury proceedings, especially because two British oil companies, Royal Dutch/Shell and the AIOC, had been included in the Justice Department's subpoena. The British worried that the investigation would hamper the companies' activities, further weaken Britain's already overstrained balance of payments, and have a prejudicial effect on the situation in Iran. In their minds the proceedings were nothing more than an election-year stunt designed "to divert public attention from charges of corruption brought against the [Truman] administration."[50] But because neither the state and defense departments nor the British government thought it proper to lobby the Justice Department to quash the investigation, it continued to move ahead during the fall of 1952.[51]

This is where the antitrust question stood on 8 October, when the State Department suggested that the U.S. majors become involved in moving Iranian oil. Throughout the next month the Justice Department continued its investigation, to the dismay of the State Department, the major oil companies, and the British government. Years later Acheson denounced "the police dogs" from the Justice Department's antitrust division who "wanted no truck with the mammon of unrighteousness . . . and had no hesitation in disagreeing with me on foreign policy aims." At the time the secretary expressed his displeasure with the Justice Department by seeking the direct intervention of "our common superior."[52]

In a 7 November memorandum to the president Acheson sketched the Iranian situation in depressing terms. The twenty-month search for a way to bridge the gap between the British and the Iranians had been fruitless, the secretary maintained, and unless the crisis was immediately resolved, Iran was doomed to economic and political collapse. To prevent this calamity Acheson asked Truman to approve two measures. The first would allow the U.S. Defense Materials Procurement Agency (DMPA) to advance Iran $100 million against future oil purchases. The second would authorize one or more U.S. oil companies to take part in the production and distribution of Iranian oil if the amount of oil taken by the AIOC proved insufficient. The Plan of Action No. 1 of the U.S. Petroleum Administration for Defense (PAD), which had helped to prevent worldwide shortages during the initial stage of the Iranian shutdown, had entailed this kind of cooperation. Enlisting the oil companies' assistance was again necessary, the secretary told the president, to avert disaster in Iran, even if it compromised the strict adherence to the antitrust laws advocated by the Justice Department. Fully convinced that the security implications of a loss of Iran overshadowed the dangers of compromising the antitrust suit, President Truman gave the State Department's plan his blessing.[53]

Meanwhile the British had been refining their earlier proposal for a two-stage settlement. In their minds the first step toward any settlement was Mossadeq's agreement to outside arbitration. Once that had been accomplished, an export company wholly owned by the AIOC would commence negotiations with the Iranian government for the movement of Iranian oil, and the DMPA would make advances to Iran against future oil purchases. Upon completion of the arbitration process the AIOC's export company would make longer-term purchase arrangements that would fulfill the terms of the compensation award. To counter probable U.S. arguments that Iran would not accept outside arbitration Whitehall enumerated the advantages of such a move. First, arbitration would allow Mossadeq "to divest himself of his reputation as a reckless fanatic" and improve Iran's financial and economic position by allowing it once again to attract foreign capital and reap the benefits of its oil industry. Second, agreeing to arbitration would show the world that Iran accepted both the impartiality of the ICJ and the strength of the country's claims against the AIOC. And, third, arbitration would not result in an unfair judgment against Iran, because it was in the AIOC's best interest to ensure that any award not exceed Iran's ability to pay. Having supported arbitration with such arguments, the British were confident of U.S. acquiescence.[54]

Acheson crushed this optimism when he told Eden at a U.N. meeting on 20 November that there was "not enough cheese" in the British proposal. With the situation in Iran deteriorating daily, the secretary said, the country might soon pass the point of no return. Unless the British undertook a "new and more vigorous effort" to solve the Iranian crisis, Acheson again intimated that the State Department might strike out on its own. In the end these threats of independent action "stirred up turgid waters in London": the British agreed to abandon their plan and to further discuss the U.S. position with Nitze in London.[55]

Acheson's hope for British cooperation and his threat of unilateral U.S. action in its absence were laid out as official U.S. policy in NSC-136/1, which the National Security Council approved in late November. According to this document, U.S. policy toward Iran should be made in "full consultation" with Great Britain and "avoid unnecessarily sacrificing legitimate" British interests or "unnecessarily impairing" Anglo-American relations. Under no circumstances, however, should the United States allow the British government to veto any U.S. actions considered essential to the achievement of U.S. goals in Iran. The NSC also endorsed the entry of U.S. oil companies into the Iranian market if necessary. This was good news for the State Department, which was already planning to hold discussions with representatives of the major U.S. oil companies based upon the president's acquiescence in Acheson's appeal of 7 November. As expected, the Department of Defense, the Office of Defense Mobilization, and the Joint Chiefs of Staff sanctioned the upcoming talks. Because of the antitrust suit, however, the Justice Department said it would reserve its position until it had seen the type of plan that might result.[56]

In two discussions with oil company officials on 4 and 9 December the State Department emphasized the importance of a speedy oil settlement. Although Acheson attributed the need for haste to Truman's desire "to avoid passing on a burden to the new Administration," it is also probable that he and the president wanted to avenge their previous failures to solve the Iranian problem with a last-minute triumph. Because such domestic political motives were unlikely to move the assembled executives, however, Acheson supplemented them with concerns about national security. In his discussions with company officials the secretary stressed the State Department's belief that Iran was deteriorating at "an accelerated rate" and that it was undergoing "a real revolution." Unless the United States took action soon, he said, Iran would experience first an "uncontrollable civil disturbance," then "a take-over by the Tudeh party." The only way to stem the tide of impending disaster, he warned, was rapid resolution of the oil crisis. But with the AIOC unable to market enough oil to satisfy Iran's requirements, all hope of such a resolution lay with the U.S. majors. In the interest of national security the secretary hoped that the majors would be willing to at least explore the possibility of marketing a substantial amount of Iranian oil.[57]

Company officials responded to the department's proposal unenthusiastically but promised to give it some thought. It was not that they lacked concern about Iran's potential fall to communism. On the contrary, they fully appreciated the dangers such a development posed. Their hesitance stemmed instead from worries about the implications of a sloppy settlement, which they sought to avoid by securing certain guarantees from the State Department. For example, the companies insisted that Iran not receive a larger return for its oil than other producing countries, lest these countries follow Iran's lead and nullify their concessionary contracts with U.S. firms. They also insisted that the British be consulted at every stage of the negotiations and that the AIOC receive immediate compensation for its assets and lost concession. This would avoid the impression that the U.S. companies were moving in on the AIOC. Finally, the U.S. companies wanted the lion's share of any cutbacks in production to be borne by Kuwait, which had profited more than the other Middle Eastern countries from the Iranian shutdown. In this way the unfavorable reaction to any reduction of output in the region would be balanced out. State Department guarantees on these matters, the executives seemed to say, would clear the way for future discussions regarding U.S. involvement in Iranian oil.[58]

Meanwhile some within the administration were trying to make the future participation of the U.S. majors in Iranian oil even more likely by quashing the ongoing antitrust suit. The campaign against the suit originated with Oscar L. Chapman, who was both secretary of the interior and petroleum administrator for defense. He presented the Interior Department's case at a meeting of the National Security Council on 17 December. In NSC-138, "National Security Problems Concerning Free World Petroleum Demands and Potential Supplies," Chapman sought to dispel any belief "that the United States could be self-sufficient with respect to its oil supply." Increased civilian and military demands for oil products since World War II, he maintained, made the entire Western world dependent on foreign supplies. But access to those supplies was endangered by the antitrust suit, which fueled nationalism throughout the oil-producing world and created a tinderbox there. To remedy this potentially catastrophic situation, which already had manifested itself in Iran's nationalization of the AIOC, Chapman recommended an evaluation of the security implications of the antitrust suit and its termination. The National Security Council approved Chapman's recommendation, commissioned such an evaluation from the interior, defense, and state departments, along with a counterpoint from the Justice Department, and agreed to reconvene on 5 January 1953 to decide the issue.[59]

At its subsequent meeting, the last under President Truman's direction, the NSC sided with the suit's opponents. The Justice Department argued aggressively that it was the international petroleum cartel that endangered Western security, not the antitrust suit. By concentrating on the development of foreign oil supplies, the department asserted, the U.S. majors had neglected to develop domestic resources and had made the United States dependent on foreign production.

Representatives of the state, defense, and interior departments disputed these assertions. In their minds the antitrust action was a real threat to U.S. national security. Because the international operations of U.S. oil companies abroad profoundly affected relations between the United States and the oil-producing countries, the national security of the United States depended on the maintenance of friendly relations between those countries and the U.S. companies. But because the grand jury's criminal investigation created tensions between the companies and the producing countries, it constituted a threat not only to U.S. national security but also to the security of the entire Western world. President Truman agreed with the state, defense, and interior departments that national security was at stake. Accordingly, he ordered Attorney General McGranery to terminate the grand jury's criminal investigation of the U.S. oil companies and prepare a civil suit against them instead. Dismissal of criminal charges against the majors removed one obstacle to their participation in Iranian oil by making them less leery of cooperative action overseas. It also signaled the U.S. government's intention to subordinate domestic concerns with antitrust to a larger conception of national security.[60]

After the State Department had secured the preliminary assent of the U.S. majors, Nitze headed to London for additional discussions with the British. It was his hope that the Foreign Office and the AIOC would agree to have Ambassador Henderson, who was then home on leave, present the State Department's plan, including the participation of the U.S. majors, to Mossadeq upon his return to Tehran. To Nitze's dismay, however, the British were not inclined to make any "concessions of substance" to the lame-duck Democrats until they knew the sentiments of the incoming Eisenhower administration. British obstinacy was most clearly revealed in their continuing insistence on outside arbitration for compensation, even though Mossadeq had rejected such an idea and even though Nitze believed that British insistence on arbitration would doom any proposal to certain rejection. U.S. officials did, however, win British acquiescence in the plan to involve the majors in the movement of Iranian oil, and in mid-December the Foreign Office agreed that Henderson could present the new plan to Mossadeq.[61]

V

In the interim Mossadeq's political position had continued to deteriorate. Senate opposition had become particularly intense, probably for the basest of political reasons. That body refused to follow the Majlis's lead in condemning Qavam as a traitor to the country and calling for the confiscation of his property. In the eyes of the Majlis this was a dangerous infringement on individual rights that would only prevent opposition elements, even those in the Senate itself, from speaking out against the government. The Senate also objected to a Majlis proposal to grant amnesty to Razmara's assassin. Its opposition was founded on the constitutional principle of the separation of powers: the legislative branch of the government should not be empowered to overturn a decision made by the judicial branch. Finally, the Senate criticized the severance of diplomatic relations with Great Britain, which the Senate saw as a dangerous move toward alliance with the Soviet Union. The Senate's opposition to this move probably also stemmed from the close relationship that had traditionally existed between that body and the British embassy. Pro-Mossadeq deputies in the Majlis attacked the Senate's opposition to these measures as self-serving and unpatriotic and in late October voted to strictly interpret Article 5 of the Iranian constitution, which limited the Senate's term to two years, thus bringing the present session, which had begun in February 1950, to an end.

Although dissolution of the Senate would drastically curtail the shah's power and eliminate the strongest voice of opposition to Mossadeq in the country, the monarch was forced to accede to the pressure of the Majlis. The dissolution may have temporarily improved Mossadeq's position by silencing some of his most vocal critics, but it also steeled many senators in their opposition to the National Front, which now seemed bent on effecting a full-scale social revolution in Iran. Ayatollah Kashani's mounting political ambitions added to the prime minister's problems by polarizing the National Front as members chose sides in this rivalry—and abandoned the common struggle against the AIOC in the process. Mossadeq also saw a decline in his popularity with Iran's most important businessmen, who interpreted his dissolution of the Senate and severance of diplomatic relations with Great Britain as threats to their political and economic positions. Disillusioned with the prime minister's continuing inability to resolve the oil crisis, these individuals lined up behind conservative opponents of the government and did what they could to undermine its position.[62]

Aside from creating political problems for Mossadeq's government, Iran's economic situation was a concern in its own right. As efforts to create an oil-less economy failed to bear fruit, government officials had become increasingly convinced that Iran's economic survival depended on oil sales. To this end, Abbas Parkhideh, the chairman of Iran's Oil Sales Committee, had ventured to Europe seeking buyers but had returned empty handed. Meanwhile Iran's earlier contracts with Italian oil companies, including the EPIM, the firm that had chartered the *Rose Mary*, were in danger of lapsing because of the companies' failure to take delivery of their oil. And until the British relaxed their boycott it was unlikely that new agreements would be negotiated in their place.[63] Kashani and others blamed the United States for allowing the boycott, and by extension Iran's economic difficulties, to continue. Mossadeq agreed and threatened to "treat the United States Government as [he] had treated Her Majesty's Government" unless U.S. officials changed their ways. Although such blustering was not likely to endear Mossadeq to U.S. hearts, it did convince the State Department of the necessity for action and was thus an indirect but important cause for the Truman administration's late autumn push for an oil settlement.[64]

Upon returning to Tehran in December Ambassador Henderson discussed the new U.S. approach in two "long and difficult" conversations with Mossadeq on Christmas Day and New Year's Eve. These general discussions did not involve specific proposals. Instead, Henderson sought Mossadeq's reaction to the idea of impartial arbitration for compensation and to a long-term sales contract with the AIOC or a multinational consortium. The first point, of course, would legitimize Iran's nationalization by paying the AIOC for its losses; the second would provide Iran with the financial wherewithal to forestall a collapse to communism. To the State Department arbitration and a long-term sales contract were the two most important components of any settlement, and it was crucial that Mossadeq agree to them before discussion of the actual proposals could begin.[65]

The prime minister's reaction to Henderson's probing was mixed. With regard to the issue of outside arbitration his attitude had softened, and he now agreed that the judges of the ICJ should constitute an arbitration panel that would determine compensation based on any nationalization law the AIOC wished to select. His new-found willingness to accept this procedure, which was amazing in itself, was all the more significant when Mossadeq stuck to it even after learning that Britain's Coal Nationalization Law, which the AIOC selected, provided for payments against the loss of future profits. What Mossadeq would not consider was a long-term sales contract with the AIOC. Although the prime minister had heretofore claimed a readiness to sign such an agreement, Henderson learned that Mossadeq "now feared it might be dangerous to trust [the] AIOC to purchase [the] bulk of Iranian oil." He was willing, however, to consider long-term sales contracts with other oil companies, including the U.S. firms, should they enter the Iranian market, but only after arrangements for arbitration had been made.[66]

Henderson's discussions with the prime minister were cautiously promising. Mossadeq had agreed to arbitration by the ICJ and to a private understanding with the British regarding the ICJ's right to consider compensation for the loss of future profits. He had also abandoned his previous insistence that the AIOC pay Iran £50 million before discussions could begin. To be sure, Mossadeq had refused to commit to a long-term contract with the AIOC and in this way seemed determined to separate the various components of the U.S. proposals in order to maximize his gains. But he had tentatively agreed to the multinational consortium the State Department had been discussing with the U.S. majors, which in Henderson's mind was a great step forward. To preserve the gains thus far achieved Henderson advised rapid progress toward a final settlement. Mossadeq, the ambassador believed, had displayed considerable courage in agreeing to arbitration and in pushing for a resolution to the crisis in the face of tremendous opposition from Ayatollah Kashani and other extremists. It would be a fatal mistake under the circumstances to delay a settlement in hopes that more favorable terms would become available. Such terms could not be struck with a successor government: as the father of the 1951 Nationalization Law, Mossadeq was in a better position to make concessions to the British than anyone else. In order to drive these points home to the British, and to secure their acceptance of what might be the last chance for an oil settlement, Assistant Secretary of State Byroade initiated discussions with policy makers in London in early January 1953.[67]

As these discussions progressed, it became clear that the British were not favorably disposed to Mossadeq's terms, especially his apparent intention to separate the various terms of the proposals by postponing the negotiation of a long-term sales contract. To the British way of thinking Mossadeq was primarily interested in receiving the DMPA advance and had no intention of ever signing a long-term sales agreement. If the United States thus failed to make the advance contingent on progress toward a sales contract, Mossadeq would have no reason to sign one. He might "be content to live as [a] pensioner" on the advance, an outcome that, according to the British, would only encourage nationalization in other countries. Nor did the British trust Mossadeq not to break a private understanding regarding the ICJ's right to consider the loss of future profits in arbitrating the compensation issue. To guard against these eventualities the British wanted 25 percent of the total DMPA advance to be placed in an escrow account that would cover compensation. They also wanted the terms of reference for the arbitration panel to mention specifically not only the Coal Nationalization Law, which provided for the payment of compensation for the loss of future profits, but also the AIOC's lost "property, rights and interests" in Iran, which clearly implied that the company intended to claim restitution for the loss of future profits. Without legal guarantees of this kind, the British feared, the arbitration panel might not compensate the AIOC fully for its lost concession. These requirements boiled down to the same sort of linkage that British officials had previously sought to insert in the Truman-Churchill proposals. Because the State Department had earlier assented to such linkage, British officials had every reason to believe that it would do so again.[68]

Yet the State Department saw as a mistake the kind of linkage the British advocated. Tying the DMPA advance to the negotiation of a sales contract would doom the new proposals by arousing Mossadeq's suspicions that the

Anglo-Americans were pressuring him into an agreement. Partially to assuage British fears that the advance would decrease Mossadeq's incentive for a settlement, U.S. officials did agree to limit the initial grant to $50 million and to pay the remainder in monthly installments once shipments of oil to the DMPA had begun. But they continued to insist that no strings be attached to the first payment, which they saw as bait to entice Mossadeq toward arbitration. Nor would U.S. officials allow the British to insert in the terms of reference for the arbitration panel a provision allowing it to consider the loss of future profits. Although Mossadeq was willing to permit such compensation, they said, he could do so only informally.[69]

These disagreements, which weeks of discussion in London failed to resolve, highlighted the different ways in which the British and the Americans still approached the oil problem. British officials were primarily concerned with protecting the commercial and economic position of Great Britain and the AIOC and thus insisted on guarantees regarding compensation for the loss of future profits and a long-term sales contract. They were also concerned about the dangerous precedent that might be set if any potential settlement was too favorable to Iran or made nationalization look easy. Other oil-producing nations had to be convinced that Iran had suffered irreparable damage by nationalizing the AIOC and that Iran would not regain its 1950 level of production for many years. Because the British had a financial stake in the outcome of the crisis and were worried about protecting their investments elsewhere, they sought an economically sound and profitable settlement that would limit Iran's gains and thus discourage nationalization in other countries.

U.S. leaders took a different tack, arguing that a "hard boiled business approach" would not work with Mossadeq, who was "highly subjective" and incapable of grasping complicated economic and financial matters. It was therefore best to keep all proposals as simple as possible. It was also best to minimize any pressure on Mossadeq for further concessions. He was already under heavy fire for conducting secret negotiations with Henderson, and British nit-picking over phraseology would only weaken his position by delaying a settlement. If the British were really serious about solving the oil crisis, Acheson told Foreign Secretary Eden, they should demonstrate more flexibility before Mossadeq's domestic pressures forced him to retreat from the concessions he had made on arbitration.[70]

U.S. criticism did push the British toward greater flexibility, and by 14 January Byroade had hammered out the terms of reference for arbitration as well as a draft agreement between the DMPA and the government of Iran. On the positive side as well the Foreign Office agreed to replace the phrase "property, rights and interests" with "enterprise in Iran" in the draft agreement and to remove references to any particular British law from the terms of reference for arbitration. On the negative side the British government insisted on signing the arbitration agreement in its name rather than on behalf of the AIOC. In addition, Whitehall added a number of legal phrases and guarantees to the agreements that Byroade worried would only end up confusing Mossadeq and diminish the likelihood that he would accept the proposals.[71]

When Henderson discussed the Anglo-American proposals with Mossadeq in a seven-hour conversation on 15 January, the prime minister seemed driven by "suspicion, pettiness, and overcaution." He "became emotionally critical of [the] DMPA agreement," "found something wrong with most provisions of [the] arbitration agreement," and "spent hours scribbling and discarding various suggestions for putting them into language acceptable to himself." The result, Henderson said, was a "confused, meaningless mass of disjointed statements." The prime minister repeated his earlier objections to the British government's intention to sign the arbitration agreement on behalf of the AIOC. Because Iran's dispute was with the AIOC, not the British government, he insisted that the company represent itself in the arbitration proceedings. Perhaps more problematic were Mossadeq's objections to two financial provisions of the DMPA contract that had not come up in his earlier discussions with Henderson. Specifically, Mossadeq balked at the idea that the DMPA should receive a 35 percent discount over prevailing Persian Gulf oil prices and that Iran should pay 4.5 percent interest on the amount of the DMPA advance that exceeded quantities of oil delivered. The first requirement amounted to giving oil away, he said, whereas the second constituted usury.

Henderson believed that the prime minister's unyielding attitude stemmed partly from the legal provisions the British had inserted into the agreements at the last moment against his advice. But he also laid part of the blame on Mossadeq himself, who approached "international politics from [the] emotional point of view of an Iranian statesman rather than from the rational view of [a] world statesman" and displayed a "complete lack of chivalry and sense of fair play." Although Henderson was disheartened at Mossadeq's reaction, he hoped that after privately studying the proposals Mossadeq would be able to accept them. Time, after all, was running out: if the agreements were not signed by 19 January, a substantial delay was likely while the incoming Eisenhower administration familiarized itself with the proposals and decided how it wished to proceed.[72]

Mossadeq, however, was less concerned with securing an expeditious agreement than with getting what he wanted. Instead of accepting the Anglo-American proposals as presented by Henderson, he redrafted them in toto. Unwilling to accept the words "enterprise in Iran," Mossadeq suggested "losses" instead. He refused to pay interest on the DMPA advance and was willing to cut it in half to avoid doing so. He also refused to sign a contract with the "Defense Materials Procurement Agency," whose name suggested, at least to him, an affiliation with the Defense Department, or to sell oil at a 35 percent discount. Finally, he tried once again to loosen the ties that bound the DMPA advance to the negotiation of a commercial contract, thereby confirming British suspicions that he was primarily interested in receiving money and had little or no intention of following through with long-term arrangements for the sale of oil.[73]

Initial Anglo-American reaction to Mossadeq's counterproposals was mixed. Washington thought that it could meet the prime minister's objections about the DMPA contract: the U.S. advance could be reduced to $50 million and the General Services Administration could sign the oil contract with Iran. London was not so flexible. It could not agree to waive Iran's negotiation of an oil sales contract as a precondition of receiving U.S. aid or to substitute "losses" for "enterprise in Iran." Without guarantees on the first score, they said, Mossadeq was likely to take the money and run; without assurances on the second it was possible that the ICJ would disallow the AIOC's claims for the loss of future profits. After considerable study the British government concluded that Mossadeq's counterproposals "fundamentally altered the shape and character" of the Anglo-American proposals, that "it was no use trying to meet them," and that "the only course was to stand firm on the proposals" Henderson had presented on 15 January. The State Department agreed, instructing Henderson to inform Mossadeq that his counterproposals were unacceptable and that the original proposals stood.[74]

Henderson did so in a meeting with the prime minister on 19 January that he described as the "most discouraging which I have had with [Mossadeq] thus far." Although Henderson had always found dealing with the prime minister to be a challenge, their last meetings were especially frustrating. Mossadeq, the ambassador reported, seemed to lack the "capacity to carry on complicated negotiations for any length of time in a single direction." He had a tendency "to change his mind, to forget, to become confused . . . to think up new ideas or to fail to state frankly what lurks in his mind." In Henderson's opinion Mossadeq's personal quirks and the pressure he felt from extreme nationalists made him unyielding. As a result, the ambassador lamented, agreement with the British seemed impossible. After his meeting with Mossadeq on 19 January Henderson for the first time expressed doubts about the chances for an agreement. The Truman administration had done its best but had simply run out of time. Perhaps the respite provided by the change in administrations in Washington would yield an acceptable settlement.[75]

In the meantime Mossadeq was moving to reconsolidate his political power. Although dissolution of the Senate had silenced that source of opposition, some critics in the Majlis still remained. To dilute their power Mossadeq on 17 December had proposed a plan for completing elections for the Seventeenth Majlis, which he had suspended in June. This plan called for an increase in the overall size of the Majlis and in the attendance requirements for a quorum, provisions that Mossadeq's critics saw as a means of paralyzing the Majlis and silencing the opposition. Additional disputes between the Majlis and Mossadeq arose over the prime minister's request in early January 1953 for renewed plenary powers, this time for a full year. As earlier, Mossadeq insisted that such extraordinary powers would help him solve the oil question and other pressing matters expeditiously.

Ayatollah Kashani was among the most vocal opponents of extending Mossadeq's powers. In his eyes the proposed bill was "absolutely contrary to the Constitution and in conflict with the interests of the country." Ultimately, 59 of 68 deputies voted for Mossadeq's plenary powers bill, but the struggle for the measure actually weakened Mossadeq's position over the long run by deepening the divide between the prime minister and Kashani that ultimately helped to destroy the National Front. Mossadeq also gave the opposition a powerful weapon—constitutionalism—on which to build its case against his government. In January 1953, however, these liabilities were not yet apparent, and Mossadeq had every reason to consider his domestic situation strong enough to withstand the pressures of dealing with a new U.S. president. U.S. intelligence analysts were not so sure. They believed that Mossadeq's continued inability to resolve the oil crisis was likely to further weaken his political position in the months ahead, creating a dangerous situation that the Tudeh might exploit.[76]

VI

Mossadeq's rejection of the Anglo-American proposals signaled the Truman administration's final failure to resolve the Iranian crisis. The administration's last-minute push for a negotiated settlement constituted the culmination of its evolution from an "honest broker" in the Anglo-Iranian dispute to a full-fledged British partner. After the severance of Anglo-Iranian diplomatic relations in October 1952, in fact, U.S. officials took the lead in seeking a settlement that followed London's blueprint. But here, as elsewhere, the Americans were unable to surmount the individual British and Iranian interests that had precluded a settlement for so long. The new Eisenhower administration, as we will see, ultimately enjoyed more success in Iran but only by adopting a more interventionist approach. Its general policy of cooperating with the British, however, was a carryover from the Truman administration.

chapter 7

The Triumph of Transatlantic Cooperation
THE UNITED STATES AND GREAT BRITAIN JOIN FORCES AGAINST MOSSADEQ

During the first seven months of the Eisenhower administration other developments in Iran took precedence over resolution of the oil crisis. Convinced that the British had no real interest in reaching a settlement that allowed Iran to control its oil industry, Mossadeq closed the door to a negotiated settlement in March and declared that the country would have to make do with small-scale sales of oil to all purchasers, including communist countries. He also tightened his grip on the country in order to combat the economic deterioration and mounting domestic opposition that were sure to follow. The prime minister's drift toward a more authoritarian rule worried the shah and other domestic critics who feared that Mossadeq was leading Iran toward communism.

Officials in London and Washington were also deeply concerned about Iran's stability, especially about Mossadeq's fitness as a leader and his chances for saving the country from a communist takeover. The British, of course, had opposed Mossadeq's premiership for quite some time but had not been able to convince the Truman administration to join them in a plan to overthrow him. They had an easier time with the Eisenhower administration, which was quickly persuaded of the danger that Mossadeq posed to continued Western access to Iran and ideologically amenable to a covert operation against him. This was especially true after the collapse in February of last-minute efforts to reach an oil agreement on terms similar to the Anglo-American proposals of 15 January. Mossadeq's apparent decision to abandon all efforts to reach a settlement with the British and his concurrent willingness to sell oil to the communist bloc pushed U.S. officials to conclude that he was a negative and dangerous force that was leading Iran to disaster. Although U.S. and British policy makers continued to pursue an oil settlement in negotiations with Mossadeq during the spring and summer of 1953, they did so with less enthusiasm than for concurrent efforts to overthrow him.

II

Prospects for resolution of the Anglo-Iranian oil crisis were not good when Dwight D. Eisenhower assumed office on 20 January 1953. As chapter 6 noted, Mossadeq had raised objections to the Anglo-American proposals that Henderson presented on 15 January and offered his own proposal instead. The Anglo-American proposals envisioned a long-term sales contract between the Iranian government and a multinational consortium that included the AIOC and the major U.S. oil companies, as well as significant purchases of Iranian oil by the U.S. government until the consortium got off the ground. In addition, the proposals would empower the ICJ to decide how much compensation the AIOC should receive as a result of Iran's nationalization. The terms of this last provision were drawn broadly enough that the AIOC could claim compensation not only for its physical assets in Iran but also for the future profits it would lose because of the premature termination of its concession.

It was the stipulation regarding compensation for future profits that emerged as the major obstacle to a settlement in the weeks after the Eisenhower administration came to office. As we have seen, Mossadeq would permit the ICJ to consider compensation for future losses. But he would not write a provision to this effect into the ICJ's terms of reference, lest he incur the wrath of the Iranian people and weaken his political position at home. Mossadeq promised instead a private understanding that the ICJ might consider lost profits, but the British considered this promise nonbinding and rejected it out of hand.[1]

With British officials insistent on a specific reference to compensation for the loss of future profits, Ambassador Henderson worried that "a hopeless deadlock" was at hand. For policy makers in the Foreign Office the Anglo-American proposals represented the "furthest limit" of their concessions to Mossadeq. They were a joint Anglo-American offer "in the full sense of the word," said the British. Modifying them to suit Mossadeq's whims would merely encourage the prime minister's intransigence and further delay a settlement. Not mentioned but clearly on their minds was the conviction that further concessions to Mossadeq, especially on the issue of future profits, would not only reward nationalization in Iran but encourage it elsewhere. For this reason, according to the Foreign Office, the British could not yield to Mossadeq "on points of substance." Past concessions had already reduced the British position in Iran "to a small beachhead"; further indulgence would lead to "a full-fledged Dunkirk." In order to protect Britain's position—not only in Iran but throughout the Middle East—the British thought it was imperative that the U.S. government stand firmly with them in an effort "to smoke out the Persians" and force Mossadeq once and for all to come to a settlement.[2]

The 15 January proposals held no sanctity for Secretary of State John Foster Dulles or for others in the new administration in Washington. On the contrary, they seemed to believe that additional British concessions might be necessary, especially on the question of compensation for the loss of future profits. Unless the British adopted a more flexible approach to the question of compensation, U.S. officials argued, the chance for an oil settlement might be lost forever.[3]

As it turned out, discussions between Ambassador Henderson and Prime Minister Mossadeq in late January and early February seemed to confirm Henderson's fears of a hopeless deadlock. Mossadeq appeared to be prepared to be as rigid as the British. He was no longer willing to strike even a private understanding with the British if it gave the ICJ unrestricted license to compensate the AIOC for the loss of future profits. Such an arrangement could not be held in confidence, he said, and would not be acceptable to either the Iranian people or the Majlis. As Ambassador Henderson reported, Mossadeq's advisers had informed him, probably in all seriousness, given what had happened to Razmara, that agreeing to such an arrangement would get him "stoned to death." Instead, Mossadeq now suggested either direct Anglo-Iranian negotiations to determine a lump-sum settlement or adjudication of the issue by the ICJ after the AIOC and the Iranian government had agreed on the "maximum amount" of compensation that might be awarded. Under either alternative, as Mossadeq explained to Henderson, the Iranian government could ensure that compensation was "not too exorbitant," did not exceed its capacity to pay, and did not stretch "indefinitely into [the] future." Mossadeq denied that his suggestions betrayed a new reluctance to reach a settlement with the British. On the contrary, he asserted, a resolution of the oil question "was important not only to Iran but to [the] world."[4]

Henderson naturally agreed that an oil settlement was internationally important, but he warned Mossadeq that restricting the ICJ's authority to determine the amount of compensation, or denying that agency any role at all, was likely to scuttle the negotiations and destroy all chances of such a settlement. The British, after all, had agreed to the Anglo-American proposals only because they permitted the ICJ to fix the amount of compensation and to consider the loss of future profits in setting that amount. Mossadeq had earlier seemed willing to strike a private understanding to this effect with the British. If that was no longer the case, Henderson said, termination of the oil discussions seemed inevitable. In reporting this conversation to the State Department Henderson assigned part of the blame for Mossadeq's change of heart to what he saw as the prime minister's inability to conduct negotiations over a sustained period of time. The ambassador, as we have seen, had made similar statements on previous occasions, arguing that Mossadeq seemed to fatigue easily and was often incapable of dealing with complicated commercial or financial information. He now assumed that Mossadeq had failed earlier to comprehend the AIOC's definition of *compensation*, which included payment for future losses, and that Mossadeq was seeking to correct the error by withdrawing his promise to consider such compensation. The ambassador's assumption was dubious, to say the least. It betrayed a tendency, far too common among the Anglo-Americans, to dismiss their Iranian critics as mentally confused and inferior or to describe them as childish and feminine. Nor did it square with the ambassador's readiness to concede a practical basis for the prime minister's position—namely, Mossadeq's fear that his political position would suffer still another blow if he appeared to compensate the AIOC for future profits.[5]

Whatever its cause, Mossadeq's refusal to consider potentially unlimited compensation for the AIOC's loss of future profits disrupted Anglo-American efforts to resolve the oil dispute. The State Department seemed willing to concede some of Mossadeq's demands, including his proposal for a lump-sum settlement. But the British would hear nothing of it. By proposing a lump-sum settlement, they said, Mossadeq was deliberately avoiding the real issue at hand—whether he would accept the proposals that Henderson had presented on 15 January, including the AIOC's unrestricted right to consider compensation for future profits as well as physical assets. In an effort to improve his domestic position, according to the British, Mossadeq was intentionally changing the basis on which the Anglo-American proposals had been formulated. Meeting his demands would only whet the prime minister's appetite for additional concessions. Instead, the Anglo-Americans should stand firmly behind the proposals that Henderson had hammered out and wait for economic pressures to force concessions from Mossadeq. This was the recommendation coming from policy makers in the Foreign Office, who were certain that Mossadeq's evasiveness would soon convince their counterparts in the Eisenhower administration that the prime minister was "unnegotiable." It was also in keeping with the thrust of British policy throughout the oil crisis, which had been to maintain a firm posture in hopes that economic difficulties would make Mossadeq more malleable.[6]

Additional Anglo-American discussions in early February brought the United States closer to the British position. U.S. officials were still "far from optimistic" that holding firm against Mossadeq would yield a solution to the oil crisis. But as the U.S. embassy in London acknowledged, "The only tactic we have not tried with Mossadeq is sustained firmness," and perhaps such a strategy was now in order. Such thinking had come to permeate all corners of the administration, and just as the Foreign Office had hoped, U.S. officials were rapidly approaching the conclusion that the oil negotiations had reached the decisive stage: the British could not be expected to make further concessions or to delay the inevitable termination of negotiations. In a major change of thinking over its predecessor's the new Eisenhower administration seemed to believe that it was time to place the onus of responsibility for the breakdown of negotiations on Mossadeq by forcing him to reject the Anglo-American proposals outright. This was a better course than allowing the prime minister to blame the Anglo-Americans for the failed negotiations and signaled the administration's ever closer relations with the British regarding Iran.[7]

Accordingly, on 20 February Henderson presented Mossadeq with a final version of the 15 January proposals. Although this version contained some cosmetic alterations, it failed to address Mossadeq's basic objection to the original proposals—the inclusion of an explicit claim for the loss of future profits—and thus assumed the character of an ultimatum, which Mossadeq rejected. There could be no agreement, the prime minister lamented to Henderson, so long as the British continued to insist on potentially unlimited compensation for the loss of future profits. Mossadeq agreed to consult his advisers before rendering a final verdict on the revised proposals, but he was sure that his colleagues would agree with his conclusion.[8]

Consultation with his advisers confirmed Mossadeq's judgment that the proposals would have to be rejected, but even then he delayed an official announcement, probably in order to use public hopes for a settlement as a means of improving his political position. As Ambassador Henderson reported, Mossadeq hoped to eliminate his political rivals, who were by now numerous, before rejecting the Anglo-American proposals. Although the Majlis had extended Mossadeq's plenary economic and financial powers through February 1954, his increasingly authoritarian stance had cost him the backing of Ayatollah Kashani and other former supporters and had split the National Front. By this time, moreover, Mossadeq was in open conflict with the shah. He sought to usurp the monarch's powers over the armed forces, the distribution of crown lands, and the revenues obtained from the Meshed Shrine in northeastern Iran. He also tried to end the shah's "unfriendly attitude" toward the government, an attitude that was evident in what the prime minister rightly believed were British-inspired court intrigues against his government and in recent court-sponsored uprisings among Bakhtiari tribesmen in southern Iran.

Unless the shah surrendered his royal prerogatives and ceased his antigovernment activities, Mossadeq vowed to resign on 24 February and to make the reasons for his resignation public. Although the shah was obviously reluctant to allow Mossadeq "to reduce [him] to [a] state of servile dependence . . . and at [the] same time publicly to humiliate him," he was also fearful of a popular outcry against Mossadeq's resignation. As a result, the shah agreed to cease contact with military figures and opponents of the government. He refused, however, to halt the distribution of the crown lands, which he said was his sovereign right as monarch.[9]

In the meantime British and U.S. officials seemed to have abandoned all hope of reaching a negotiated oil settlement with Mossadeq. They were now actively "looking for alternatives," in the words of Foreign Secretary Eden.[10] The British, of course, had long believed that Mossadeq had to go but had been unable to sway the Truman administration. To be sure, Truman and his advisers had been concerned for Iran's security. But an aversion to covert operations and prior commitments in Western Europe and Korea had prevented them from acquiescing in British plans to topple Mossadeq.

The Eisenhower administration proved more receptive to these plans. According to Mark J. Gasiorowski, who has studied the Anglo-American effort to remove Mossadeq, the administration agreed in principle on 3 February to support a British scheme to overthrow the Iranian prime minister.[11] U.S. officials justified their decision as necessary to save Iran from communist domination, interpreting recent developments as further proof that the country was headed in that direction. As they saw it, for example, Mossadeq's assault against the shah had created a power vacuum that could only benefit the communists, tribal discontent among the Bakhtiaris and the

Qashqais threatened a civil war that would weaken the central state and leave it vulnerable to Soviet domination, and the communist Tudeh Party had become increasingly active, apparently with Mossadeq's sanction. In addition, the Eisenhower administration did not face the same constraints that had often handicapped its predecessor. The U.S. commitment to Western European recovery was winding down, spending for the war in Korea had leveled off, and the war would soon be over. Under these circumstances the new administration had room to maneuver. It also saw covert operations as an inexpensive and relatively risk-free way of attaining its foreign policy goals throughout the developing world. In its mind, moreover, a covert operation against Mossadeq offered certain advantages: it would allow the administration to score an early foreign policy success, signal the world that the United States would do whatever it could to prevent the spread of communism, and guarantee continued Western access to Iran's valuable oil fields.[12]

By early February, then, even before Henderson had presented Mossadeq with his final proposals, the U.S. and British governments had become committed to undermining the prime minister's government and to removing him from office. Perhaps this commitment lessened their willingness to make additional concessions to Mossadeq; no doubt it steeled their determination to make the 20 February proposals their final offer. It is even possible that the revised Anglo-American proposals were presented as a smokescreen for the Anglo-American plans to overthrow Mossadeq, which were just beginning to solidify. U.S. officials clearly assumed that by rejecting those proposals, Mossadeq would dim the last prospects for an oil settlement, further damage his position with the Iranian people, and pave the way for Anglo-American action against him.[13]

A hint of what was to come for the prime minister occurred at the end of February, following the shah's announcement that he intended to leave the country. Although the shah and his courtiers claimed, then and later, that Mossadeq had demanded the shah's departure, recent scholarship supports Mossadeq's assertion that the decision originated with the shah.[14] It soon became clear that the shah's supposed trip was part of a concerted plan against the government, if not against the prime minister's life. After joining other government officials in a farewell ceremony at the shah's palace on 28 February, Mossadeq was summoned to an important impromptu meeting with Ambassador Henderson and was forced to leave the palace before the shah's scheduled departure. Upon approaching the main palace gate, however, the prime minister heard the rumblings of an angry crowd on the other side, including calls for his death. With the assistance of one of the shah's guards Mossadeq departed the palace grounds through another gate, successfully eluded the enraged mob, and fled to his nearby home. The crowd gave chase, but the iron gates surrounding Mossadeq's residence kept it at bay long enough for the prime minister to arrange another escape, this time to army headquarters and then to the Majlis building, where he related the assassination attempt to a closed session of the legislature.[15]

The picture the prime minister painted for the Majlis was of a far-flung antigovernment conspiracy that extended even to the U.S. embassy. Mossadeq first implicated the shah, who had supposedly engineered the episode by threatening to go abroad and by leaking his plans to Kashani and others, who then incited the anti-Mossadeq crowd by accusing the prime minister of driving the shah from the country. The prime minister next accused members of the Retired Officers' Association, including future prime minister Fazlollah Zahedi and other high-ranking current and former army officers, of either direct participation in the uprising or of supporting it indirectly by failing to take action against the rioters. Finally, Mossadeq fingered U.S. Ambassador Loy Henderson, whose supposedly urgent need to see the prime minister had almost delivered him to the angry throng outside the shah's palace. The prime minister was especially vehement about Henderson's culpability, saying that when he finally reached the ambassador, he learned that Henderson had summoned him for a trivial and unimportant matter. Although Mossadeq did not immediately make his charges public, he threatened to resign and to reveal his account of the incident unless the Majlis asked him to remain in office. Unwilling to see Mossadeq open a scandal involving the shah, the court, and the military, the Majlis complied by reiterating its 6 January vote of confidence in the prime minister.[16]

For the next several weeks Mossadeq's preoccupation with domestic matters prevented him from seriously considering the modified Anglo-American oil proposals of 20 February.[17] He personally ordered the arrest of the ringleaders of the 28 February episode; appointed a loyal supporter, Taqi Riyahi, as army chief of staff; and thwarted several efforts by speaker of the Majlis Kashani to decrease the government's power over the legislature.

Mossadeq was also busy reporting to an eight-man committee of Majlis deputies that was charged with settling the prime minister's outstanding differences with the shah. The committee's report, presented to the Majlis on 12 March, supported Mossadeq's contention that the shah should reign, not rule, by which it meant that the prime minister and his cabinet, not the shah, had sole responsibility over the country's civil and military matters. Although opposition deputies blocked its ratification by the Majlis, the report was a clear victory for Mossadeq. By mid-March the prime minister appeared to have recovered much of his political clout: he had silenced the shah and his other domestic critics at least temporarily and was working to reconsolidate his support among the Iranian masses. He was still concerned about Iran's economic situation, though, and increasingly convinced that U.S. assistance was the only way to stave off the country's collapse in the absence of an oil settlement with Great Britain.[18]

In a desperate effort to raise revenue that only fueled U.S. fears that he was heading toward communism, Mossadeq again sought U.S. purchases of Iranian oil. When asked how the United States could justify such purchases in the absence of an Iranian settlement with Great Britain, Mossadeq said that the purchases would help "to prevent Iran from becoming Communist." If the U.S. government refused to buy Iranian oil, according to the prime minister, he would have to sell it at any price to all buyers—even to countries behind the iron curtain. In truth, the staunchly anticommunist Mossadeq had no intention of selling oil to Soviet bloc nations. But threats to do so had worked to good advantage in the past. They had pushed the Truman administration, for example, into waiving restrictions regarding the dispersal of U.S. military aid in early 1952, and the prime minister had every reason to believe that they would work again. What he did not know was that Anglo-American officials saw these threats as justification for their plans against his government. Although the Eisenhower administration continued to search for an oil settlement throughout the spring of 1953, it had already abandoned the hope of reaching any settlement with Mossadeq and was determined to join the British in a plot to topple his government. Mossadeq's own words and apparent drift toward communism only strengthened their resolve.[19]

III

Mossadeq publicly rejected the most recent Anglo-American oil proposals in an address to the Iranian people on 20 March 1953 that contained no surprises. It reiterated his determination to set some limits on the amount of compensation to the AIOC, because any other course would surrender the Iranian oil industry to Great Britain and thereby defeat "the purpose of nationalization." From Mossadeq's point of view the address did not necessarily close the door to negotiations with the British government; he was still willing to talk directly to the British in order to determine the amount of compensation or to submit the question to arbitration by the ICJ after both sides had stated their maximum claims.

As noted earlier, however, the British had already rejected these terms. The Anglo-American proposals were fair and equitable, they repeated, and represented the limit of their concessions. The prime minister's speech, in their opinion, "placed [a] fallacious interpretation on both [the] letter and [the] spirit" of the Anglo-American proposals, especially concerning the question of compensation. Surrendering to Mossadeq on this point would endanger British commercial interests the world over and call into question the authority of the ICJ as an international mediator. For Whitehall the only course of action was to stand firm on the revised Anglo-American proposals and wait for Mossadeq to give in. This was the official position of the British government. But unofficially, as we have seen, British policy makers had exhausted their patience with Mossadeq and were laying plans to topple his government.[20]

Much the same can be said of the Eisenhower administration. U.S. officials supported the British decision to hold firm on the revised Anglo-American proposals. They affirmed the fairness of these proposals and were willing to back their conviction with tough talk to Mossadeq. This was good news for British officials, who believed that the Eisenhower administration was more sympathetic to Britain's position vis-à-vis Mossadeq than its predecessor. In keeping with its new firmer posture the State Department remained unwilling to purchase Iranian oil in the absence of an Anglo-Iranian settlement, in this way continuing to support the British-led boycott that was taking a severe toll on the Iranian economy. The State Department also ignored Mossadeq's pleas for budgetary assistance and other forms of aid to forestall a collapse of the Iranian economy. Such assistance could not be justified, the department repeatedly told the prime minister, when Iran could secure substantial revenues merely by reaching an agreement on compensation with the British. What the department did not say was that the U.S. government, like the British government, was now committed in principle to Mossadeq's ouster and was already working on a plan "for some alternative to [him]." U.S. policy makers were thus in no mood to make concessions on the revised Anglo-American proposals or to bolster the Iranian government with additional aid. On the contrary, the sketchy evidence available suggests that both the British and U.S. governments were busy adding to the economic and political troubles that confronted Mossadeq.[21]

These troubles were considerable. To be sure, the Iranian government had previously negotiated oil sales with Italian and Japanese firms, and these sales had been upheld by courts in Venice and Tokyo. But they failed to break the international boycott by generating significant revenues or long-term contracts. And with world oil production outstripping demand, extended contracts were unlikely in the near future, even though Iran was now offering its oil at less than half the world price. By April, according to the U.S. embassy in Tehran, Iran had "psychologically entered a new economic era, characterized by general acceptance of the fact that no oil settlement is in prospect." If Iranians accepted this fact, however, they were not reconciled to the hardships that accompanied the deterioration of their economy. Inflationary pressures generated by the government's still secret issuance of 3.1 billion rials in the autumn of 1952 were inciting workers across the country to strike for higher wages. Unless the government did something soon to stabilize prices and improve the standard of living for working-class Iranians, the embassy predicted increased work stoppages and eventual economic collapse.[22]

Political as well as economic factors were now working against Mossadeq. In April opponents of the government made another attempt to bring down the government, this time by kidnapping key officials in order to create chaos throughout the country and thereby force Mossadeq's resignation. Because all the information about the plot has yet to come to light, determining a complete list of intended victims or alleged conspirators is impossible. Early discovery of the plot by the Iranian government prevented its full implementation; the conspirators abducted only one official—chief of police Mahmud Afshartus. And when their plot began to unravel, they murdered Afshartus in order to keep him from identifying members of the conspiracy, who were thought to include Mozaffar Baqai, Husain Khatibi, Mostafa Kashani (the ayatollah's son), and other prominent members of the opposition. Recent scholarship has also implicated the shah in this conspiracy, along with other members of the royal family and high-ranking military officers, including Fazlollah Zahedi. The British intelligence organization MI-6 and the U.S. Central Intelligence Agency (CIA) were almost certainly involved as well, although details of their involvement remain classified. The murder of Afshartus and the antigovernment plot were serious blows to Mossadeq's regime that contributed to the National Front's declining morale and decaying fortunes. They also highlighted the growing strength, determination, and ruthlessness of the anti-Mossadeq forces in Iran and signaled as well that the conspiracy against the prime minister now included the U.S. and British governments.[23]

Making matters worse for Mossadeq, the April conspiracy was only the most dramatic evidence of the pervasive political instability that wracked Iran in the months following the incident of 28 February. By late spring the Majlis had become divided between Mossadeq's supporters and his opponents. It usually lacked a quorum, because opposition deputies refused to attend. And when they were present, the deputies spent most of their time debating the merits of the government rather than conducting constructive business. Opposition deputies accused the government of beating suspects in the Afshartus murder in order to extract confessions. They also charged the government with trying to eliminate the shah by seeking ratification of the Committee of Eight report. They even resorted to "guerrilla tactics" that led to periodic fistfights on the floor of the Majlis and within its chambers. Violence often spilled out into the streets of Tehran, where Mossadeq's supporters and detractors clashed regularly. The Tudeh Party was invariably involved in these confrontations on the side of the government, which further fueled Anglo-American suspicions that a tacit alliance between the party and Mossadeq was delivering Iran into Soviet hands.[24]

If Iran's mounting economic and political problems troubled U.S. officials, they also troubled Mossadeq, whose attempt to deal with them only added to Washington's mounting suspicion of his government. To forestall economic disaster Mossadeq made a final desperate bid for U.S. economic and financial assistance. In several meetings with Ambassador Henderson in May the prime minister asserted that without such aid his government would be overthrown and Iran would cease to be an independent country. Given the country's strategic value in the cold war, he cautioned, a lack of U.S. aid might even turn Iran into "a second Korea." He asked the ambassador to convey Iran's serious economic and political problems to Secretary of State Dulles, who spent May touring the Middle East with Mutual Security Director Harold E. Stassen. Because the administration was determined to do nothing that might bolster Mossadeq's political position and was in fact working to overthrow him, Dulles had excluded Iran from his itinerary, which included virtually every other nation in the region.

The State Department probably hoped that such an obvious snub would discredit the prime minister with the Iranian people, who had been led to believe that Mossadeq enjoyed the best of relations with Washington. Ambassador Henderson met with Secretary Dulles in Karachi on 24 May. Despite the prime minister's oblique warning that without economic aid Iran might lose its independence to the communists, Henderson and Dulles decided to reject Mossadeq's appeal, perhaps because they were now firmly committed to the Anglo-American plan to topple Mossadeq's government. On the following day Henderson conveyed the rejection of economic aid to the prime minister, adding that the only solution to Iran's problems lay in a resolution of the oil dispute.[25]

Mossadeq was disappointed by Dulles's response but not deterred in his search for U.S. aid. Unaware of the Anglo-American plot being hatched against him, the prime minister decided to appeal directly to President Eisenhower. On 28 May he sent a written message to the president through Ambassador Henderson, who was returning to Washington for consultations with the State Department. The message warned again of Iran's imminent collapse and lamented that the new administration in Washington had failed to be more sympathetic to Iran's plight. It also referred several times to the "serious consequences" that would result from a failure to address Iran's economic problems, consequences that presumably included a communist takeover of the country. "If prompt and effective aid is not given [to] this country now," Mossadeq warned, "any steps that might be taken tomorrow to compensate for the negligence of today might well be too late." Sounding very much like an ultimatum, the prime minister's message sought to exploit U.S. fears of a communist coup in Tehran in order to enlist Washington's aid on behalf of Iran's imperiled economy.[26]

U.S. policy makers interpreted Mossadeq's message as a transparent attempt at blackmail and ignored it for almost a month. When President Eisenhower did reply on 29 June, he reaffirmed earlier U.S. pronouncements that neither large-scale economic grants nor U.S. purchases of Iranian oil were possible so long as Iran refused to settle the oil crisis through international arbitration and to compensate the AIOC for more than its physical assets. Eisenhower went on to note his distress at the "present dangerous situation in Iran" and to express his hope that Mossadeq's government would "take such steps as are in its power to prevent further deterioration of that situation . . . before it is too late."[27]

In retrospect, of course, it now is clear that it already was too late for Mossadeq. Eisenhower; Secretary of State Dulles; his brother, CIA director Allen W. Dulles; and other high-ranking officials had decided that Mossadeq's ouster was the only way to "prevent further deterioration" in Iran. Even Ambassador Henderson was now forced to acknowledge that "nothing whatever was to be hoped for from [him]" and that Mossadeq would therefore have to be replaced if Iran was to be saved from communism.[28]

Indeed, contrary to Iranian hopes that Henderson's return to Washington in early June would result in an offer of a lump-sum compensation agreement, the ambassador had actually been recalled in order to participate in final planning for Mossadeq's removal. By that time, of course, transatlantic talks on this subject had gone on for several months. They had led to Anglo-American involvement in the abortive April conspiracy, if not the failed coup d'état of late February. When the April plot collapsed, British and U.S. policy makers decided to join with Iranian opposition elements in planning still another coup against Mossadeq's government. Kermit Roosevelt, a CIA operative who had worked in the Office of Strategic Services during World War II, headed the Anglo-American effort in Iran. A grandson of Theodore Roosevelt and a cousin of FDR, the younger Roosevelt was quiet and retiring, "the last person you would expect to be up to his neck in dirty tricks," according to Kim Philby, the British agent who later defected to the Soviet Union.[29] These attributes, of course, made Roosevelt an excellent candidate for espionage work. He had worked in Iran during World War II and was acquainted with a number of prominent Iranians, including the shah. Assisting him on location in Iran would be other CIA agents, members of MI-6, and Iranian dissidents in the employ of the U.S. or British governments.[30]

Official U.S. approval of the plan for a coup d'état came in a meeting at the State Department on 25 June. Restricted access to the written minutes of this meeting, as well as to other documents, make it impossible to determine precisely what transpired. Indeed, limited access to most U.S. documents on the subject prevents a full and complete assessment of the U.S. and British roles in overthrowing Mossadeq. There can be no doubt of U.S. and British involvement, however, or of the underlying reasons for that involvement, which included the collapse of the oil negotiations and the mounting economic and political instability in Iran. The United States believed that these developments ran the risk of putting Iran's oil resources into the hands of the Soviet Union, thereby adding to its economic and military strength, and of clearing a path for Soviet expansion through the Persian Gulf to the strategically important and oil-rich Middle East. Mossadeq's regime was thus a serious threat to Western security and had to be eliminated. As Ambassador Henderson reportedly asserted at the 25 June meeting, Mossadeq was "a madman who would ally himself with the Russians. We have no choice but to proceed with this undertaking. May God grant us success."[31]

Ironically, Mossadeq had recognized the overriding importance that officials in Washington placed on security concerns, as is evident in his efforts to win U.S. aid by raising the danger of communist expansion into Iran. But unfortunately, as we have seen, his warnings only confirmed Anglo-American suspicions and sealed the prime minister's fate. Secretary of State Dulles probably spoke for the entire administration when he acknowledged that although a "wily oriental" like Mossadeq might only be "trying to blackmail [the West] by using the Communist bogy [sic]," the U.S. government could take no chances and had to be prepared to move against the prime minister just in case he was serious.[32]

While U.S. and British officials were plotting the demise of Mossadeq's government, forces in Iran were conspiring toward the same end. Although Mossadeq prevented Ayatollah Kashani's reelection as speaker of the Majlis on 1 July, this proved little more than a Pyrrhic victory. With opposition deputies determined to obstruct the government at every turn Mossadeq's chances of controlling the Majlis in the future still looked grim. Only thirty deputies were unconditionally behind the government, whereas another twenty or so claimed independent status but usually backed Mossadeq. Twenty-five others, or roughly one-third of the Majlis—enough to prevent a quorum and block passage of government-sponsored legislation—were working tirelessly for the prime minister's defeat. Already Mossadeq was losing ground. On 9 July the Majlis elected his former ally and now bitter enemy Hossein Makki to the supervisory board of the Bank Melli, which controlled the note reserve of the government. In this powerful position Makki was likely to learn of the secret issuance of 3.1 billion rials in the autumn of 1952 and to make this information public, thereby weakening the government by calling into question its ability to manage the country's economy.[33]

Adding to Mossadeq's troubles was the concurrent revelation that Eisenhower had refused the request for economic assistance. Because Mossadeq had often claimed U.S. support for his policies, including a willingness by U.S. leaders to provide Iran with substantial aid, he had tried to keep the president's rebuff a secret. In early July, however, after word of his recent exchange with Eisenhower had been leaked in Tehran, Mossadeq was forced to release both his letter of 28 May and Eisenhower's response. The revelation dealt a serious blow to the prime minister's prestige. Workers who had seen U.S. aid as a means of improving their sorry living conditions now demonstrated openly against Mossadeq, and opposition elements in the Majlis launched new attacks against the government, including a motion of censure over the alleged mistreatment of suspects in the Afshartus case.[34]

To counter this mounting resistance within the Majlis, which could lead only to a vote of no confidence in the government, Mossadeq decided to dissolve the legislature. This was a difficult decision for a prime minister who had dedicated his life to expanding the powers of the Majlis and to making it more responsive to the Iranian people. But now that his opponents were threatening to use the Majlis to bring down the government— and by extension the popular movement against Great Britain—Mossadeq came to see dissolution as the only way to guard the Iranian people against an eternity of "imperialist domination."[35]

Having resigned himself to dissolution, Mossadeq then set about formulating a plan to bring it about. This would not be easy, because the constitution of 1949 gave the shah sole authority to dissolve the Majlis. But with the shah unlikely to accept Mossadeq's demand for dissolution the prime minister would have to circumvent the monarch by appealing directly to the Iranian people. Accordingly, he devised a two-part plan that aimed to force the shah's compliance by presenting him with the fait accompli of an already dissolved Majlis. First, Mossadeq asked his supporters in that body to resign in order to deprive it of a quorum. On 14 July twenty-eight deputies surrendered their seats; by 28 July twenty-six others had followed suit, many of them convinced that doing so was the only way to guarantee their reelection to the next legislature. With only the twenty-five hard-core opposition deputies remaining the Majlis ceased to function the following day. At that point Mossadeq moved to the second stage of his plan—a public referendum to determine the fate not only of the Majlis but of the government as well. A vote to dissolve the Majlis and initiate elections for a new one, Mossadeq declared, would be a vote for the government and give his regime a popular mandate. A vote against the measure would demonstrate public dissatisfaction with the regime and lead to his resignation.[36]

Mossadeq's decision to appeal directly to the people was consistent with his long-standing belief that the public should have a say in its governance. But the way in which the prime minister carried out the referendum belied his faith in the democratic process and highlighted his increasingly authoritarian character. Instead of being conducted, like most Iranian elections, over a long period of time in order to give residents of outlying rural areas a chance to vote, the referendum lasted only a few hours and was held only in the cities, where the government's position was strongest. Instead of being conducted by secret ballot, moreover, separate polling places were erected for yeas and nays, with the government keeping individual voting records. Given these restrictive and blatantly progovernment conditions, the outcome of the referendum was a foregone conclusion, as 99.9 percent of those voting on 3 August supported Mossadeq's decision to terminate the Majlis.[37]

The prime minister's opponents immediately attacked the referendum as an undemocratic and unlawful affront to the constitution. On a procedural level they denounced the government's use of segregated polling places, an unprecedented step even in Iran, where free elections had never been the norm. On a constitutional level they condemned the prime minister's illegal attempt to allow the Iranian people to pass judgment on a question that fell exclusively within the purview of the shah. Because the referendum was illegal, they said, the results meant nothing.

This was the shah's position as well. He refused to bow to the prime minister's call for an official *firman* dissolving the Majlis and authorizing new elections, even after Mossadeq delivered a nationwide radio address on 12 August calling upon the shah to heed "popular wishes."[38] Instead, the shah and other opponents of the prime minister derided the referendum as concrete proof that Mossadeq was determined to overturn the constitution and make himself dictator of Iran. They charged the prime minister with destroying the Senate and robbing the shah of his royal prerogatives, such as nominal control over the armed forces. Now Mossadeq was trying to eliminate the Majlis, the only remaining source of opposition to the government except the press. The referendum handed Mossadeq's opponents the vehicle they had been waiting for to discredit his government. They could now claim that ousting the prime minister was the only way to preserve the Iranian constitution, and they could count on substantial U.S. support for their efforts.[39]

Indeed, policy makers in Washington had watched Iran's economic and political deterioration with growing trepidation. The country's worsening economy, which had always given them cause for alarm, now seemed locked on a downward spiral that would lead inevitably to the kind of environment in which communism flourished. U.S. officials were also concerned about Iran's unstable political situation. They too believed that Mossadeq was trying to eliminate all rival political forces in Iran and to create a dictatorship that left him unchallenged and in complete control. According to Ambassador Henderson, this was Mossadeq's usual course of action when frustrated. Over the course of his premiership he had "thrown out [the] British, . . . emasculated [the] Majlis, . . . eliminated [the] Senate," and "deposed all [of the country's] prominent civilian and military officials."

In the process, as Henderson and other U.S. officials believed, Mossadeq had alienated legitimate sources of authority and become increasingly dependent on the Tudeh Party for moral support. Party members had participated in a massive demonstration to commemorate the first anniversary of Mossadeq's return to office on 21 July, rivaling the prime minister's National Front supporters in both numbers and discipline. In the words of the U.S. chargé d'affaires in Tehran, Gordon H. Mattison, the prime minister was "making a careful play for Tudeh support," the probable results of which were "too obvious to need elaboration." As the situation continued to degenerate, he and other U.S. officials feared, mass demonstrations against the government would grow into a full-scale revolution, Western influence in Iran would come to an end, and the country would be delivered into the hands of the Soviet Union. The shah agreed, asserting that Mossadeq's alliance with the Tudeh would turn him into "the Dr. Benes of Iran."[40]

It was to keep Iran from going the way of Czechoslovakia that the Eisenhower administration had earlier decided to remove Mossadeq from office. By early August it had decided that Fazlollah Zahedi would succeed Mossadeq, despite London's initial objections to the general's anti-British activities during World War II and the shah's uncertainties about his trustworthiness. U.S. policy makers saw Zahedi as the only figure in Iran strong enough to challenge Mossadeq and win. U.S. officials also secured the shah's support for the coup d'état against Mossadeq. This was not an easy task and took longer than expected. After the failed efforts in February and April to remove Mossadeq from office, the shah was no doubt reluctant to participate in any operation that was not supported completely by the British and U.S. governments. Both the shah's twin sister Princess Ashraf and General H. Norman Schwarzkopf Sr., who commanded the Iranian gendarmerie from 1942 to 1948, had tried and failed to win the monarch's support for another covert operation against the prime minister. It was only in early August, after meeting with Kermit Roosevelt and being assured of full Anglo-American backing, that the shah agreed to go along.[41]

Other scholars have described the subsequent coup d'état in some detail, so a thorough examination need not detain us here. Besides, illuminating the situation is not possible without the release of additional documentation, which is unlikely to occur in the near future. Suffice it to say that after three days of tense fighting in Tehran that resulted in at least three hundred deaths and many more injuries, the anti-Mossadeq forces triumphed, ousted the prime minister on 19 August, and installed Zahedi in his place. The shah, who had fled Tehran before the coup got under way, returned to cheering crowds three days later. Mossadeq and his remaining close advisers were arrested and charged with treason. The members of other political groups, such as the Tudeh, were also rounded up as part of a general effort by the shah and the new government to silence political opposition.[42]

The U.S. contribution to what Iranians call the 28 Mordad coup was substantial, even decisive. Kermit Roosevelt held the operation together after several early setbacks threatened failure. U.S. money helped to produce both the "Tudeh" mobs that marched through the streets of Tehran on 17 and 18 August, prompting fears of an imminent communist takeover, and the pro-shah mobs that took their place on 19 August. Ambassador Henderson engineered a critical break between Mossadeq and the Tudeh by demanding that Mossadeq order the police to protect U.S. citizens and property from the marauding mobs. By acquiescing in Henderson's demand and ordering action against the Tudeh demonstrations Mossadeq alienated the party, prevented it from effectively opposing the pro-shah forces, and guaranteed the success of what Anthony Eden later called the "royalist *coup d'etat*." Following the coup, moreover, the United States promptly offered the new government an emergency package of economic aid, presumably to bolster it against potential opponents and to entice it into negotiating an acceptable oil agreement with the British.[43]

IV

By the time Eisenhower assumed the presidency on 20 January Iran's economic and political conditions had disintegrated almost to the point of collapse. Prime Minister Mossadeq had abandoned hope of reaching a negotiated oil settlement with the British and sought instead to base the country's economy on nonoil exports and small-scale oil sales to all purchasers, even Soviet bloc nations. Because these measures were sure to bring serious economic hardship to Iran and fuel the fires of dissent throughout the country, Mossadeq accompanied them with a campaign of suppression that some observers viewed as tantamount to authoritarian rule and a subversion of the Iranian constitution.

These trends worried the new Eisenhower administration in Washington, especially Mossadeq's apparent flirtation with communism and his drift toward authoritarianism. To be sure, Republican policy makers were just as concerned about Iran's deteriorating economic situation as their Democratic predecessors had been. But Iran's economy had been in bad shape for some time, and most officials in Washington were still inclined to accept British assertions that collapse was a long way off.

What troubled U.S. officials more was the possibility that Mossadeq might sell oil to Soviet bloc nations or scuttle democratic governance and ally himself with the Tudeh Party in order to remain in office. These were possibilities that the Eisenhower administration could not countenance, and top U.S. officials became increasingly convinced that Mossadeq was leading Iran to disaster. To prevent such a development the Eisenhower administration was amenable to a course of action long favored by the British but consistently rejected by its predecessor: Anglo-American covert action to replace Mossadeq with a prime minister who was willing to allow Western control of Iran's oil industry. Although U.S. officials publicly professed their interest in a negotiated settlement to the Anglo-Iranian oil dispute, these pronouncements masked a private commitment to join the British in a covert operation against Mossadeq. Protecting U.S. national security was the administration's overriding concern, and it had no qualms about intriguing against Iran's government if such action served the larger interest of U.S. national security. In fact, the successful covert operation against Mossadeq served as a model for subsequent operations—some successful, some not—in Guatemala, Egypt, Syria, Indonesia, and Cuba.[44]

Despite the important role played by the United States, it is essential to remember that the coup would have been impossible without significant opposition to Mossadeq within Iran. The prime minister's drift toward authoritarianism alienated many of his supporters. In addition, Mossadeq's inability to make the nationalized oil industry profitable had weakened his support among the Iranian masses, who could ill afford the economic hardships that were certain to accompany his continuing tenure as prime minister. These two developments created a vicious circle: decreased popular support inspired Mossadeq's drift toward authoritarianism, which in turn further weakened his popular support. Mossadeq's nationalistic crusade against the AIOC, which had so inspired Iranians during 1950 and early 1951, ultimately generated demands that it could not satisfy.

When this became clear, Mossadeq was toppled from his place as the head of the Iranian government by a coalition of domestic dissidents working in partnership with covert operatives within the British and U.S. governments. His removal from office drove the remnants of the National Front underground, where it continued to work for Iranian independence from foreign influence. For all intents and purposes, however, Mossadeq's effort to drive the AIOC from Iran had received a major setback. By the autumn of 1954 Zahedi's government had effectively reversed nationalization and cleared the way for the reappearance of Iranian oil on world markets. In this way the immediate legacy of the 28 Mordad coup was a new oil agreement that allowed the British and other Western interests to regain control of Iran's petroleum, something Mossadeq would never have permitted.

chapter 8

The "Miraculous Second Chance"
THE CREATION OF THE IRANIAN OIL CONSORTIUM

Ousting Mossadeq did not remove all the obstacles to a resolution of the Anglo-Iranian oil dispute. The Zahedi government still needed time to consolidate its position and to convince the Iranian people that some degree of foreign involvement would be necessary if Iranian oil was to reenter world markets. In addition, the British had to persuade the Iranian government to accept a settlement that allowed the AIOC to return to Iran as a major shareholder in an international consortium of companies. The U.S. government had to convince the major U.S. companies to enter the Iranian oil industry and then make their participation legal by skirting the antitrust laws. Finally, the international consortium, once organized, had to reach agreement with the Iranian government for the renewed production and marketing of Iranian oil. By the autumn of 1954 progress along all these fronts had allowed Iranian oil to again make its way onto world markets.

The consortium that replaced the AIOC in Iran was more a product of U.S. thinking than anything else. It reflected the commercial concerns of the U.S. oil companies and the strategic concerns of the U.S. government. By skirting domestic antitrust laws to allow the majors to enter the new consortium, the agreement revealed the willingness of U.S. officials to subordinate other issues to national security.

It also increased the U.S. stake in Iran's affairs and kept that country and its resources within the U.S. rather than the Soviet orbit. In this sense the final settlement was a major Anglo-American victory. It held fewer advantages for the Iranians, of course, and surely contributed over the long term to the anti-Western sentiment that exploded in Iran twenty-five years later.

II

Zahedi's government faced tremendous economic obstacles when it assumed office on 20 August 1953. The thirty-month oil crisis had drained Iran's treasury and destroyed its economy. During its final months in office Mossadeq's regime had racked up a substantial debt to the Bank Melli, which now lacked sufficient supplies of both rials and foreign currencies. In addition to liquidating this debt and improving the nation's balance of payments Zahedi had to find the resources to pay government employees, reimburse private contractors and suppliers, and secure the international credit that Iran needed to import sugar and other crucial commodities. He also had to improve conditions generally for the Iranian people, whose economic troubles had mounted during Mossadeq's last months in office. Housing for the urban poor was inadequate, working-class wages had failed to keep pace with inflation, and the nation's transportation, education, and health care systems were outdated and woefully inadequate.[1]

The government's political troubles were also substantial. The Tudeh remained a formidable foe, despite its humiliating defeat in the 28 Mordad coup. Although the new government was determined from the outset to crush the movement completely, it knew that this goal could be accomplished only by eliminating the economic conditions that drove people to support the Tudeh in the first place. In the meantime the government initiated a concerted campaign of repression designed to deprive the Tudeh of its leadership and decimate its membership. What remained of the National Front was an even bigger worry. Many of Mossadeq's strongest supporters seized every opportunity to assail the new government. Moreover, the general population still strongly supported Mossadeq's nationalist goals— "freedom from foreign political influence and economic exploitation"— and doubted that Zahedi would uphold them. Clearly, the government faced an uphill battle in silencing opposition groups and rerouting public support from the National Front to itself.[2]

To improve the nation's sagging economic situation and bolster his own political position Zahedi set out to show the Iranian people that he had something to offer them. With emergency aid from the United States worth approximately $45 million the prime minister initiated new housing developments in the slums of Tehran and began modernizing the Iranian road system. He also laid plans, in the hope of future aid from the Export-Import Bank and other lending agencies, to improve Iran's health care system and correct other social problems.[3]

As Zahedi understood, however, emergency assistance from the United States could not last forever, whereas aid from international agencies took months to arrange and could not be used to support the government's day-to-day expenses.[4] Iran's economic prosperity, and indeed Zahedi's political fortunes, depended on revenue from the sale of the country's oil in international markets, which depended in turn on a successful resolution of the oil crisis. When the new government assumed office, popular opinion still supported Mossadeq's position that an oil-less economy was preferable to foreign control of the oil industry. As the seriousness of Iran's economic plight became clear, however, more and more people concluded that only an oil settlement that allowed for some foreign involvement could save Iran from economic collapse.[5] This was where Zahedi's government might offer some hope. The prime minister and his advisers lacked Mossadeq's nationalist credentials, but in their minds they had something of potentially equal value: close ties to the Western powers, especially the United States, and the promise that those ties would lead to an oil settlement and other financial rewards. With the Iranian economy near collapse the lure of such assistance was strong and probably accounts in part for the rise in the government's fortunes by November 1953.[6]

Besides working successfully to convince the general population of the need for an oil settlement, the Iranian government took a number of steps to clear the way for one. The prime minister and the shah dissolved the rump Majlis left in Mossadeq's wake, which lacked a quorum in any case; selected a slate of candidates for its successor, as well as for a new Senate; and moved to initiate national elections at the earliest date possible. A new Majlis, they proclaimed, was necessary to lend legitimacy to any oil agreement with Great Britain and to provide the government with legislative support for its other programs and projects.[7] The government also intensified its campaign against the National Front and the Tudeh. In the months after assuming power it declared both organizations illegal, imprisoned or murdered many of their leaders, and forced the remaining members either underground or out of the country. In December, moreover, the regime won the conviction in a military court of former prime minister Mossadeq on charges of defying the shah, attempting to overthrow the monarchy, and illegally dissolving the Majlis. With Mossadeq sentenced to three years of solitary confinement Zahedi's regime had every reason to expect that it could put the 28 Mordad coup behind it, concentrate on resolving the oil dispute, and begin to reinvigorate the Iranian economy.[8]

Perhaps more important than these developments was Zahedi's decision to reestablish diplomatic relations with Great Britain. For some months after taking office Zahedi's government, heeding popular opinion, had demanded some gesture of British goodwill on the oil issue before resuming diplomatic relations.[9] But the British had refused to make such a gesture in the absence of direct diplomatic contact between the two nations. Renewed relations, they believed, would bolster their flagging prestige in the Middle East, enable them to deal directly with the government in Tehran, rather than through Washington, and put them on a more equal footing with the Americans at a time when the United States was threatening to supplant Great Britain throughout the region. U.S. officials had already assumed the position of mediator in Britain's dispute with Egypt over control of the military base at Suez, and British officials were loath to allow the same thing to happen in Iran. It was thus imperative, in their minds at least, that the resumption of Anglo-Iranian relations not be tied to progress on the oil crisis and that U.S. officials support them.[10]

U.S. officials did support the British position and exerted "friendly pressure" on Zahedi to restore relations without progress on the oil issue. In numerous discussions with the prime minister and his cabinet throughout the autumn months Ambassador Henderson told the Iranians that it was unreasonable to expect the British to make oil concessions to a government that would not conduct relations with them. If the Iranian government was to get anywhere on the oil question, he intoned, it would first have to reestablish diplomatic relations with London, even if this meant going against public opinion, which Henderson did not think entirely bad. On the contrary, standing up to opposition elements would improve the government's political position by convincing the Iranian public that the government favored a "policy of action rather than drift," Henderson said.[11]

Ultimately, Prime Minister Zahedi followed Henderson's advice. He discussed the resumption of relations with legislative leaders and other important public figures at meetings held on 30 November, won their overwhelming support, and then joined the British government in a joint communiqué of 5 December reestablishing relations and announcing plans to exchange diplomatic representatives at the earliest opportunity.[12] Public reaction to the communiqué was more unfavorable than Zahedi had anticipated and set the tone for the government's fortunes through the early months of 1954.[13] Protest marches were commonplace in Tehran, as were violent efforts on the part of the government to quash them. Zahedi and his ministers were especially brutal in pursuing members of the National Front, who continued to preach Mossadeq's nationalist message and to champion the cause of oil nationalization. As British chargé d'affaires Denis H. Wright reported, the government's policy of repression commanded respect but no "appreciable measure of active support." Zahedi, who lacked the charisma of his predecessor, found it difficult to win the hearts and minds of the Iranian people. Nor did it help that his regime set a new high for political corruption and that he was thought to have engaged in illicit, if not illegal, financial dealings.[14] Although elections for the Eighteenth Majlis, which concluded in March, resulted in a legislature dominated by pro-Zahedi forces, a number of opposition figures secured seats as well, and their presence made it difficult for the new government to successfully dominate the Majlis.[15] Given the regime's general unpopularity, it was clear that Zahedi would have his hands full in winning public support for the kinds of concessions that would be necessary to settle the oil crisis.

III

Although Zahedi's government was working to solidify its political position and prepare the way for an oil settlement, U.S. officials were eager to take advantage of what Secretary of State Dulles called their "miraculous second chance" in Iran. The overthrow of Mossadeq and the installation of Zahedi opened up the possibility of a settlement that would restore Iran's oil to international markets, stabilize economic and political conditions in that country, and close the door to an expansion of Soviet influence.[16]

But as Dulles and other U.S. officials realized, Zahedi was constrained by Iranian public opinion. He could not "rush with open arms" to the West and conclude a quick oil settlement. He had to "shape his program on the basis of nationalist aspirations," which meant that the Anglo-Americans had to view the oil crisis not as a technical or commercial problem primarily but as a "dynamic political and psychological" one. They had to frame an oil settlement that took account of Iran's hatred of the AIOC and allowed for some degree of Iranian control of the industry. Only then, said Ambassador Henderson, could they hope to achieve an enduring settlement.[17] Henderson and other U.S. policy makers also believed that any agreement with Iran depended on Anglo-American cooperation. By supporting the British in Iran U.S. officials had "burned [their] bridges behind [them]." They had staked Iran's future on the successful resolution of the oil crisis and had to play a role in the formulation of any settlement. "We are in this together," Henderson asserted. If the British wanted to resolve the oil crisis they could "make no move without consulting" the United States and giving "weight to [U.S.] points of view."[18]

Officials in the British government agreed with the U.S. assessment. They too believed that "political stability and the closing of the door to Communist infiltration" in Iran were more important than "compensation for the Anglo-Iranian Oil Company or the availability of Persian oil." For this reason they were willing "to seek a rapid, if not very satisfactory, settlement rather than prolong negotiations in the hope of eventually getting something better."[19] In addition, the British placed just as much importance on Anglo-American cooperation as did officials in the State Department. They had worked hard to achieve a "common front" with Washington and were determined to preserve it at all costs. For this reason the British were eager to make concessions on the oil issue, appear flexible and generous, and consult the United States at every stage of the game.[20]

Yet, when the British outlined their specific demands for an oil settlement in a memorandum to the State Department of 11 September, prospects for Anglo-American cooperation seemed to dim. The memorandum listed three requirements: compensation for the AIOC, assurances that Iran would not receive a better return than its oil-producing neighbors, and guarantees against adverse effects on Britain's balance of payments. The best way to guarantee these principles, the memorandum proclaimed, was a settlement based on the abortive 20 February proposals. These proposals called for a long-term sales contract between the Iranian government, which would produce and refine its oil, and a multinational consortium that included the AIOC and the major U.S. oil companies, as well as significant U.S. purchases of Iranian oil until the consortium got off the ground. In addition, the proposals would empower the International Court of Justice to decide how much compensation the AIOC should receive as a result of Iran's nationalization. The terms of this last provision were drawn broadly enough to allow the AIOC to claim compensation not only for its physical assets in Iran but also for the profits it would lose because of the premature cancellation of its concession. Finally, the proposals provided for Iranian ownership of the oil installations once compensation to the AIOC had been settled. Although the British were willing "to consider variations of detail and form" in these proposals, "modifications of substance," they said, "would be inconsistent with their minimum requirements."[21]

U.S. officials backed the principles outlined in the memorandum but rejected the idea of basing discussions with Zahedi on the 20 February proposals. Well-known oil consultant Herbert Hoover Jr., whom Eisenhower had appointed as special adviser to the State Department, viewed the proposals with horror. He thought that the British "should be grateful to Mussadiq" for rejecting them. In his estimation the proposals endangered concessions everywhere by giving the Iranians ownership of the oil installations after they had compensated the AIOC. He and other U.S. officials also thought that "conditions had changed so much" since the proposals were first formulated as to make them "no longer . . . feasible." Increased production and refining capacity in other areas had negated the need to reintegrate Iranian oil into the world market, and the U.S. government's commitment of emergency aid to Iran now prevented it from making the advance against future oil purchases provided for in the proposals. With the United States unalterably opposed to using the 20 February proposals as the basis for oil negotiations with Zahedi's government, the British agreed to search for an alternative.[22]

As the Anglo-American discussions progressed, it became clear that the only solution lay in the creation of what the British called an "international syndicate to purchase Iranian oil." According to Victor Butler of the British Ministry of Fuel and Power, the AIOC knew "in its heart of hearts" that it could not recover its previous position in Iran. It had "to let in other oil companies," including Royal Dutch/Shell and the U.S. majors—Standard Oil of New Jersey, the Socony–Vacuum Oil Company, the Texas Company, Standard Oil of California, and the Gulf Oil Corporation. Only such a strategy could satisfy the Iranians and only such a group had the marketing and distribution networks to ensure significant international sales of Iranian oil without disturbing the petroleum industry's delicate price structure and worldwide production patterns. Although U.S. officials agreed on the need for a truly international solution to the Iranian problem, they understood that such a solution would violate the U.S. antitrust laws and would therefore make no commitments without consulting the Justice Department. In the meantime they secured Whitehall's agreement that Hoover should initiate preliminary fact-finding talks with the Iranian government in Tehran.[23]

Hoover's meetings with Zahedi, Foreign Minister Abdollah Entezam, and members of Iran's Oil Advisory Committee in late October and early November were a positive step toward an oil settlement. Hoover easily achieved his primary goal—to educate the Iranian government about "the basic facts underlying [the] world oil situation" and about the "technical problems likely to arise in response to [the] reappearance [of] Iranian production in world markets." Prime Minister Zahedi "expressed disgust at [the] manner in which Mosadeq had been deceiving [the] Iranian people."

The former prime minister had decimated the country's economy, Zahedi asserted, and reintegrating Iranian oil into world markets was the only way to avert a total collapse. Although public opinion prevented the AIOC from returning as the sole operator of the oil industry, the prime minister was willing to see the company participate as a minority member in an international consortium. However unpalatable the idea of foreign involvement in the industry might be, Zahedi acknowledged that it was the only way to ensure that Iranian oil reentered world markets competitively priced and in significant quantities. The problem, the prime minister noted, would be accommodating these facts to the Iranian nationalization laws.[24]

At the conclusion of Hoover's stay in Tehran Entezam presented him with a memorandum that summarized "current Iranian thinking" on how best to arrange such an accommodation. He asked Hoover to deliver the memorandum to the Foreign Office, because diplomatic relations between Iran and Great Britain had not yet been resumed. The memorandum began with a vituperative denunciation of the AIOC's "colonial aims in Iran," which Hoover feared would probably raise British tempers. But he believed that the "document in general" showed a realistic grasp of the situation and might be used as the basis for future Anglo-Iranian discussions. By calling for negotiations between the Iranian government and the large international companies the memorandum gave real hope of an ultimate resolution of the oil crisis. So did Iran's willingness to grant the AIOC a minority interest in this multinational company, to concede total British participation of up to 50 percent, and to invest the company with full responsibility for the "sale, transportation and distribution" of Iranian oil. These were major concessions, Hoover proclaimed. They showed that Zahedi's government recognized its inability to reintegrate Iran's oil into world markets. Although the memorandum did not go so far as to allow for foreign control over the production of Iranian oil, Hoover was confident that in time a compromise on this issue could be arranged. The important thing was that Iran had finally taken the initiative in suggesting a solution to the oil crisis—a point that Hoover thought British officials should take into account when considering the Iranian memorandum.[25]

Even before Hoover's arrival in London both the AIOC and the British government were signaling that they would be responsive to the Iranian démarche. Hoover had made "a very good impression" on Basil Jackson and Neville A. Gass of the AIOC, who found him sensible and "well balanced." They welcomed his efforts to educate the Iranian government to the realities of the international petroleum situation, so long as he kept firmly in mind the company's two essential demands: adequate compensation and

a guarantee that the Iranians not receive better terms than other oil producers. Jackson and Gass were also willing to consider an international consortium for the production and distribution of Iranian oil, provided that the
AIOC would receive a substantial portion of its shares. Officials in the
Foreign Office shared these sentiments. "Subject to our essential safe-
guards," they said, "the important thing [was] to reach some kind of a settlement," even if it was "not ideal or very workmanlike." They also agreed
that an international organization was probably the only way to restart the
Iranian oil industry and that the British share in such an organization should
be no less than 50 percent.[26]

As Hoover found out when he met with British officials, however, agreeing to a consortium in principle did not necessarily mean that Anglo-Iranian
discussions would be based on the Iranian memorandum. Foreign Secretary
Eden found Iran's assault on the AIOC "entirely unacceptable," as did Sir
William Fraser, who chaired the AIOC's board of directors. Fraser was
especially negative, dismissing as unproved Iran's charges of misconduct
by the AIOC and warning that any Iranian restrictions on the company's
participation in the oil industry would constitute a dangerous precedent.
Although British officials considered a consortium the "only practicable
solution," they believed that the initiative on this score should come from
the AIOC, not from the Iranians. "If the AIOC had to withdraw from
Persia," they said, it "should walk out through the front-door and not be
kicked out through the back-door."[27]

An even more serious objection to the Iranian memorandum was the
continuing British belief that the resumption of diplomatic relations should
precede agreement on the principles for future oil discussions. Because
these discussions were bound to be complex and protracted, Whitehall
thought they were best conducted directly rather than through intermedi-
aries. In addition, British officials still saw the resumption of relations as
the only way for them to assess conditions in Iran for themselves, determine
whether the Iranians would block the AIOC from returning under its old
concession, and therefore clear the way for a multinational consortium.[28]
For these reasons the British declined to accept the Iranian memorandum
as the basis for Anglo-Iranian discussions and handed it back to Hoover.[29]
They also tried again to win Iranian agreement to resume diplomatic relations, this time by promising publicly to strike a fair deal on the oil issue.
As we saw earlier, this final effort, coupled with U.S. pressure to resume
relations, was ultimately successful.[30]

Hoover assessed the results of his fact-finding mission in balanced
terms. It was true, he noted, that the Iranians and the British could not agree

on the potential British share in any international oil consortium, particularly the share that might be held by the AIOC, or on whether the consortium should control production as well as marketing. Nor could they decide whether diplomatic relations should be resumed before or after an agreement on the principles of any settlement. Despite these differences, however, Hoover was optimistic about the prospects for a settlement. To his way of thinking the Iranian memorandum, though rejected by the British, had been "absolutely the best thing that [had] happened so far" in the oil dispute. Iran's "aggressive initiative" had a "most salutary effect" on thinking in London, where officials were now more realistic about the AIOC's chances of restoring its Iranian monopoly. For reasons of prestige the British had to assess the Iranian situation for themselves. But they were clearly ready, as were the Iranians, to consider replacing the AIOC with an international consortium to market Iranian oil.[31]

Based upon Hoover's findings, U.S. officials formulated a policy that split the differences between Iran and Great Britain. They agreed with Tehran that Britain's share of the proposed consortium should amount to no more than 50 percent, with "no more than a minority position for [the] AIOC." These terms were necessary to assuage nationalist aspirations in Iran. But U.S. officials supported face-to-face contact between the British and Iranian governments and endorsed Britain's call for the resumption of relations before oil discussions.[32] To ensure that time was not lost once relations were resumed Hoover also worked with the Justice Department to clear the way for a consortium. In November Attorney General Herbert Brownell decided to consider the legality of participation by the major U.S. oil companies in discussions regarding the formation of an international consortium. Although Brownell reserved final judgment until he had seen "specific proposals," Hoover was nonetheless buoyed by the decision. He advised industry representatives to prepare for talks with the AIOC, which he wanted British officials to initiate as soon as possible.[33]

When he resumed discussions with the British in late November and early December, Hoover stressed that time and money were running out in Iran. Zahedi's government would exhaust its emergency aid from the United States by the end of March 1954 and was likely to be overthrown unless it could show concrete progress toward an oil settlement. Speed was also essential to preempt independent oil companies from negotiating separate contracts with the Iranian government and thereby hampering the negotiation of an Anglo-Iranian arrangement. Representatives of some of these companies, Hoover said, already had approached Iranian officials. Zahedi had taken a great risk, Hoover told the Foreign Office, in resuming diplomatic relations without progress toward an oil settlement. It was now time for the British to take a risk by going ahead with a consortium before they had directly assessed the situation in Iran. Otherwise, too much time would be lost between the resumption of relations and the first moves toward a settlement.[34]

Hoover's pleas for prompt action led Eden and other British officials to adopt a much more flexible position. The foreign secretary now acknowledged that it was impractical for the AIOC to return to Iran alone and that the British should move ahead with plans for a consortium. Fraser agreed and promised to put the idea to the AIOC's board of directors. He still insisted, for reasons of prestige, that "first-hand reports" by British officials in Iran must precede a public endorsement of the consortium idea. In the meantime Fraser invited the heads of the major international oil companies—Standard Oil of New Jersey, Socony–Vacuum Oil, Texas, Standard Oil of California, Gulf, and Royal Dutch/Shell—to London for "preliminary and hypothetical" discussions on the Iranian situation.[35]

The U.S. majors did not immediately accept Fraser's offer. These firms had their own operations in other countries. They did not need Iranian oil and were not eager to see the resumption of Iranian production cause adjustments elsewhere in the Middle East, where output had skyrocketed during the Iranian crisis. Clearly, their participation required assurances that operations in Iran would not jeopardize their global production, marketing, and pricing arrangements. They were also reluctant to join an international consortium if doing so would strengthen the case of the U.S. Justice Department, which in April 1953 had filed a civil antitrust suit accusing the U.S. majors of "conspiracy to restrain interstate and foreign trade."[36]

The executives feared that accepting Fraser's invitation would only validate the antitrust suit and open them up to renewed attacks by the Justice Department. To prevent such untoward developments they delayed their response until the state and justice departments had ruled on the legality of their participation in the proposed discussions. Neither department's response was surprising. The State Department was enthusiastic about the impending talks, saying that resolution of the Iranian oil problem was in the national interest and that a "cooperative arrangement among the oil companies seemed to be an essential element in such a solution." The Justice Department, although acquiescing in the proposed talks, continued to reserve its right to pass on the legality of any agreement that might result. It also insisted that Hoover attend the meetings as an official representative of the U.S. government.[37]

After thus receiving a formal go-ahead oil company executives left for

London, where discussions with the AIOC began on 14 December. The three days of talks were exploratory and merely allowed the companies to exchange information. Fraser again said the AIOC intended to ask for a 50 percent share in the proposed consortium, although he also insisted that detailed discussions should await British evaluations. These evaluations would determine whether the company could recapture its monopoly, which, incidentally, the assembled executives all thought desirable, Fraser said. In addition, Fraser revealed the company's intention to request compensation not only in the form of payments by its consortium partners but also as free oil from the Iranian government. In keeping with the fact-finding nature of the talks the U.S. executives did not comment on Fraser's demands, with which they did not necessarily agree. But they did join with representatives of Royal Dutch/Shell and the Compagnie Française des Pétroles (CFP), which also participated in the talks, to assert that any settlement with Iran must guarantee that production and refining, as well as marketing, remained in foreign hands. This was necessary, the company leaders believed, to protect the large foreign investment needed to restart the industry, ensure that adequate oil supplies were available to the consortium partners, and deter other nations from following Iran's lead. At the conclusion of the talks the U.S. group asserted that "considerable progress" had been made toward a solution to the Iranian crisis. They said that "adequate sources [of] supply elsewhere" made the acquisition of Iranian oil unnecessary from a strictly "commercial standpoint." Still, they promised to "consider any constructive solution" to the Iranian problem, including their participation in a multinational consortium, at the request of the U.S. government. By this they meant guarantees from the government that the consortium would not constitute the kind of joint ownership and production agreement that the antitrust suit sought to eliminate.[38]

Even as the U.S. executives agreed to participate in a consortium, British officials were hoping for Iranian agreement to the resumption of the AIOC's monopoly, which would make such an arrangement unnecessary. Instructions to Britain's new chargé d'affaires in Tehran, Denis Wright, asserted that the "most satisfactory outcome" to the oil crisis would be "a direct settlement between the Persian Government and the A.I.O.C." The Foreign Office urged Wright to work toward this end. He was to tell the Iranians that the company was in a position to make a "very real contribution . . . to a mutually satisfactory [oil] solution" and that, in fact, "no-one [was] so well qualified" to run the Iranian oil industry "as the people who did it before: the A.I.O.C." In considering solutions to the dispute the Iranians should take account of the company's "decades of patient explo-

ration" in Iran and disregard Mossadeq's "false propaganda" about its supposed misdeeds. Foreign Secretary Eden did "not want to appear to be hus-
tling the Persians unduly," but he was eager to determine Iranian sentiment
on the return of the AIOC as the sole operator of Iranian oil so he would
know whether to proceed with discussions regarding a consortium.[39]

Wright's initial discussions with Iranian officials quickly revealed the
folly of the Foreign Office's strategy. Zahedi and officials in his cabinet all
agreed that the AIOC's return was "quite impossible" and "entirely out of
[the] question." Prevailing public sentiment that the company "had taken
much out of [Iran] and put little into it" could not easily be dispelled. Nor
could the government "face being accused of preparing the way" for the
company's return. Instead, leaders in Tehran continued to call for a consortium of oil companies, including but not dominated by the AIOC, to distribute Iranian oil to world markets, and for a separate Iranian company to
handle production and refining. The Iranians understood the need for a certain amount of foreign assistance to run their oil industry, but they were
clearly unwilling to surrender control to a single company. Given the
importance to both nations of reaching a satisfactory settlement, Zahedi
hoped that the British would be generous in their future dealings with Iran
over oil and would "be governed by strategic and not merely material and
economic considerations."[40]

If Wright's reports were not exactly what officials in the Foreign Office
and the AIOC had hoped for, nor were they surprising, and by the middle
of January 1954 both had conceded "that the A.I.O.C. could not expect to
regain exclusive rights in the production and marketing of Persian oil." In
the company's place they were willing to consider the multinational consortium favored by the Iranians but only on two conditions. First, the proposed consortium must consist only of the major multinational oil companies, which alone had the marketing networks to dispose of significant
quantities of Iranian oil, and these companies must "buy their interest" in
the consortium by "paying the A.I.O.C. either in capital, in revenue or in
free oil." Second, Whitehall demanded that the AIOC receive what it described as "an appropriate share" in the consortium. The British deliberately avoided telling the Iranians exactly what they considered appropriate,
but internal discussions and communications with the U.S. government
confirmed their intention to seek a 50 percent interest in the consortium.
This share was "only just," officials in the Foreign Office asserted, because
the AIOC alone had undertaken the risky venture of exploring for oil in Iran
in the first place and was now "in the best position to absorb [that] oil."
Additional justifications were to be found in the expectations of "British

public opinion" and in the "standing of the A.I.O.C. in the Middle East." Although the British took a firm public stand on this issue, in private they conceded that it might be a "matter for negotiation" with the Iranians. As a last resort they might have to settle for a total British interest—the shares of the AIOC and the British portion of Royal Dutch/Shell combined—of "not less than" 50 percent.[41]

If winning British support for a consortium was relatively easy, securing Washington's final acquiescence to U.S. participation in such an enterprise was more difficult and brought Hoover up against two conflicting strands of U.S. policy. One strand was embodied in the determination of the National Security Council that the U.S. government play a major role in arranging an Iranian settlement. U.S. national security depended on long-term political and economic stability in Iran, which depended in turn on substantial sales of Iranian oil. As British policy makers and Hoover realized, the only way to ensure these sales was an international consortium that included the five largest U.S. oil companies.[42]

At the same time, however, the Justice Department's antitrust suit threatened to ban participation by the U.S. majors and wreck the chances for a consortium. Because the new arrangement would constitute the kind of joint ownership and production that the antitrust suit sought to eliminate, securing U.S. participation required the permission of Attorney General Brownell. Hoover pressed for Brownell's approval, as did Secretary of State Dulles, Ambassador Henderson, Secretary of Defense Charles E. Wilson, Secretary of the Navy Robert B. Anderson, Chairman of the Joint Chiefs of Staff Arthur W. Radford, and President Eisenhower.

Admiral Radford summed up their common sentiments when he declared that "it was almost impossible to overestimate the importance of an Iranian oil settlement from the point of view of national security." The reintegration of Iranian oil into world markets, he asserted, was far more important than the antitrust concerns of the Justice Department. Representatives of the major U.S. oil companies made the same argument in a meeting with government officials in early January, and by the end of the month Brownell had relented. Under his ruling the U.S. firms could participate in a consortium for the "production, refining, and acquisition" of Iranian oil without violating the antitrust laws. They could not, however, jointly control the sale of Iranian oil in world markets; each company had to market its share of Iranian oil individually. Nor could the attorney general drop the antitrust suit, which the president had charged him to pursue.[43] Brownell's decision cleared the path to U.S. participation in the consortium that Hoover envisioned and pointed up how national security considerations had come to overshadow other concerns in U.S. policy making. It also marked the end of the first stage of the negotiations leading to resolution of the Iranian oil crisis.

IV

After all the interested parties—the Iranian, British, and U.S. governments, the AIOC, and the U.S. majors—had assented to an Iranian consortium, Hoover and other U.S. officials moved to the more arduous task of actually creating the new agency. Success required agreement on a broad range of thorny issues, including the division of interests in the new organization, especially the share to be allotted to the AIOC, the kind of compensation that the company would be owed, and the type of arrangement to be offered the Iranian government. Although the participating companies and the U.S. and British governments were forced to compromise in order to reach final agreements on each issue, U.S. interests prevailed more often than British ones.

Unlike other stages of the Iranian crisis, when U.S. officials had allowed their British counterparts to lead the way, discussions toward the creation of the Iranian consortium were dominated by U.S. ideas, and the final settlement was shaped primarily by U.S. commercial and strategic concerns. The U.S. oil companies were able to use their government's desire to settle the Iranian crisis and the AIOC's inability to return as sole operator in Iran as vehicles for their entry into the Iranian oil industry on terms that guaranteed huge profits for years to come and safeguarded their supplies in other areas of the world. Given then-prevailing world conditions and Britain's growing dependence on the United States, Whitehall had no choice but to go along.

All sides had hoped that final arrangements for a consortium would quickly follow Brownell's decision, but these hopes were dashed when the British government continued to demand a 50 percent interest for the AIOC. In private the British were willing to settle for an arrangement whereby the combined shares of the AIOC and the British portion of Royal Dutch/Shell equaled "not less than" 50 percent, but they gave no hint of such a compromise when they met with U.S. officials in January. On the contrary, they said that the AIOC must control at least 50 percent of the consortium, lest it appear that U.S. companies had replaced the British firm in Iran. Such an appearance, they argued, would upset British opinion, which expected the AIOC to play a large role in any settlement, and damage

Britain's standing at a time when its prestige and power were being challenged in Egypt and elsewhere in the Middle East. Sir William Fraser supported this contention. He reminded U.S. officials that the AIOC had already given up sole control of the Iranian oil industry and had made other concessions to nationalist sentiment in Iran. Under the circumstances, he concluded, it was unreasonable to expect the company to settle for less than 50 percent, especially when the Iranians had never suggested such a condition officially.[44]

U.S. oil company executives and officials in the State Department rejected these arguments. They had earlier refused to take the British demand seriously and were distressed to learn that the Foreign Office intended to push it aggressively. Company executives categorically declined to participate in the consortium if the AIOC held a 50 percent interest. Their opposition, so they said, did not stem from a desire to secure a larger share of the consortium for themselves. It grew out of their conviction that such a large British share would be unacceptable to the Iranians, who would then deny the consortium the control over the production, refining, and marketing arrangements that U.S. executives considered essential to the security of their investment. Consortium control over these arrangements, rather than ownership of Iran's oil resources, was the sine qua non of any settlement, according to the U.S. companies. And it was exactly this kind of control that Tehran would veto if the consortium became a vehicle for the restoration of British dominance.[45]

The State Department raised another concern, namely, that any agreement giving the AIOC 50 percent participation would be open to attack by the Tudeh and by extreme Iranian nationalist elements. Both groups had extensive support among the Iranian people, and their concerns had to be assuaged if an oil agreement was going to endure. The political nature of the Iranian oil problem, especially the widespread Iranian distrust of the AIOC, made the question of the company's participation in the consortium a matter that was best discussed between governments.[46] This was Hoover's opinion, and it was shared by the U.S. companies. Until a government agreement regarding relative participation had been hammered out, the companies refused to proceed with high-level discussions in London, and progress toward a resolution of the Iranian dispute came to a standstill.[47]

To prevent a collapse of the consortium idea Dulles raised the issue with Eden when the two were in Berlin in February for a conference on Germany. The Iranian discussions, Dulles explained, were "not [an] ordinary commercial negotiation"; political considerations, such as Iranian opposition to the AIOC, were overriding. Dulles stressed that the U.S. companies did not want a larger share than the AIOC and proposed as a compromise the same arrangement that British officials had considered privately—that the combined participation of the AIOC and the British portion of Royal Dutch/Shell amount to 50 percent of the consortium. This kind of division, he asserted, should allay any fear in London that the U.S. companies were seeking to "control or dominate" the consortium. When confronted with a firm U.S. position and a compromise the British already considered acceptable, Eden agreed to go along. He pledged that the AIOC would not insist on 50 percent of the new enterprise, so long as the "total British share" was "about that proportion" and the U.S. share was not larger than the British one.[48]

Ultimately, the State Department and the Foreign Office agreed that the AIOC and the five U.S. companies as a group would each hold 40 percent of the consortium, with the remaining 20 percent divided between Royal Dutch/Shell and the CFP. Before getting to this point, however, progress faltered again on another British attempt to gain control, at least indirectly, of the proposed consortium. The British proposed to give the AIOC and the CFP 44 and 8 percent of the consortium, respectively. According to the State Department, such an arrangement would alienate Iranian nationalists by giving the two companies, which normally moved "on parallel lines," a combined share of 52 percent and working control of the consortium. It would also alienate the U.S. companies. Portraying themselves as reluctant patriots driven more by the spirit of public service than by the profit motive, the U.S. majors refused to subordinate themselves to the AIOC or to support any agreement that might inflame nationalist sentiment in Iran. Although the companies' claims of altruism should not be taken at face value, the State Department was able to whittle the AIOC down to a 40 percent share of the consortium, instead of the 44 percent it had originally sought.[49]

By the end of March British officials had also surrendered on the share that would go to the CFP, specifically the AIOC's proposal to offer 8 percent of the remaining 20 to that enterprise, with Shell taking only 12 percent. The State Department considered the proposal unrealistic. The CFP lacked the capital to purchase 8 percent of the consortium, nor could it market 8 percent of Iranian oil, roughly 800,000 tons in the first year alone, when it was already finding it difficult to dispose of its 23.75 percent share of oil from the Iraq Petroleum Company. Shell, on the other hand, had a large cash reserve to cover its initial investment in the consortium. It also had ten times the marketing volume of the CFP and was much better equipped to handle large volumes of Iranian oil without causing "unfortunate repercussions elsewhere." Unlike the CFP, in other words, Shell could market Iranian oil without selling it at cutthroat prices and destabilizing the entire global petroleum industry. Even the French government understood the "commercial considerations" enumerated by the United States. In the end the French national oil company settled for 6 percent of the new consortium, whereas 14 percent went to Royal Dutch/Shell and 40 percent each to the AIOC and a group of the five U.S. companies. To be sure, the British had a substantial interest in Royal Dutch/Shell, but the 14 percent going to that firm did not disturb the United States as much as the 8 percent originally proposed for the CFP. Perhaps this was because the Dutch owned 60 percent of the enterprise, so that the total British share of the companies came to less than 50 percent of the consortium. Or perhaps it was because the British and the Americans needed another partner to appease Iran—one, like Royal Dutch/Shell, that also satisfied important "commercial considerations."[50]

The British had hoped that their concessions regarding the consortium's composition might bring a U.S. quid pro quo on the question of compensation owed the AIOC—a key British demand and a major sticking point in negotiations with Mossadeq. The AIOC demanded substantial payments from its consortium partners for their 60 percent interest in what had once been an AIOC operation and from the Iranian government for the losses it had sustained as a result of nationalization. Its claims in both areas covered the loss of future profits as well as physical assets. In the first area they totaled $1.267 billion, consisting of an immediate cash payment and a small charge per barrel of oil produced over the next twenty years; in the second they amounted to 110 million tons of free oil, worth approximately $1.463 billion and payable over the same period. Fraser was especially adamant regarding compensation from the Iranian government, which he said was necessary to show other countries that nationalization did not pay and to reassure foreign investors that Iran would deal fairly with them in the future. By taking payments in free oil rather than cash, he added, the AIOC would protect the Iranian treasury from the burdens of compensation and allow Iran to use more of its oil revenue for economic development and modernization.[51]

U.S. oil executives refused to support the AIOC's claims in either area of compensation. Regarding the $1.267 billion the AIOC expected from the consortium partners, the U.S. firms considered the amount "fantastically unrealistic" and without "any commercial basis." The Iranian oil industry was not exactly a "going enterprise in a stable and convenient area," they pointed out. Besides, the British had been out of Iran since October 1951 and their hold over Iranian operations was nonexistent. Because of these liabilities the U.S. majors believed that a reasonable price for their participation was $800 million, an amount they later increased to $1 billion.[52]

The U.S. companies were less flexible when it came to the AIOC's demand for compensation from Iran in the form of free oil. Such an arrangement would deny the Iranian government, not to mention the consortium companies, a share of the profits from the sale of 110 million tons of oil. In the process it would violate U.S. hopes for an equal division of profits between the consortium and the Iranian government. Since World War II the principle of fifty-fifty profit sharing had become a common feature of agreements negotiated between U.S. companies and oil-producing countries. The majors had used that principle to assuage nationalist sentiment in countries like Venezuela and Saudi Arabia, and they wanted to do the same thing in Iran, where politicians and the public alike saw an equal division of profits as a key component of any settlement with the consortium.

The majors also complained about the AIOC's demand to be compensated for the loss of future profits. The British company was "asking to be paid twice" for the same loss, the U.S. majors pointed out, "once by [the] consortium and once by Iran," even though its profits under the consortium would more than offset the future profits it would forgo as a result of nationalization. What is more, British claims for compensation were bound to provoke Iranian counterclaims, lead to international arbitration, and delay a settlement indefinitely. The other companies believed that the AIOC need only be compensated for the internal production and distribution facilities that would be transferred to Iranian hands once the consortium began operations. To ask for more would rekindle Iranian fears of unreasonable compensation and place the entire consortium scheme in jeopardy. Unless the company abandoned its claims for compensation against future losses, the U.S. oil executives threatened to withdraw from the negotiations.[53]

Government officials in Washington were just as critical of the AIOC's demands. Unwilling to see the negotiations break down, they lobbied the British to adopt a "more realistic, flexible attitude." At one level U.S. policy makers assailed the AIOC's demands as commercially unsound. Secretary of Defense Charles E. Wilson said, "The British are trying to sell something for twice what it is worth and they don't [even] have clear title." Secretary Dulles concurred. Noting that the consortium companies were prepared to pay the British "one billion dollars more than [they] have now—which is nothing," Dulles warned ominously that the British would continue to have nothing "if they [didn't] change their tune."[54]

At another level the objections of U.S. policy makers stemmed from the belief that the AIOC's demands endangered their dual efforts to protect Iran from communist expansion and to act in concert with Great Britain in the Middle East. As Dulles told British Ambassador Roger Makins in Washington, the United States hoped to achieve an oil settlement that "preserve[d] Iran's political independence and [gave] a fair deal to British interests." But if the AIOC insisted on taking an unfair and "totally unrealistic attitude" that ignored political conditions in Iran, not to mention international commercial considerations, Washington would have to "concentrate on the former, and salvage what was possible."[55]

As Dulles's comments suggest, U.S. officials were concerned about the whole Anglo-American partnership in the Middle East, which in their minds "always end[ed] in dismal failure." To their way of thinking Washington had already suffered a loss of prestige by supporting London's unwise and rigid policy in Egypt, where the British had been struggling to retain control of the military base at Suez. It was not about to suffer the same fate in Iran, where the Zahedi government offered the best chance yet of resolving the oil crisis. But this was exactly what would happen if the U.S. government supported the AIOC's claim for compensation. Dulles told Makins that "a turning point had been reached, not only in the oil dispute, but in the policy of Anglo-American solidarity in Middle Eastern affairs." Unless the Foreign Office brought its influence to bear on the AIOC, the United States would reconsider its policy in Iran and throughout the region.

On 18 March a working group of the National Security Council evaluated four different courses of unilateral U.S. action to support Iran: U.S. government purchases of Iranian oil, similar action by the U.S. oil companies, U.S. subsidies to the Iranian government, and "exceptional pressure to induce the British to offer a reasonable proposal for an early settlement." Although the working group saw dangers in each of these alternatives, it concluded that direct pressure on Britain was preferable to the other three. Eisenhower agreed at an NSC meeting later that same day,[56] and still later Secretary of Defense Wilson and others hinted at the kind of pressure Washington had in mind. The "attitudes of Congress re aid to [the] U.K.," they said, "may be greatly influenced by [the] British attitude on Iran[ian] oil."[57] U.S. assistance, it now seemed, could be used as leverage against Britain as well as Iran.

British leaders appreciated the dangers of an independent U.S. policy in Iran and the Middle East. They had worked hard throughout the Iranian crisis to win U.S. support for their position and were not about to see the chances of Anglo-American solidarity sacrificed on the altar of the AIOC's profit-and-loss statement. Eden told Fraser that the Iranian crisis concerned "not only the commercial interests of the A.I.O.C., but the wider interests of the United Kingdom in the Middle East." The company's inability to see beyond its own interests had delayed progress toward an Iranian settlement and was now threatening the chances of reaching one altogether. As a result, the Foreign Office decided that the question of Iranian compensation to the AIOC should be removed from the company's purview and become a subject for discussion between the British and U.S. governments.[58]

Anglo-American talks on the subject did not immediately yield agreement on what might be demanded of the Iranian government. Both agreed that Iran should pay "an appreciable sum in compensation," so as to "preserve commercial decency in the Middle East," but they had markedly different views regarding the amount of compensation and what it might encompass.[59] The Foreign Office started by taking a position similar to Fraser's. The AIOC, it said, would settle for a low level of compensation from its partners so long as its total compensation, from the government in Tehran as well as from its partners, bore "some reasonable relation" to the value of its Iranian enterprise before nationalization. According to the Foreign Office, it would not be unreasonable if Iran paid $280 million over twenty years. This figure was high enough to deter Iran's neighbors from nationalizing their oil resources and to cover the "loss and damage" the AIOC had suffered as a result of nationalization, a vague phrase that was probably intended to cover actual property losses as well as forgone future profits. Officials in the Foreign Office considered Iranian compensation in that amount to be an integral part of any settlement, and they implored policy makers in Washington to support them.[60]

U.S. officials, however, were unable to back what they considered an exorbitant demand. According to Ambassador Henderson, Zahedi's government was ready to surrender operating control of the Iranian oil industry in order to guarantee large-scale oil production. But giving in on compensation as well would damage the government's credibility and endanger the prospects for an agreement. Henderson worried as well that Iranian nationalists might interpret these payments as punishment for their efforts to nationalize the oil industry. As he and other U.S. officials reminded the Foreign Office, the Iranians had learned the folly of their actions; they had "endured appalling losses" while the AIOC appeared "to have thrived." In their view it would also be unfair for policy makers in Washington to demand a fixed sum for compensation from the Iranians when these same policy makers had not weighed the relative merits of the various claims and counterclaims. Finally, Henderson and others worried that compensation in the amount demanded by the British might entitle the Iranians to ownership or control of the oil industry. For all these reasons they wanted the AIOC to forgo any compensation whatsoever from the Iranian government or at least to settle for a sum equal to the value of the internal refining, production, and distribution facilities that Iran would be taking over, which Hoover put at a meager $5 million.[61]

To prevent the complete breakdown of the negotiations and to preserve the appearance of Anglo-American unity officials in Whitehall again decided to soften their demands. If a satisfactory fifty-fifty profit-sharing arrangement could be worked out with the Iranians, the British would settle for compensation somewhere between the $280 million finally agreed to by the AIOC and the $5 million favored by the State Department. The Foreign Office also agreed to negotiate the amount of compensation directly with the Iranian government instead of permitting the AIOC to handle the negotiations. Hoover applauded the new proposals because the Foreign Office "would undoubtedly take [a] much broader view of [the] situation than [the] AIOC." In return he and other U.S. officials agreed to champion the principle of just compensation with the Iranians.[62] It is worth noting that this action, if taken earlier, might have broken the deadlock that led the British and U.S. governments to overthrow Mossadeq's regime.

In the meantime the consortium companies had formulated a tentative proposal for presentation to the Iranian government. Under their proposal the consortium would effectively control Iranian oil operations and split the profits from those operations equally with the Iranian government. The first point was a sine qua non as far as the U.S. companies were concerned because it was the only way to ensure the production of sufficient quantities of Iranian oil. The second point was designed to placate the Iranians by giving them a financial return that was just as favorable as that received by other Middle Eastern oil producers.[63] Iranian oil would be sold only in its former markets, which were primarily in the eastern hemisphere, so as to protect pricing, production, and distribution arrangements in other parts of the world, including the arrangements of the U.S. companies in the western hemisphere and elsewhere. To protect Great Britain's gold and dollar reserves the proposal also provided that Iranian oil would be sold for sterling and that sterling would be used by the consortium to pay royalties and taxes to the Iranian government.[64]

To handle its day-to-day operations the consortium would form separate operating and refining companies domiciled in Britain. Although the U.S. companies had no vested interest in this particular matter, they agreed to support the British position in exchange for promises from the British treasury to convert their sterling profits from Iran into dollars.[65] Finally, the consortium representatives formulated a tentative plan for Iranian oil production that would not disrupt their arrangements with other Middle Eastern countries. That plan called for the annual production of 10, 20, and 25 million tons of crude oil in the first three years of the contract, respectively, and for annual production at the Abadan refinery of 6.5, 10, and 12.5 million tons over the same period. Sticking as near as possible to these amounts would make it unnecessary to curtail production in other countries and thus safeguard oil company relationships with the governments involved.[66]

While the consortium was negotiating on these points with the Iranian government, representatives of the British and Iranian governments were to conduct separate discussions regarding Iran's compensation to the AIOC and the currency arrangements that would surround the new oil contract. The British agreed that Iran could convert its sterling into the currencies of the countries represented in the European Payments Union (EPU), a customs union comprised of the Western European nations. They even agreed in principle to a "reasonable measure of convertibility" into dollars. Despite some trepidation, the United States intended to leave the currency arrangements to the British and Iranian governments. U.S. officials hoped that London would accord Tehran favorable terms, however, including a guarantee against losses resulting from the devaluation of sterling and a generous right to convert sterling into dollars.[67]

V

If organizing the consortium—which Hoover later called "perhaps the largest commercial deal ever put together"—had been a difficult process, much the same would be true of the negotiations leading to a final agreement between the new enterprise and the Iranian government.[68] Reconciling the commercial needs of the consortium with the aspirations of Iran and the prestige of the AIOC was no easy task.[69] All sides had to compromise, although the commercial concerns of the U.S. companies took precedence over all others.[70] The U.S. group was able to shape the final agreement in ways that limited the gains to the AIOC and the Iranian government, in part because of the strong support it received from U.S. policy makers, who were willing to do whatever was necessary to bring the Iranian oil crisis to an end. They took the lead with company officials in negotiating the final agreement, demonstrating in the process that the mantle of Western power in Iran had truly passed from London to Washington.

Initial discussions between the Iranian government and the consortium negotiating team—which consisted of Orville Harden of Standard Oil of New Jersey (who headed the delegation); John Hugo Loudon, president of Royal Dutch/Shell; and Harold Snow, managing director of the AIOC—did not bode well for a prompt resolution of the oil dispute. The Iranian negotiators, led by Finance Minister Ali Amini, initially took issue with every important aspect of the consortium's proposals. Any agreement with the consortium, they said, would have to conform to the nationalization laws, which gave control to Iran and guaranteed the nation better commercial terms than those available to nations that had not nationalized their oil industries. By giving the consortium control of the oil industry the proposed agreement violated these laws and was therefore unacceptable. The Iranian negotiators also balked at the proposed production schedule, demanded a guaranteed percentage of Middle Eastern production, preferably one-third of the regional total, and wanted the consortium's operating and refining companies to be Iranian rather than British.[71]

In addition, the Iranians raised objections on the two points that would be reserved for direct discussions with the British: payment arrangements and compensation to the AIOC. On the first, the Iranians rejected out of hand the proposal that the consortium pay its taxes and royalties to the Iranian government in sterling. They wanted at least part of these payments in dollars, which was the international reserve currency and as good as gold. On the second point, they questioned the AIOC's apparent intention to claim compensation for its loss of profits between the date of nationalization and the coming into force of the new agreement.[72]

Although the Iranians were more conciliatory in subsequent discussions, thus confirming the Foreign Office's somewhat condescending belief that their initial hard line was nothing more than "tactics to employ in buying a carpet," the only concrete accomplishment after six weeks was a draft Anglo-Iranian payment arrangement. Under this agreement the consortium would conduct its business in sterling. The Iranians would have no guarantees against losses resulting from British devaluation and would be banned from freely converting their sterling from oil operations into gold. They could convert up to 40 percent into dollars, however, a percentage equal to the U.S. share of the consortium, and the remainder into currencies of the European Payments Union.[73] U.S. officials were satisfied with the proposed arrangement; it dispelled an earlier fear that the British would pursue a rigid payments policy in hopes of regaining their pre-1951 position in

Iran.[74] But U.S. officials were less happy about the pace of negotiations on the two main issues of management control and company nationality.

By the middle of May the Iranians had agreed to give the consortium effective management control over Iranian oil operations but only under cover of language that made the consortium Iran's agent. That condition was essential, according to the Iranian negotiating team, because public opinion in their country would accept only an agreement that recognized Iran's nationalization of the oil industry. Negotiators for the consortium referred the Iranian proposal to their home offices but were not optimistic about an arrangement that reduced the consortium to an agency of the Iranian government. The U.S. negotiators, at least, worried that other oil-producing countries would demand agency arrangements if Iran received one and were loath to make any concessions to Iran that might jeopardize their arrangements elsewhere.[75]

A similar impasse developed over the nationality of the consortium's producing and refining companies. The Iranians moved a long way from their original demand for domicile in Iran: they agreed that the companies could be any nationality except British. This proposal satisfied U.S. officials but not the British, whose economic interests and national prestige required a degree of control that surpassed what the United States had in mind. As an alternative to the Iranian proposal the British suggested the incorporation of separate Iranian producing and refining companies operating under the supervision of a British holding company.[76] With deadlocks on this and the agency issue threatening to disrupt the negotiations, the consortium representatives headed to London for discussions with their company principals.

Policy makers in Washington worried that a breakdown of the negotiations would endanger U.S. economic and national security interests in the Middle East. It might contribute to worsening economic and political conditions in Iran and force the United States into steps to "save Iran from communist control," such as propping up the government there with long-term financial assistance or sponsoring an independent venture to produce and market Iranian oil. U.S. officials relished neither of these options, both of which would involve significant expenditures, alienate the British, and tie the U.S. government too deeply to the final Iranian settlement. Nor did they believe that either option would provide Iran with the long-term economic stability necessary to steel itself against communism. Instead, U.S. officials reaffirmed their belief that only a commercially viable consortium could solve Iran's ills and vowed to do whatever they could to encourage such a development when negotiations resumed in mid-June. On 27 May, for example, the NSC recommended "heavy pressure" on the Iranian and British governments in the next round of negotiations, especially if the talks had not yielded significant results by mid-July. Failure to reach a settlement, the council concluded, promised consequences too dire to allow any other policy.[77]

If U.S. officials saw the Iranian crisis in global terms, British officials continued to be more concerned with protecting their status as a "Middle East oil power." Unlike the United States, whose oil operations in the region were marginal and easily "compromised for the sake of political objectives," Great Britain received 90 percent of its crude oil from the Middle East. It could not afford to jeopardize its regional position by granting Iran concessions that other oil-producing nations might also demand. This explained Whitehall's reluctance, when it came to the producing and refining companies or to the issue of agency, to sanction agreements that allowed Iran any real control over its oil industry.[78]

At the same time, however, British officials realized that a successful agreement was their last hope of keeping any share of the Iranian oil industry. The company's embargo of Iranian oil sales had weakened considerably. Zahedi's government was preparing to honor contracts negotiated earlier for the annual sale of almost three million tons of oil to Italian and Japanese firms. If the embargo collapsed, Iran could be expected to take charge of its own oil operations and to export five to six million tons of oil annually. Sales of this magnitude did not approach the potential production of the consortium. But as A. V. Allen, assistant secretary of the British treasury, pointed out, they could "put the Persian industry as far out of [Britain's] reach as the Mexican oil industry" by convincing the Iranians that they no longer needed to settle with the AIOC.[79]

The challenge for Anglo-American policy makers was to formulate a settlement generous enough to assuage Iranian nationalism but not so generous as to wound British pride or endanger other Western oil arrangements in the Middle East. Balancing these two concerns with regard to management control was essentially a search for the right wording. Needed was some way to express the opinion of both sides that the consortium would exercise effective control of the industry while paying lip service to Iranian nationalization. State Department officials and executives of the U.S. companies wrestled with this problem at a meeting in late May. The executives accepted the department's assertion that an agency arrangement was the only practical solution, so long as it guaranteed the consortium fifty-fifty profit sharing, a contract with Iran that was at least as long as the AIOC's former concession, and true management control. When the consortium companies met in London the following month, the U.S. firms won support for a proposal drawn along these lines. The proposal accepted nationalization in principle and gave the Iranian government limited powers to inspect the consortium's operations but left operational control of the Iranian oil industry in the hands of the Western enterprise. By accepting some type of agency arrangement the consortium broke the deadlock on a difficult issue and cleared the way for continued progress toward a settlement.[80]

Securing an acceptable arrangement on the nationality of the producing and refining companies was more difficult, but in the end the British surrendered to U.S. and Iranian demands for non-British nationality. U.S. officials joined the British in opposing Iranian nationality, even under the supervision of a British holding company. Such an arrangement would not be durable or workable and might lead other oil-producing countries to make similar demands. To them Dutch nationality was the best alternative. The Dutch had extensive experience in international oil operations, and the Iranians had signaled their willingness to domicile the companies in the Netherlands. To make this option more attractive to London U.S. officials would not object to a British holding company if the Iranians went along.[81]

At first, British officials had considered the only "politically acceptable" arrangement to be one that incorporated the producing and refining companies in Great Britain. But subsequent discussion in the Foreign Office revealed that Dutch domicile had numerous advantages. It would be easy to defend before the British Parliament and public, in part because of close ties between the two countries, in part because of the British connection to Royal Dutch/Shell. It would also provide the producing and refining companies with greater diplomatic support than incorporation in a neutral country, give at least the appearance of some British control, and make it easier for the British to win U.S. support for other "measures to keep control in London."[82] It took some doing to convince Sir William Fraser that such gains were worth the risk of weakening the AIOC's position as leader of the international petroleum industry. But Foreign Office pressure to concede what was essentially a matter of prestige ultimately proved too much for even Fraser to ignore. He ultimately agreed to go along if provision was made for a British holding company.[83]

The consortium negotiators returned to Tehran confident of their ability to achieve agreement in principle on the questions of nationality and management. By 28 June the Iranians had accepted the consortium's proposed nationality scheme, including a British holding company.[84] Within a week the two sides had also reached an agreement on management control, which, according to the shah, "went to the root of the whole Iranian position." Because the consortium had agreed to state explicitly that the producing and refining companies would act as the agents of the Iranian government, the only real difficulty was "finding words not offensive to [the] Majlis and [the Iranian] public."[85] The issues included the duration of the consortium's contract, the level of its production, and the fees it would pay to the Iranian government. The two sides wrestled with all these issues during the summer until compromises were arranged on each one.[86]

In early August negotiators on both sides initialed a preliminary agreement that favored the consortium more than Iran. To maintain the facade of nationalization, the Iranian government, through the National Iranian Oil Company, would retain formal title to the nation's oil. But because Iran lacked the technical know-how to develop the oil or the ability to market it worldwide, actual control would be vested in the producing and refining companies owned by the consortium—which were later designated the Iranian Oil Exploration and Producing Company and the Iranian Oil Refining Company. These companies would be registered in Iran but subject to Dutch commercial laws. Each would have seven directors, only two of whom would be appointed by Iran. Iran was to receive 50 percent of the industry's net profits from production but nothing from its marketing or distribution operations. These and other features of the agreement were to run for twenty-five years, until 1979, at which point the consortium had the option of three 5-year renewals. With each five-year renewal the area of the consortium was to be reduced, so that after forty years it would cover only half its initial 100,000 square miles.[87]

The British and Iranian governments signed a separate agreement covering the issue of compensation. Although the Iranian government had long acknowledged its obligation to compensate the AIOC, it refused at first to pay the £100 million ($280 million) the company demanded. It tried instead to reduce the amount by pressing counterclaims for the losses Iran had suffered during the international embargo of its oil exports. The Iranians eventually abandoned their counterclaims, however, and agreed on 26 July to pay the AIOC a net sum of £25 million, £10 million for the internal distribution facilities it would be taking over and £15 million "for the damage done to [the] A.I.O.C.'s business between 1951 and 1954." The total would be payable in ten equal annual installments beginning 1 January 1957.

These concessions convinced some officials in the Foreign Office that the Iranian government's initial hard line on compensation had been little more than a public relations ploy to assuage nationalist sentiment. But actually the Iranians had gotten something in return for their concession: a figure for their compensation to the AIOC that was so low even Mossadeq might have accepted it, as well as a promise from the AIOC to fork over the £50 million that Iran would have received had it ratified the 1949 supplemental agreement. The exchange of concessions apparently cost the AIOC approximately $70 million, although the actual cost was considerably less. As Fraser realized, by paying Iran the $140 million, which would otherwise appear as profit on the company's books, the AIOC could reduce its tax bill by about $56 million.[88]

Although these terms were a mixed bag for the Iranians, the coup de grâce to their hopes to control the oil industry came in the provision permitting the consortium alone to decide how much oil the country would produce after the third year of the contract. Production during the first three years was to be approximately 15, 23, and 30 million tons, respectively. From then on a complicated and secret arrangement gave the eight participating companies complete control over production levels, which they termed the "aggregate programmed quantity (APQ)." The specifics of the APQ formula are not as important as its results: it restricted Iranian production so that the consortium companies could maintain their production levels in other parts of the world and prevent a price-depressing surplus of oil on the world market. This clandestine agreement, made public in 1974, was apparently the price the U.S. majors exacted for their participation in the consortium. It was their way of guaranteeing that the Iranian settlement would not disrupt their relations with Kuwait, Saudi Arabia, and other oil-producing countries. By placing Iran at the mercy of the consortium, however, this secret production agreement laid the basis for future Iranian discontent with Western control of its oil.[89]

The proposed consortium agreement had many points to recommend it. It enabled Iranian oil to reenter world markets, thereby generating substantial revenues for the government in Tehran. Indeed, the fifty-fifty profit-sharing arrangement provided Zahedi's government with oil royalties larger than earlier Iranian governments had received under previous contracts with the AIOC. The agreement also gave Iran the right to appoint members to the boards of the producing and refining companies and included a low figure for Iran's compensation to the AIOC. The provisions regarding profit sharing and compensation in particular suggest that Anglo-American officials were not able to ignore public opinion in Iran or run roughshod over the government they had installed there. Nevertheless, the agreement was a far cry from the nationalization that Mossadeq had once envisioned. Under its terms Iran would surrender real control of its petroleum industry to the consortium's producing and refining companies. It would receive no profits from the consortium's refining and marketing operations and exert no control over how much oil the consortium produced. By accepting the agreement the Iranian government in effect would be signing away these and other rights until as late as 1994.

Given these shortcomings, it is not surprising that neither the shah nor Zahedi was particularly pleased with the proposed agreement. In their opinion it did not go far enough to meet Iranian desires for large-scale oil production. Nor did it really conform to the nationalization laws, which called for total Iranian control of the oil industry. Still, they and other Iranian officials thought they had no choice but to go along. The shah and his prime minister were well aware of their debt to the Anglo-Americans, which had to be repaid with an oil agreement favorable to the West. They also realized that Iran's weak economic position made them vulnerable to Anglo-American pressure for a settlement and that future economic and military assistance from the West depended on satisfactory resolution of the oil crisis.

The promise of aid was especially important to the shah, who had been urging reluctant U.S. policy makers to drastically increase such aid since the Mossadeq coup. Ostensibly, the lack of enthusiasm on the U.S. side stemmed from doubts about the Iranian army's ability to handle sophisticated military equipment and from hopes that such aid might be tied to Iranian membership in a regional defense plan. These concerns may have played a part, but it was just as likely that U.S. leaders withheld aid in order to leverage Iran into an oil agreement that rolled back nationalization and kept control of Iran's petroleum industry firmly in the hands of the Western powers. Hoover, in fact, had suggested such a tactic at an NSC meeting on 27 May 1954.[90]

Because the agreement reached in Tehran was only a preliminary one, it would not come into force until it had won the approval of Attorney General Brownell, the eight oil companies involved, and the Iranian Majlis and Senate. Brownell's earlier acquiescence in the proposed consortium plan led him to approve the final agreement on 15 September, even though the secret production agreement constituted a cartel-like arrangement and even though his approval compromised the Justice Department's antitrust suit against the U.S. majors.[91] As Burton Kaufman has noted, the compromise was the price the Eisenhower administration paid to get the U.S. majors into a consortium that safeguarded U.S. economic and strategic interests in Iran and the Middle East.[92]

In the interim the Iranian government wanted to reopen the discussions on issues on which it felt it had been shortchanged during the negotiations, such as production levels, loans to the NIOC, and the use of Iranian shipping. Although the consortium finally consented to make advances to the NIOC and to pay its taxes to the Iranian government on a monthly rather than a yearly basis, it refused to renegotiate any part of the final agreement. It also moved rapidly toward ratification once the Justice Department had approved U.S. participation in the consortium. On 21 September the companies cabled their assent to the Iranian government.[93]

The shah and the Iranian government were determined to do what they could to secure a favorable outcome in the legislature, where the long delay in winning the approval of the Justice Department and the consortium principals had allowed critics of the agreement time to coordinate their opposition. To outmaneuver them the government presented the final agreement in the form of a single-article bill that prevented any amendments. Finance Minister Amini described the agreement as the best obtainable under the circumstances. He proclaimed that the Iranian negotiators "had extracted every ounce from the other side which present-day conditions [would] permit" and asserted that the government was "not prepared [to] renegotiate." In a foreshadowing of things to come, however, Amini also implied that Iran could obtain a more favorable agreement once it "possessed the technical, material and economic resources to compete all over the world with powerful trusts supported by the Great Powers."[94]

For the next several weeks a commission composed of eighteen Majlis deputies and eighteen senators discussed the oil agreement in minute detail. At least twenty-seven of the commission's members favored the agreement and kept dissent to a minimum. The only real problem concerned the level of the consortium's production after the third year of the contract. By allowing the consortium "to produce and sell just as much Iranian oil as it pleased" the proposed agreement, as the commission saw it, left "Iran economically at [the] mercy" of the new enterprise. The prospects for ratification and for long-term harmony between the consortium and the Iranian government would improve if the consortium specified its intended production levels.[95]

With this goal in mind Amini sought clarification of the consortium's intentions from Howard Page, who had replaced Orville Harden as the consortium's chief negotiator in Tehran. At first the consortium companies saw the Iranian request as an effort to obtain additional concessions at their expense. But in time they came to a different conclusion, which was shared by the British and U.S. governments. In light of Iran's "delicate political situation" they now concluded that supporters of the agreement in Tehran required assurances regarding production schedules if they were going to carry the day in the legislature. The result was a promise from the consortium that Iranian production would follow the same patterns as those of other regional oil producers. The promise was vague, but it satisfied the commission, which approved the oil agreement and reported on it favorably before a public session of the Majlis on 10 October.[96]

A lively debate followed in both the Majlis and the Senate, but at no time was the bill in real danger of being rejected. Minister of Finance Amini disarmed the oil agreement's opponents early on by branding them "enemies of Iran," "self-seeking opportunists," or "blind isolationists." Although some members of both chambers spoke against the agreement anyway, they were not able to sway their colleagues who saw the agreement as the only way to save the Iranian economy from complete collapse. Even Mostafa Kashani, who shared his father's long-standing opposition to any settlement with the British, was forced to concede that Mossadeq's economic mismanagement required the government to accept any agreement it could get. On 21 October the Majlis approved the consortium bill by a vote of 113 to 5, with 1 abstention; the Senate vote a week later was nearly as one sided. The large majorities may be attributed to the "argument, cajolement and threats" of the shah, who worked diligently to bring the legislators "to the right state of mind"; he happily signed the oil bill into law on 29 October.[97]

In what may be seen as a postscript to the oil agreement the United States agreed in late 1954 to increase its economic and military assistance to Iran. U.S. officials believed that a comprehensive aid package would keep Iran from falling to communism and help to cement its ties to the West. They may also have seen such assistance as a way to assuage Iranian opposition to the less-than-perfect oil pact. Economic and financial assistance would amount to $127.3 million in fiscal year 1955 alone and would continue on a large scale for the next three years, until Iran began receiving substantial oil revenues.[98] Military assistance would be significantly higher, amounting to a projected total of $360 million over the next three fiscal years. This money was to be used to expand and develop the Iranian armed forces, both for internal defense and in anticipation that they might be needed to stave off a Soviet invasion. Although U.S. officials doubted the likelihood of the latter eventuality, they went along with the shah's plans for a large and grandiose military establishment.[99]

In the months immediately before and after the ratification of the oil agreement, both the shah and Prime Minister Zahedi worked to solidify their respective positions throughout the country and to consolidate their relationships with U.S. policy makers. The shah, who had distinguished himself during the later phases of the oil negotiations as a strong and forceful leader, began to take a more active role in Iranian politics. He sought to influence the government's legislative agenda and to extend his control over the Iranian armed forces. In a visit to the United States in December he also promised closer ties between Iran and the West.[100] Zahedi too tried to strengthen his position during this period. His government launched an extensive anticommunist campaign that included death penalty specifications "for leadership activity directed at [the] overthrow [of the] government." It also uncovered and destroyed a communist cell of about five hundred men and officers within the Iranian military.[101] These developments, plus the significant amounts of U.S. economic and military aid that flowed into Iran in the immediate aftermath of the oil settlement, demonstrated that by the end of 1954 Iran was indeed becoming a U.S. client state.[102]

VI

In a demonstration that Western leadership in Iran had passed from London to Washington, U.S. interests dominated the negotiations that led to the Iranian consortium agreement. Officials in the Foreign Office knew that a consortium was the only way for the AIOC to retain any share whatsoever in future Iranian oil operations and that reaching a satisfactory consortium arrangement depended on the participation of the U.S. majors. They also realized that their declining world status by 1954 made them dependent on U.S. support in Iran and throughout the Middle East. These factors forced British officials to yield to U.S. points of view on all issues of importance during the consortium talks.

Similar realities were responsible for Iranian acquiescence in a final settlement that was a far cry from nationalization. The international oil industry had done a remarkable job of accommodating to the loss of Iranian supplies after 1951, a fact that diminished Tehran's bargaining position in negotiations with the consortium. Also important in forcing Zahedi's government to limit its demands was the precarious position of the Iranian economy, which could not be propped up indefinitely by U.S. assistance; both needed the benefits that would accrue from a resumption of large-scale oil production.

Western interests won a substantial victory in the Iranian settlement. The U.S. companies and the U.S. government got what they wanted. The companies got a stake in Iranian oil on terms that squared with agreements they had negotiated elsewhere and that protected their international production and marketing arrangements. The government stabilized a friendly regime in Tehran without seriously alienating the British. The prospect of significant oil sales seemed to stave off the chances of a communist takeover in Iran; Western interests would continue to dominate Iran's oil, thereby denying that precious resource to the Soviet Union. With Iran squarely in the Western camp, moreover, at least one door had been closed to Soviet expansion into the oil-rich and strategically important region of the Middle East.

chapter 9

The Anglo-Iranian Oil Crisis

AN APPRAISAL

As we have seen, the Anglo-Iranian oil dispute was not a spontaneous, isolated, or self-contained development. Its roots reached back to Iran's early opposition to the AIOC's domination of the nation's oil industry, and its effects stretched beyond Iran to the world petroleum market and the international economy.

II

To recap, the Anglo-Iranian dispute originated in the opposition of Iranian nationalists to the Supplemental Oil Agreement negotiated in July 1949 between the government of Iran and the AIOC. Although the supplemental agreement provided Iran with additional royalties from the AIOC, along with other financial benefits, it did not address such long-standing Iranian demands as access to the AIOC's books, representation on its board of directors, and periodic review of the oil concession. Successive Iranian governments tried for eighteen months to win British concessions that would give Tehran greater control over the oil industry and a larger share of the revenue it generated. Winning greater control over the oil industry was a matter of national pride, whereas higher revenues would finance the ambitious Seven-

Year Plan, which was designed to modernize Iran's economy and improve its standard of living. When efforts to renegotiate the supplemental agreement failed, a new government under Mohammed Mossadeq nationalized the AIOC in the spring of 1951. It laid plans to assume the AIOC's operations and invited the company to discuss the question of compensation. Rather than settle the oil dispute, however, the AIOC and the British government, with the support of the U.S. majors, boycotted Iranian oil sales in hope of winning concessions by preventing the Iranian government from reaping the benefits of nationalization. The boycott was immediately successful: Iranian oil production declined from thirty-two million tons in 1950 (the AIOC's last full year of operation) to one million tons in 1952.

The oil boycott crippled Iran's economy but failed to moderate Mossadeq's policy. To be sure, his government had nationalized the AIOC in order to better the standard of living of the Iranian people, not to make an already wealthy foreign corporation even wealthier. But the drive to nationalize the AIOC was motivated by more than a desire for profits. It was also designed to remove the last vestiges of Britain's colonial control over Iran. Convinced that the AIOC and the British government had interfered in Iran's domestic affairs for decades, nationalists like Mossadeq believed that such interference would stop only after Iran had gained control of its rich oil holdings. Because this was precisely the concession that the British would not make, the oil dispute dragged on interminably.

Certainly, the Iranians had a right to nationalize their oil, a right that the United States conceded, and to seek a fair settlement of the issue with the AIOC. Also clear is that in the early days of the dispute, Iranian expectations, though difficult to pin down, offered a reasonable basis for a settlement. Before Mossadeq became prime minister, for example, the Iranians would probably have settled for a fifty-fifty profit-sharing arrangement that left the AIOC in control of the oil industry. Indeed, these terms were not much different from what the Anglo-Americans conceded at the end of the crisis.

By the time Mossadeq came to power, however, the Iranians could no longer settle on these terms, not so much because Mossadeq was unreasonable—as the Anglo-Americans so often charged—but because the crisis had escalated and the political situation in Tehran limited the prime minister's freedom to maneuver. On the one hand, Mossadeq exposed his government to criticism from members of the National Front and especially from the Tudeh if he did not appear to get the maximum advantage from the British. Having come to office promising full and complete nationalization of the oil industry, he was unable to accept anything less. Even the hint of a compromise might net him the same fate as Razmara. On the other hand, the more determined Mossadeq was to get the best settlement for Iran, the more likely he was to alienate the shah, elements in the military, and other conservative forces that were critical of his regime and maintained generally close, if covert, relations with the British. A firm stand in defense of Iran's position also fostered difficulties for the prime minister with the British. Faced with what seemed to be an impossible balancing act, the prime minister found it difficult to work constructively toward a settlement.

Although Mossadeq made some concessions during his tenure as prime minister, he remained uncompromising on the central point: operational control of the oil industry had to rest in Iranian hands. Price, production levels, and other technical details, although difficult to resolve, could ultimately be agreed upon. The obstacle to an acceptable settlement was who would be in charge of the oil industry and, by extension, Iran's internal affairs. For Mossadeq oil operations became a symbol of Iran's national independence. The country could hope to attain its freedom only if it controlled its resources. Thus no settlement with the AIOC was possible that left control in any hands but Iran's.

British leaders, public and private alike, would not agree to Iran's nationalization without a fight. The AIOC's operations in Iran made a contribution to Britain's balance of payments that grew in importance during the financial crisis of 1951. They provided Britain with £100 million annually in foreign exchange, as well as twenty-two million tons of oil products and seven million tons of crude oil per year. Under these circumstances the British did not believe that they could surrender control of the company to the Iranians. Instead, they first offered cosmetic and financial inducements that created the facade of Iranian ownership but vested actual control elsewhere. This was the thrust of every British proposal for resolution of the dispute—from the Jackson and Stokes plans of 1951 to the Truman-Churchill proposals of 1952—and explains why Mossadeq could accept none of them. When efforts to reach a negotiated settlement on their terms failed, officials in London boycotted Iranian oil exports.

Given their concerns about losing control of Iranian oil, the British adopted a stubborn policy that always seemed one concession short of a final settlement, especially in the early years of the controversy. This was true of their reluctance to renegotiate the supplemental agreement, even when the new agreement of the Arabian-American Oil Company (ARAMCO) and Saudi Arabia introduced the fifty-fifty profit-sharing principle to the Middle East and made it unlikely that the Iranians would accept anything less from the AIOC. It was also the case with regard to the Stokes and Jackson proposals, which would simply perpetuate the AIOC's traditional dominance of the Iranian oil industry. In fact, this book has suggested that British policy makers sought throughout the dispute to block any settlement that involved a loss of their traditional control over Iranian oil. They were convinced that this strategy would leave the United States with no choice but to support them and the Iranians with no choice but to concede or face certain economic and political disaster.

British policy throughout the oil dispute was based officially on the rule of law and the sanctity of contracts. Company executives and government officials alike saw Iran's nationalization as tantamount to confiscation because the government in Tehran failed to offer prompt and adequate compensation for the AIOC's assets. Their complaints had some merit. But the delay in arranging compensation did not stem from an Iranian unwillingness to pay. Provision for such payment was included in the nationalization laws, and Mossadeq remained willing until the end to arrange a satisfactory compensation settlement. The real difficulty regarding compensation was that the British-inspired boycott of Iranian oil sales deprived Mossadeq's government of the means of paying. Without oil money the government was hard pressed to meet its day-to-day expenses, let alone handle the burdens of compensating the AIOC for its Iranian property. Seen in this light, Britain's complaints that Iran's nonpayment of compensation invalidated the nationalization of the AIOC seem disingenuous, to say the least. Had the British not prevented Iran from reaping the financial benefits of nationalization, it would have been able to compensate the AIOC. But relaxing the boycott and allowing Iranian nationalization to proceed would have run counter to British national interests and led to the complete collapse of its position in Iran and throughout the Middle East. So officials in London maintained a campaign of economic warfare against Iran instead.

The Anglo-Iranian oil crisis marked a turning point in the relationship between the AIOC and the British government. Although the British government had owned a majority of the company's stock since 1914, it had by tradition remained uninvolved in the company's operations. All that changed with the crisis of the 1950s. Many within the British government blamed the company's troubles in Iran on the unwise and narrow-minded policies of Sir William Fraser, who had chaired the AIOC's board of directors since 1941. Fraser's refusal to modify the supplemental agreement, which he had helped to draft, fueled Iranian discontent with the AIOC and contributed mightily to the passage of the nationalization laws. It also ultimately brought him into conflict with officials in the British government, who feared that such a hard-line stance would lead to a total loss of British influence in Iran.

The chairman was "in cloud cuckoo land" when it came to the best course of action in Iran, noted Foreign Secretary Eden in the summer of 1952, and Fraser's refusal to compromise led to greater efforts by the Foreign Office to influence company policy.[1] These efforts did not amount to a government takeover. Nor were they edicts or orders for the company to give in to all of Iran's demands. But they did constitute a more active government role in the shaping of AIOC policy than had been the case previously. As this book makes clear, moreover, the government did have some success in getting the company to moderate its stance, most notably during the negotiations that led to the formation of the international cartel in 1954.

In addition to working actively to influence the policies of the AIOC, the British government sought the assistance of several international organizations in arranging a settlement of the oil dispute. None of these appeals was successful. After first issuing an injunction that called for a temporary moratorium in the dispute, the International Court of Justice ultimately ruled that it lacked the authority to even consider the matter, a judgment widely recognized as a victory for Iran because it declared the oil dispute an internal Iranian problem. Much the same thing happened when Britain tried to get the U.N. Security Council to declare the Iranian imbroglio a threat to world peace. The British government found little council support for its resolution; even the Americans doubted the chances of success and were lukewarm in their backing. Britain's failure to sway these two legally oriented bodies to its position appeared to punch holes in its contention that Iran's nationalization of the AIOC was illegal. Had that been the case, it seems likely that the ICJ and the Security Council would have ruled in Britain's favor and ordered a halt to Iranian efforts to take over the company. The absence of such orders suggests that international legal opinion rested with Iran, rendering British contentions regarding Iran's lawlessness suspect in the process.

Although British officials detailed many reasons for their opposition to Iranian nationalization of the AIOC, the crux of the matter for them was the danger such a move posed for their status as a great power. As Britain's largest overseas investment, the Abadan refinery and the AIOC's Iranian operations symbolized British power in the Middle East. Losing control of these assets would be a deadly blow to British prestige the world over, especially considering Britain's recent withdrawals from India and Palestine. It might also imperil other British holdings around the world, foremost among them the Suez Canal. At a time when British policy makers were keenly aware of their diminishing status as a global power it is not surprising that they were also sensitive to anything that might undermine their position in Iran, such as concessions to Mossadeq that would give Iran control of its oil industry. In other words, even had satisfactory arrangements regarding compensation and other technical details been possible, British reluctance to surrender operational control to the Iranians—which was, after all, the heart of the matter for Tehran—doomed the chances of a satisfactory settlement. Ultimately, the British were just as constrained and inflexible as Mossadeq when it came to compromising on the key issue of control.

The resulting Anglo-Iranian stalemate threatened Western interests throughout the Middle East and thus gave policy makers in the Truman administration cause for alarm. As the only direct land barrier between the Soviet Union and the Persian Gulf Iran served as a vital link in the Western alliance's security chain; Soviet control of its territory would make the defense of Greece, Turkey, and the eastern Mediterranean all but impossible. Compounding Iran's importance were its rich oil reserves, which the United States considered crucial to the reconstruction and rearmament of Western Europe. Loss of these reserves would have dire consequences. In the short term it would create serious shortages of aviation gasoline and other fuels needed for the military effort in Korea and raise the specter of civilian rationing in the United States and throughout the West. In the long term it might compromise the West's ability to fight a protracted war with the Soviets, force augmentation of its military establishments, and result in an expansion of Soviet military bases in the Middle East.

In seeing the oil dispute's broad implications U.S. policy makers revealed their inclination to place that conflict in a cold war context. This was especially the case after the outbreak of the Korean War, which highlighted both Iran's importance as a vital supplier of oil to the Western alliance and its vulnerability as a potential victim of Soviet attack. With so much resting on Iran's continued alliance with the West U.S. policy makers did not think they could stand idly by while Iran surrendered to communism or fell victim to Soviet control. They had to seek a negotiated Anglo-Iranian settlement.

Initially, the Truman administration acted as an honest broker in the search for a settlement that paid lip service to the idea of nationalization but also recognized the contractual rights of the AIOC. On the one hand, U.S. policy makers called for a firm, commercially acceptable agreement between Iran and the AIOC, one that did not set a dangerous precedent or encourage nationalization elsewhere. On the other, they advocated a flexible approach to the oil question that would make a settlement possible before Iran collapsed internally or succumbed to Soviet penetration. Although the British government pressed for more active U.S. involvement in the dispute, Truman and Acheson at first resisted such an approach. They preferred instead to work toward a peaceful mediation of the dispute. With this goal in mind Truman lobbied for concessions from both sides, warning that "too much 'take'" on the part of the Iranians was as dangerous as "too little 'give'" on the part of the British. He commissioned Averell Harriman to harmonize Anglo-Iranian differences in 1951 and pursued similar efforts, including the discussions between Mossadeq and McGhee, after the Harriman mission collapsed.

As the oil dispute continued, administration officials grew increasingly concerned about its potentially disastrous effects on Western security. They began to recognize that preserving British oil interests in Iran would go a long way toward defending Western interests there and throughout the Middle East. The attitude of the major U.S. oil companies probably contributed to the administration's more pro-British posture as well. By the fall of 1951 U.S. oil company executives had abandoned their initial support for Iran's position in favor of solidarity with the AIOC. Standing shoulder to shoulder with the AIOC in Iran, they came to believe, was the best way to protect their operations against any takeover attempts by nationalists in other places. The force of their arguments may help to account for the hardening of the Truman administration's position, suggesting in the process that the oil companies wielded more influence in Washington than other scholars have maintained.[2]

An inability to bridge the Anglo-Iranian gap, which U.S. officials increasingly attributed to what they came to view as Mossadeq's unreasonableness and inflexibility, also contributed to the administration's drift toward the British. Influenced by these factors, and by their growing dependence on a global partnership with Great Britain, officials in the Truman administration ultimately abandoned their middle-of-the-road stance and decided to prop up the British position in Iran, just as they were doing in Egypt and would soon do for the French in Indochina. This shift in U.S. policy culminated during the summer of 1952, when Truman joined with Churchill in a last-ditch effort at a compromise solution that wedded the U.S. government to the British position in Iran.

British officials had been woefully disappointed with the Truman administration's efforts to mediate an Iranian settlement and had pushed instead for explicit U.S. support for their position. In their minds only Anglo-American cooperation could save the informal British empire in the

Middle East and deter other nations from following Iran's lead and nationalizing Western-owned property. Accordingly, Whitehall called for joint Anglo-American action in Iran, for a unified approach to Mossadeq that would demonstrate the inviolability of the transatlantic alliance and the folly of trying to sway the United States to Iran's side. When it became obvious that Mossadeq would not back down, even in the face of economic pressure and the British-led boycott of Iranian oil sales, British leaders even went so far as to advocate joint Anglo-American action to remove the prime minister from office.

If the Truman administration was willing to become increasingly involved in seeking an oil settlement, even to join with the British in a common proposal to Mossadeq, it was not willing to become part of a joint effort to overthrow his government. In part their refusal to go along with repeated British entreaties for a joint operation against Mossadeq's government stemmed from an ideological opposition to covert intervention in the internal affairs of other countries. In part they were restrained by commitments in other parts of the world—to economic and military aid for Western Europe and to the struggle in Korea—that made it difficult for the administration to contemplate involvement in an expensive covert operation against Mossadeq. The administration would go only so far in backing the British in Iran. As a result, the oil crisis remained unresolved when Truman left office in January 1953.

The Eisenhower administration assumed office just as Iran's political and economic deterioration was fueling U.S. fears about the nation's safety. Although earlier fears of Iran's collapse had been unfounded, by early 1953 disaster really did seem inevitable. The loss of oil revenue was taking a serious toll on the country's economy, and economic dislocation was causing mass demonstrations that U.S. officials believed would grow into full-scale revolution. Making matters worse, Mossadeq forged closer ties with the communist Tudeh Party and threatened to sell oil to the Soviet Union and its satellites. In truth, Mossadeq was a staunch anticommunist who hoped such moves would win additional U.S. assistance for his financially strapped government. Given the anticommunist hysteria of the early 1950s, however, officials in the Eisenhower administration could not easily dismiss the prime minister's apparent flirtation with communism. To them he was a dangerous radical whose policies could lead Iran into the Soviet bloc. They thought they had no choice but to get rid of him. Accordingly, only two weeks after assuming office the new administration in February 1953 accepted British plans for joint action against Mossadeq that Truman had earlier rejected.

Several factors contributed to the shift in U.S. policy. Unlike their predecessors, Eisenhower and Dulles were ideologically predisposed to covert operations. In their eyes such tactics were an acceptable way to square the administration's limited resources with its growing global commitments. Covert missions were swift, relatively low cost, and comparatively risk free. They would allow the United States to maintain its worldwide struggle against communism but not compromise the administration's quest for a balanced budget. After the termination of both the European Recovery Program and the Korean War the administration was also in a position to devote more of its resources to Iran. Freed from the financial considerations that had earlier forced Truman to depend on the British, Eisenhower could contemplate, and initiate, direct U.S. intervention in Iran. To be sure, the administration preserved the facade of negotiations by offering a settlement based on the revised Anglo-American proposals of 20 February. But these proposals represented little more than an extension of unsuccessful schemes first hammered out in the Truman administration. In addition, they came at a time when the new administration in Washington was committing itself in principle to toppling the Iranian government. Under these circumstances it is difficult to escape the conclusion that Eisenhower and his colleagues were convinced from the start that serious negotiations with Mossadeq had to give way to a covert operation.

Preserving Iran's Western orientation and preventing Soviet control of its oil reserves ultimately doomed all thought of a compromise, as did a set of cultural prejudices on all sides of the controversy. On the Iranian side these were apparent in Mossadeq's tendency to demonize the British, to blame them for all of Iran's troubles, and to ascribe to them the basest of motives during the oil negotiations—all of which made it difficult for him to be flexible and realistic in seeking a settlement.

These prejudices were even more pronounced on the Anglo-American side, where policy makers found Mossadeq different from themselves in many ways. One startling difference, of course, was that Mossadeq often worked from his bed while dressed in pajamas. To Anglo-American diplomats used to conducting negotiations under formal circumstances, conversing with a pajama-clad Mossadeq who worked from his bed was a strange experience. In their minds real leaders wore suits or other professional attire when conducting business, not pajamas, and they conducted their business from an upright position, not from their beds. Never mind that Winston Churchill often wore pajamas and worked from his bed. That Mossadeq did so marked him as an eccentric at best, a lunatic at worst.[3]

Compounding the problem for Western diplomats was what they believed to be Mossadeq's fragile and emotional temperament.[4] On many occasions throughout his premiership Mossadeq became teary-eyed when speaking of the misdeeds the AIOC and the British government had perpetrated on the Iranian people. In part these outbursts were genuine reflections of his outrage at the sufferings wrought upon his country by the evil Anglo-Iranian Oil Company. In part, though, these episodes were carefully choreographed plays to the balcony designed to garner important popular support for the prime minister during the long and economically devastating oil crisis. Anglo-American officials never considered the possibility that Mossadeq's tears might have come from something other than uncontrolled emotionalism. To them they were signs of weakness and effeminacy that diminished Mossadeq's standing as a statesman and absolved them of the need to deal with him as an equal.[5]

Mossadeq's tears were not the only thing that made him feminine in Western eyes. The prime minister also displayed a host of other traits that earned him the opprobrium of officials in the Foreign Office and the State Department and that yielded descriptions thick with gender-coded language. He was moody, impractical, and unrealistic, they said.[6] He had a tendency "to change his mind, to forget, to become confused."[7] And he lacked the capacity "to carry on complicated negotiations for any length of time in a single direction."[8] Nor was the language always gender coded. Sometimes it was explicit and obvious, as when Peter Ramsbotham of the Foreign Office railed against the prime minister's "negative and feminine tactics."[9] Like most women, it seemed, Mossadeq apparently had trouble making up his mind, sought to avoid final decisions, and always wanted something better. The cumulative effect of such characterizations was the conclusion that Mossadeq was an irrational and fickle adversary who was prone to emotional outbursts, likely to change his mind, and could not be trusted.

Many of Mossadeq's policies contributed to Western descriptions of him as weak and incapable. By eschewing the economic gains that would come from a compromise settlement and insisting on total Iranian control of the oil industry, even if that meant operating at a reduced output, Mossadeq saw himself as safeguarding his nation's independence against the rapacious imperialism of the West. Anglo-American officials, however, saw things differently. For them such a stance was further proof of Mossadeq's simple mind and unfitness for office.

Mossadeq's efforts to steer a middle course in the cold war, which at the time took the name of "negative equilibrium," also made him look weak in Western eyes. Such a course revised the traditional Iranian policy of playing the great powers against each other by proclaiming instead that no foreign power should have influence in Iran. As the prime minister saw it, what would later come to be called nonalignment was the only way to ensure the attainment of Iran's national goals.[10] For U.S. officials, though, refusing to stand with the West against the communist menace was unmanly, even perfidious. In the "if you're not with us you're against us" climate that characterized the early 1950s, especially once the Republicans returned to power in 1953, Mossadeq's neutralism only further confirmed suspicions that his regime was leading Iran toward disaster.[11]

Also telling were the frequent Anglo-American references to Mossadeq's childishness and immaturity and the attendant assumption that the West needed to save Iran from his unrealistic and naive policies. The prime minister was called insolent and intransigent when he refused to accept British and U.S. plans for resolving the oil crisis, and during negotiations he allegedly had to be humored like a "fractious child."[12] In contrast to the British, who had been "saints" throughout the oil crisis, Mossadeq had been "the naughty boy" who needed to be disciplined. By describing Mossadeq in these ways Anglo-American officials were questioning his fitness for office and justifying their opposition to his regime.[13]

Finally, Anglo-American officials revealed their cultural biases when describing Iranian society and the Iranian people in general. Those Iranians who followed Mossadeq were little more than "mad and suicidal . . . lemmings" who needed to be saved from their folly by Western benevolence.[14] They were motivated by the "Iranian mentality" and the "Oriental mind," terms that Anglo-American officials used quite frequently but never really defined. Whatever these terms entailed, they became all-too-easy rationalizations for the failure to reach an acceptable oil agreement and prevented Western officials from searching for the real root of the impasse in oil talks; blaming the inability to reach a settlement on the inherent differences between the Iranians and themselves offered Anglo-American officials an honorable way to escape blame for the continued stalemate.[15] Not surprisingly, descriptions of Mossadeq fit with these general assessments of the Iranian people. The prime minister was a "wily Oriental" whose approach to the oil question was "almost mystical."[16] Patronizing remarks about the Iranian people's inability to choose and follow the right leader and stereotypical remarks about the mysterious East did more than reveal the cultural biases of Anglo-American officials. By assuming an air of superiority they also suggested, at least implicitly, an imperialist mentality that justified Western intervention to save Iran from self-destruction.

In characterizing Mossadeq as feminine and incapable Anglo-

American officials made two serious mistakes. One was their failure to recognize that Iranian standards of acceptable and normal behavior differed greatly from those that prevailed in the West. Whereas Mossadeq's tears symbolized weakness and emotionalism to them, for the Iranian people they were proof of Mossadeq's deep concern for the welfare of the country. Whereas his proclivity to conduct business from his bed while dressed in pajamas proved his quirkiness to Westerners, for Iranians these things were, as Andrew F. Westwood has noted, "deeply symbolic . . . of their personal plight and that of their nation, symbolic of the frailty of righteousness beset by powerful forces of evil." And whereas his fainting spells were for the Anglo-Americans something to mock and laugh about, they were the kinds of public displays of emotion and feeling that Iranians expected from a leader.[17]

Anglo-American officials also erred by never stopping to consider that perhaps Mossadeq's emotionalism was intentional, something he used to serve his own ends. Maybe he fainted and cried on purpose. In fact, evidence suggests this is precisely what the prime minister did. The best example of the depth of Mossadeq's theatrical talent came from a Majlis deputy who related the following personal experience. One day during an emotional speech on the floor of the Majlis Mossadeq collapsed in a heap. Fearing that the elderly premier had suffered a heart attack, the deputy, who also happened to be a medical doctor, rushed to check Mossadeq's pulse, which he expected to find weak and fluttering. He was quite surprised when it was strong and regular—and even more surprised when the prime minister opened one eye and winked at him, as if to say, "My trick has worked. You were taken in, and so were the others. I have won you over."[18]

When judged by Western standards, Mossadeq obviously did not measure up. He wept; he wore pajamas; he did not understand the intricacies of the international oil industry; he eschewed involvement in the cold war. These were not things real men did, and they set Mossadeq apart from the Anglo-Americans.

Like all of us, British and U.S. policy makers judged others, including Mossadeq, in relation to how they saw themselves. They developed in their own minds standards of acceptable behavior, action, and appearance and used them as a yardstick to measure others. Those who met the minimum were respected as equals; those who did not were denigrated and dismissed. As scholars such as Carol Cohn and Emily Rosenberg have noted, these standards for the most part consisted of opposing pairs of traits and behaviors with the positive element of each pair denoting acceptable (or Western norms) and the negative element signifying unacceptable (or other) norms.[19] For Westerners the positive traits were coded as male, the negative traits as female. Thus, in the pairs strong and weak, rational and irrational, and realistic and emotional, *strong, rational,* and *realistic* are seen as male and therefore desirable traits, whereas *weak, irrational,* and *emotional* are seen as female and therefore undesirable traits.

In the case of Mossadeq everything he did fed Western perceptions of him as weak and unmanly, which in turn made it much easier for Anglo-American officials to discount his position—and that of his country. Because Mossadeq neither looked nor acted like a Western leader and refused to kowtow to Western pressures for continued control of Iran's oil industry, he was described as an irrational lunatic unfit to hold the office of prime minister.

Iranians who were willing to work with the West received more positive reviews from British and U.S. officials. One member of the Iranian opposition who was willing to see the British return to Iran "as partners in the oil industry," for example, was praised for his physical and mental strength and for an ability to drink "his whisky manfully" (always the mark of a competent leader).[20] Mossadeq's successor as prime minister, Fazlollah Zahedi, also won plaudits as "a realistic man who [could] recognize a need to cooperate with the West in order to obtain revenue from the sale of Iranian oil."[21] In accepting the necessity of Western influence in and control over Iranian affairs these men differed from Mossadeq. They went along with Western schemes and tacitly accepted the idea of Western superiority that was built into the Orientalist thinking that so condemned and denigrated Mossadeq. In other words, in order to win Western acceptance they had put aside their Iranianness and embraced Westernness. They had abandoned the idea of national independence that spurred Mossadeq to defy the Anglo-Americans in order to receive Western support and assistance.

Assessing the immediate influence of Anglo-American characterizations of Mossadeq on the formulation of policy is tricky, because it is not possible to determine a direct causal relationship between Anglo-American perceptions and specific events. We cannot say, for example, that Western stereotypes led linearly to the coup that removed Mossadeq from office in the summer of 1953. But this does not mean that these stereotypes were unimportant. On the contrary, by shaping the mind-set of Anglo-American officials the stereotypes were part of the context within which those officials formulated policy. They buttressed claims of Western superiority over Iranian and other Middle Eastern peoples by perpetuating the idea that those peoples were weak and incapable. And their cumulative effect was to paint Mossadeq and others like him in unfavorable ways that rationalized and justified Western control.

Out of this three-way clash came the overthrow of Mossadeq's regime and the 1954 consortium agreement. The August 1953 coup brought the U.S. and British governments together with a coalition of Mossadeq's domestic opponents. The consortium agreement gave the major U.S. oil companies a 40 percent interest in the Iranian oil industry. This interest was an important economic and strategic asset that allowed the U.S. companies to conserve domestic petroleum supplies when analysts were warning of the nation's growing dependence on foreign oil supplies and of its vulnerability should hostile forces seize control of those supplies. In the short term, of course, the British, the Americans, and the oil companies appeared to be substantial winners. Under the consortium agreement Iranian nationalization became a facade for continued Western domination of the Iranian oil industry. But because the Iranian consortium laid the seeds of future Iranian discontent, the Western gain was actually short lived.

The coup against Mossadeq and the subsequent consortium agreement exacerbated Iranian nationalism, which, as we know, had inspired the initial drive for nationalization of the AIOC. Iranian nationalists were forced underground in the immediate aftermath of the 28 Mordad coup, as the shah and Zahedi crushed all potential opponents in a ruthless drive for supremacy. But the National Front remained loyal to the struggle against foreign domination. It worked clandestinely against ratification of the consortium agreement in 1954 and criticized the agreement thereafter as a sell-out that robbed Iran of its right to control its resources. In the long term it may well be true that the inability of the British and the United States to deal with Mossadeq, whose policies seem moderate in hindsight, cleared the path not so much for the shah and his agents over the next several decades but for the far more radical, dangerous, and anti-Western regimes that would follow after 1979.

III

The Iranian nationalization controversy was one of the first major post–World War II confrontations between the developed and developing worlds, between what historians of world systems call the core and the periphery. As such, it has much to tell us about relations between those two worlds, about how policy makers on each side perceived the other, how their perceptions helped to shape policy, how leaders in Washington and London envisioned the global economy, and how they tried to integrate a nation like Iran and a resource like oil into that economy.

As this discussion suggests, the question of perceptions—or, perhaps more accurately, misperceptions—proved to be an important one throughout the oil crisis. Mossadeq misread the willingness of U.S. officials to come to Iran's assistance, the difficulties of selling nationalized oil on the open market, and the degree of British opposition to surrendering control of Iranian oil. He also miscalculated the usefulness of communism as a way to win U.S. support. For their part Anglo-American officials had tremendous misperceptions about Mossadeq—that he was senile, mentally unbalanced, and unfit for office. Exacerbating these misperceptions was that key U.S. diplomats in Iran were not Middle Eastern or Iranian experts but career Foreign Service officers, like Henry Grady and Loy Henderson, who moved from trouble spot to trouble spot with some frequency. With little or no understanding of Iranian history, culture, or traditions they did not appreciate the role that emotion or public tears played in the political culture of Iran or why Mossadeq might have worn pajamas and worked from his bed. Instead of taking Mossadeq on his terms, Western leaders chose to judge him according to their standards and to dismiss him when he failed to measure up to expectations. Their sentiments were perhaps best reflected in the story that accompanied *Time* magazine's designation of Mossadeq as 1951's Man of the Year. While calling the prime minister a "dizzy old wizard" who "put Scheharazade in the petroleum business" by nationalizing the AIOC, *Time*'s editors labeled him "by Western standards an appalling caricature of a statesman." No policy maker in London or Washington could have said it better.[22] This tendency was not unique to Iran, of course, but applied throughout the world's developing countries. It reflected an Anglo-American sense of cultural superiority that used the set of stereotypes (termed orientalism by Edward Said) to denigrate anyone who came from the developing world as inferior, incapable, and unworthy. And it helps to explain why the Iranian crisis, which was at its heart a North-South conflict, ultimately proved so difficult to resolve.

The oil crisis was also part of the East-West cold war in which policy makers on both sides sought to control raw materials and strategic resources, like Iranian oil, and deny them to their opponents. For officials in the United States and Great Britain Iranian oil could best be safeguarded by fostering political and economic stability in Iran and by containing what they saw as the radical nationalism of an underdeveloped country. Both strategies involved subordinating Iran's needs and desires to those of the West; neither yielded long-term benefits. Although Iran did not fall behind the iron curtain, it ultimately did not become a permanent fixture in the Western sphere of influence in the Middle East. Instead, U.S. involvement in the 28 Mordad coup and the 1954 consortium agreement convinced the Iranian people that the United States cared little for their interests, that it was more concerned with propping up British imperialism than with assisting their national self-determination and independence. These convictions led Iranian nationalists to dub the United States the Great Satan and to blame it for all their nation's ills during the next twenty-five years. In a sense Ayatollah Khomeini finally realized Mossadeq's dream of expelling foreign influence from Iran, demonstrating to Anglo-American officials in the process the long-term repercussions of their suppression of Iranian nationalism during the 1950s.

As this book makes clear, the Anglo-Iranian oil dispute was also a major episode in the postwar history of the Anglo-American relationship. Although the oil crisis generated a great deal of transatlantic squabbling, Washington's fears for Iran's safety did not lead to a U.S. alliance with Iran against Great Britain. Instead, the Iranian oil dispute fostered Anglo-American cooperation. Hamstrung by their commitments in other parts of the world, U.S. officials had no choice but to follow Britain's lead in Iran in order to prevent a disaster there. During the Truman administration the British helped to shape U.S. policy in ways that favored their purposes. The Harriman mission, the McGhee-Mossadeq talks, and the Truman-Churchill proposals all brought U.S. and British policies toward the Iranian oil dispute closer together, so that by the time Truman left office the two had become virtually indistinguishable. Transatlantic cooperation continued during the Eisenhower administration but with U.S. officials now assuming the dominant role in the Anglo-American relationship. Freed from the responsibilities that had made its predecessor dependent on the British, the new administration took the lead in planning for the covert operation that overthrew Mossadeq and in the negotiations that led to the formation of an international cartel that restarted the Iranian oil industry. Indeed, by 1954 the United States had replaced Great Britain as the major Western power in Iran and was on its way to becoming the major Western power in the Middle East as a whole. The Anglo-American reversal of roles would be complete after Britain's humiliation at Suez in 1956.

In addition to being a catalyst for the rise of U.S. power in the Middle East, the Iranian nationalization crisis was a key development in the rise of indigenous nationalism throughout that region. Just as British and U.S. officials had feared, Iran's nationalization of the Anglo-Iranian Oil Company was prelude to similar efforts in other nations, most notably in Egypt, where the target was the Suez Canal. As the Egyptian and other episodes attest, Middle Eastern nationalism became a force to be reckoned with after the Iranian oil crisis. Nationalism remained an important force in Iran as well, for even though the National Front and other opponents of foreign influence in Iran were suppressed after 1953, they continued to operate underground, gaining support as the excesses and abuses of the shah became increasingly egregious and ultimately helping to drive him into exile in early 1979.

The Anglo-Iranian crisis also provides a good example of how a preoccupation with the communist threat led the U.S. government to stifle a developing country's nationalism in favor of traditional European-style imperialism. For the first several years of the Anglo-Iranian dispute, as we have seen, the Truman administration pushed the British to accommodate Iranian nationalism and allow the Iranians a greater role in the operation of the oil industry. As the United States saw it, dealing generously with the Iranians offered the best hope of attaining an oil settlement that preserved Iran's Western orientation and prevented it from falling to communism. As the crisis dragged on, however, Washington's determination to protect Iran from the communists, its commitments in other parts of the world, and its growing global partnership with London led it to identify more closely with the British position, even if this meant abandoning Iran's nationalist ambitions in the process.

Although U.S. officials acknowledged Iran's right to nationalize its oil industry, they were reluctant to see control of that industry pass to Iranian hands, as such a development might imperil continued Western access to a vital and seemingly irreplaceable resource. This concern explained their eventual decision to side with the British over the Iranians in the oil dispute. It also explains their strong opposition to Mossadeq's apparent antidemocratic drift during the summer of 1953. Officials in the Eisenhower administration were probably being honest when they expressed concern that the instability caused by Mossadeq's authoritarianism would lead to a triumph of communism. This is the same kind of thinking that guided U.S. policy in other developing countries and helps to explain why U.S. officials saw nationalist leaders like Mossadeq as threats to U.S. interests. Because they would not side solidly with the West against the Soviet Union, and because they challenged traditional Western control over key resources, these leaders were seen as communists and targeted for removal from office. Instability from whatever source was the enemy for Western leaders in Iran, as it would later be in places like Guatemala and Egypt. But in a somewhat ironic twist the administration's pursuit of stability, in Iran and elsewhere, ultimately contributed to the very chaos and instability it so feared.[23]

IV

When Iran first nationalized the Anglo-Iranian Oil Company's holdings in the spring of 1951, both parties believed, albeit for different reasons, that coming to a satisfactory resolution of the conflict would be a simple and rapid process. As this book has shown, the process was anything but. Both sides ultimately came to invest so much symbolic meaning in determining the terms of the final settlement that arriving at such a settlement was all but impossible, even with the intervention of the United States. And when the dispute was finally resolved to the advantage of the Anglo-Americans, to Iranian observers it seemed that might, not right, had prevailed—at least temporarily. By subverting Iranian nationalism the oil dispute of the 1950s laid the seeds for the Islamic Revolution that would come twenty-five years later and that would usher in even more anti-Western regimes in Tehran than Mossadeq's. As a result, its consequences continue even now to cast a shadow over the Persian Gulf and beyond.

As a courtesy to readers who may be unfamiliar with the abbreviations and archival sources used in the notes that follow, these terms have been abbreviated throughout: telegram (tel.), Record Group (RG), Foreign Office (FO), President's Secretary's Files (PSF). PREM is the record class designation for British prime ministers' records.

Citations to the General Records of the Department of State (RG 59) consist of three combinations of numbers; the first refers to the general subject and referent nation of the document cited, the second contains modifiers of the first, more general subject, and the third provides the date of the document. In the citation *RG 59, 888.2553AIOC/1-2150*, for example, 888 refers to economic conditions in Iran, .2553AIOC refers to oil (and specifically to the Anglo-Iranian Oil Company), and 1-2150 dates the document as 21 January 1950. Guides to the State Department's numbering system are available at the National Archives in Washington, D.C.

Citations to the Political Correspondence of the British Foreign Office (FO 371) consist of three elements. The first refers to the specific bundle of documents ordered from the document inventory, the second represents a particular subject or topic, and the third provides the item number of the specific document cited. In the citation *FO 371, 82374/EP1531/1*, 82374 is the bundle of documents ordered from the central document inventory,

EP1531 is the general heading for the Anglo-Iranian oil crisis, and 1 shows it is the first item in the bundle. Explanations of the Foreign Office's numbering system are available at the Public Record Office in Kew.

1. The Anglo-Iranian Oil Crisis: An Overview

1. On this point see Robert B. Stobaugh, "The Evolution of Iranian Oil Policy, 1925–1975," in *Iran Under the Pahlavis*, ed. George Lenczowski (Stanford, Calif.: Hoover Institution Press, 1978), p. 207.

2. Representative of this literature are Ervand Abrahamian, *Iran Between Two Revolutions* (Princeton, N.J.: Princeton University Press, 1982); Fakhreddin Azimi, *Iran: The Crisis of Democracy, 1941–1953* (London: I. B. Tauris, 1989); Farhad Diba, *Mohammad Mossadegh: A Political Biography* (London: Croom Helm, 1986); L. P. Elwell-Sutton, *Persian Oil: A Study in Power Politics* (London: Lawrence & Wishart, 1955); M. Reza Ghods, *Iran in the Twentieth Century: A Political History* (Boulder, Colo.: Lynne Rienner, 1989); Homa Katouzian, *The Political Economy of Modern Iran: Despotism and Pseudo-Modernism, 1926–1979* (New York: New York University Press, 1981), and *Musaddiq and the Struggle for Power in Iran* (London: I. B. Tauris, 1990); and Sepehr Zabih, *The Mossadegh Era: Roots of the Iranian Revolution* (Chicago: Lake View, 1982).

3. For examples see Diba, *Mohammad Mossadegh*; and Amir Taheri, *Nest of Spies: America's Journey to Disaster in Iran* (London: Hutchinson, 1988).

4. See, for example, Elwell-Sutton, *Persian Oil*.

5. Characteristic are Robert Engler, *The Politics of Oil: A Study of Private Power and Democratic Directions* (Chicago: University of Chicago Press, 1961); Walter Levy, *Oil Strategy and Politics, 1941–1981* (Boulder, Colo.: Westview, 1982); Stephen Helmsley Longrigg, *Oil in the Middle East: Its Discovery and Development*, 3d ed. (London: Oxford University Press, 1968); Henry Longhurst, *Adventure in Oil: The Story of British Petroleum* (London: Sidgwick and Jackson, 1959); and Anthony Sampson, *The Seven Sisters: The Great Oil Companies and the World They Shaped* (New York: Viking, 1975). The official company history is J. H. Bamberg, *The History of the British Petroleum Company*, vol. 2: *The Anglo-Iranian Years, 1928–1954* (Cambridge, England: Cambridge University Press, 1994).

6. See, for example, James A. Bill, *The Eagle and the Lion: The Tragedy of American-Iranian Relations* (New Haven, Conn.: Yale University Press, 1988); James A. Goode, *The United States and Iran, 1946–1951: The Diplomacy of Neglect* (New York: St. Martin's, 1989); Wm. Roger Louis, *The British Empire in the Middle East, 1945–1951: Arab Nationalism, the United States, and Postwar Imperialism* (Oxford, England: Oxford University Press, 1984); Mark Hamilton Lytle, *The Origins of the Iranian-American Alliance, 1941–1953* (New York: Holmes & Maier, 1987); David S. Painter, *Oil and the American Century: The Political Economy of U.S. Foreign Oil Policy, 1941–1954* (Baltimore: Johns Hopkins University Press, 1986); and Barry Rubin, *Paved with Good Intentions: The American Experience and Iran* (New York: Oxford University Press, 1980).

7. See Alan W. Ford, *The Anglo-Iranian Dispute of 1951–1952: A Study of the Role of Law in the Relations of States* (Berkeley: University of California Press, 1954); Sunil Kanti Ghosh, *The Anglo-Iranian Oil Dispute: A Study of the Problems of Nationaliza-*

tion of Foreign Investment and Their Impact on International Law (Calcutta: Firma K. L. Mukhopadhjay, 1960); and International Court of Justice, *Pleadings, Oral Arguments, Documents, Anglo-Iranian Oil Co. Case (United Kingdom v. Iran)* (The Hague: International Court of Justice, 1952).

8. Mostafa Elm, *Oil, Power, and Principle: Iran's Oil Nationalization and Its Aftermath* (Syracuse, N.Y.: Syracuse University Press, 1992).

9. For this revisionist argument see, for example, Alan S. Milward, *The Reconstruction of Western Europe, 1945–1951* (Berkeley: University of California Press, 1984); and Fraser J. Harbutt, *The Iron Curtain: Churchill, America, and the Origins of the Cold War* (New York: Oxford University Press, 1986).

10. Edward W. Said, *Orientalism* (New York: Vintage, 1978). For an excellent exploration of the use of such stereotypes see Andrew J. Rotter, "Gender Relations, Foreign Relations: The United States and South Asia, 1947–1964," *Journal of American History* 81 (September 1994): 518–42.

11. The best examination of the U.S. relationship with the shah is Mark J. Gasiorowski, *U.S. Foreign Policy and the Shah: Building a Client State in Iran* (Ithaca, N.Y.: Cornell University Press, 1991).

12. James A. Bill and Wm. Roger Louis, eds., *Musaddiq, Iranian Nationalism, and Oil* (Austin: University of Texas Press, 1988), p. 11.

13. On the early years of British involvement in Iranian oil see J. R. L. Anderson, *East of Suez: A Study of Britain's Greatest Trading Enterprise* (London: Hodder & Stoughton, 1969), pp. 26–43; Ronald W. Ferrier, "The Development of the Iranian Oil Industry," in *Twentieth-Century Iran*, ed. Hossein Amirsadeghi (London: Heinemann, 1977), pp. 93–97, and Ferrier, *The History of the British Petroleum Company*, vol. 1: *The Developing Years, 1901–1932* (Cambridge, England: Cambridge University Press, 1982), pp. 15–201; Longhurst, *Adventure in Oil*, pp. 19–53; Longrigg, *Oil in the Middle East*, pp. 16–22; B. S. McBeth, *British Oil Policy, 1919–1939* (London: Frank Cass, 1986); Benjamin Shwadran, *The Middle East, Oil, and the Great Powers* (New York: Wiley, 1973), pp. 13 19; and Stobaugh, "Evolution of Iranian Oil Policy," pp. 201–202.

14. Unless otherwise stated, the statistics are taken from Longrigg, *Oil in the Middle East*, pp. 35–36.

15. Again, the statistics are taken from Longrigg, *Oil in the Middle East*, p. 58.

16. For developments discussed in the four preceding paragraphs see Anderson, *East of Suez*, pp. 43–48; Ferrier, *History of British Petroleum*, pp. 202–61, 350–97, 588–635; Longhurst, *Adventure in Oil*, pp. 54–80; Longrigg, *Oil in the Middle East*, pp. 48–60; Shwadran, *Middle East*, pp. 20–47; and Stobaugh, "Evolution of Iranian Oil Policy," pp. 202–205. See also Peter Beck, "The Anglo-Persian Dispute of 1932–33," *Journal of Contemporary History* 9 (October 1974): 123–51.

17. Among the available accounts of the wartime occupation are Bruce Robellet Kuniholm, *The Origins of the Cold War in the Near East: Great Power Conflict and Diplomacy in Iran, Turkey, and Greece* (Princeton, N.J.: Princeton University Press, 1980); Lytle, *Origins of the Iranian-American Alliance*, pp. 16–27; Stephen L. McFarland, "A Peripheral View of the Origins of the Cold War: The Crisis in Iran, 1941–1947," *Diplomatic History* 4 (Fall 1980): 333–51; Eduard M. Mark, "Allied Relations in Iran, 1941–1947: The Origins of a Cold War Crisis," *Wisconsin Magazine of History* 59 (Autumn 1975): 51–63; Rouhollah K. Ramazani, *Iran's Foreign Policy,*

1941–1973: A Study of Foreign Policy in Modernizing Nations (Charlottesville: University of Virginia Press, 1975), pp. 30–62; and Shwadran, *Middle East*, pp. 47–51.

18. For U.S. oil policy see Edward W. Chester, *United States Oil Policy and Diplomacy: A Twentieth-Century Overview* (Westport, Conn.: Greenwood, 1983); Engler, *Politics of Oil*; Levy, *Oil Strategy and Politics*; Gerald Nash, *United States Oil Policy, 1880–1964: Business and Government in Twentieth-Century America* (Pittsburgh, Pa.: University of Pittsburgh Press, 1968); Painter, *Oil and the American Century*; Stephen J. Randall, *United States Foreign Oil Policy, 1919–1948: For Profits and Security* (Kingston, Ontario, Canada: McGill-Queen's University Press, 1985); Sampson, *Seven Sisters*; Michael B. Stoff, *Oil, War, and American Security: The Search for a National Policy on Foreign Oil, 1941–1947* (New Haven, Conn.: Yale University Press, 1980); and Daniel Yergin, *The Prize: The Epic Quest for Oil, Money, and Power* (New York: Simon & Schuster, 1991). For developments in Iran see Kuniholm, *Origins of the Cold War*; George Lenczowski, *Russia and the West in Iran, 1918–1948: A Study in Big Power Rivalry* (New York: Greenwood, 1968); Longrigg, *Oil in the Middle East*; Lytle, *Origins of the Iranian-American Alliance*, pp. 63–99; McFarland, "A Peripheral View"; Mark, "Allied Relations"; Richard A. Pfau, "Avoiding the Cold War: The United States and the Iranian Oil Crisis, 1944," *Diplomatic History* 1 (Fall 1977): 359–72; and Shwadran, *Middle East*, pp. 51–53.

19. These developments are described in Terry H. Anderson, *The United States, Great Britain, and the Cold War, 1944–1947* (Columbia: University of Missouri Press, 1981), pp. 100–107, 119–30; Ferrier, "Development of the Iranian Oil Industry," pp. 102–104; Lytle, *Origins of the Iranian-American Alliance*, pp. 164–88; Ramazani, *Iran's Foreign Policy*, pp. 91–153, 167–69; Shwadran, *Middle East*, pp. 313–19; and Stobaugh, "Iranian Oil Policy," pp. 201–202.

20. See Richard W. Cottam, *Iran and the United States: A Cold War Case Study* (Pittsburgh, Pa.: University of Pittsburgh Press, 1988), and "The United States, Iran, and the Cold War," *Iranian Studies* 3 (Winter 1970): 3–33; Fraser J. Harbutt, "American Challenge, Soviet Response: The Beginning of the Cold War, February–March 1946," *Political Science Quarterly* 96 (Winter 1981–1982): 623–39; Gary R. Hess, "The Iranian Crisis of 1945–1946 and the Cold War," *Political Science Quarterly* 89 (March 1974): 117–46; George Lenczowski, "United States' Support for Iran's Independence and Integrity, 1945–1959," *Annals of the American Academy* 401 (May 1972): 45–55; Lytle, *Origins of the Iranian-American Alliance*, pp. 156–63; and Michael K. Sheehan, *Iran: The Impact of United States Interests and Policies, 1941–1954* (New York: Gaus, 1986).

21. For the wartime U.S. agreements see Lytle, *Origins of the Iranian-American Alliance*, pp. 27–32, 103–17, and Ramazani, *Iran's Foreign Policy*, pp. 70–90.

22. For this argument see Lytle, *Origins of the Iranian-American Alliance*, pp. 177–78.

23. Ibid., 138–39, 144, 174–75; see also Kuniholm, *Origins of the Cold War*, p. 422; and Ramazani, *Iran's Foreign Policy*, pp. 154–66.

24. The best study of the postwar independence movements in the Middle East is Louis, *British Empire*. Also of use are Elizabeth Monroe, *Britain's Moment in the Middle East, 1917–1971*, rev. ed. (Baltimore: Johns Hopkins University Press, 1981), and M. A. Fitzsimons, *Empire by Treaty: Britain and the Middle East in the Twentieth Century* (Notre Dame, Ind.: University of Notre Dame Press, 1964).

25. On Iranian nationalism see Richard W. Cottam, *Nationalism in Iran*, 2d rev. ed. (Pittsburgh, Pa.: University of Pittsburgh Press, 1979), and "Nationalism in Twentieth-Century Iran and Dr. Muhammad Musaddiq," in *Musaddiq*, ed. Bill and Louis, pp. 23–46.

26. See Louis, *British Empire*, pp. 46–47.

27. See sources cited in note 25.

28. On Venezuela see Rómulo Betancourt, *Venezuela: Oil and Politics* (Boston: Houghton Mifflin, 1979); Stephen G. Rabe, *The Road to OPEC: United States Relations with Venezuela, 1919–1976* (Austin: University of Texas Press, 1982); and Franklin Tugwell, *The Politics of Oil in Venezuela* (Stanford, Calif.: Stanford University Press, 1958). On Saudi Arabia see Irvine H. Anderson, "The American Oil Industry and the Fifty-Fifty Agreement of 1950," in *Musaddiq*, ed. Bill and Louis, pp. 143–63; Anderson, *ARAMCO, the United States, and Saudi Arabia: A Study in the Dynamics of Foreign Oil Policy, 1933–1950* (Princeton, N.J.: Princeton University Press, 1980); and Aaron David Miller, *Search for Security: Saudi Arabian Oil and American Foreign Policy, 1939–1949* (Chapel Hill: University of North Carolina Press, 1980).

29. This and the paragraphs that follow are based on Ronald W. Ferrier, "The Anglo-Iranian Oil Dispute: A Triangular Relationship," in *Musaddiq*, ed. Bill and Louis, pp. 168–74; Longrigg, *Oil in the Middle East*; Lytle, *Origins of the Iranian-American Alliance*, pp. 193–96; Ramazani, *Iran's Foreign Policy*, pp. 181–86; and Shwadran, *Middle East*, pp. 89–91.

30. See Ferrier, "Development of the Iranian Oil Industry," p. 106.

31. Text of the supplemental agreement may be found in Ghosh, *Anglo-Iranian Oil Dispute*, pp. 298–99.

32. On Majlis debate regarding the supplemental agreement see Elwell-Sutton, *Persian Oil*, pp. 178–81.

2. Too Little, Too Late

1. Overseas Consultants, Inc., *Report on the Seven-Year Development Plan for the Plan Organization of the Imperial Government of Iran*, vol. 5 (New York: Overseas Consultants, 1949), p. 11. See also vols. 1–4; Barry Rubin, *Paved with Good Intentions: The American Experience and Iran* (New York: Oxford University Press, 1980), pp. 40–42; and Mark Hamilton Lytle, *Origins of the Iranian-American Alliance, 1941–1953* (New York: Holmes & Maier, 1987), pp. 195–96.

2. Fakhreddin Azimi, *Iran: Crisis of Democracy, 1941–1953* (London: I. B. Tauris, 1989), p. 213. See also Wiley tel. (telegram) to State Department, 8 January 1950, U.S. Department of State, *Foreign Relations of the United States, 1950*, vol. 5 (Washington, D.C.: Government Printing Office, 1978), pp. 445–46 (hereafter *FRUS*); Sir John Le Rougetel (British ambassador, Tehran) tel. 16 to Foreign Office (FO), 9 January 1950, Political Correspondence of the Foreign Office, Record Class FO 371, 82374/EP1531/1, Public Record Office, Kew, England (hereafter FO 371, with filing information); Wiley tel. 115 to State Department, 21 January 1950, General Records of the Department of State, Record Group 59, 888.2553/1-2150, National Archives, Washington, D.C. (hereafter RG 59, with filing information); and Azimi, *Iran*, pp. 100, 201.

3. Ervand Abrahamian, *Iran Between Two Revolutions* (Princeton, N.J.: Princeton University Press, 1982), p. 260. For a discussion of the rising power of the National

Front coalition see Richard W. Cottam, *Iran and the United States: A Cold War Case Study* (Pittsburgh, Pa.: University of Pittsburgh Press, 1988), pp. 73, 88, 91, and *Nationalism in Iran*, 2d rev. ed. (Pittsburgh, Pa.: University of Pittsburgh Press, 1979), pp. 264–68; Farhad Diba, *Mohammad Mossadegh: A Political Biography* (London: Croom Helm, 1986), pp. 96–112; Abrahamian, *Iran Between Two Revolutions*, pp. 252–67, and "The Crowd in Iranian Politics, 1905–53," in *Iran: A Revolution in Turmoil*, ed. Haleh Afshar (London: Macmillan, 1985), pp. 137–40; Azimi, *Iran,* pp. 220–21; Homa Katouzian, *Musaddiq and the Struggle for Power in Iran* (London: I. B. Tauris, 1990), pp. 71–77; and James A. Bill, *Eagle and the Lion: The Tragedy of American-Iranian Relations* (New Haven, Conn.: Yale University Press, 1988), pp. 67–72.

4. See Diba, *Mohammad Mossadegh*, pp. 3–63; Azimi, *Iran*, p. 258; and Homa Katouzian, ed., *Musaddiq's Memoirs* (London: JEBHE, National Movement of Iran, 1988), chaps. 5, 12–14, 17, 20–24.

5. In addition to the sources cited in note 4 see Francis Shepherd (British ambassador, Tehran) dispatch 106 to FO, 7 May 1950, FO 371, 82310/EP1016/27; Shepherd dispatch 140 to FO, "Monthly Report for April 1950," 5 May 1950, FO 371, 82308/EP1013/23; and Katouzian, *Musaddiq and the Struggle for Power*, pp. 71–77.

6. On the establishment of the Senate see Azimi, *Iran*, pp. 203–204; and James A. Goode, *The United States and Iran, 1946–51: The Diplomacy of Neglect* (New York: St. Martin's, 1989), pp. 21–23.

7. See Marvin Zonis, *The Political Elite of Iran* (Princeton, N.J.: Princeton University Press, 1971); and Azimi, *Iran*.

8. On the Tudeh see Sepehr Zabih, *The Communist Movement in Iran* (Berkeley: University of California Press, 1966), esp. pp. 166–207.

9. See Wiley tel. 311 to State Department, 23 February 1950, RG 59, 888.2553/2-2450; Wiley tel. to State Department, 27 February 1950, *FRUS, 1950*, vol. 5, pp. 479–80; and Azimi, *Iran*, pp. 213–14.

10. Wiley tel. 44 to State Department, 9 January 1950, RG 59, 788.00/1-950; Alan Leavett (FO Eastern Department) minute, 11 January 1950, FO 371, 82374/EP1531/1; Wiley dispatch to State Department, 30 January 1950, *FRUS, 1950*, vol. 5, p. 460. Foreign Office sentiment was not entirely united about the benefits of a take-it-or-leave-it attitude, however. Valentine G. Lawford (counselor, British embassy, Tehran) and Lancelot F. L. Pyman (Oriental counselor, British embassy, Tehran) disagreed with such a strategy. See Wiley tel. 115 to State Department, 21 January 1950, RG 59, 888.2553/1-2150; and Wiley dispatch, 30 January 1950, *FRUS, 1950*, vol. 5, p. 460.

11. Dean G. Acheson, *Present at the Creation: My Years in the State Department* (New York: Norton, 1969), p. 503. For similar sentiment see George C. McGhee oral history interview, Harry S Truman Library, Independence, Missouri.

12. Wiley tel. 44 to State Department, RG 59, 788.00/1-950. See also Bill, *Eagle and the Lion*, p. 52.

13. Harlan B. Clark (officer in charge of Lebanon-Syria-Iraq affairs, Bureau of African and Near Eastern Affairs, State Department) memorandum of conversation re discussion with Anglo-Iranian Oil Company officials, 24 January 1950, RG 59, 888.2553AIOC/1-2450.

14. Wiley tel. 44 to State Department, 9 January 1950, RG 59, 788.00/1-950; C. Vaughan Ferguson (officer in charge of Iranian affairs, Office of Greek, Turkish, and Iranian Affairs, State Department) memorandum of conversation re Anglo-Iranian Oil

Company concession, 7 February 1950, RG 59, 888.2553AIOC/2-750. See also Holmes tel. 550 to State Department, 31 January 1950, Records of the Foreign Service Posts of the Department of State, Record Group 84, Tehran Embassy Confidential File, 523.1 AIOC, Washington National Records Center, Suitland, Maryland (hereafter RG 84, with filing information); Acheson tel. 157 to U.S. embassy, Tehran, 14 February 1950, RG 59, 888.2553AIOC/2-2650; and Acheson tel. 1037 to U.S. embassy, London, 23 February 1950, RG 59, 841.2553/2-2350.

15. Acting Secretary of State James E. Webb tel. to U.S. embassy, London, 22 May 1950, *FRUS, 1950*, vol. 5, pp. 550–51. See also F. Garner Ranney (Office of British Commonwealth and Northern European Affairs [NEA]) memorandum for Henry Labouisse (director, NEA), "Anglo-American Cooperation in the Near East," 30 January 1950, *FRUS, 1950*, vol. 5, pp. 123–24.

16. Le Rougetel tel. 70 to FO, 7 February 1950, FO 371, 82374/EP1531/5.

17. Le Rougetel to Wright, with enclosed copy of Le Rougetel to Fraser, 6 February 1950, FO 371, 82374/EP1531/11.

18. Lawford dispatch 62 to FO, 21 February 1950, FO 371, 82310/EP1016/18; Leavett and Furlonge minutes, 16 February 1950, FO 371, 82374/EP1531/11; Shepherd tel. 181 to FO, 21 April 1950, FO 371, 82374/EP1531/14. See also Furlonge to Shepherd, 10 March 1950, FO 371, 82310/EP1016/18; and Wright record of conversation with the Iranian ambassador, 8 June 1950, FO 371, 82374/EP1531/23.

19. Lawford dispatch 62 to FO, 21 February 1950, FO 371, 82310/EP1016/18; Leavett et al. minutes re Lawford dispatch 62, 7 March 1950, FO 371, 82310/EP1016/18. See also Leavett and Furlonge minutes, 16 February 1950, FO 371, 82374/EP1531/11; and Bevin tel. 174 to British embassy, Tehran, 1 May 1950, FO 371, 82374/EP1531/14.

20. Bevin tel. 174 to British embassy, Tehran, 1 May 1950, FO 371, 82374/EP1531/14; Le Rougetel tel. 70 to FO, 7 February 1950, FO 371, 82374/EP1531/5. See also Douglas tel. 2335 to State Department, 28 April 1950, RG 59, 888.2553/4-2850; and Bevin tel. 181 to British embassy, Tehran, 5 May 1950, FO 371, 82311/EP1016/33.

21. For Sa'ed's premiership see Shepherd dispatch 39 to FO, 1 February 1950, FO 371, 82310/EP1016/10; Wiley tel. 311 to State Department, 23 February 1950, RG 59, 888.2553/2-2450; Wiley tel. to State Department, 27 February 1950, *FRUS, 1950*, vol. 5, pp. 479–80; and Azimi, *Iran*, pp. 201–17.

22. For Sa'ed's resignation see Wiley tel. to State Department, 23 March 1950, *FRUS, 1950*, vol. 5, pp. 490–91; H. A. Dudgeon minute, "Change of Government in Persia," 27 March 1950, FO 371, 82310/EP1016/24; Azimi, *Iran*, pp. 213–17; and Katouzian, *Musaddiq and the Struggle for Power*, p. 76.

23. Wiley dispatch to State Department, "General Foreign and Domestic Political Situation of Iran," 30 January 1950, *FRUS, 1950*, vol. 5, pp. 459–64; Azimi, *Iran*, p. 222. For opposition to Mansur's appointment see Wiley tel. to State Department, 23 March 1950, *FRUS, 1950*, vol. 5, pp. 490–91; Acheson tel. to U.S. embassy, Tehran, 25 March 1950, *FRUS, 1950*, vol. 5, pp. 504–505; Shepherd dispatch 106 to FO, 7 April 1950, FO 371, 82310/EP1016/27; and Azimi, *Iran*, p. 219. For more on the shah's failure to support Mansur see Wiley tel. to State Department, 22 May 1950, *FRUS, 1950*, vol. 5, pp. 548; Wiley tels. (2) to State Department, 26 May 1950, *FRUS, 1950*, vol. 5, pp. 556–58; and Shepherd dispatch 177 to FO, 12 June 1950, FO 371, 82311/EP1016/53.

24. Wiley tel. 1116 to State Department, 13 June 1950, RG 59, 888.2553AIOC/6-1350; Shepherd to FO, 26 June 1950, FO 371, 82312/EP1016/62.

25. Douglas tel. 2336 to State Department, 28 April 1950, RG 59, 888.2553/4-2850; FO tel. 174 to British embassy, Tehran, 1 May 1950, FO 371, 82374/EP1531/14; Richards tel. 798 to State Department, 3 May 1950, RG 59, 888.2553AIOC/5-350.

26. Webb tel. 2275 to U.S. embassy, London, 12 May 1950, RG 59, 888.2553AIOC/5-1250; U.S. delegation at the Tripartite Preparatory Meetings tel. to State Department, 6 May 1950, *FRUS, 1950*, vol. 3, p. 987. See also unsigned memorandum, "AIOC Negotiations," 16 June 1950, RG 59, 888.2553/6-1650.

27. Shepherd to Furlonge, 5 June 1950, FO 371, 82311/EP1016/46. See also Diba, *Mohammad Mossadegh*, p. 102.

28. Paper prepared by the Bureau of Near Eastern, South Asian, and African Affairs, "May Foreign Ministers Position Paper on Iran," 27 April 1950, and Ferguson paper, "May Foreign Ministers Meeting Supplement to Position Paper on Iran," 3 May 1950, *FRUS, 1950*, vol. 5, pp. 529, 541. See also unsigned memorandum for the file, "Under Secretary's Meeting April 26, 1950," undated, *FRUS, 1950*, vol. 5, pp. 518–21.

29. U.S. delegation at the Tripartite Foreign Ministers Meeting tel. to State Department, 11 May 1950, *FRUS, 1950*, vol. 3, pp. 1027–31; U.S. delegation at the Tripartite Foreign Ministers Meeting tel. to State Department, 2 May 1950, *FRUS, 1950*, vol. 3, pp. 975–79. See also FO tel. 181 to British embassy, Tehran, 5 May 1950, FO 371, 82311/EP1016/33.

30. For the decision to reevaluate the U.S. aid program to Iran see Acheson tel. 312 to U.S. embassy, Tehran, 20 March 1950, RG 59, 888.00/3-2050; and Acheson tel. 369 to U.S. embassy, Tehran, 30 March 1950, RG 59, 888.00/3-3050.

31. See Ferguson memorandum of conversation with Ambassador Ala and State Department aide-mémoire to Iranian embassy, both 26 January 1950, *FRUS, 1950*, vol. 5, pp. 447–57; and Ferguson memorandum of conversation with Ala, 7 February 1950, RG 59, 788.5MAP/2-750. For U.S. military assistance see Ferguson memorandum of conversation with Ala et al., 24 March 1950, *FRUS, 1950*, vol. 5, pp. 500–501; Lytle, *Origins of Iranian-American Alliance*, pp. 195–96; and Bill, *Eagle and the Lion*, pp. 39–42.

32. Undated State Department paper, "The Present Crisis in Iran," *FRUS, 1950*, vol. 5, pp. 513, 516. See also Ferguson memorandum of conversation with Iranian Ambassador Nemazee, 12 April 1950, RG 59, 888.00/4-1250; and Richards tel. 680 to State Department, 14 April 1940, RG 59, 888.00/4-1450.

33. Wiley to Acheson, 15 and 27 February 1950, and Rountree to Jernegan, 23 March 1950, *FRUS, 1950*, vol. 5, pp. 470, 481–82, 492. See also Wiley tel. 416 to State Department, 11 March 1950, RG 59, 398.14/3-1150.

34. McGhee memorandum for Acheson re the Iranian crisis, 25 [26] April 1950, *FRUS, 1950*, vol. 5, pp. 521–26. See also paper prepared in the Department of State, UM D-97, "The Present Crisis in Iran," [21 April 1950], and paper prepared by the State Department's Bureau of Near Eastern, South Asian, and African Affairs, "May Foreign Ministers Meetings Position Paper on Iran," 27 April 1950, *FRUS, 1950*, vol. 5, pp. 509–18, 529–32.

35. Paper prepared in the Department of State, "The Present Crisis in Iran," undated, *FRUS, 1950*, vol. 5, pp. 509–19. In addition to the documents cited in note 34 see unsigned report prepared in the Department of State, "Regional Security Arrangements in the Eastern Mediterranean and Near East Areas," 11 May 1950, *FRUS, 1950*, vol. 5, pp. 152–59.

36. U.S. delegation at the London Tripartite Foreign Ministers Meeting tel. to State Department, 16 May 1950, *FRUS, 1950*, vol. 5, pp. 546–48.

37. Wiley tel. 947 to State Department, 23 May 1950, RG 59, 888.2553AIOC/5-2350. For the importance of using assistance as a means of exacting Iranian reforms see Richards tel. 673 to State Department, 13 April 1950, RG 59, 888.00/4-1350; and McGhee memorandum of conversation with Ambassador Ala, 1 May 1950, *FRUS, 1950*, vol. 5, pp. 536–40.

38. Bevin tel. 181 to British embassy, Tehran, 5 May 1950, FO 371, 82311/EP1016/33. For various demands by individual Iranians and their generally amorphous nature see Ferguson memorandum of conversation with Iranian ambassador et al. re Anglo-Iranian Oil Company concession, 7 February 1950, RG 59, 888.2553AIOC/2-750; Acheson tel. 157 to U.S. embassy, Tehran, 14 February 1950, RG 59, 888.2553AIOC/1-2650; Richards tel. 680 to State Department, 14 April 1950, RG 59, 888.00/4-1450; and Acheson tel. 751 to U.S. embassy, Tehran, 22 June 1950, RG 59, 888.2553AIOC/6-2250.

39. Shepherd to Furlonge, 5 June 1950, FO 371, 82311/EP1016/46. See also Albert F. Lager (U.S. petroleum attaché for Middle East, Cairo) memorandum, "Late Developments in the Iranian Oil Situation," 21 June 1950, RG 84, Tehran Embassy, Confidential File, 523.1 AIOC.

40. See Leavett et al. minutes, 7 March 1950, FO 371, 82310/EP1016/18; Wiley tel. to State Department, 26 May 1950, *FRUS, 1950*, vol. 5, pp. 558–59; Shepherd tel. 247 to FO (with Leavett minute), 2 June 1950, FO 371, 82311/EP1016/45; Cottam, *Iran and the United States*, pp. 83, 87–90; L. P. Elwell-Sutton, *Persian Oil: A Study in Power Politics* (London: Lawrence & Wishart, 1955), p. 183; and Azimi, *Iran*, pp. 222–28.

41. The shah's fears of Razmara are discussed in M. Reza Ghods, *Iran in the Twentieth Century: A Political History* (Boulder, Colo.: Lynne Rienner, 1989), p. 180.

42. Shepherd tel. 247 to FO, 2 June 1950, FO 371, 82311/EP1016/45; Richards tel. 1168 to State Department, *FRUS, 1950*, vol. 5, pp. 560–62. See also Acheson tel. to U.S. embassy, Tehran, 23 June 1950, *FRUS, 1950*, vol. 5, pp. 562–63; Douglas tel. 3680 to State Department, 28 June 1950, RG 59, 888.2553AIOC/6-2850; and McGhee memorandum for Acheson, "The Present Situation in Iran," 7 July 1950, *FRUS, 1950*, vol. 5, pp. 564–65.

43. Wiley tel. to State Department, 26 May 1950, *FRUS, 1950*, vol. 5, pp. 558–59; Wiley tel. 997 to State Department, 31 May 1950, RG 59, 888.2553AIOC/5-3150. See also Shepherd tel. 271 to FO, 16 June 1950, FO 371, 82311/EP1016/51; and Shepherd tel. 275 to FO, 19 June 1950, FO 371, 82311/EP1016/52.

44. See Furlonge to Shepherd, 30 June 1950, FO 371, 82312/EP1016/60; and Shepherd to Furlonge, 10 July 1950, with attached Shepherd memorandum and FO minutes, FO 371, 82375/EP1531/32.

45. See Richards tel. to State Department, 21 June 1950, Acheson tel. to U.S. embassy, Tehran, 23 June 1950, and McGhee memorandum for Acheson, "The Present Situation in Iran," 7 July 1950, *FRUS, 1950*, vol. 5, pp. 560–66; Cottam, *Iran and the United States*, p. 88; and Ghods, *Iran in the Twentieth Century*, pp. 180–81.

46. Bill, *Eagle and the Lion*, p. 73; Grady tel. to State Department, 15 August 1950, *FRUS, 1950*, vol. 5, pp. 581–83. See also Azimi, *Iran*, pp. 229, 232–33.

47. Furlonge to Shepherd, 30 June 1950, FO 371, 82312/EP1016/60; Shepherd to Furlonge, 26 June 1950, FO 371, 82374/EP1531/29.

48. Grady tel. 13 to State Department, 3 July 1950, RG 59, 888.2553AIOC/7-350; Grady tel. to State Department, 13 July 1950, *FRUS, 1950*, vol. 5, pp. 566–69. See also Richards dispatch 108 to State Department, 11 August 1950, RG 59, 788.00/8-1150.

49. Shepherd to Furlonge, with attached memorandum, 10 July 1950, FO 371, 82375/EP1531/32; Leavett minute on Shepherd letter to Furlonge of 10 July 1950, 13 July 1950, FO 371, 82374/EP1531/29.

50. See editorial note, *FRUS, 1950*, vol. 5, pp. 551–52.

51. For post-Korea thinking in Washington see Acheson tel. 89 to U.S. embassy, Tehran, 15 July 1950, RG 59, 888.00/7-1550; Grady tel. 164 to State Department, 20 July 1950, RG 59, 888.00/7-2050; McGhee memorandum to Acheson, "The United States Position in the Event of a Soviet Attack on Iran," 21 July 1950, *FRUS, 1950*, vol. 5, pp. 572–74; and Lytle, *Origins of the Iranian-American Alliance*, p. 198.

52. In addition to the sources cited in note 51 see Philip C. Jessup (American ambassador at large) memorandum of conversation with General Omar Bradley (U.S. Army chief of staff), 12 July 1950, *FRUS, 1950*, vol. 3, pp. 1655–57.

53. Grady tel. to State Department, 13 July 1950, *FRUS, 1950*, vol. 5, pp. 566–69; Wagner memorandum, "The Peculiar Position of the British in Iran," in Arthur L. Richards (counselor, U.S. embassy, Tehran) dispatch 83 to State Department, 29 July 195, RG 59, 641.88/7-2950. See also P. S. Stephens (British embassy, Washington) to Furlonge, 19 July 1950, FO 371, 82347/EP11345/28.

54. Acheson tel. 225 to U.S. embassy, London, 14 July 1950, RG 59, 888.2553/7-1450; Joseph J. Wagner (second secretary, U.S. embassy, Tehran) memorandum, "The Peculiar Position of the British in Iran," in Richards dispatch 83 to State Department, 29 July 1950, RG 59, 641.88/7-2950.

55. Bevin record of conversation with Ambassador Douglas, 12 August 1950, FO 371, 82375/EP1531/37. See also Douglas tel. to State Department, 12 August 1950, *FRUS, 1950*, vol. 5, pp. 580–81.

56. Acheson tel. 225 to U.S. embassy, London, 14 July 1950, RG 59, 888.553/7-1450; Douglas tel. 839 to State Department, 10 August 1950, RG 59, 888.2553AIOC/8-1050. For American assessments of the strategic importance of Iran see McGhee memorandum for Webb re suggested discussion of Iranian problem with Senator Tom T. Connally (D-Tex.), 25 April 1950, RG 59, 611.88/4-2550; Acheson tel. 781 to U.S. embassy, London, 11 August 1950, RG 59, 841.2553/8-1150; and background paper prepared in the Department of State for 11 September meeting with oil company executives, "Middle East Oil," September 1950, *FRUS, 1950*, vol. 5, pp. 76–96.

57. Bevin record of conversation with Ambassador Douglas, 12 August 1950, FO 371, 82375/EP1531/37.

58. See Grady tel. 215 to State Department, 25 July 1950, RG 59, 888.2553/7-2550; H. M. A. Hankey (FO) minute, 28 July 1950, FO 371, 87375/EP1531/42; L. Barnett memorandum, "Royalty Rates in Persia and Iraq" with attached minutes, 17 August 1950, FO 371, 82375/EP1531/53; and Shepherd to Furlonge, 21 August 1950, FO 371, 82375/EP1531/44.

59. Grady tel. 243 to State Department, 28 July 1950, RG 59, 888.2553AIOC/7-2850; Richards dispatch 92 to State Department, "Transmittal of Summaries of Conversations with Prime Minister Ali Razmara and Minister of Finance Taqi Nasr," 3 August 1950, RG 59, 788.00/8-350.

60. See Grady tel. 243 to State Department, 28 July 1950, RG 59, 888.2553AIOC/7-2850; and Acheson tel. 251 to U.S. embassy, Tehran, 7 August 1950, RG 59, 888.2553AIOC/8-750.

61. Acheson tel. to U.S. embassy, London, 7 August 1950, *FRUS, 1950*, vol. 5, pp. 576–77. See also Douglas tel. 792 to State Department, 8 August 1950, RG 59, 888.2553AIOC/8-850.

62. Shepherd dispatch 258 to FO, "Monthly Economic Report for August 1950," 2 September 1950, FO 371, 82309/EP1013/43. See also Shepherd tel. 341 to FO, 29 July 1950, FO 371, 82375/EP1531/36; and Barnett memorandum, 2 August 1950, FO 371, 82375/EP1531/43.

63. Furlonge memorandum, 11 August 1950, FO 371, 82375/EP1531/38. See also Douglas tel. 792 to State Department, 8 August 1950, RG 59, 888.2553AIOC/8-850; and Furlonge to Shepherd, 26 August 1950, FO 371, 82375/EP1531/44. For a refutation of Acheson's assertion regarding Anglo-American solidarity see Douglas tel. 839 to State Department, 10 August 1950, RG 59, 888.2553AIOC/8-1050.

64. Furlonge memorandum, 11 August 1950, FO 371, 82375/EP1531/38. See also Douglas tel. to State Department, 12 August 1950, *FRUS, 1950*, vol. 5, pp. 580–81.

65. See Bevin record of conversation with Ambassador Douglas, 12 August 1950, FO 371, 82375/EP1531/37; and Douglas tels. (2) to State Department, 10 and 12 August 1950, *FRUS, 1950*, vol. 5, pp. 578–81.

66. Acheson tel. 978 to U.S. embassy, London, 12 August 1950, RG 59, 888.2553AIOC/8-1250. See also Douglas tel. 792 to State Department, 8 August 1950, RG 59, 888.2553AIOC/8-850.

67. See Barnett minutes of meeting held on 2 August 1950 with Fraser, Gass et al., 3 August 1950, FO 371, 82375/EP1531/40; and Douglas tel. 839 to State Department, 10 August 1950, RG 59, 888.2553AIOC/8-1050.

68. Richards dispatch 92 to State Department, 3 August 1950, RG 59, 788.00/8-350; Barnett minutes of meeting held on 2 August 1950 with Fraser, Gass et al., 3 August 1950, FO 371, 82375/EP1531/40; the characterizations of Fraser are quoted in Anthony Sampson, *The Seven Sisters: The Great Oil Companies and the World They Shaped* (New York: Viking, 1975), p. 120. See also Wright's remarks in Douglas tel. 792 to State Department, 8 August 1950, RG 59, 888.2553AIOC/8-850; Shepherd tel. 330 to FO, 9 August 1950, FO 371, 82375/EP1531/36; and J.H. Bamberg, *The History of the British Petroleum Company*, vol. 2: *The Anglo-Iranian Years, 1928–1954* (Cambridge, England: Cambridge University Press, 1994), pp. 326–28.

69. For more on these talks see editorial note, *FRUS, 1950*, vol. 5, pp. 192–93.

70. Emphasis in original, Richard Funkhouser (Office of African and Near Eastern Affairs) memorandum for McGhee re discussions with British on AIOC, 14 September 1950, *FRUS, 1950*, vol. 5, p. 97.

71. Funkhouser memorandum for McGhee, "Summary—11 September Meeting with Oil Officials," 18 September 1950, in U.S. Congress, Senate Committee on Foreign Relations, Subcommittee on Multinational Corporations, *Multinational Corporations and United States Foreign Policy*, part 8, 93d Cong., 2d sess., 1974, p. 345; Funkhouser memorandum for McGhee, 14 September 1950, *FRUS, 1950*, vol. 5, p. 99. See also George McGhee, *Envoy to the Middle World: Adventures in Diplomacy* (New York: Harper & Row, 1983), p. 321.

72. Franks tel. 2498 to FO, 18 September 1950, FO 371, 82375/EP1531/51.

73. Unsigned record of informal U.S.-U.K. discussions, Thursday morning, 21 September 1950, *FRUS, 1950*, vol. 5, p. 597. See also unsigned record of informal U.S.-U.K. discussions, Saturday morning, 23 September 1950, *FRUS, 1950*, vol. 5, pp. 600–602; David K. E. Bruce (American ambassador, Paris) tel. 1606 to State Department (from McGhee), 27 September 1950, RG 59, 888.2553/9-2750; and McGhee, *Envoy to the Middle World*, pp. 322–24.

74. Richards dispatch 212 to State Department, "Transmission of a Report Entitled 'Iran at the End of Summer, 1950,'" 25 September 1950, RG 59, 788.00/9-2550; Bruce tel. 1606 to State Department, 27 September 1950, RG 59, 888.2553/9-2750; Rountree memorandum to McGhee re U.S.-U.K. divergences on Iran, 20 December 1950, *FRUS, 1950*, vol. 5, p. 634.

75. C.P.(50)250, "Persia: Labour Situation in the Oil Areas, Memorandum by the Secretary of State for Foreign Affairs, Minister of Labour and National Service and Minister of Fuel and Power," 26 October 1950, Cabinet Papers, Record Class CAB 129/42, PRO (hereafter CAB 129, with filing information); Grady tel. to State Department, 31 October 1950, *FRUS, 1950*, vol. 5, pp. 612–13. See also Acheson tel. to U.S. embassy, Tehran, 18 November 1950, *FRUS, 1950*, vol. 5, pp. 613–15; and Acheson to Bevin, 20 November 1950, *FRUS, 1950*, vol. 5, pp. 616–18.

76. P. E. Ramsbotham minute with enclosures, 19 December 1950, FO 371, 82377/EP1531/105; G. F. Rogers (British Middle East Office) to Wright, 16 November 1950, enclosing E. W. Noonan memorandum, "AIOC," 15 November 1950, FO 371, 82377/EP1531/82; Barnett memorandum, "Possible Modifications to the Supplemental Oil Agreement," 18 September 1950, FO 371, 82375/EP1531/54.

77. FO minutes, 21 December 1950, FO 371, 91521/EP1531/13; Wright memorandum, 16 October 1950, FO 371, 82376/EP1531/70.

78. See Richards dispatch 183 to State Department, 9 September 1950, RG 59, 788.00/9-950; Holmes tel. 1554 to State Department, 12 September 1950, RG 59, 888.2553AIOC/9-1250; Grady tel. 658 to State Department, 14 September 1950, RG 59, 888.2553AIOC/9-1450; and Shepherd dispatch 294 to FO, 6 October 1950, FO 371, 82309/EP1013/48. For the company's reaction to these demands and general statements about its willingness to make concessions outside the supplemental agreement see Holmes tel. 1499 to State Department, 9 September 1950, RG 59, 888.2553AIOC/9-950; Shepherd tel. 488 to FO, 6 October 1950, FO 371, 82375/EP1531/56; Douglas tel. 2238 to State Department, 18 October 1950, RG 59, 888.2553AIOC/10-1850; Wright record of conversation with Fraser and N. A. Gass (managing director, AIOC), 23 October 1950, FO 371, 82376/EP1531/71; and Gass to Furlonge, 26 October 1950, FO 371, 82376/EP1531/72. For additional Iranian demands see also Bevin tel. 580 to British embassy, Tehran, 29 December 1950, FO 371, 82377/EP1531/106.

79. Shepherd to Bevin, 14 October 1950, FO 371, 82376/EP1531/67. See also Richards dispatch 183 to State Department, 9 September 1950, RG 59, 788.00/9-950; Shepherd tel. 488 to FO, 6 October 1950, FO 371, 82375/EP1531/56; Grady tel. 828 to State Department, 9 October 1950, RG 59, 888.2553AIOC/10-950; Shepherd tel. 510 to FO, 15 October 1950, FO 371, 82376/EP1531/63; and Grady tel. 1015 to State Department, 2 November 1950, RG 59, 888.2553AIOC/11-250.

80. See Shepherd tel. 330 to FO, 9 August 1950, FO 371, 82375/EP1531/36; Holmes tel. 1499 to State Department, 9 September 1950, RG 59, 888.2553AIOC/9-950; Wright memorandum, 16 October 1950, FO 371, 82376/EP1531/70; Gass to Furlonge, 26

October 1950, FO 371, 82376/EP1531/72; and Douglas tel. 2489 to State Department, 31 October 1950, RG 59, 888.2553/10-3150.

81. Barnett record of meeting with Gass and Rice (AIOC) and Bowker and Furlonge (FO), 23 November 1950, FO 371, 82376/EP1531/84. See also Shepherd tel. 488 to FO, 6 October 1950, FO 371, 82375/EP1531/56; Shepherd tel. 489 to FO, 6 October 1950, FO 371, 82375/EP1531/57; and Holmes tel. to State Department, 14 December 1950, *FRUS, 1950*, vol. 5, pp. 632–33.

82. For British fears that the oil commission might reject the supplemental agreement see Ramsbotham minute with attachments, 19 December 1950, FO 371, 82377/EP1531/105.

83. See Richards dispatch 183 to State Department, 9 September 1950, RG 59, 788.00/9-950; and Shepherd to Bevin, 14 October 1950, FO 371, 82376/EP1531/671.

84. Wagner memorandum, "The Peculiar Position of the British in Iran," in Richards dispatch 83 to State Department, 29 July 1950, RG 59, 641.88/7-2950. See also British embassy, Tehran, dispatch 333 to Bevin, 13 November 1950, FO 371, 82376/EP1531/79.

85. On the National Front's political power see Goode, *The United States and Iran,*, pp. 59–60.

86. For the oil commission see Richards tel. 1179 to State Department, 23 June 1950, RG 59, 888.2553AIOC/6-2350; Rouhollah K. Ramazani, *Iran's Foreign Policy, 1941– 1973: A Study of Foreign Policy in Modernizing Nations* (Charlottesville: University of Virginia Press, 1975), pp. 189–94; Ronald W. Ferrier, "The Anglo-Iranian Oil Dispute: A Triangular Relationship," in *Musaddiq, Iranian Nationalism, and Oil*, ed. James A. Bill and Wm. Roger Louis (Austin: University of Texas Press, 1988), pp. 175–78; Sepehr Zabih, *The Mossadegh Era: Roots of the Iranian Revolution* (Chicago: Lake View, 1982), pp. 24–25; Diba, *Mohammad Mossadegh*, pp. 101–10; Elwell-Sutton, *Persian Oil*, pp. 182–84; and Katouzian, *Musaddiq and the Struggle for Power*, pp. 90–92.

87. See "Press Extracts No. 877," Report of the Oil Committee on Oil Bill, 23 December 1950, FO 371, 91521/EP1531/4; and Ramazani, *Iran's Foreign Policy*, pp. 189–94.

88. See British embassy, Tehran, dispatch 333 to FO, 13 November 1950, FO 371, 82376/EP1531/79; and Ramazani, *Iran's Foreign Policy*, pp. 189–94.

89. On Razmara's secret talks with the AIOC see, for example, Furlonge to Shepherd, 9 December 1950, FO 3711, 82377/EP1531/94; Richards tel. 1333 to State Department, 13 December 1950, RG 59, 888.00/12-1350; and Alfred F. Lager (regional petroleum attaché, U.S. embassy, Tehran) memorandum of conversation with prime minister of Iran and Max Thornburg, "Revision of Supplemental Agreement," 27 December 1950, RG 59, 888.2553/12-2750.

90. See Shepherd tel. 525 to FO, 19 October 1950, FO 371, 82376/EP1531/65; Shepherd tel. 526 to FO, 20 October 1950, FO 371, 82376/EP1531/66; Grady tel. 934 to State Department, 20 October 1950, RG 59, 888.2553AIOC/10-2050; Grady tel. 1015 to State Department, 2 November 1950, RG 59, 888.2553AIOC/11-250; and Ramazani, *Iran's Foreign Policy*, p. 190.

91. Mossadeq quoted in Ramazani, *Iran's Foreign Policy*, p. 194; Richards tel. 1199 to State Department, 27 November 1950, RG 59, 888.2553/11-2750. See also Shepherd to Furlonge, 27 November 1950, FO 371, 82377/EP1531/89; Richards tel. to State Department, 14 December 1950, *FRUS, 1950*, vol. 5, pp. 630–32; Shepherd to FO, 23 December

1950, enclosing "Report of Oil Committee on Oil Bill," FO 371, 91521/EP1531/4; and the sources cited in note 89.

92. Richards tel. to State Department, 14 December 1950, *FRUS, 1950*, vol. 5, pp. 630–32; Holmes tel. to State Department, 14 December 1950, *FRUS, 1950*, vol. 5, pp. 632–33. See also Richards tel. 1199 to State Department, 27 November 1950, RG 59, 888.2553/11-2750; Shepherd to Furlonge, 27 November 1950, FO 371, 82377/EP1531/89; and Holmes tel. 3186 to State Department, 30 November 1950, RG 59, 888.2553/11-3050.

93. Holmes tel. 3186 to State Department, 30 November 1950, RG 59, 888.2553/11-3060; Shepherd tel. 626 to FO, 7 December 1950, FO 371, 91521/EP1531/13; Holmes tel. to State Department, 14 December 1950, *FRUS, 1950*, vol. 5, pp. 632–33; Richards dispatch 404 to State Department, 4 December 1950, enclosing Stutesman memorandum, "Oil Industry," RG 59, 888.2553/12-450. See also Richards tel. to State Department, 14 December 1950, *FRUS, 1950*, vol. 5, pp. 630–32.

94. On Kashani see Shahrough Akhavi, "The Role of the Clergy in Iranian Politics, 1949–1954," in *Musaddiq, Iranian Nationalism, and Oil*, ed. Bill and Louis, pp. 91–94; and Yann Richard, "Ayatollah Kashani: Precursor to the Islamic Republic?" in *Religion and Politics in Iran*, ed. and trans. Nikki R. Keddie (New Haven, Conn.: Yale University Press, 1983), pp. 101–10.

95. Richards dispatch 465 to State Department, "Public Statement by Mullah Kashani Demanding Nationalization of the Oil Industry in Iran," 21 December 1950, RG 59, 888.2553/12-2150. See also Richards tel. 1307 to State Department, 11 December 1950, RG 59, 788.00/12-1150; Richards tel. 1344 to State Department, 14 December 1950, RG 59, 888.2553AIOC/12-1450; and Richards dispatch 471 to State Department, 22 December 1950, RG 59, 888.2553/12-2250. Additional public demands for nationalization are discussed in Richards tel. 1344 to State Department, 14 December 1950, RG 59, 888.2553AIOC/12-1450; Shepherd tel. 654 to FO, 21 December 1950, FO 371, 82377/EP1531/98; and Richards dispatch 471 to State Department, "Two Published Demands for the Nationalization of the Oil Industry in Iran," 22 December 1950, RG 59, 888.2553/12-2250.

96. Shepherd to Bevin, 22 December 1950, FO 371, 82377/EP1531/108. See also Shepherd dispatch 348 to FO, 4 December 1950, FO 371, 82313/EP1016/90.

97. See Shepherd tel. 654 to FO, 21 December 1950, FO 371, 82377/EP1531/98; and Shepherd to Bevin, 22 December 1950, FO 371, 82377/EP1531/108.

98. Holmes tel. to State Department, 14 December 1950, *FRUS, 1950*, vol. 5, p. 633. See also Shepherd dispatch 368 to FO, 29 December 1950, FO 371, 91521/EP1531/6.

99. E. A. Gilmore Jr. (first secretary of the U.S. embassy, Tehran) dispatch 544, "Reaction to Finance Minister Forouhar's Speech Withdrawing Supplementary Oil Agreement from the Majlis," 12 January 1951, RG 59, 888.2553/1-1251. See also Ramazani, *Iran's Foreign Policy*, p. 194.

100. Shepherd dispatch 368 to FO, 29 December 1950, FO 371, 91521/EP1531/6. See also Shepherd tel. 654 to FO, 21 December 1950, FO 371, 82377/EP1531/98; Shepherd to Bevin, 22 December 1950, FO 371, 82377/EP1531/108; Grady tel. 1432 to State Department, 29 December 1950, RG 59, 888.2553AIOC/12-2950; Shepherd tel. 675 to FO, 31 December 1950, FO 371, 91521/EP1531/1; C.P.(51)28, "Persia: Memorandum by the Secretary of State for Foreign Affairs," 22 January 1951, CAB 129/44; and Azimi, *Iran*, pp. 236–37.

101. Paul C. Parker (U.S. Treasury representative in the Middle East) to McGhee, 27 December 1950, RG 59, 888.2553/12-2750; CIA National Intelligence Estimate 15, "Probable Soviet Moves to Exploit the Present Situation," 11 December 1950, Harry S Truman Papers, President's Secretary's File (PSF), Subject File: National Security Council, box 191, folder: Central Intelligence, Truman Library. See also Ferguson memorandum of conversation, "Military Assistance to Iran," 8 December 1950, *FRUS, 1950*, vol. 5, pp. 620–24; report to the National Security Council (NSC), Annexes to NSC-68/3, "United States Objectives and Programs for National Security," 8 December 1950, *FRUS, 1950*, vol. 1, pp. 432–46; and paper prepared in the Office of Greek, Turkish, and Iranian Affairs, "Regional Policy Statement: Greece, Turkey, and Iran," 28 December 1950, *FRUS, 1950*, vol. 5, pp. 254–70.

3. Washington in the Middle

1. Shepherd dispatch 376 to FO, "Conduct of the Anglo-Persian Question: Analysis of Persian Objections to the Supplemental Oil Agreement and Suggested Future Policy," 31 December 1950, FO 371, 91521/EP1531/7.

2. Record of 3 January 1951 meeting between Gass and Rice (AIOC), Nuttall (Ministry of Fuel and Power), and Furlonge, Fry, Ramsbotham, and Barnett (FO), 7 January 1951, FO 371, 91521/EP1531/19. See also Barnett minute, 3 January 1951, FO 371, 91521/EP1531/11.

3. Burrows to Furlonge, 3 January 1951, FO 371, 91521/EP1531/16; Furlonge to Burrows, 10 January 1951, FO 371, 91521/EP1531/16; Shepherd dispatch 376 to FO, 31 December 1950, FO 371, 91521/EP1531/7; record of meeting between Butler and Nuttall and Furlonge, Fry, Ramsbotham, and Barnett, 3 January 1951, FO 371, 91521/EP1531/12; record of 3 January 1951 meeting between Gass and Rice, Nuttall, and Furlonge, Fry, Ramsbotham, and Barnett, 7 January 1951, FO 371, 91521/EP1531/19.

4. Furlonge to Burrows, 10 January 1951, FO 371, 91521/EP1531/16; Shepherd dispatch 376 to FO, 31 December 1950, FO 371, 91521/EP1531/7. See also Shepherd tel. 26 to FO, 10 January 1951, FO 371, 91521/EP1531/17.

5. Record of interdepartmental meeting between representatives of the Treasury, Ministry of Fuel and Power, and Foreign Office, 13 January 1951, FO 371, 91522/EP1531/31 (which also details the opposing Treasury position); Furlonge memorandum, 19 January 1951, FO 371, 91522/EP1531/32; N. E. Young (Treasury) memorandum, 18 January 1951, Records of the Central Economic Planning Staff, Record Class T236/2824, Public Record Office (hereafter T236, with filing information); Furlonge to Burrows, 10 January 1951, FO 371, 91521/EP1531/16; Burrows to Furlonge, 3 January 1951, FO 371, 91521/EP1531/16.

6. Grady tel. 1455 to State Department, 3 January 1951, RG 59, 888.2553/1-351; Acheson tel. 1122 to U.S. embassy, Tehran, 6 January 1951, RG 84, London Embassy, Classified Records, 523.1 Middle East.

7. Richards dispatch 509 to State Department, 5 January 1951, RG 59, 788.00/1-551. See also record of 3 January 1951 meeting of Gass and Rice, Nuttall, and Furlonge, Fry, Ramsbotham, and Barnett, 7 January 1951, FO 371, 91521/EP1521/19; and Grady tel. 1504 to State Department, 8 January 1951, RG 59, 888.2553/1-851.

8. Richards dispatch 540 to State Department, 11 January 1951, RG 59, 788.00/1-1151. See also Grady tel. 1549 to State Department, 12 January 1951, RG 59, 888.2553/1-

1251; and Fakhreddin Azimi, *Iran: The Crisis of Democracy, 1941–1953* (London: I. B. Tauris, 1989), pp. 235–36.

9. Record of meeting of Gass, Northcroft, and Rice, Young, Potter, Serpell, and Hedley-Miller, Nuttall and Butler, and Bowker, Furlonge, Fry, Ramsbotham, and Barnett, 16 January 1951, T236/2821; Shepherd dispatch 376 to FO, 31 December 1950, FO 371, 91521/EP1531/7. See also FO tel. 17 to British embassy, Tehran, 19 January 1951, FO 371, 91521/EP1531/23; and Furlonge memorandum, with attached record of meeting, 24 January 1951, FO 371, 91522/EP1531/35.

10. Grady tel. 549 to State Department, 12 January 1951, RG 59, 888.2553/1-1251; Shepherd to Furlonge, with attached "Note to Persian Government or to Persian Ambassador in London," and FO minutes, 14 January 1951, FO 371, 91521/EP1531/25.

11. Grady tel. 1563 to State Department, 13 January 1951, RG 59, 888.2553/1-1351; Richards dispatch 540 to State Department, 11 January 1951, RG 59, 788.00/1-1151.

12. For more on Iran's precarious economic situation see Nikki R. Keddie, *Roots of Revolution: An Interpretive History of Modern Iran* (New Haven, Conn.: Yale University Press, 1981), pp. 131–32.

13. See aide-mémoire handed to Shepherd by Razmara on 30 December 1950, with attached minutes, 10 January 1951, FO 371, 91521/EP1531/24; FO tel. 18 to British embassy, Tehran, 19 January 1951, FO 371, 91521/EP1531/23; FO tel. 24 to British embassy, Tehran, 24 January 1951, FO 371, 91522/EP1531/35; and Grady tel. 1722 to State Department, 1 February 1951, RG 84, London Embassy, Classified Records, 523.1 Middle East.

14. Furlonge memorandum with attached record of meeting, 24 January 1951, FO 371, 91522/EP1531/35; Serpell (Treasury) to Fry, 6 February 1951, FO 371, 91522/EP1531/39; Carr dispatch 652, "British Motives Behind £25 Million AIOC Advance to Iran," 15 March 1951, RG 59, 888.2553/2-1551.

15. See Young memorandum, 18 January 1951, T236/2824; Serpell to Fry, with attached FO minutes, 6 February 1951, FO 371, 91522/EP1531/39; Grady tel. 1767 to State Department, 7 February 1951, RG 59, 888.2553AIOC/2-751; and Furlonge to Shepherd, 27 February 1951, FO 371, 91522/EP1531/35.

16. Shepherd tel. 73 to FO, 4 February 1951, FO 371, 91522/EP1531/37. See also Shepherd tel. 87 to FO, 8 February 1951, FO 371, 91522/EP1531/40; and Shepherd tel. 93 to FO, 10 February 1951, FO 371, 91522/EP1531/41.

17. See Shepherd tel. 87 to FO, 8 February 1951, FO 371, 91522/EP1531/40; Shepherd tel. 93 to FO, 10 February 1951, FO 371, 91522/EP1531/41; Shepherd tel. 95 to FO, 11 February 1951, FO 371, 91522/EP1531/42; and Shepherd tel. 99 to FO, 14 February 1951, FO 371, 91522/EP1531/50.

18. FO tel. 25 to British embassy, Tehran, 24 January 1951, FO 371, 91522/EP1531/35; Shepherd tel. 93 to FO, 10 February 1951, FO 371, 91522/EP1531/41.

19. Shepherd tel. 95 to FO, 11 February 1951, FO 371, 91522/EP1531/42; Richards (Tehran) tel. 1847 to State Department, 16 February 1951, RG 59, 888.2553AIOC/2-1651.

20. Northcroft to Rice, 22 February 1951, FO 371, 91522/EP1531/62. See also Shepherd tel. 119 to FO, 21 February 1951, FO 371, 91522/EP1531/60; and Shepherd tel. 120 to FO, 21 February 1951, FO 371, 91522/EP1531/62.

21. See Shepherd tel. 73 to FO, 4 February 1951, FO 371, 91522/EP1531/37; Shepherd tel. 119 to FO, 21 February 1951, FO 371, 91522/EP1531/60; FO minutes, 23

February 1951, FO 371, 91522/EP1531/62; Shepherd tel. 122 to FO, 25 February 1951, FO 371, 91523/EP1531/66; and Shepherd tels. 128 and 133 to FO, 28 February 1951, FO 371, 91523/EP1531/69 and 91523/EP1531/73.

22. Shepherd tel. 99 to FO, 14 February 1951, FO 371, 91522/EP1531/50; Shepherd tel. 137 to FO, 1 March 1951, FO 371, 91523/EP1531/74. See also Shepherd tel. 119 to FO, 21 February 1951, FO 371, 91522/EP1531/160; Shepherd tel. 122 to FO, 25 February 1951, FO 371, 91523/EP1531/66; Shepherd tel. 133 to FO, 28 February 1951, FO 371, 91523/EP1531/73; Shepherd tel. 141 to FO, 2 March 1951, FO 371, 91523/EP1531/77; and Shepherd dispatch 99 to FO, 25 March 1951, FO 371, 91449/EP1013/16.

23. Gifford tel. 4754 to State Department, 3 March 1951, RG 84, London Embassy, Classified Records, 523.1 Middle East. See also Shepherd tel. 145 to FO, 4 March 1951, FO 371, 91523/EP1531/80; Shepherd tel. 149 to FO, 5 March 1951, FO 371, 91523/EP1531/81; Rothnie minute, 6 March 1951, FO 371, 91523/EP1531/81; and Gifford tel. 4792 to State Department, 6 March 1951, RG 59, 888.2553AIOC/3-651.

24. Shepherd tel. 144 to FO, 4 March 1951, FO 371, 91523/EP1531/79. See also Shepherd tel. 154 to FO, 6 March 1951, FO 371, 91523/EP1531/86.

25. Gifford tel. 4934 to State Department, 14 March 1951, RG 84, London Embassy, Classified Records, 523.1 Middle East. Scc also minutes of the undersecretary's meeting, 7 March 1951, RG 59, General Records of the Executive Secretariat, Minutes of Under Secretary's Meetings, lot 58 D 609 (hereafter RG 59, lot 58 D 609); Berry memorandum for the secretary, "The Iranian Situation," 14 March 1951, *Foreign Relations of the United States, 1952–1954*, vol. 10 (Washington, D.C.: Government Printing Office, 1978), pp. 9–11 (hereafter *FRUS*); and undated National Security Council staff study, "The Position of the United States with Respect to Iran," *FRUS, 1952–1954,* vol. 10, pp. 11–21.

26. Gifford tel. 4829 to State Department, 8 March 1951, RG 59, 788.00/3-851. See also minutes of the undersecretary's meeting, 7 March 1951, RG 59, lot 58 D 609; Grady tel. 2013 to State Department, 9 March 1951, RG 59, 788.00/3-951; and Azimi, *Iran*, pp. 246–54.

27. Shepherd tel. 173 to FO, 9 March 1951, FO 371, 91523/EP1531/93; Furlonge to Shepherd, 10 March 1951, FO 371, 91523/EP1531/98; Gifford tel. 4934 to State Department, 14 March 1951, RG 84, London Embassy, Classified Records, 523.1 Middle East. See also Furlonge memorandum, "Anglo-Iranian Oil Company Affairs in Persia," 10 March 1951, FO 371, 91523/EP1531/98; and Shepherd tel. 183 to FO, 12 March 1951, FO 371, 91523/EP1531/97.

28. "Exchange of Notes Between the British and Persian Governments on the Proposed Nationalization of the Oil Industry," 14 March 1951, Royal Institute of International Affairs, *Documents on International Affairs, 1951* (London: Oxford University Press, 1952), pp. 475–78 (hereafter *DIA*). See also Furlonge memorandum, "Anglo-Iranian Oil Company Affairs in Persia," 10 March 1951, FO 371, 91523/EP1531/98; Shepherd tel. 189 to FO, 13 March 1951, FO 371, 91524/EP1531/101; Eden to Shepherd, 17 March 1951, FO 371, 91524/EP1531/113; E. A. Bayne to W. A. B. Iliff (loan director, International Bank for Reconstruction and Development [IBRD]), 17 March 1951, RG 84, Tehran Embassy, Confidential File, 523.1 AIOC; and record of 20 March 1951 interdepartmental meeting, 21 March 1951, FO 371, 91525/EP1531/149.

29. Grady tel. 2094 to State Department, 16 March 1951, RG 59, 888.2553/3-1651;

Farhad Diba, *Mohammad Mossadegh: A Political Biography* (London: Croom Helm, 1986), p. 111.

30. See Shepherd tel. 196 to FO, 15 March 1951, FO 371, 91524/EP1531/108; and Shepherd dispatch 97 to FO, 19 March 1951, FO 371, 91524/EP1531/125. For the internal dynamics of Majlis support for nationalization see Richard W. Cottam, *Nationalism in Iran*, 2d rev. ed. (Pittsburgh, Pa.: University of Pittsburgh Press, 1979), pp. 269–70; and Keddie, *Roots of Revolution*, p. 133.

31. Grady tel. 2094 to State Department, 16 March 1951, RG 59, 888.2553/3-1651. See also Shepherd tel. 196 to FO, 15 March 1951, FO 371, 91524/EP1531/108; and Azimi, *Iran*, pp. 248–49.

32. Acheson tel. to U.S. embassy, Tehran, 17 March 1951, *FRUS, 1952–1954*, vol. 10, pp. 25–26; Acheson tel. to U.S. embassy, Cairo, 28 March 1951, *FRUS, 1952–1954*, vol. 10, pp. 28–30. See also Steel (Washington) tel. 753 to FO, 14 March 1951, FO 371, 91570/EP1023/1; and Acheson tel. 925 to U.S. embassy, Cairo, 28 March 1951, *FRUS, 1952–1954*, vol. 10, pp. 26–28.

33. Webb (acting secretary of state) tel. 4143 to U.S. embassy, London, 10 March 1951, RG 59, 888.2553AIOC/3-1051; Gifford tel. 4991 to State Department, 19 March 1951, RG 84, London Embassy, Classified Records, 523.1 Middle East.

34. Shepherd tel. 205 to FO, 18 March 1951, FO 371, 91524/EP1531/117; Shepherd tel. 261 to FO, 28 March 1951, FO 371, 91525/EP1531/137; Gifford tel. 5044 to State Department, 21 March 1951, RG 59, 888.2553/3-2151; Rodney E. Willoughby (U.S. petroleum adviser, London) to Edwin G. Moline (acting chief, petroleum policy staff, State Department), 17 April 1951, RG 84, London Embassy, Classified Records, 523.1 Middle East.

35. See Gifford tel. 4871 to State Department, 10 March 1951, RG 59, 888.2553AIOC/3-1051; Acheson tel. 4209 to U.S. embassy, London, 16 March 1951, RG 59, 888.2553/3-1651; and Jefferson Caffery (American ambassador to Egypt) tel. 1000 to State Department, 1 April 1951, RG 59, 880.2553/4-151.

36. Crocker (U.S. embassy, Baghdad) tel. to State Department, 29 March 1951, *FRUS, 1951*, vol. 5, pp. 292–93; minutes of undersecretary's meeting, 6 April 1951, RG 59, lot 58 D 609; Gifford tel. 5239 to State Department, 4 April 1951, RG 59, 888.2553/4-451; FO tel. 1149 to British embassy, Washington, 24 March 1951, FO 371, 91470/EP1023/5. See also undated National Security Council staff study, "The Position of the United States with Respect to Iran," *FRUS, 1952–1954*, vol. 10, pp. 11–21; Steel tels. 775 and 776 to FO, 15 March 1951, FO 371, 91524/EP1531/110 and 91524/EP1531/111; FO tel. 1062 to British embassy, Washington, 19 March 1951, FO 371, 91524/EP1531/114; and Shepherd tel. 246 to FO, 24 March 1951, FO 371, 91524/EP1531/127.

37. U.K. record of 9 April 1951 meeting between U.S. and U.K. delegations, 11 April 1951, FO 371, 91471/EP1023/36; U.S. record of 10 April meeting between U.S. and U.K. delegations, 13 April 1951, FO 371, 91471/EP1023/37; George McGhee, *Envoy to the Middle World: Adventures in Diplomacy* (New York: Harper & Row, 1983), p. 335. For U.S. estimates of the importance of Iranian oil see National Intelligence Estimate NIE-14, "The Importance of Iranian and Middle East Oil to Western Europe Under Peacetime Conditions," 8 January 1951, *FRUS, 1951*, vol. 5, pp. 268–76; NSC-107, "The Position of the United States with Respect to Iran," 14 March 1951, Truman Papers, NSC Meetings, box 212, folder: NSC Meeting #87, 21 March 1951; CIA Special Estimate, "The Current Crisis in Iran," SE-3, 16 March 1951, Truman Papers,

NSC Meetings, box 212, folder: NSC Meeting #89, 21 March 1951; and NIE-6, "Iran's Position in the East-West Conflict," 5 April 1951, Truman Papers, Intelligence File, box 253, folder: Central Intelligence Reports, NIE 1–6.

38. U.K. record of 9 April 1951 meeting between U.S. and U.K. delegations, 12 April 1951, FO 371, 91471/EP1023/36; Franks tels. 1079 and 1080 to FO, 10 April 1951, FO 371, 91470/EP1023/16 and 91470/EP1023/17.

39. Franks tel. 1194 to FO, 18 April 1951, FO 371, 91471/EP1023/39.

40. U.K. record of second meeting (10 April 1951) between U.S. and U.K. delegations, 13 April 1951, FO 371, 91471/EP1023/37; Rountree memorandum of conversation with British ambassador, 18 April 1951, RG 59, 641.88/4-1851. See also FO tel. 1481 to British embassy, Washington, 13 April 1951, FO 371, 91470/EP1023/20; and Sir Donald Fergusson to Edward Bridges (Treasury), 14 April 1951, FO 371, 91526/EP1531/187. For additional British thinking on what type of arrangement would best meet Iranian demands see Ramsbotham minute, 13 April 1951, FO 371, 91527/EP1531/193; and C.P.(51)114, "Persian Oil: Memorandum by the Secretary of State for Foreign Affairs," 20 April 1951, Cabinet Papers, Record Class CAB 129/45, Public Record Office (hereafter CAB 129, with filing information).

41. Franks tel. 1194 to FO, 18 April, 1951, FO 371, 91471/EP1023/39; summary of meeting with the secretary, 23 April 1951, RG 59, lot 58 D 609; McGhee memorandum for the secretary, "Discussion of the Iranian Situation with the British Ambassador," 27 April 1951, RG 59, 788.00/4-1751.

42. "Exchange of Notes Between the British and Persian Governments on the Proposed Nationalization of the Oil Industry," 14 March 1951, *DIA, 1951*, pp. 475–78; Grady tel. 2328 to State Department, 10 April 1951, RG 84, London Embassy, Classified Records, 523.1 Middle East; Grady tel. 2322 to State Department, 8 April 1951, RG 59, 888.2553/4-851. See also Richards dispatch 308, "Statement on Oil Nationalization Released by Dr. Mosadeq, National Front Leader, at Press Conference April 8," 10 April 1951, RG 59, 888.2553/5-151.

43. Grady tel. 2399 to State Department, 13 April 1951, RG 59, 888.2553/4-1351; Franks to Strang, 21 April 1951, FO 371, 91529/EP1531/241; Grady tel. 2465 to State Department, 18 April 1951, RG 59, 888.2553/4-1851.

44. Grady tel. 2535 to State Department, 24 April 1951, RG 59, 888.2553/4-2451; Shepherd tel. 363 to FO, 20 April 1951, FO 371, 91529/EP1531/242; Grady tel. 2514 to State Department, RG 59, 888.2553/4-2351. See also Ferguson memorandum of conversation with Iranian ambassador (Entezam), 9 April 1951, RG 59, 888.2553/4-951; C.M.(51)30th Conclusions, 23 April 1951, CABINET 30(51), Cabinet Minutes, Conclusions, and Memoranda, Record Class CAB 128/19, Public Record Office (hereafter CAB 128, with filing information); and Azimi, *Iran*, pp. 252–54.

45. Franks tel. 1128 to FO, 13 April 1951, FO 371, 91471/EP1023/26; Shepherd tel. 392 to FO, 26 April 1951, FO 371, 91528/EP1531/220. See also Strang record of conversation with Sir William Fraser, 19 April 1951, FO 371, 91527/EP1531/199; C.M.(51)30th Conclusions, 23 April 1951, CABINET 30(51), CAB 128/19; Strang record of conversation with Sir William Fraser, 23 April 1951, FO 371, 91528/EP1531/219; and Rountree memorandum of conversation with Burrows, 25 April 1951, RG 59, 888.2553AIOC/4-2551.

46. Shepherd tel. 378 to FO, 24 April 1951, FO 371, 91527/EP1531/209; Grady tel. 2583 to State Department, 27 April 1951, RG 59, 888.2553/4-2751. See also Shepherd

tel. 379 to FO, 24 April 1951, FO 371, 91527/EP1531/210; and Grady tel. 2533 to State Department, 24 April 1951, RG 59, 888.2553/4-2451.

47. Franks tel. 1304 to FO, 28 April 1951, FO 371, 91528/EP1531/235.

48. Furlonge note for Morrison, 29 April 1951, FO 371, 91529/EP1531/256. See also Grady tel. 2604 to State Department, 29 April 1951, RG 59, 788.00/4-2951; Grady tel. 2605 to State Department, 29 April 1951, RG 59, 788.00/4-2951; Grady tel. 2607 to State Department, 29 April 1951, RG 59, 788.00/4-2951; C.M.(51)32d Conclusions, CABINET 31(51), 30 April 1951, CAB 128/19; Homa Katouzian, ed., *Musaddiq's Memoirs* (London: JEBHE, National Movement of Iran, 1988), pp. 264–67, and Homa Katouzian, *Musaddiq and the Struggle for Power in Iran* (London: I. B. Tauris, 1990), pp. 92–94.

49. See N. R. Seddon (AIOC representative in Tehran) to Mossadeq, 28 April 1951, International Court of Justice, *Pleadings, Oral Arguments, Documents: Anglo-Iranian Oil Case (United Kingdom v. Iran)* (The Hague: International Court of Justice, 1952), p. 35; and Richards dispatch 872, "AIOC Protest Re Majlis Oil Commission Resolution," 30 April 1951, RG 59, 888.2553/4-3051. The British legal position is explained in detail in "Expropriation of Foreign Private Property: Statement of the General Position Under International Law with Particular Relation to the Recent Persian Law Purporting to Nationalize the Anglo-Iranian Oil Company," 28 April 1951, FO 371, 91530/EP1531/270.

50. Grady tel. 2580 to State Department, 27 April 1951, RG 59, 888.2553AIOC/4-2751. See also FO tel. 314 to British embassy, Tehran, 28 April 1951, FO 371, 91528/EP1531/225; Franks tel. 1310 to FO, 29 April 1951, FO 371, 91528/EP1531/237; FO tel. 1791 to British embassy, Washington, 30 April 1951, FO 371, 91528/EP1531/237; C.M.(51)32d Conclusions, 30 April 1951, CABINET 32(51), CAB 128/19; and "Extract from Statement in House of Commons by the Secretary of State for Foreign Affairs, Mr. Herbert Morrison, on the United Kingdom's Attitude Towards the Negotiations with the Persian Government," 1 May 1951, *DIA, 1951*, pp. 480–81.

51. Franks tel. 1297 to FO, 27 April 1951, FO 371, 91528/EP1531/223; FO tel. 1766 to British embassy, Washington, 28 April 1951, FO 371, 91528/EP1531/223; Gifford tel. 5654 to State Department, 28 April 1951, RG 59, 888.2553/4-2851; FO tel. 1755 to British embassy, Washington, 28 April 1951, FO 371, 91528/EP1531/223.

52. Shepherd tel. 426 to FO, 2 May 1951, FO 371, 91529/EP1531/251; Shepherd tel. 425 to FO, 2 May 1951, FO 371, 91529/EP1531/252; Furlonge minute, 3 May 1951, FO 371, 91533/EP1531/300; Bowker minute, 4 May 1951, FO 371, 91534/EP1531/327. See also "Law Nationalizing the Oil Industry in Persia," 1 May 1951, *DIA, 1951*, pp. 481–82; and Shepherd tel. 418 to FO, 1 May 1951, FO 371, 91529/EP1531/244.

53. Furlonge notes for secretary of state, 29 April 1951, FO 371, 91529/EP1531/256; Bowker to Shepherd, 5 May 1951, FO 371, 91531/EP1531/294; Gifford tel. 6005 to State Department, 18 May 1951, RG 59, 888.2553AIOC/5-1851; M. R. Starkey (resident clerk, FO) minute, 14 May 1951, FO 371, 91534/EP1531/321; Franks tel. 136 to FO, 3 May 1951, FO 371, 91530/EP1531/264. On the Persian Oil Working Party (POWP) see Furlonge memorandum with attached POWP paper, "U.K. Objectives and Possible Approaches to the Problem," 7 May 1951, FO 371, 91453/EP1531/573.

54. Morrison message to Mossadeq, 2 May 1951, *DIA, 1951*, pp. 482–83. See also "Extract from the Statement in the House of Commons by the Secretary of State for

Foreign Affairs, Mr. Herbert Morrison, on the United Kingdom's Attitude Towards the Negotiations with the Persian Government," 1 May 1951, *DIA, 1951*, pp. 480–81; FO tel. 350 to British embassy, Tehran, 5 May 1951, FO 371, 91530/EP1531/262; R. J. Bowker to Shepherd, 5 May 1951, FO 371, 91531/EP1531/294; Shepherd tel. 450 to FO, 7 May 1951, FO 371, 91531/EP1531/387; Shepherd, "Interview with the Prime Minister (Mossadegh)," 7 May 1951, FO 371, 91534/EP1531/338; and Shepherd tel. 469 to FO, 11 May 1951, FO 371, 91533/EP1531/305.

55. "Reply from Dr. Mossadegh to Mr. Morrison's Note," 8 May 1951, *DIA, 1951*, pp. 484–85; Shepherd tel. 425 to FO, 2 May 1951, FO 371, 91529/EP1531/252.

56. Richards dispatch to State Department, enclosing memorandum of conversation of Mossadeq, Grady, and Shepherd, 31 May 1951, *FRUS, 1952–1954*, vol. 10, pp. 57–59; Richards dispatch 2800, enclosing copy of British note to Iran, 21 May 1951, RG 59, 888.2553/5-2151.

57. Grady tel. 2721 to State Department, 9 May 1951, RG 59, 888.2553AIOC/5-951; Grady tel. 2917 to State Department, 22 May 1951, RG 59, 788.13/5-2251; Carr dispatch 1016, "Monthly Economic Review," 29 May 1951, RG 59, 888.00/5-2951.

58. Acheson tel. 2067 to U.S. embassy, Tehran, 10 May 1951, RG 59, 788.13/5-1051. See also NIE-26, "Key Problems Affecting U.S. Efforts to Strengthen the Near East," 25 April 1951, Truman Papers, Intelligence File, box 253, folder: Intelligence Reports, NIE 21–26; Grady dispatch 889 to State Department re 2 May 1951 conversation with Mossadeq, 4 May 1951, RG 59, 611.88/5-451; and Acheson tel. 2194 to U.S. embassy, Tehran, 24 May 1951, RG 59, 888.2553/5-2451.

59. Richards dispatch 899 to State Department, 4 May 1951, RG 59, 788.00/5-451.

60. Gifford tel. 5748 to State Department, 4 May 1951, RG 59, 888.2553AIOC/5-451; Shepherd to Bowker, 22 May 1951, FO 371, 91542/EP1531/547.

61. Furlonge minute, 17 May 1951, FO 371, 91536/EP1531/379; Shepherd tel. 539 to FO, 30 May 1951, 91538/EP1531/445; Shepherd to Morrison, 18 June 1951, FO 371, 91547/EP1531/646.

62. Grady tel. 2787 to State Department, 13 May 1951, RG 59, 888.2553/5-1351; Arthur L. Richards (counselor, U.S. embassy, Tehran) dispatch 1006 to State Department, 26 May 1951, RG 59, 788.13/5-2651. See also Grady tel. 2650 to State Department, 2 May 1951, RG 59, 788.13/5-251; Franks tel. 1361 to FO, 3 May 1951, FO 371, 91530/EP1531/264; Franks tel. 1387 to FO, 4 May 1951, FO 371, 91530/EP1531/264; and FO tel. 391 to British embassy, Tehran, 18 May 1951, FO 371, 91534/EP1531/335.

63. Grady tel. to State Department, 7 May 1951, *FRUS, 1952–1954*, vol. 10, pp. 46–47; Furlonge minute, 4 May 1951, FO 371, 91531/EP1531/288.

64. Gifford tel. 5774 to State Department, 5 May 1951, RG 59, 888.2553AIOC/5-551; Franks tel. 1361 to FO, 3 May 1951, FO 371, 91530/EP1531/264; Grady tel. 3174 to State Department, 8 June 1951, RG 59, 888.2553AIOC/6-851; Grady tel. 2787 to State Department, 13 May 1951, RG 59, 888.2553/5-1351.

65. For the initial British military buildup see Rouhollah K. Ramazani, *Iran's Foreign Policy, 1941–1973: A Study of Foreign Policy in Modernizing Nations* (Charlottesville: University of Virginia Press, 1975), pp. 205–206; Leonard Mosley, *Power Play: The Tumultuous World of Middle East Oil, 1890–1973* (London: Weidenfeld and Nicolson, 1973) p. 205; and Dean G. Acheson, *Present at the Creation: My Years in the State Department* (New York: Norton, 1969), pp. 505–506.

66. See Gifford tel. 5142 to State Department, 30 March 1951, RG 59, 888.2553/3-

3051; FO tel. 2022 to British embassy, Washington, 14 May 1951, FO 371, 91534/EP1531/305; Franks tel. 1547 to FO, 17 May 1951, FO 371, 91535/EP1531/354; and FO tel. 2103 to British embassy, Washington, 18 May 1951, FO 371, 91535/EP1531/354. For the internal British debate over the use of force in Iran see the documents in Records of the Chiefs of Staff Committee, Record Class DEFE4, Public Record Office; the papers in CAB 21/1982; Wm. Roger Louis, *The British Empire in the Middle East, 1945–1951: Arab Nationalism, the United States, and Postwar Imperialism* (Oxford, England: Oxford University Press, 1984), pp. 657–66; and H. W. Brands, "The Cairo-Tehran Connection in Anglo-American Rivalry in the Middle East, 1951–1953," *International History Review* 9 (August 1989): 438–39.

67. See Acheson, *Present at the Creation*, p. 506. See also Acheson tel. 5199 to U.S. embassy, London, 5 May 1951, RG 59, 888.2553AIOC/5-551; Franks tel. 1488 to FO, 12 May 1951, FO 371, 91533/EP1531/304; and FO tel. 2103 to British embassy, Washington, 18 May 1951, FO 371, 91535/EP1531/354.

68. See McGhee memorandum for the secretary, "The Iranian Situation," 30 January 1951, RG 59, 788.00/1-3051; Acheson tel. 1698 to British embassy, Tehran, 28 March 1951, RG 59, 611.88/3-2851; and Franks tel. 1594 to FO, 21 May 1951, FO 371, 91493/EP11345/11.

69. FO tel. 2103 to British embassy, Washington, 18 May 1951, FO 371, 91535/-EP1531/354; Gifford tel. 5774 to State Department, 5 May 1951, RG 59, 888.2553AIOC/-5-551; Gifford tel. 5850 to State Department, 9 May 1951, RG 59, 888.2553/5-951; Sir Roger Makins record of conversation, 12 May 1951, FO 371, 91535/EP1531/358.

70. Funkhouser memorandum of conversation re Discussion of AIOC Problem with U.S. Oil Companies Operating in the Middle East, 14 May 1951, RG 59, 888.2553AIOC/5-1451. See also Acheson tel. 2119 to U.S. embassy, Tehran, 16 May 1951, RG 84, Tehran Embassy, Confidential File, 523.1 AIOC. The Royal Dutch Shell Company had earlier voiced similar concerns to the British government. See George Leigh-Jones (Shell) to Fergusson, with attached FO minutes, 7 May 1951, FO 371, 92050/UES15327/1; and unsigned memorandum, 7 May 1951, FO 371, 92050/UES15327/1. For evidence of the importance of this kind of neutrality see Gifford tel. 5850 to State Department, 9 May 1951, RG 59, 888.2553/5-951.

71. *Parliamentary Debates* (Commons), 5th ser., vol. 488 (1951), col. 42; M. R. Starkey (resident clerk, FO) minute, 14 May 1951, FO 371, 91534/EP1531/321. See also C.M.(51)37th Conclusions, 28 May 1951, CABINET 37(51), CAB 128/19; and Office of Intelligence Research Paper, "Iran Briefs," OIR 5557.1, 31 May 1951, RG 59, 888.2553/6-151.

72. Shepherd tel. 547 to FO, 31 May 1951, FO 371, 91539/EP1531/472. See also Franks tel. 1653 to FO, 26 May 1951, FO 371, 91537/EP1531/420; Iranian aide-mémoire to AIOC, 30 May 1951, FO 371, 91542/EP1531/560; Acheson tel. to U.S. embassy, London, 31 May 1951, RG 59, 888.2553/5-3151; minutes of Cabinet meeting, GEN 363/5th meeting, 1 June 1951, CAB 21/1982; FO tel. 470 to British embassy, Tehran, 2 June 1951, FO 371, 92540/EP1531/483; and Acheson memorandum for the president, 7 June 1951, Truman Papers, PSF—Subject File, box 180, folder: Iran.

73. Berthoud minute, 6 June 1951, FO 371, 91551/EP1531/733.

74. Richards dispatch to State Department, enclosing memorandum of conversation between Mossadeq, Grady, and Shepherd, 31 May 1951, *FRUS, 1952–1954*, vol. 10, pp.

57–59; Grady tel. 3027 to State Department, 29 May 1951, RG 84, Tehran Embassy, Confidential File, 523.1 AIOC. See also Grady tel. 3042 to State Department, 30 May 1951, RG 59, 888.2553AIOC/5-3051; Richards dispatch 1023 to State Department, transmitting memorandum of conversation between Grady and Mossadeq, 31 May 1951, RG 59, 888.2553/5-3151; minutes of Cabinet meeting, GEN 363/5th Meeting, 1 June 1951, CAB 21/1982; and Franks tel. 504 to FO, 2 June 1951, FO 371, 91540/EP1531/496.

75. See minutes of meeting between Sir A. E. C. Drake (AIOC general manager in Tehran) and Iranian Temporary Management Commission, 12 June 1951, FO 371, 91550/EP1531/717; Grady tel. 3283 to State Department, 14 June 1951, RG 59, 888.2553AIOC/6-1451; Shepherd tel. 637 to FO, 14 June 1951, FO 371, 91545/EP1531/612; and Richards dispatch 1081 to State Department, including memorandum of conversation between Grady and Mossadeq, 15 June 1951, RG 59, 888.2553/6-1551.

76. FO tel. 549 to British embassy, Tehran, 16 June 1951, FO 371, 91548/EP1531/669. The abortive AIOC-Iranian negotiations may be followed in minutes of discussions between Drake (AIOC general manager) and members of the Mixed Parliamentary Commission and Temporary Management Commission, 12 and 13 June 1951, FO 371, 91550/EP1531/717 and 91550/EP1531/721; Grady tel. 3266 to State Department, 14 June 1951, RG 59, 888.2553AIOC/6-1451; Gifford tel. 6597 to State Department, 15 June 1951, RG 59, 888.2553AIOC/6-1551; Shepherd tel. 639 to FO, 15 June 1951, FO 371, 91545/EP1531/611; Shepherd tels. 657 and 660 to FO, 17 June 1951, FO 371, 91546/EP1531/635 and 91546/EP1531/638; and British record of 17 June 1951 meeting between AIOC delegation and Iranian government representatives, 19 June 1951, FO 371, 91575/EP1531/1287.

77. Strang minute, 23 June 1951, FO 371, 91556/EP1531/884; Acheson tel. 6049 to U.S. embassy, London, 22 June 1951, RG 59, 888.2553/6-2251. See also Holmes (London) tel. 6667 to State Department, 18 June 1951, RG 59, 888.2553AIOC/6-1851; Richards dispatch 1102 to State Department, including memorandum of conversation with George H. Middleton (counselor, British embassy, Washington), 19 June 1951, RG 59, 888.2553/6-1951; Grady tel. 3358 to State Department, 20 June 1951, RG 59, 888.2553AIOC/6-2051; and Furlonge brief for ministerial meeting, 21 June 1951, FO 371, 91550/EP1531/724.

78. Steel tel. 1952 to FO, 25 June 1951, FO 371, 91551/EP1531/736; Acheson tel. 6049 to U.S. embassy, London, 22 June 1951, RG 59, 888.2553/6-2251.

79. Steel tel. 1952 to FO, 25 June 1951, FO 371. 91551/EP1531/736; Shepherd tel. 667 to FO, 18 June 1951, FO 371, 91547/EP1531/659.

80. See Acheson tel. 2446 to U.S. embassy, Tehran, 20 June 1951, RG 59, 888.2553AIOC/6-2051; Shepherd tel. 677 to FO, 20 June 1951, FO 371, 91548/EP1531/666; FO tel. 573 to British embassy, Tehran, 20 June 1951, FO 371, 91531/EP1531/666; Grady tel. 3373 to State Department, 21 June 1951, RG 59, 888.2553AIOC/6-2151; minutes of meeting between Drake and Iranian government representatives, 20 June 1951, FO 371, 91554/EP1531/823; C.M.(51)45th Conclusions, 21 June 1951, CABINET 45(51), CAB 128/19; and Grady tel. 3399 to State Department, 22 June 1951, RG 59, 888.2553AIOC/6-2251.

81. See "Draft Anti-Sabotage Bill to the Majlis," 21 June 1951, *DIA, 1951*, pp. 495–96; FO tel. 653 to British embassy, Tehran, 28 June 1951, FO 371, 91553/EP1531/801; and Shepherd tel. 753 to FO, 29 June 1951, FO 371, 91553/EP1531/796.

82. See David K. E. Bruce (Paris) tel. 7956 to State Department, 21 June 1951, RG 59, 888.2553/6-2151; Grady tel. 3419 to State Department, 23 June 1951, RG 59, 888.2553AIOC/6-2351; and British consul general, Khorramshahr, tel. 166 to FO, 23 June 1951, FO 371, 91550/EP1531/702.

83. For the British belief that it was useless to negotiate with Mossadeq and that the best strategy was to wait for his successor see, for example, Makins et al. minutes, 1 June 1951, FO 371, 91542/EP1531/539; unsigned memorandum, "Persia: Next Steps," 20 June 1951, FO 371, 91550/EP1531/709; and Shepherd tel. 746 to FO, 28 June 1951, FO 371, 91553/EP1531/778.

84. Steel tel. 1952 to FO, 25 June 1951, FO 371, 91551/EP1531/736; Strang minute, 23 June 1951, FO 371, 91556/EP1531/884; Berthoud minute, 21 June 1951, FO 371, 91550/EP1531/713. See also C.M.(51)45th Conclusions, 21 June 1951, CABINET 45(51), CAB 128/19; Ministry of Fuel and Power paper, "Policy on Oil Supplies if We Have to do without Persian Oil," 22 June 1951, FO 371, 92050/UES15327/10; Grady tel. 3414 to State Department, 23 June 1951, RG 59, 888.2553AIOC/6-2351; and Gifford tel. 6938 to State Department, 30 June 1951, RG 59, 888.2553AIOC/6-3051.

85. Grady dispatch 1159 to State Department, 29 June 1951, RG 59, 788.00/6-2951; Shepherd dispatch 177 to FO, 18 June 1951, FO 371, 91548/EP1531/676. See also Mossadeq message to Truman, 28 May 1951, Truman Papers, PSF—Press Release File, box 72, folder: May 1951; Grady tel. 3468 to State Department, 28 June 1951, RG 59, 888.2553/6-2851; and Shepherd tel. 746 to FO, 28 June 1951, FO 371, 91553/EP1531/778.

86. Steel tel. 1952 to FO, 25 June 1951, FO 371, 91551/EP1531/736; Acheson statement, "Developments in Iran Cause Increased Concern," 27 June 1951, U.S. Department of State *Bulletin* 25 (9 July 1951): 73; NSC-107/2, "The Position of the United States with Respect to Iran," 27 June 1951, Truman Papers, PSF—NSC Meetings, box 213, folder: NSC Meeting #95, 27 June 1951. See also Acheson tel. 6184 to U.S. embassy, London, 27 June 1951, RG 59, 888.2553/6-2751; Acheson tel. 6234 to U.S. embassy, London, 28 June 1951, RG 59, 888.2553/6-2951; FO tel. 658 to British embassy, Tehran, 28 June 1951, FO 371, 91553/EP1531/802; C.M.(51)47th Conclusions, 28 June 1951, CABINET 47(51), CAB 128/19; Furlonge brief for the secretary of state, 29 June 1951, FO 371, 91554/EP1531/851; and Gifford tel. 6908 to State Department, 29 June 1951, RG 59, 888.2553/6-2951.

87. Gifford tel. to State Department, 26 June 1951, *FRUS, 1952–1954*, vol. 10, pp. 69–71; *Parliamentary Debates* (Commons), 5th ser. (1951), vol. 489, col. 827. The entire debate, which ran for four hours, spans cols. 746–833. See also Holmes tel. 6771 to State Department, 22 June 1951, RG 84, London Embassy, Classified Records, 523.1 Middle East.

88. See Churchill to Truman, 29 June 1951, RG 59, 888.2553/7-1051; Gifford tel. 6870 to State Department, 28 June 1951, RG 59, 888.2553/6-2851; and "Notes of Meeting to Discuss Persia at House of Commons Between Churchill, Eden, Chancellor of Exchequer and Minister of Defence (Salisbury unable to attend)," 28 June 1951, FO 371, 91555/EP1531/870. Churchill proposed the bipartisan meeting after Prime Minister Morrison reported to the House of Commons on 28 June that no further progress had been made on the Iranian front. See *Parliamentary Debates* (Commons), 5th ser. (1951), vol. 489, col. 1380.

4. From Honest Broker to British Partner

1. L. P. Elwell-Sutton, "Statement on the Persian Oil Dispute," 12 July 1951, FO 371, 91572/EP1531/1232.

2. Arthur L. Richards (counselor, U.S. embassy, Tehran) dispatch 9 to State Department, 2 July 1951, RG 59, 788.13/7-251. See also Grady tel. 35 to State Department, 3 July 1951, RG 59, 888.2553AIOC/7-351; Gifford tel. 59 to State Department, 4 July 1951, RG 59, 888.2553AIOC/7-451; and D. A. Logan (FO) minute, 4 July 1951, FO 371, 91560/EP1531/928.

3. Gifford tel. 125 to State Department, 6 July 1951, RG 59, 888.2553/7-651. See also C.P.(51)192, "Persia: Ruling of the Hague Court, Memorandum by the Secretary of State for Foreign Affairs," 6 July 1951, CAB 129/46; Gifford tel. 118 to State Department, 6 July 1951, RG 59, 888.2553AIOC/7-651; Grady tel. 76 to State Department, 7 July 1951, RG 59, 888.2553/7-751; Grady tel. 109 to State Department, 9 July 1951, RG 59, 888.2553/7-951; and Richards dispatch 42 to State Department, 11 July 1951, RG 59, 888.2553/7-1151. For the British appeal to the ICJ see International Court of Justice, *Pleadings, Oral Arguments, Documents: Anglo-Iranian Oil Case (United Kingdom v. Iran)* (The Hague: International Court of Justice, 1952), pp. 8–19, 45–53.

4. Mostafa Elm, *Oil, Power, and Principle: Iran's Oil Nationalization and Its Aftermath* (Syracuse, N.Y.: Syracuse University Press, 1992), p. 121; Richards dispatch 21, "Confidential Papers from AIOC Information Office," 5 July 1951, RG 59, 888.2553/7-551; British consul general, Khorramshahr, tel. 247 to FO, 13 July 1951, FO 371, 91584/EP1531/1471; Grady tel. 380 to State Department, 25 July 1951, RG 59, 888.2553/7-2551.

5. Churchill to Attlee, 9 July 1951, FO 371, 91563/EP1531/1012. See also C.M.(51)48th Conclusions, 2 July 1951, CABINET 48(51), CAB 128/19; Morrison record of conversation with Gifford, 3 July 1951, FO 371, 91555/EP1531/869; unsigned FO memorandum to Morrison, 4 July 1951, FO 371, 91561/EP1531/955; R. J. Bowker to Shepherd, 7 July 1951, FO 371, 91563/EP1531/1010; C.M.(51)50th Conclusions, 9 July 1951, CABINET 50(51), CAB 128/19; C.P.(51)200, "Persia: Memorandum by the Secretary of State for Foreign Affairs," 11 July 1951, CAB 129/46; and Shepherd tel. 868 to FO, 15 July 1951, FO 371, 91563/EP1531/1026. For the public declaration to remain in Iran see Morrison statement, 9 July 1951, *Parliamentary Debates*, Commons, 5th ser., vol. 490 (1951), col. 35.

6. Shepherd tel. 190 to FO, 2 July 1951, FO 371, 91529/EP1531/253. See also C.M.(51)50th Conclusions, 9 July 1951, CABINET 50(51), CAB 128/19; Churchill to Attlee, 9 July 1951, FO 371, 91563/EP1531/1012; C.P.(51)200, "Persia: Memorandum by the Secretary of State for Foreign Affairs," 11 July 1951, CAB 129/46; and C.M.(51)51st Conclusions, 12 July 1951, CABINET 51(51), CAB 128/20. Detailed military plans may be followed in Chiefs of Staff Committee, Confidential Annex to C.O.S.(51)111th Meeting, 4 July 1951, CAB 21/1983; Chiefs of Staff Committee, Minutes, C.O.S.(51)116th Meeting, 16 July 1951, DEFE 4/45; Chiefs of Staff Committee, Minutes, C.O.S.(51)117th Meeting, 17 July 1951, DEFE 4/45; and C.P.(51)212, "Persia: Memorandum by the Secretary of State for Foreign Affairs," 20 July 1951, CAB 129/46.

7. See Shepherd tel. 788 to FO, 4 July 1951, FO 371, 91555/EP1531/854; Shepherd tel. 840 to FO, 11 July 1951, FO 371, 91584/EP1531/1471; FO tel. 2991 to British embassy, Washington, 12 July 1951, FO 371, 91561/EP1531/964; FO tel. 668 to British

embassy, Paris, 13 July 1951, FO 371, 91562/EP1531/997; and FO tel. 826 to British embassy, Tehran, 14 July 1951, FO 371, 91562/EP1531/997.

8. Dean G. Acheson, *Present at the Creation: My Years in the State Department* (New York: Norton, 1969), p. 507.

9. Grady tel. 197 to State Department, 16 July 1951, RG 59, 888.2553/7-1651.

10. See Grady tel. 6 to State Department, 1 July 1951, RG 59, 888.2553/7-151; Grady tel. 39 to State Department, 4 July 1951, RG 59, 888.2553/7-451; L. P. Elwell-Sutton, "Statement on the Persian Oil Dispute," 12 July 1951, FO 371, 91572/EP1531/1232; and unsigned memorandum, "'Neutral' Management of the Iranian Oil Industry," 14 July 1951, RG 59, 888.2553/7-1451.

11. Acheson tel. 72 to U.S. embassy, London, 4 July 1951, RG 59, 888.2553/7-451; Franks tel. 2060 to FO, 4 July 1951, FO 371, 91555/EP1531/864. See also Franks tel. 2068 to FO, 5 July 1951, FO 371, 91555/EP1531/864; and Acheson, *Present at the Creation*, pp. 506–508.

12. See Franks tel. 2060 to FO, 4 July 1951, FO 371, 91555/EP1531/864; Acheson tel. 72 to U.S. embassy, London, 4 July 1951, RG 59, 888.2553/7-451; Franks tel. 2068 to FO, 5 July 1951, FO 371, 91555/EP1531/864; FO tel. 2897 to British embassy, Washington, 7 July 1951, FO 371, 91555/EP1531/867; Franks tel. 2098 to FO, 8 July 1951, FO 371, 91559/EP1531/913; and C.M.(51)51st Conclusions, 12 July 1951, CAB-INET 51(51), CAB 128/20.

13. Acheson tel. 45 to U.S. embassy, Tehran, 8 July 1951, Truman Papers, OF, file: 134-B, box 569. See also Acheson tel. 44 to U.S. embassy, Tehran, 8 July 1951, RG 59, 888.2553/7-851; Acheson tel. 49 to U.S. embassy, Tehran, 9 July 1951, RG 59, 888.2553/7-951; and Grady tel. 147 to State Department, 11 July 1951, RG 59, 888.2553/7-1151.

14. Gifford tel. 276 to State Department, 13 July 1951, RG 59, 888.2553/7-1351. See also Franks tel. 2068 to FO, 5 July 1951, FO 371, 91555/EP1531/864; Shepherd tel. 846 to FO, 12 July 1951, FO 371, 91561/EP1531/975; Gifford tel. 275 to State Department, 13 July 1951, RG 59, 888.2553/7-1351; and FO tel. 668 to British embassy, Paris, 13 July 1951, FO 371, 91562/EP1531/997.

15. See Franks tel. 2143 to FO, 11 July 1951, FO 371, 91561/EP1531/964; McGhee memorandum of conversation, 11 July 1951, Acheson Papers, box 66, folder: Memoranda of Conversations, July 1951; Franks tel. 2164 to FO, 12 July 1951, FO 371, 91562/EP1531/997; McGhee memorandum of conversation, 12 July 1951, RG 59, 888.2553/7-1251; FO tel. 826 to British embassy, Tehran, 14 July 1951, FO 371, 91562/EP1531/997; and Acheson tel. 303 to U.S. embassy, London, 14 July 1951, RG 59, 888.2553/7-1451.

16. Grady (Harriman) tel. 240 to State Department, 17 July 1951, RG 59, 888.2553/7-1751; Shepherd tel. 879 to FO, FO 371, 91564/EP1531/1048; Vernon Walters, *Silent Missions* (Garden City, N.Y.: Doubleday, 1978), p. 247. See also Shepherd tel. 880 to FO, 17 July 1951, FO 371, 91566/EP1531/1086; Shepherd tel. 890 to FO, 18 July 1951, FO 371, 91566/EP1531/1076; Grady (Harriman) tel. 276 to State Department, 19 July 1951, RG 59, 888.2553/7-1951; Grady (Harriman) tel. 285 to State Department, 19 July 1951, RG 59, 888.2553/7-1951; Shepherd tel. 900 to FO, 20 July 1951, FO 371, 91567/EP1531/1099; and Grady (Harriman) tel. 287 to State Department, 20 July 1951, RG 59, 888.2553/7-2051. Walters, *Silent Missions*, pp. 241–58, details both the Harriman and subsequent Stokes missions.

17. Shepherd tel. 890 to FO, 18 July 1951, FO 371, 91566/EP1531/1076; Shepherd

tel. 900 to FO, 20 July 1951, FO 371, 91567/EP1531/1099; Grady (Harriman) tel. 276 to State Department, 19 July 1951, RG 59, 888.2553/7-1951.

18. See the sources cited in note 17.

19. See Grady (Harriman) tel. 276 to State Department, 19 July 1951, RG 59, 888.2553/7-1951; Shepherd tel. 900 to FO, 20 July 1951, FO 371, 91567/EP1531/1099; McGhee memorandum for Acheson re: Weekend Developments in Iranian Situation, 23 July 1951, RG 59, 888.2553/7-2351. For figures see N. Spencer Barnes (first secretary, U.S. embassy, Tehran) dispatch 136 to State Department, 30 July 1951, RG 59, 888.00/7-3051; and Grady tel. 39 to State Department, 4 July 1951, RG 59, 888.2553/7-451.

20. "Harriman Formula—Resolution of the Persian Cabinet Containing Proposals as a Basis for Discussion, Proposed to Mr. Harriman for Transmission to the British Government," 23 July 1951, Royal Institute of International Affairs, *Documents on International Affairs, 1951* (London: Oxford University Press, 1952), p. 501 (hereafter *DIA*); Shepherd tel. 925 to FO, 24 July 1951, FO 371, 91568/EP1531/1124; Shepherd tel. 926 to FO, 24 July 1951, FO 371, 91568/EP1531/1127; Shepherd tel. 927 to FO, 24 July 1951, FO 371, 91568/EP1531/1129; Grady (Harriman) tel. 340 to State Department, 24 July 1951, RG 59, 888.2553/7-2451; Grady (Harriman) tel. 341 to State Department, 24 July 1951, RG 59, 888.2553/7-2451; and FO memorandum with attached summary of telegrams, 25 July 1951, FO 371, 91571/EP1531/1196. See also Wm. Roger Louis, *The British Empire in the Middle East, 1945–1951: Arab Nationalism, the United States, and Postwar Imperialism* (Oxford, England: Oxford University Press, 1984), p. 676.

21. See Grady (Harriman) tel. to State Department, 23 July 1951, *Foreign Relations of the United States, 1952–1954*, vol. 10 (Washington, D.C.: Government Printing Office, 1978), pp. 107–8 (hereafter *FRUS*); Grady (Harriman) tel. 340 to State Department, 24 July 1951, RG 59, 888.2553/7-2451; Grady (Harriman) tel. 341 to State Department, 24 July 1951, RG 59, 888.2553/7-2451; Grady (Harriman) tel. 348 to State Department, 24 July 1951, RG 59, 888.2553/7-2451; Grady (Harriman) tel. 352 to State Department, 24 July 1951, RG 59, 888.2553/7-2451; Grady (Harriman) tel. 353 to State Department, 24 July 1951, RG 59, 888.2553/7-2451; and Grady (Harriman) tel. 380 to State Department, 25 July 1951, RG 59, 888.2553/7-2551.

22. Shepherd to Bowker, 23 July 1951, FO 371, 91571/EP1531/1217. For Britain's terms see Morrison record of conversation with American ambassador, 25 July 1951, FO 371, 91570/EP1531/1186.

23. Grady (Harriman) tel. 380 to State Department, 25 July 1951, RG 59, 888.2553/7-2551. See also Shepherd tel. 950 to FO, 27 July 1951, FO 371, 91569/EP1531/1162; Grady (Harriman) tel. 397 to State Department, 27 July 1951, Truman Papers, PSF—Subject File, box 180, folder: Iran—W. Averell Harriman; Grady (Harriman) tel. 404 to State Department, 27 July 1951, Truman Papers, PSF—Subject File, box 180, folder: Iran—W. Averell Harriman; and Grady (Harriman) tel. 407 to State Department, 27 July 1951, RG 59, 888.2553/7-2751.

24. See FO tel. 927 to British embassy, Tehran, 28 July 1951, FO 371, 91572/EP1531/1233; Acheson tel. 211 to U.S. embassy, Tehran, 28 July 1951, Truman Papers, PSF—Subject File, box 180, folder: Iran—W. Averell Harriman; Gifford (Harriman) tel. 581 to State Department, 28 July 1951, Truman Papers, PSF—Subject File, box 180, folder: Iran—W. Averell Harriman; Grady tel. 424 to State Department, 29 July 1951, RG 59, 888.2553/7-2951; Grady tel. 425 to State Department, 29 July 1951, RG 59,

888.2553/7-2951; and McGhee memorandum for Acheson, "Latest Developments in the Iranian Situation," 2 August 1951, RG 59, 788.00/8-251.

25. See Middleton tel. 988 to FO, 30 July 1951, FO 371, 91570/EP1531/1189; Gifford (Harriman) tel. 584 to State Department, 30 July 1951, Truman Papers, PSF—Subject File, box 180, folder: W. Averell Harriman; Grady tel. 442 to State Department, 30 July 1951, Truman Papers, PSF—Subject File, box 180, folder: Iran—W. Averell Harriman; McGhee memorandum for the secretary, "Weekend Developments in the Iranian Situation, for Discussion with the President," 30 July 1951, RG 59, 888.2553/7-3051; C.M.(51)57th Conclusions, 1 August 1951, CABINET 57(51), CAB 128/20; Gifford tel. 648 to State Department, 1 August 1951, RG 59, 888.2553/8-151; FO tel. 952 to British embassy, Tehran, 1 August 1951, FO 371, 91570/EP1531/1182; FO tel. 953 to British embassy, Tehran, 1 August 1951, FO 371, 91570/EP1531/1182; and FO tel. 969 to British embassy, Tehran, 3 August 1951, FO 371, 91575/EP1531/1282.

26. For discussion of Harriman's remaining in Tehran see H. Freeman Matthews memorandum of conversation, 2 August 1951, Acheson Papers, box 66, folder: Memoranda of Conversations, August 1951; McGhee memorandum for Acheson, re: "Desirability of Mr. Harriman's Remaining in Iran Until Conclusion of Negotiations He Has Arranged," 3 July 1951, RG 59, 888.2553/8-351; and Grady (Harriman) tel. 489 to State Department, 3 July 1951, Truman Papers, PSF—Subject File, box 180, folder: Iran—W. Averell Harriman.

27. Grady to Willard M. Kiplinger (Dear Kip), 20 July 1951, Grady Papers, Alphabetic File, box 1, folder: Iran, Amb Appointment to.

28. *Parliamentary Debates* (Commons), 5th ser., vol. 491 (1951), col. 991. The entire Middle Eastern debate runs from cols. 959 to 1072. See also Louis, *British Empire in the Middle East*, pp. 666–71.

29. Stokes, quoted in Louis, *British Empire in the Middle East*, p. 678; H. Freeman Matthews memorandum of conversation, 2 August 1951, Acheson Papers, box 66, folder: Memoranda of Conversations, August 1951. On Stokes's background see also Louis, *British Empire in the Middle East*, pp. 677–82. For Stokes's attitude toward the Iranian people see, for example, "History of Events on 21st August 1951: Note by the Lord Privy Seal," 22 August 1951, FO 371, 91583/EP1531/1453; and Averell Harriman quoted in Truman Library, Princeton Seminar, 15 May 1954, reel 2, track 2, page 6.

30. Ramsbotham memorandum of interdepartmental meeting, 31 July 1951, FO 371, 91575/EP1531/1292. See also record of meeting, 29 July 1951, FO 371, 91585/EP1531/1492; Berthoud memorandum with attached paper, "Notes for Lord Privy Seal's Mission," 3 August 1951, FO 371, 91574/EP1531/1266; Furlonge minute with attached paper, "Lord Privy Seal's Mission to Persia," 4 August 1951, FO 371, 91571/EP1531/1267; and FO tel. 1009 to British embassy, Tehran, 11 August 1951, FO 371, 91575/EP1531/1291.

31. See Shepherd tel. 1039 to FO, 5 August 1951, FO 371, 91573/EP1531/1251; Berry memorandum, 16 August 1951, RG 59, 888.2553/8-1651; Shepherd tel. 1163 to FO, 20 August 1951, FO 371, 91579/EP1531/1363; and Shepherd tel. 1196 to FO, 22 August 1951, FO 371, 91580/EP1531/1390.

32. Shepherd minute, 5 August 1951, FO 371, 91577/EP1531/1338; Shepherd (Stokes) tel. 1043 to FO, 7 August 1951, FO 371, 91573/EP1531/1258.

33. Shepherd (Stokes) tel. 1038 to FO, 5 August 1951, FO 371, 91573/EP1531/1250.

34. See Shepherd (Stokes) tel. 1047 to FO, 7 August 1951, FO 371, 91574/

EP1531/1260; Grady (Harriman) tel. 531 to State Department, 8 August 1951, RG 59, 888.2553/8-851; Shepherd (Stokes) tel. 1056 to FO, 9 August 1951, FO 371, 91574/EP1531/1277; McGhee memorandum for Acheson, 9 August 1951, RG 59, 888.2553/8-951; and Shepherd (Stokes) tel. 1066 to FO, 10 August 1951, FO 371, 91575/EP1531/1284.

35. Shepherd (Stokes) tel. 1077 to FO, 11 August 1951, FO 371, 91576/EP1531/1295; Shepherd tel. 1082 to FO, 12 August 1951, FO 371, 91575/EP1531/1297; "British Embassy Press Release Concerning Additional Information on the 8-Point Proposal, Provided by Mr. Stokes, August 13, 1951," 13 August 1951, RG 59, 888.2553/8-1351.

36. Mossadeq in Grady (Harriman) tel. 675 to State Department, 17 August 1951, RG 59, 888.2553/8-1751. See also Shepherd (Stokes) tel. 1085 to FO, 12 August 1951, FO 371, 91576/EP1531/1298; Grady (Harriman) tel. 601 to State Department, 13 August 1951, Truman Papers, PSF—Subject File, box 180, folder: Iran—W. Averell Harriman; and Elm, *Oil, Power, and Principle*, pp. 137–38.

37. Grady (Harriman) tel. 601 to State Department, 13 August 1951, Truman Papers, PSF—Subject File, box 180, folder: Iran—W. Averell Harriman; Berry memorandum, 13 August 1951, RG 59, 888.2553/8-1351; Shepherd (Stokes) tel. 1086 to FO, 13 August 1951, FO 371, 91576/EP1531/1209; Shepherd to Bowker, 13 August 1951, FO 371, 91578/EP1531/1344; unsigned memorandum [Stokes], "Meeting with the President of the Senate and About 20 Senators," 16 August 1951, FO 371, 91580/EP1531/1383; Shepherd (Stokes) tel. 1105 to FO, 14 August 1951, FO 371, 91577/EP1531/1316.

38. See sources cited in note 34.

39. Ramsbotham to Logan, 20 August 1951, FO 371, 91580/EP1531/1391; "Mr. Stokes' Statement to the Press," 17 August 1951, RG 59, 888.2553/8-1751.

40. Grady (Harriman) tel. 704 to State Department, 18 August 1951, RG 59, 888.2553/8-1851; L. P. Elwell-Sutton, *Persian Oil: A Study in Power Politics* (London: Lawrence & Wishart, 1955), p. 252.

41. For Harriman's initial private support of the Eight Point Proposal see Grady (Harriman) tel. 589 to State Department, 12 August 1951, Truman Papers, PSF—Subject File, box 180, folder: Iran—W. Averell Harriman.

42. Grady (Harriman) tel. 705 to State Department, 19 August 1951, Truman Papers, PSF—Subject File, box 180, folder: Iran—W. Averell Harriman. See also Grady (Harriman) tel. 709 to State Department, 19 August 1951, RG 59, 888.2553/8-1951; Shepherd (Stokes) tel. 1150 to FO, 19 August 1951, FO 371, 91578/EP1531/1355; and Shepherd (Stokes) tel. 1152 to FO, 19 August 1951, FO 371, 91578/EP1531/1357.

43. Grady (Harriman) tel. 736 to State Department, 22 August 1951, RG 59, 888.2553/8-2251. See also Shepherd (Stokes) tel. 1163 to FO, 20 August 1951, FO 371, 91579/EP1531/1363; Shepherd to Bowker, 20 August 1951, FO 371, 91580/EP1531/1396; Grady (Harriman) tel. 724 to State Department, 20 August 1951, RG 59, 888.2553/8-2051; Grady (Harriman) tel. 734 to State Department, 22 August 1951, RG 59, 888.2553/8-2251; Grady (Harriman) tel. 737 to State Department, 22 August 1951, Truman Papers, PSF—Subject File, box 180, folder: Iran—W. Averell Harriman; Grady (Harriman) tel. 756 to State Department, 22 August 1951, Truman Papers, PSF—Subject File, box 180, folder: Iran—W. Averell Harriman; Grady (Harriman) tel. 781 to State Department, 23 August 1951, Truman Papers, PSF—Subject File, box 180, folder: Iran—W. Averell Harriman; "Mr. Stokes' Statement to Press on Departure from Iran,

August 23, 1951," 23 August 1951, RG 59, 888.2553/8-2351; "Dr. Mosadeq's Reply to Mr. Harriman's Letter of August 21," 24 August 1951, RG 59, 888.2553/8-2451; and "Short Account of Talks on Wednesday Morning, 22 August 1951, Before Leaving Tehran," 27 August 1951, FO 371, 91584/EP1531/1481.

44. See FO tel. 1109 to British embassy, Tehran, 28 August 1951, FO 371, 91581/EP1531/1408; and Strang record of 27 August meeting between Attlee, Harriman, et al., 28 August 1951, T236/3657. For evidence that Mossadeq's attitude might have been softening see Grady (Harriman) tel. 786 to State Department, 24 August 1951, Truman Papers, PSF—Subject File, box 180, folder: Iran—W. Averell Harriman; and Shepherd tel. 1212 to FO, 24 August 1951, FO 371, 91581/EP1531/1408.

45. FO tel. 1009 to British embassy, Tehran, 25 August 1951, FO 371, 91582/EP1531/1428. See also minutes of Cabinet meeting, GEN.363/20th Meeting, 24 August 1951, T236/2657; and Shepherd tel. 1234 to FO, 26 August 1951, FO 371, 91582/EP1531/1429.

46. See Furlonge memorandum, "AIOC Personnel," 20 August 1951, FO 371, 91580/EP1531/1385; minutes of Cabinet meeting, GEN.363/19th meeting, 22 August 1951, T236/3657; note by the Persian Oil Working Party, "Action Consequent upon the Withdrawal of the Stokes Mission," 22 August 1951, GEN.363/11, T236/3657; FO tel. 1078 to British embassy, Tehran, 22 August 1951, FO 371, 91580/EP1531/1387; record of interdepartmental meeting, 23 August 1951, T236/3657; minutes of Cabinet meeting, GEN.363/21st meeting, 27 August 1951, T236/3657; C.M.(51)58th Conclusions, 4 September 1951, CABINET 58(51), CAB 128/20; and FO tel. 1170 to British embassy, Tehran, 8 September 1951, FO 371, 91586/EP1531/1517.

47. Shepherd tel. 1234 to FO, 26 August 1951, FO 371, 91582/EP1531/1429; Fergusson (MFP) to Strang, 1 September 1951, FO 371, 91587/EP1531/1540. See also David S. Painter, *Oil and the American Century: The Political Economy of U.S. Foreign Oil Policy, 1941–1954* (Baltimore: Johns Hopkins University Press, 1986), p. 179; Louis, *British Empire in the Middle East*, pp. 657–62, 674–76; and C. M. Woodhouse, *Something Ventured* (London: Granada, 1982), pp. 108–11.

48. See PAD press release #114, 3 July 1951, Records of the Office of Civil and Defense Mobilization, Record Group 304, Oil and Gas Staff Records, box 1, National Archives (hereafter RG 304, with filing information); PAD press release #116, 6 July 1951, RG 304, box 1; PAD memorandum, "Supplying Petroleum to Free World without Iran," 12 July 1951, and PAD 126, Plan Approved for Joint Action to Offset Loss of Iranian Oil, 2 August 1951, both in Oscar L. Chapman Papers, Misc. Records, box 99, folder: Petroleum Administration for Defense (1), Truman Library; PAD press release #132, "Special Efforts by United States Oil Industry Needed to Offset Iranian Losses, Brown Says," 7 August 1951, Records of the Office of the Secretary of the Interior, Record Group 48, Press Releases for Various Defense Agencies, 1950–1953, Petroleum Administration for Defense, box 1, National Archives (hereafter RG 48, with filing information); "Co-Operative Action Approved," *Petroleum Press Service* 18 (September 1951): 310–11; Burton I. Kaufman, *The Oil Cartel Case: A Documentary Study of Antitrust Activity During the Cold War Era* (Westport, Conn.: Greenwood, 1978), pp. 42–43; and Gerald Nash, *United States Oil Policy, 1880–1964: Business and Government in Twentieth-Century America* (Pittsburgh, Pa.: University of Pittsburgh Press, 1968), pp. 195–96.

49. Oscar L. Chapman to James M. Mead (chair, FTC), 8 July 1952, Stephen J.

Spingarn Papers, FTC File, box 55, folder: International Petroleum Cartel Report, Truman Library.

50. See Bruce K. Brown, *Oil Men in Washington: An Informal Account of the Organization and Activities of the Petroleum Administration for Defense During the Korean War, 1950–1952* (Evanil Press, 1965), pp. 149–65; and Painter, *Oil and the American Century*, pp. 179–81. For an in-depth look at the interpenetration of the public and private sectors with regard to oil policy see Robert Engler, *The Politics of Oil: A Study of Private Power and Democratic Directions* (Chicago: University of Chicago Press, 1961).

51. Shepherd tel. 1296 to FO, 6 September 1951, FO 371, 91586/EP1531/1509; Shepherd dispatch 253 to FO, 15 September 1951, FO 371, 91589/EP1531/1591.

52. Shepherd to Strang, 4 September 1951, T236/2825. For Iranian opposition see Shepherd dispatch 253 to Younger, 15 September 1951, FO 371, 91589/EP1531/1591; Shepherd dispatch 283 to Morrison, 11 October 1951, FO 371, 91451/EP1013/40; Sepehr Zabih, *The Mossadegh Era: Roots of the Iranian Revolution* (Chicago: Lake View, 1982), pp. 29–30; Farhad Diba, *Mohammad Mossadegh: A Political Biography* (London: Croom Helm, 1986), pp. 129–30; Fakhreddin Azimi, *Iran: The Crisis of Democracy, 1941–1953* (London: I. B. Tauris, 1989), p. 271; and Anthony Eden, *The Memoirs of Anthony Eden: Full Circle* (Boston: Houghton Mifflin, 1960), pp. 222–23.

53. See Franks tel. 3046 to FO, 20 September 1951, FO 371, 91589/EP1531/1588; Shepherd tel. 1374 to FO, 20 September 1951, FO 371, 91589/EP1531/1580; Shepherd tel. 1375 to FO, 20 September 1951, FO 371, 91589/EP1531/1584; FO tel. 1238 to British embassy, Tehran, 21 September 1951, FO 371, 91589/EP1531/1581; FO tel. 1261 to British embassy, Tehran, 25 September 1951, FO 371, 91590/EP1531/1619; and Shepherd tel. 1425 to FO, 26 September 1951, FO 371, 91591/EP1531/1628.

54. Shepherd to Strang, 23 September 1951, FO 371, 91472/EP1024/4; Franks tel. 3223 to FO, 5 October 1951, FO 371, 91596/EP1531/1769; Shepherd tel. 1421 to FO, 26 September 1951, FO 800/653; FO tel. 4572 to British embassy, Washington, 25 September 1951, FO 371, 91590/EP1531/1619; FO tel. 1261 to British embassy, Tehran, 25 September 1951, FO 371, 91590/EP1531/1619. For British assessments of the shah see Furlonge et al. minutes, 20 September 1951, FO 371, 91472/EP1024/2; Shepherd tel. 1389 to FO, 21 September 1951, FO 800/653; Makins minute, 21 September 1951, FO 371, 91591/EP1531/1639; Shepherd tel. 1389 to FO, 21 September 1951, FO 371, 91591/EP1531/1633; Furlonge memorandum, 22 September 1951, FO 371, 91595/EP1531/1736; and Franks tel. 3074 to FO, 22 September 1951, FO 371, 91590/EP1531/1606.

55. See Webb tel. 5 to U.S. delegation, San Francisco, 1 September 1951, RG 59, 888.2553/9-151; Franks tel. 3061 to FO, 21 September 1951, FO 371, 91589/EP1531/1598; Franks tel. 3097 to FO, 25 September 1951, FO 371, 91462/EP1024/3; and Furlonge to Shepherd, 14 October 1951, FO 371, 91591/EP1531/1624.

56. C.M.(51)60th Conclusions, 27 September 1951, CABINET 60(51), CAB 128/20. For continuing British military plans see, for example, Chiefs of Staff Committee, Minutes, C.O.S.(51)129th meeting, 13 August 1951, DEFE4/46; Chiefs of Staff Committee, Confidential Annex to C.O.S.(51)129th Meeting, 13 August 1951, DEFE4/46; Chiefs of Staff Committee, Minutes, C.O.S.(51)130th Meeting, 14 August 1951, DEFE4/46; and Chiefs of Staff Committee, Minutes, C.O.S.(51)134th Meeting, 22 August 1951, DEFE4/46.

57. For domestic British politics and Labour-Conservative discussions see Root to John E. Utter (U.S. embassy, Paris), 25 July 1951, RG 84, London Embassy, Classified Records, 523.1 Middle East; Margaret Woon (research analyst, U.S. embassy, London) dispatch 1022 to State Department, 23 August 1951, RG 59, 741.00/8-2351; Holmes tel. 1270 to State Department, 7 September 1951, RG 59, 741.00/9-751; Harriman to Dwight D. Eisenhower, 19 September 1951, Eisenhower Pre-Presidential Papers, Principal File, box 55, folder: Harriman, W. Averell (1) [September 1951–April 1952], Dwight D. Eisenhower Library, Abilene, Kansas; George W. Perkins (EUR) memorandum for Acheson, 26 September 1951, RG 59, 741.00/9-2651; and Holmes tel. 1531 to State Department, 26 September 1951, RG 59, 741.00/9-2651.

58. Berry memorandum to the acting secretary of state, 4 October 1951, RG 59, 788.00/10-451.

59. See Shepherd tel. 1456 to FO, 30 September 1951, FO 371, 91593/EP1531/1681; and Webb tel. 1840 to U.S. embassy, London, 4 October 1951, RG 59, 888.2553/10-451.

60. See C.M.(51)60th Conclusions, 27 September 1951, CABINET 60(51), CAB 128/20; Franks tel. 3138 to FO, 28 September 1951, FO 371, 91592/EP1531/1656; FO tel. 4675 to British embassy, Washington, 30 September 1951, FO 371, 91592/EP1531/1665; and Webb tel. to U.S. embassy, London, 30 September 1951, *FRUS, 1952–1954*, vol. 10, pp. 183–85.

61. Although debate was originally scheduled to begin on 11 October, it was postponed until 15 October at Mossadeq's request.

62. Gifford tel. 1607 to State Department, 2 October 1951, RG 59, 888.2553/10-251. For a colorful account of the AIOC's withdrawal from Abadan see Henry Longhurst, *Adventure in Oil: The Story of British Petroleum* (London: Sidgwick and Jackson, 1959), pp. 143–44. For domestic British reaction see "Speeches on the Persian Situation Made During the British General Election Campaign," October 1951, *DIA, 1951*, pp. 520–26; Gifford tel. 1623 to State Department, 3 October 1951, RG 59, 741.00/10-351; Gifford tel. 1624 to State Department, 3 October 1951, RG 59, 741.00/10-351; Gifford tel. 1673 to State Department, 4 October 1951, RG 59, 741.00/10-451; and Gifford tel. 1722 to State Department, 8 October 1951, RG 59, 741.00/10-851.

63. Gifford tel. to State Department, 5 October 1951, RG 59, 888.2553/10-551; FO tel. 4804 to British embassy, Washington, 6 October 1951, FO 371, 91596/EP1531/1763; FO tel. 4687 to British embassy, Washington, 30 September 1951, FO 371, 91598/EP1531/1815; Shepherd to Bowker, 8 October 1951, FO 371, 91606/EP1531/1994; L. D. Battle memorandum of conversation between Acheson and Truman, 10 October 1951, Acheson Papers, box 66, folder: Memoranda of Conversations, October 1951.

64. For detailed coverage of the Security Council debate see Alan W. Ford, *The Anglo-Iranian Dispute of 1951–1952: A Study of the Role of Law in the Relations of States* (Berkeley: University of California Press, 1954), pp. 124–53; and ICJ, *Pleadings*, pp. 372–78.

65. Acheson, *Present at the Creation*, p. 511; Acheson tel. 2808 to State Department, 10 November 1951, RG 59, 888.2553/11-1051. See also Acheson tel. to State Department, 14 November 1951, *FRUS, 1952–1954*, vol. 10, pp. 281–83.

66. Vernon A. Walters memorandum of conversation between McGhee and Mossadeq, 14 October 1951, in William O. Baxter (GTI) memorandum for the files re

McGhee-Mossadeq conversations, 1951, 28 January 1953, RG 59, 888.2553/1-2853 (hereafter Baxter memorandum). For McGhee's account of the discussions see McGhee, "Recollections of Dr Muhammad Musaddiq," in *Musaddiq, Iranian Nationalism, and Oil*, ed. James A. Bill and Wm. Roger Louis (Austin: University of Texas Press, 1988), pp. 296–302; George McGhee, *Envoy to the Middle World: Adventures in Diplomacy* (New York: Harper & Row, 1983), pp. 388–404. See also Walters, *Silent Missions*, pp. 259–63.

67. See Walters memorandums of conversation, 8, 9 (2 conversations), 11 (2 conversations), 12, and 13 October 1951, in Baxter memorandum, 23 January 1953, RG 59, 888.2553/1-2853; Franks tel. 3280 to FO, 11 October 1951, FO 371, 91600/EP1531/1854; Acheson tel. 801 to U.S. embassy, Tehran, 12 October 1951, RG 59, 888.2553/10-1215; and Franks tel. 3321 to FO, 13 October 1951, FO 371, 91601/EP1531/1884.

68. See the documents cited in note 63.

69. Funkhouser memorandum of conversation, "Meeting with Representatives of U.S. Oil Companies to Discuss Developments in Iran," 14 September 1951, RG 59, 788.00/9-1451; Jebb tel. 332 to FO, 12 October 1951, FO 371, 91601/EP1531/1889. See also McGhee memorandum of conversation with Acheson and representatives of U.S. oil companies, 10 October 1951, Acheson Papers, box 66, folder: Memoranda of Conversations, October 1951; McGhee memorandum of conversation for the president, RG 59, 788.00/10-1051; and Butler record of conversation, 10 October 1951, FO 371, 91612/EP1531/2176.

70. See Walters memorandums of conversation, 24 (2 conversations), 27, 28, 29, and 30 October, in Baxter memorandum, 28 January 1953, RG 59, 888.2553/1-2853.

71. Walters memorandum of conversation, 24 October 1951, in Baxter memorandum, 28 January 1953, RG 59, 888.2553/1-2853; Franks tel. 3434 to FO, 25 October 1951, FO 371, 91606/EP1531/2011. For discussions of price see Walters memorandums of conversation, 25, 29, and 30 October 1951, in Baxter memorandum, 28 January 1953, RG 59, 888.2553/1-2853.

72. Mossadeq quoted in Walters memorandum of conversation, 30 October 1951, in Baxter memorandum, 28 January 1953, RG 59, 888.2553/1-2853. See also the sources cited in note 67.

73. Webb (acting secretary of state) tel. to U.S. embassy, London, 1 November 1951, *FRUS, 1952–1954*, vol. 10, pp. 248–55. Quotes are from p. 253.

74. Acheson memorandum of conversation, 4 November 1951, *FRUS, 1952–1954*, vol. 10, pp. 256–58; unsigned minutes of interdepartmental meeting, 1 November 1951, FO 371, 91608/EP1531/2045. See also Furlonge, "Notes on Washington tel. 3485," 1 November 1951, FO 371, 91607/EP1531/2032; Treasury record of meeting with Harold Linder with attached FO minutes, 3 November 1951, FO 371, 91609/EP1531/2080; minutes of meeting of Persian Oil Working Party with attached FO minutes, 6 November 1951, FO 371, 91609/EP1531/2098; FO memorandum, "Discussion with Mr. Acheson," 6 November 1951, FO 371, 91612/EP1531/2161; and FO tel. 1596 to British embassy, Paris (for Eden), 6 November 1951, FO 371, 91608/EP1531/2059.

75. Acheson actel. [Acheson telegram] to State Department, 7 November 1951, *FRUS, 1952–1954*, vol. 10, pp. 265–67; FO memorandum, "Discussion with Mr. Acheson," 6 November 1951, FO 371, 91612/EP1531/2161. See also Treasury record of meeting with Harold Linder with attached FO minutes, 3 November 1951, FO 371, 91609/EP1531/2080; FO tel. 1596 to British embassy, Paris (for Eden), 6 November

1951, FO 371, 91608/EP1531/2059; C.C.(51)5th Conclusions, 8 November 1951, CAB 128/23; Franks tel. 3409 to FO, 23 November 1951, FO 371, 91606/EP1531/1992; and Franks tel. 3434 to FO, 25 November 1951, FO 371, 91606/EP1531/2011.

76. Bruce tel. to State Department, 9 November 1951, *FRUS, 1952–1954*, vol. 10, pp. 272–74; Acheson tel. 2808 to State Department, 10 November 1951, RG 59, 888.2553/11-1051. See also Persian Oil Working Party on Persian Oil memorandum with attached FO minutes, 29 October 1951, FO 371, 91608/EP1531/2061; Webb tel. to U.S. embassy, Paris (for Acheson), 9 November 1951, *FRUS, 1952–1954*, vol. 10, pp. 275–78; FO minutes re conversation between Eden, Acheson, and Harriman, 14 November 1951, FO 371, 91612/EP1531/2174; Webb memorandum for Truman, 16 November 1951, Truman Papers, PSF—Subject File, box 180, folder: Iran; and Eden, *Full Circle*, pp. 219–25.

77. See Ministry of Fuel and Power note on Iran, P.O.W.P. (51) 25, 29 October 1951, FO 371, 91607/EP1531/2036.

78. Acheson actel. to State Department, 7 November 1951, *FRUS, 1952–1954*, vol. 10, pp. 265–67. See also FO memorandum, "Discussion with Mr. Acheson," 6 November 1951, FO 371, 91612/EP1531/2161; Harvey (Eden) tel. 501 to FO, 7 November 1951, FO 800/812; and Acheson tel. 2808 to State Department, 10 November 1951, RG 59, 888.2553/11-1051.

79. Mossadeq, quoted in Walters, *Silent Missions*, p. 262. For continuing McGhee-Mossadeq discussions see Walters memorandums of conversation, 1, 3, 5, 8, 9 (2 conversations), 13, 15 (2 conversations), 16, and 17 (2 conversations) November 1951, in Baxter memorandum, 28 January 1953, RG 59, 888.2553/1-2853. For Mossadeq's appeals for financial assistance see Walters memorandum of conversation, 8 November 1951, in Baxter memorandum, 28 January 1953, RG 59, 888.2553/1-2853; and Mossadeq to Truman, 9 November 1951, Truman Papers, OF, file 134-B, box 569.

80. Acheson memorandum for Truman, 22 October 1951, Truman Papers, PSF—Subject File, box 180, folder: Iran—W. Averell Harriman.

5. Stalemate

1. Dean G. Acheson, *Present at the Creation: My Years in the State Department* (New York: Norton, 1969), p. 679.

2. See Richards dispatch 516 to State Department, 16 October 1951, RG 59, 788.13/10-1651; Robert M. Carr (counselor for economic affairs, U.S. embassy, Tehran) dispatch 584 to State Department, 2 November 1951, RG 59, 888.00/11-251; M. T. Flett (Treasury) note with enclosed paper by Persian Oil Working Party, "Economic Sanctions against Persia," 4 November 1951, T236/3660; and Middleton to Furlonge, 19 November 1951, FO 371, 91472/EP1024/10. For figures see Henderson tel. 1479 to State Department, 22 October 1951, RG 59, 888.2553/10-2251.

3. For Iranian opposition see Shepherd tel. 1585 to FO, 24 October 1951, FO 371, 91606/EP1531/2002; Middleton dispatch 310 to FO, 14 November 1951, FO 371, 91451/EP1013/41; and Middleton dispatch 333 to FO, 12 December 1951, FO 371, 91451/EP1013/44. For British efforts to encourage anti-Mossadeq sentiment see Wm. Roger Louis, *The British Empire in the Middle East, 1945–1951: Arab Nationalism, the United States, and Postwar Imperialism* (Oxford, England: Oxford University Press, 1984), pp. 657–61.

4. See Central Intelligence Agency (CIA), "Analysis of Iranian Political Situation," 12 October 1951, Truman Papers, PSF—Subject File, box 180, folder: Iran—W. Averell Harriman; Henderson tel. to State Department, 7 November 1951, *Foreign Relations of the United States, 1952–1954*, vol. 10 (Washington, D.C.: Government Printing Office, 1978), pp. 262–65 (hereafter *FRUS*); Acheson tel. 2808 to State Department, 10 November 1951, RG 59, 888.2553/11-1051; FO minutes, 19 November 1951, FO 371, 91613/EP1531/2209; McGhee memorandum of conversation, 21 November 1951, RG 59, 611.88/11-2151; Churchill note to FO, 24 November 1951, Records of the Prime Minister's Office, Record Class PREM11/725, Public Record Office; and Eden note, 4 December 1951, PREM11/625.

5. Henderson tel. 1935 to State Department, 26 November 1951, RG 59, 788.13/11-2651. See also Franklin C. Gowen (counselor, U.S. embassy, Mexico City) dispatch 849 to State Department, 5 October 1951, RG 59, 888.2553/10-551; and Middleton dispatch 333 to FO, 12 December 1951, FO 371, 91451/EP1013/44. For Mossadeq's visit to Cairo see Melbourne dispatch 645 to State Department, 27 November 1951, RG 59, 888.2553/11-2751.

6. Leslie Rowan to Sir Ernest Rowe-Dutton, 30 October 1951, T236/3666; FO tel. 5930 to British embassy, Washington, 7 December 1951, FO 371, 91614/EO1531/2280. See also AIOC memorandum on International Bank for Reconstruction and Development (IBRD) proposals re Iranian oil with attached FO minutes, 28 November 1951, FO 371, 91615/EP1531/2250; P.O.(M)(51)6, "International Bank Proposals: Note by Persia (Official) Committee," 29 November 1951, PREM11/725; Berry memorandum for Acheson, "IBRD Plan for Iranian Oil" with enclosed draft of IBRD plan and British memorandum on International Bank proposal, 14 December 1951, RG 59, 888.2553/12-1451; C.(51)46, "Persia: International Bank Proposal, Memorandum by the Secretary of State for Foreign Affairs," 17 December 1951, CAB 129/48; Harold N. Graves Jr., "The Bank as International Mediator: Three Episodes," in *The World Bank Since Bretton Woods*, ed. Edward S. Mason and Robert E. Asher (Washington, D.C.: Brookings Institution, 1973), pp. 595–603, and L. P. Elwell-Sutton, *Persian Oil: A Study in Power Politics* (London: Lawrence & Wishart, 1955), pp. 274–76.

7. See Henderson tel. to State Department, 14 December 1951, *FRUS, 1952–1954*, vol. 10, pp. 291–95; FO minutes, 15 December 1951, FO 371, 91617/EP1531/2294; Franks tel. 3877 to FO, 16 December 1951, FO 371, 91617/EP1531/2308; and Acheson tel. to U.S. embassy, Tehran, 21 December 1951, and Henderson tel. to State Department, 26 December 1951, *FRUS, 1952–1954*, vol. 10, pp. 295–300.

8. For the domestic Iranian context see Fakhreddin Azimi, *Iran: Crisis of Democracy, 1941–1953* (London: I. B. Tauris, 1989), pp. 273–76; and "Chronology," *Middle Eastern Affairs* (January 1952): 29–30.

9. See Ortiz (PED) memorandum of conversation re: International Bank Mission to Tehran Regarding Possible Iranian Oil Agreement, 26 December 1951, RG 59, 888.2553/12-2651; Franks tel. 3995 to FO, 29 December 1951, FO 371, 91619/EP1531/2354; FO tel. 6318 to British embassy, Washington, 31 December 1951, FO 371, 91619/EP1531/2354; and Graves, "The Bank as International Mediator," pp. 602–603.

10. For "non-oil economics" see Homa Katouzian, "Oil Boycott and the Political Economy: Musaddiq and the Strategy of Non-Oil Economics," in *Musaddiq, Iranian Nationalism, and Oil*, ed. James A. Bill and Wm. Roger Louis (Austin: University of Texas Press, 1988), pp. 203–27; and Patrick Clawson and Cyrius Sassanpour,

"Adjustment to a Foreign Exchange Shock: Iran, 1951–1953," *International Journal of Middle East Studies* 19 (February 1987): 1–22. For Mossadeq's warnings about financial collapse see Henderson tel. 2609 to State Department, 14 January 1952, RG 59, 888.00TA/1-1452. See also J. S. Earman (executive director, CIA) memorandum for Rear Admiral R. L. Dennison, 18 January 1952, enclosing Paul A. Borel memorandum, "Mosadeq's Demand for Emergency U.S. Aid," 17 January 1952, Truman Papers, PSF—Subject File, box 180, folder: Iran—W. Averell Harriman.

11. See Middleton to Bowker, 4 January 1952, FO 371, 98618/EP1051/8; Office of Intelligence Research, OIR-5735, "Mosadeq and the Current Iranian Elections," 10 January 1952; Azimi, *Iran*, pp. 275–77; and Sepehr Zabih, *The Mossadegh Era: Roots of the Iranian Revolution* (Chicago: Lake View, 1982), pp. 33–34.

12. Acheson tel. to U.S. embassy, Tehran, 22 January 1952, *FRUS, 1952–1954*, vol. 10, pp. 336–38. See also Burton Y. Berry (acting assistant secretary of state for Near Eastern, South Asian, and African affairs) memorandum to Acheson, "Application to Iran of Section 511(a), Mutual Security Act," 8 January 1952, Henderson tel. to State Department, 15 January 1952, Paul A. Borel (Office of National Estimates) memorandum for Walter Bedell Smith (director of the CIA), "Mosadeq's Demand for Emergency US Aid," 17 January 1952, contained in J. S. Earman (executive assistant to Smith) memorandum for R. L. Dennison (naval aide to the president), 18 January 1952, James K. Penfield (chargé d'affaires, U.S. embassy, London) tel. to State Department, 18 January 1952, Henderson tel. to State Department, 19 January 1952, and Henderson tel. to State Department, 19 January 1952, *FRUS, 1952–1954*, vol. 10, pp. 305–11, 323–35.

13. Henderson tel. 2549 to State Department, 9 January 1952, RG 59, 888.2553/1-952; FO tel. 29 to British embassy, Tehran, 10 January 1952, FO 371, 98618/EP1051/4. See also Shepherd tel. 18 to FO, 9 January 1952, FO 371, 98618/EP1051/2; Richards dispatch 809 to State Department, 15 January 1952, RG 59, 641.88/1-1552; Melbourne (first secretary, U.S. embassy, Tehran) dispatch 896 to State Department, 7 February 1952, RG 59, 641.88/2-752; and Azimi, *Iran*.

14. In addition to the sources cited in note 13 see Henderson tel. 2670 to State Department, 17 January 1952, RG 59, 788.99/1-1752; and Azimi, *Iran*, p. 276.

15. State Department Paper, "Approach and Objectives for the Churchill Talks," 21 December 1951, *FRUS, 1952–1954*, vol. 6 (Washington, D.C.: Government Printing Office, 1989), pp. 709–16; minutes of Third Formal Session, Truman-Churchill Talks, 9 January 1952, Truman Papers, PSF—General File, box 116, folder: Churchill-Truman Meetings, Memos and Minutes; Omar Bradley (chairman, Joint Chiefs of Staff) notes of Anglo-American meeting, 5 January 1952, *FRUS, 1952–1954*, vol. 6, pp. 740–41.

16. Steering Group on Preparations for the Talks between the President and Prime Minister Churchill, paper on Iran, 5 January 1952, Truman Papers, PSF—General File, box 116, folder: Churchill-Truman Meetings, Negotiating Papers (#1); Steering Group on Preparations for Talks between the President and Prime Minister Churchill, Negotiating Paper: General Middle East, 21 December 1951, Truman Papers, PSF—General File, box 116, folder: Churchill-Truman Meetings, Papers Prepared for; NSC Staff Study, "The Position of the United States with Respect to the Area Comprising the Arab States, Iran and Israel," 18 January 1952, Records of the Policy Planning Staff, Country and Area Files, box 30, folder: Near and Middle East, 1952–1953, National Archives.

17. Acheson memorandum of 5 January 1952 meeting between Truman and Churchill, 6 January 1952, Truman Papers, PSF—General File, box 116, folder:

Churchill-Truman Meetings, Memos and Minutes. See also Acheson memorandum of conversation between Truman and Churchill, 6 January 1952, *FRUS, 1952–1954*, vol. 6, pp. 742–46; and U.S. minutes of Anglo-American meeting, 8 January 1952, *FRUS, 1952–1954*, vol. 9, pp. 171–76.

18. Memorandum of meeting between the foreign ministers of the United States and the United Kingdom, 9 January 1952, *FRUS, 1952–1954*, vol. 10, pp. 311–20. See also Acheson tel. 1624 to U.S. embassy, Tehran, 7 February 1952, RG 59, 641.88/2-752.

19. Memorandum of meeting between the foreign ministers of the United States and the United Kingdom, 9 January 1952, *FRUS, 1952–1954*, vol. 10, pp. 311–20. See also Franks tel. 68 to FO, 18 January 1952, FO 371, 98684/EP1531/2; and Acheson memorandum of Anglo-American meeting, 6 January 1952, *FRUS, 1952–1954*, vol. 6, pp. 742–46.

20. FO tel. 521 to British embassy, Washington, 26 January 1952, FO 371, 98684/EP15314/2; Franks (Makins) tel. 204 to FO (for Sir William Strang), 18 January 1952, FO 371, 98684/EP15314/1; FO tel. 520 to British embassy, Washington, 26 January 1952, FO 371, 98684/EP15314/2.

21. Franks tel. 68 to FO, 18 January 1952, FO 371, 98684/EP15314/2; memorandum of meeting between the foreign ministers of the United States and the United Kingdom, 9 January 1952, *FRUS, 1952–1954*, vol. 10, pp. 311–20; Middleton (acting chargé d'affaires, British embassy, Tehran) tel. 107 to FO, 26 January 1952, FO 371, 98684/EP15314/10.

22. National Intelligence Estimate, NIE-46, "Probable Developments in Iran in 1952 in the Absence of an Oil Settlement," 31 January 1952, Truman Papers, PSF—Intelligence File, box 253, folder: Central Intelligence Reports, NIE 44–52. See also Ramsbotham memorandum on Persia (Official) Committee meeting, 29 January 1952, FO 371, 98685/EP15314/21; record of Ramsbotham discussion with Nitze on "Possible Long-Term Solutions, Persia (Official) Committee, 2/13/52, Item 2," 13 February 1952, FO 371, 98608/EP1022/21; and British record of Anglo-American meeting, 14 February 1952, FO 371, 98608/EP1022/9.

23. Franks tel. 439 to FO, 12 February 1952, FO 371, 98685/EP15314/32; FO tel. 774 to British embassy, Washington, 9 February 1952, FO 371, 98685/EP15314/24.

24. Truman message to Mossadeq, 9 February 1952, Truman Papers, White House Central Files (WHCF)—Confidential File, box 39, folder: State Department Correspondence 1952. See also Acheson tel. to U.S. embassy, Tehran, 26 January 1952, *FRUS, 1952–1954*, vol. 10, pp. 338–41; Henderson tel. 3031 to State Department, 11 February 1952, RG 59, 888.2553/2-1153; and record of Ramsbotham discussion with Nitze, "Possible Long-Term Solutions, Persia (Official) Committee, 2/13/52, Item 2," 13 February 1952, FO 371, 98608/EP1022/21.

25. Berry memorandum to Acheson, "Application to Iran of Section 511(a) Mutual Security Act," 8 Janaury 1952, *FRUS, 1952–1954*, vol. 10, p. 310. See also Henderson tel. to State Department, 19 January 1952, *FRUS, 1952–1954*, vol. 10, pp. 334–35.

26. Franks tel. 439 to FO, 12 February 1952, FO 371, 98685/EP15314/32; Franks tel. 427 to FO, 11 February 1952, FO 371, 98685/EP15314/31. See also FO tel. 776 to British embassy, Washington, 9 February 1952, FO 371, 98685/EP15314/24; and FO tel. 894 to British embassy, Washington, 19 February 1952, FO 371, 98608/EP1022/9. For the Anglo-American joint assessment see Middleton tel. 168 to FO, 17 February 1952, FO 371, 98608/EP1022/10.

27. Graves, "The Bank as International Mediator," pp. 602–603.

28. Ibid., p. 604.

29. Henderson tel. to State Department, 19 February 1952, *FRUS, 1952–1954*, vol. 10, pp. 358–59. See also Homa Katouzian, ed., *Musaddiq's Memoirs* (London: JEBHE, National Movement of Iran, 1988), p. 367.

30. See Henderson tel. 2598 to State Department, 12 January 1952, RG 59, 888.2553/1-1252; and Franks tel. 271 to FO, 25 January 1952, FO 371, 98684/EP15314/6.

31. See FO tel. 32 to British embassy, Tehran, 1 March 1952, FO 371, 98649/EP1531/67; and Bowker record of conversation with Prud'homme, 3 March 1952, FO 371, 98650/EP1531/82.

32. Concerning the bank's thinking see Middleton tel. 167 to FO, 17 February 1952, FO 371, 98647/EP1531/38; FO tel. 184 to British embassy, Tehran, 18 February 1952, FO 371, 98647/EP1531/38; and IBRD paper, 8 March 1952, World Bank General Archives (WBGA), Central Files, 1946–1971: Operational Correspondence, Iran, box 32, folder: 1. I am grateful to my friend Amy L. S. Staples for providing me with copies of her research in the records of the World Bank.

33. Mossadeq to Garner, 3 January 1952, WBGA, Central Files, 1946–1971: Operational Correspondence, Iran, box 31, folder: 10. See also Henderson tel. to State Department, 4 January 1952, *FRUS, 1952–1954*, vol. 10, pp. 301–303; Henderson tel. 3139 to State Department, 17 February 1952, RG 59, 888.2553/2-752; Middleton tel. 167 to FO, 17 February 1952, FO 371, 98647/EP1531/38; Graves, "The Bank as International Mediator," pp. 605–606; and Katouzian, *Musaddiq's Memoirs*, p. 367.

34. See Henderson tel. 2598 to State Department, 12 January 1952, RG 59, 888.2553/1-1252; and Franks tel. 271 to FO, 25 January 1952, FO 371, 98684/EP15314/6.

35. See "Suggestions for Consideration by International Bank in Connection with the Points Raised in Mossadeq's Letter of January 3rd, 1952," 6 February 1952, WBGA, Central Files, 1946–1971: Operational Correspondence, Iran, box 32, folder: 1.

36. See Franks tel. 387 to FO, 5 February 1952, FO 371, 98685/EP15314/24; Acheson tel. to U.S. embassy, London, 6 February 1952, *FRUS, 1952–1954*, vol. 10, pp. 343–46; and Acheson tel. 1623 to U.S. embassy, Tehran, 7 February 1952, RG 59, 888.2553/2-752.

37. Makins memorandum, 6 February 1952, FO 371, 98675/EP1536/17; Franks tel. 273 to FO, 25 February 1952, FO 371, 98684/EP15314/5. See also Franks tel. 387 to FO, 5 February 1952, FO 371, 98685/EP15314/24; and FO tel. 775 to British embassy, Washington, 9 February 1952, FO 371, 98685/EP15314/24.

38. Record of meeting at State Department about IBRD proposals, 11 February 1952, FO 371, 98685/EP15314/36; Franks tel. 427 to FO, 11 February 1952, FO 371, 98685/EP15314/31. See also FO tel. 774 to British embassy, Washington, 9 February 1952, FO 371, 98685/EP15314/24; FO tel. 790 to British embassy, Washington, 11 February 1952, FO 371, 98685/EP15314/34; and Acheson tel. to U.S. embassy, Tehran, 12 February 1952, *FRUS, 1952–1954*, vol. 10, pp. 352–54.

39. Henderson tel. 3141 to State Department, 17 February 1952, RG 59, 888.2553/2-1752; Ross minute, 18 February 1952, FO 371, 98648/EP1531/51. See also Henderson tel. 3123 to State Department, 16 February 1952, RG 59, 888.2553/2-1652; Ramsbotham memorandum of meeting with Garner, 21 February 1952, FO 371, 98648/EP1531/57; and Azimi, *Iran*, p. 278.

40. Bowker minute, 5 March 1952, FO 371, 98685/EP15314/48; Middleton tel. 232

to FO, 11 March 1952, FO 371, 98686/EP15314/65. See also Henderson tel. to State Department, 28 February 1952, *FRUS, 1952–1954*, vol. 10, pp. 361–64; Henderson tel. 3421 to State Department, 7 March 1952, RG 59, 888.2553/3-752; and Middleton tel. 237 to FO, 12 March 1952, FO 371, 98650/EP1531/87.

41. Henderson tel. 3513 to State Department, 13 March 1952, RG 59, 888.2553/3-1352; Middleton tel. 237 to FO, 12 March 1952, FO 371, 98650/EP1531/87; Middleton letter to Eden, 8 March 1952, FO 371, 98707/EP15317/4; Middleton tel. 239 to FO, 13 March 1952, FO 371, 98650/EP1531/90; Henderson tel. 3540 to State Department, 16 March 1952, RG 59, 888.2553/3-1652.

42. Transcript of proceedings of 27 March 1952 IBRD 38th Special Meeting of Executive Directors, 1 April 1952, T236/3671; press accounts of IBRD mission to Iran, undated, WBGA, Central Files, 1946–1971: Operational Correspondence, Iran, box 31, folder: 2.

43. Hector Prud'homme to Robert Garner, 1 and 3 January 1952, and Prud'homme to Loy Henderson, 14 January 1952, all in WBGA, Central Files, 1946–1971: Operational Correspondence, Iran, box 31, folder: 10; and Hector Prud'homme oral history interview, 2 May 1985, WBGA.

44. C.C.(52)31st Conclusions, 18 March 1952, CAB 128/24; Franks tel. 373 to FO, 9 April 1952, FO 371, 98688/EP15314/107. See also Ramsbotham minute with attached Persia (Official) Committee paper, 2 April 1952, FO 371, 98687/EP15314/103; and FO tel. 1756 to British embassy, Washington, 2 April 1952, FO 371, 98688/EP15314/107.

45. Ramsbotham minute with attached Persia (Official) Committee paper, 2 April 1952, FO 371, 98687/EP15314/102. See also Makins et al. minutes, 9 April 1952, FO 371, 98677/EP1538/4.

46. For British policy see Franks tel. 442 to FO, 29 April 1952, FO 371, 98688/EP15314/120; and Franks tel. 450 to FO, 30 April 1952, FO 371, 98688/EP15314/123.

47. John A. Samford (director of intelligence, USAF) memorandum, "Implications of the Soviet-Communist Threat in Iran," 16 May 1952, Records of the Office of the Secretary of Defense, Record Group 330, CCS 092 Iran (4-23-48) sec. 6, National Archives.

48. Hoskins (acting regional planning adviser, Bureau of Near Eastern, South Asian, and African affairs) memorandum to Byroade (assistant secretary of state for Near Eastern South Asian, and African Affairs), "Re-appraisal of US Policies in the NEA Area," 7 April 1952, *FRUS, 1952–1954*, vol. 9, pp. 204–13; "Britain's Position in the World and Its Implications for Our Middle East Policy," 3 June 1952, RG 59, Records of the Policy Planning Staff, Country and Area Files, box 30, folder: Near and Middle East, 1952–1953.

49. Carr dispatch 1067, "Monthly Economic Report," 7 April 1952, RG 59, 888.00/4-752; Henderson tel. 3922 to State Department, 14 April 1952, RG 59, 788.00/4-1452; Henderson tel. 3939 to State Department, 15 April 1952, RG 59, 641.88/4-1552.

50. Carr dispatch 1067, "Monthly Economic Report," 7 April 1952, RG 59, 888.00/4-752; Henderson tel. 3939 to State Department, 15 April 1952, RG 59, 641.88/4-1552. See also Henderson tel. 3865 to State Department, 10 April 1952, RG 59, 788.00/4-1052; and Melbourne dispatch 1077, "The Iranian Political Situation, April 1, 1952," 11 April 1952, RG 59, 788.00/4-1152.

51. Henderson tel. to State Department, 19 April 1952, *FRUS, 1952–1954*, vol. 10, pp. 371–75. See also Acheson tel. to U.S. embassy, Tehran, 21 April 1952, Henderson

tel. to State Department, 23 April 1952, and Acheson tel. to U.S. embassy, Tehran, 23 April 1952, *FRUS, 1952–1954*, vol. 10, pp. 375–79.

52. See Henderson tel. 3861 to State Department, 10 April 1952, RG 59, 788.00/4-1052; Henderson tel. 4138 to State Department, 26 April 1952, RG 59, 788.00/4-2652; Azimi, *Iran*, pp. 279–80; Richard W. Cottam, *Nationalism in Iran*, 2d rev. ed. (Pittsburgh, Pa.: University of Pittsburgh Press, 1979), pp. 100–101; and Zabih, *Mossadegh Era*, pp. 33–34.

53. Henderson tel. to State Department, 28 May 1952, *FRUS, 1952–1954*, vol. 10, pp. 384–86. See also Acheson tel. to U.S. embassy, Tehran, 30 May 1952, Henderson tel. to State Department, 6 June 1952, and Henderson tel. to State Department, 13 June 1952, *FRUS, 1952–1954*, vol. 10, pp. 386–92, 396–400.

54. For British activities against Mossadeq's government see Mark J. Gasiorowski, *U.S. Foreign Policy and the Shah: Building a Client State in Iran* (Ithaca, N.Y.: Cornell University Press, 1991), pp. 63–65.

55. Brief for meeting of the Persia (Official) Committee, 6 May 1952, FO 371, 98675/EP1436/41; draft tel. to British embassy, Washington, 13 May 1952, FO 371, 98689/EP15314/137; Fergusson to Makins, 27 May 1952, FO 371, 98689/EP15314/146.

56. W. J. McWilliams memorandum of conversation with the secretary, 16 May 1952, RG 59, lot 58 D 609. See also Acheson tel. to U.S. embassy, Tehran, 11 June 1952, *FRUS, 1952–1954*, vol. 10, pp. 393–95; U.S. minutes of Anglo-American discussion on the Middle East, 24 June 1952, *FRUS, 1952–1954*, vol. 10, pp. 400–403; and U.S. minutes of U.S.-U.K. ministerial meeting in London, 28 June 1952, *FRUS, 1952–1954*, vol. 10, pp. 406–408.

57. Philip Clock (secretary, U.S. embassy, The Hague) dispatch 2275, "Dr. Mosadeq's Appearance before the International Court of Justice," 19 June 1952, RG 59, 788.13/6-1952. See also Chapin (The Hague) tel. 1362 to State Department, 17 June 1952, RG 59, 788.13/6-1752; and Chapin tel. 1400 to State Department, 23 June 1952, RG 59, 788.13/6-2352. Mossadeq's speech may be found in International Court of Justice, *Pleadings, Oral Arguments, Documents: Anglo-Iranian Oil Case (United Kingdom v. Iran)* (The Hague: International Court of Justice, 1952), pp. 437–42.

58. See ICJ, *Pleadings*, pp. 445–669; and Chapin tel. 1400 to State Department, 23 June 1952, RG 59, 788.13/6-2352.

59. Middleton to Eden, 7 July 1952, FO 371, 98661/EP1532/230. See also Carr dispatch 1265, "Monthly Economic Report," 2 June 1952, RG 59, 888.00/6-252; Carr dispatch 7, "Monthly Economic Report," 3 July 1952, RG 59, 888.00/7-352; and Acheson, *Present at the Creation*, p. 679.

60. Hickinbotham (Aden) tel. 156 to FO, 21 June 1952, FO 371, 98660/EP1532/204.

61. National Front declaration quoted in Zabih, *Mossadegh Era*, p. 38; Henderson tel. to State Department, 27 June 1952, *FRUS, 1952–1954*, vol. 10, pp. 404–406. See also Henderson tel. 5048 to State Department, 27 June 1952, RG 59, 788.13/6-2752; Cottam, *Nationalism in Iran*, pp. 100–101; and Azimi, *Iran*, pp. 285–87.

62. See Henderson tel. 98 to State Department, 7 July 1952, RG 59, 788.13/7-752; Henderson tel. 108 to State Department, 8 July 1952, RG 59, 788.13/7-852; Gifford tel. 153 to State Department, 9 July 1952, RG 59, 788.13/7-952; and Acheson tel. 262 to U.S. embassy, London, 9 July 1952, RG 59, 788.13/7-952. See also Azimi, *Iran*, pp. 281–86; and Zabih, *Mossadegh Era*, pp. 35–39.

63. Henderson tel. 182 to State Department, 14 July 1952, RG 59, 788.00/7-1452.

See also Henderson tel. 251 to State Department, 18 July 1952, RG 59, 788.13/7-1852; Zabih, *Mossadegh Era*, pp. 39–41; and Azimi, *Iran*, pp. 286–87.

64. See FO tel. 2864 to British embassy, Washington, 18 July 1952, FO 371, 98690/EP15314/170; Franks tel. 1378 to FO, 18 July 1952, FO 371, 98690/EP15314/171; Gifford tel. 359 to State Department, 19 July 1952, RG 59, 888.2553/7-1952; Homa Katouzian, *Musaddiq and the Struggle for Power in Iran* (London: I. B. Tauris, 1990), pp. 121–25; and Zabih, *Mossadegh Era*, pp. 41–42.

65. See Henderson tel. 287 to State Department, 20 July 1952, RG 59, 788.00/7-2052; Francis E. Meloy Jr., memorandum of 9:30 meeting in the secretary's office, 21 July 1952, RG 59, lot 58 D 609; Azimi, *Iran*, pp. 288–91; and Zabih, *Mossadegh Era*, pp. 44–48.

66. Henderson tel. 287 to State Department, 20 July 1952, RG 59, 788.00/7-2052. See also Henderson tel. 353 to State Department, 23 July 1952, RG 59, 788.00/2-2352; Zabih, *Mossadegh Era*, pp. 56–64; and Azimi, *Iran*, pp. 290–92.

67. See ICJ, *Pleadings*.

6. Washington Takes the Lead

1. For these U.S. concerns see unsigned memorandum, "The Progressive Threat to the U.S. Position in Foreign Oil," 25 July 1952, Oscar L. Chapman Papers, box 102, folder: Petroleum Cartel 1952 (folder #1), Truman Library.

2. Middleton tel. 531 to FO, 27 July 1952, FO 371, 98691/EP15314/186; Franks tel. 1428 to FO, 26 July 1952, FO 371, 98691/EP15314/182.

3. Henderson tel. 580 to State Department, 8 August 1952, RG 59, 788.13/8-852. See also Acheson tel. 585 to U.S. embassy, London, 26 July 1952, RG 59, 888.2553/7-2652; Roy M. Melbourne (first secretary, U.S. embassy, Tehran) dispatch 514, "Political Trends from Mosadeq's Return to Power to the Effective Break in Relations with Britain," 3 January 1953, RG 59, 788.00/1-353; Richard W. Cottam, *Nationalism in Iran*, 2d rev. ed. (Pittsburgh, Pa.: University of Pittsburgh Press, 1979), pp. 216–17; and Sepehr Zabih, *The Mossadegh Era: Roots of the Iranian Revolution* (Chicago: Lake View, 1982), p. 73.

4. Henderson tel. 377 to State Department, 24 July 1952, RG 59, 788.00/7-2452. See also Middleton tel. 531 to FO, 27 July 1952, FO 371, 98691/EP15314/186; Farhad Diba, *Mohammad Mossadegh: A Political Biography* (London: Croom Helm, 1986), p. 138; and Homa Katouzian, "Oil Boycott and the Political Economy: Musaddiq and the Strategy of Non-oil Economics," in *Musaddiq, Iranian Nationalism, and Oil*, ed. James A. Bill and Wm. Roger Louis (Austin: University of Texas Press, 1988), pp. 203–27.

5. Middleton tel. 518 to FO, 25 July 1952, FO 371, 98691/EP15314/179; Middleton tel. 519 to FO, 25 July 1952, FO 371, 98691/EP15314/180.

6. Franks tel. 1428 to FO, 26 July 1952, FO 371, 98691/EP15314/182. See also Middleton tel. 523 to FO, 25 July 1952, FO 371, 98691/EP15314/181; and Middleton tel. 531 to FO, 27 July 1952, FO 371, 98691/EP15314/186.

7. Middleton tel. 534 to FO, 28 July 1952, FO 371, 98691/EP1531/190; Henderson tel. to State Department, 28 July 1952, *Foreign Relations of the United States, 1952–1954*, vol. 10 (Washington, D.C.: Government Printing Office, 1978), pp. 416–21 (hereafter *FRUS*). See also Henderson tel. 460 to State Department, 30 July 1952, RG 59,

788.13/7-3052; and Henderson tel. 480 to State Department, 31 July 1952, RG 59, 788.13/7-3152.

8. Franks tel. 1448 to FO, 29 July 1952, FO 371, 98691/EP15314/195; memorandum of discussion of the 121st meeting of the NSC, 6 August 1952, *FRUS, 1952–1954*, vol. 10, pp. 430–32. See also Middleton tel. 531 to FO, 27 July 1952, FO 371, 98691/EP15314/186; and Henderson tel. to State Department, 31 July 1952, *FRUS, 1952–1954*, vol. 10, pp. 427–28.

9. Acheson tel. to U.S. embassy, London, 31 July 1952, *FRUS, 1952–1954*, vol. 10, pp. 429–30; Henderson tel. 514 to State Department, 3 August 1952, RG 59, 788.00/8-352; J. C. Holmes (chargé d'affaires ad interim, U.S. embassy, London) dispatch 787, "The British Situation," 13 August 1952, RG 59, 741.00/8-1352.

10. C.(52)276, "Persia: Memorandum by the Secretary of State for Foreign Affairs," 5 August 1952, CAB 129/54; Eden message to Acheson, 9 August 1952, *FRUS, 1952–1954*, vol. 10, pp. 433–37.

11. Jernegan memorandum of conversation between Franks, Acheson, and Burrows, 11 August 1952, Acheson Papers, box 67, folder: Memoranda of Conversations, August 1952; Eden message to Acheson, 9 August 1952, *FRUS, 1952–1954*, vol. 10, pp. 433–37; "Preliminary NEA Comments on Mr. Eden's Message to Secretary Acheson, 8 August 1952," 9 August 1952, RG 59, 888.2553/8-952; "Memorandum Analyzing the Message from Mr. Eden to Mr. Acheson dated 9 August 1952," 12 August 1952, RG 59, 888.2553/8-1252; "Message from Mr. Eden to Mr. Acheson," 12 August 1952, RG 59, 888.2553/8-1252; Bruce tel. to U.S. embassy, London, 18 August 1952, *FRUS, 1952–1954*, vol. 10, pp. 445–47.

12. Bruce tel. to U.S. embassy, London, 18 August 1952, *FRUS, 1952–1954*, vol. 10, pp. 445–47; Franks tel. 1510 to FO, 12 August 1952, FO 371, 98693/EP15314/225; Eden message to Acheson, 9 August 1952, *FRUS, 1952–1954*, vol. 10, pp. 433–37. See also C.(52)285, "Persia: Mr. Middleton's Conversation with Dr. Musaddiq on 14th August, Memorandum by the Minister of State," 19 August 1952, CAB 129/54; C.C.(52)77th Conclusions, 20 August 1952, CAB 128/25; and Middleton tel. 589 to FO, 18 August 1952, FO 371, 98693/EP15314/243.

13. FO tel. 3403 to British embassy, Washington, 20 August 1952, FO 371, 98694/EP15314/254; minutes of meeting held on Iranian oil at the White House, 21 August 1952, Acheson Papers, box 67, folder: Memoranda of Conversations, August 1952.

14. Franks tel. 1612 to FO, 24 August 1952, FO 371, 98694/EP15314/261; Henderson tel. to State Department, 25 August 1952, *FRUS, 1952–1954*, vol. 10, pp. 458–60. See also Bruce tel. to U.S. embassy, Tehran, 25 August 1952, *FRUS, 1952–1954*, vol. 10, pp. 461–62; and Bruce tel. 481 to U.S. embassy, Tehran, 25 August 1952, RG 59, 888.2553/8-2552.

15. Henderson tel. 892 to State Department, 27 August 1952, *FRUS, 1952–1954*, vol. 10, pp. 464–69.

16. FO tel. 3596 to British embassy, Washington, 28 August 1952, FO 371, 98695/EP15314/282; FO tel. 3605 to British embassy, Washington, 29 August 1952, FO 371, 98695/EP15314/282; Middleton to Bowker, 1 September 1952, FO 371, 98697/EP15314/331.

17. C.C.(52)78th Conclusions, 4 September 1952, CAB 128/25; Henderson tel. 1031 to State Department, 7 September 1952, RG 59, 788.13/9-752. See also Middleton tel.

648 to FO, 1 September 1952, FO 371, 98695/EP15314/290; and Henderson tel. 1024 to State Department, 6 September 1952, RG 59, 888.2553/8-652.

18. Ramsbotham minute re Persia: Oil, 8 September 1952, FO 371, 98697/EP15314/332; Middleton tel. 676 to FO, 8 September 1952, FO 371, 98696/EP15314/319.

19. C.(52)295, "Persian Oil: Memorandum by the Secretary of State for Foreign Affairs," 10 September 1952, CAB 129/54; FO tel. 667 to British embassy, Tehran, 12 September 1952, FO 371, 98696/EP15314/319; Paper for Persia (Official) Committee meeting, 18 September 1952, FO 371, 98695/EP15314/67.

20. See Middleton tel. 676 to FO, 8 September 1952, FO 371, 98696/EP15314/319; C.(52)295, "Persian Oil: Memorandum by the Secretary of State for Foreign Affairs," 10 September 1952, CAB 129/54; and D. A. H. Wright (FO) to E. J. Joint (British embassy, Rome), 12 September 1952, FO 371, 98662/EP1532/272.

21. See C.C.(52)81st Conclusions, 26 September 1952, CAB 128/25; FO tel. 4085 to British embassy, Washington, 28 September 1952, FO 371, 98698/EP15314/370; and Makins record of conversation, 29 September 1952, FO 371, 98699/EP15314/390.

22. Middleton tel. 750 to FO, 27 September 1952, FO 371, 98698/EP15314/379; Logan memorandum, "Brief for the Minister of State for the Meeting of the Cabinet on the 26th of September 1952" with enclosed annex, "Persian Reply to Joint U.S./U.K. Offer," 25 September 1952, FO 371, 98700/EP15314/412.

23. Churchill message to Truman, 1 October 1952, Truman Papers, PSF—General File, box 115, folder: Churchill, 1951–1953.

24. FO tel. 4106 to British embassy, Washington, 30 September 1952, FO 371, 98699/EP15314/384; Churchill message to Truman, 1 October 1952, Truman Papers, PSF—General File, box 115, folder: Churchill, 1951–1953.

25. Henderson tel. 1295 to State Department, 27 September 1952, RG 59, 888.2553/9-2752; Franks tel. 1857 to FO, 30 September 1952, FO 371, 98699/EP15314/390.

26. FO tel. 4176 to British embassy, Washington, 3 October 1952, FO 371, 98699/EP15314/397; Franks tel. 1883 to FO, 3 October 1952, FO 371, 98700/EP15314/404.

27. Acheson tel. to U.S. embassy, Tehran, 3 October 1952, *FRUS, 1952–1954*, vol. 10, pp. 482–83.

28. See source cited in note 27; and FO tel. 749 to British embassy, Tehran, 4 October 1952, FO 371, 98700/EP15314/406.

29. Middleton tel. 771 to FO, 5 October 1952, FO 371, 98700/EP15314/408; Henderson tel. to State Department, 5 October 1952, *FRUS, 1952–1954*, vol. 10, pp. 484–85.

30. Middleton tel. 784 to FO, 7 October 1952, FO 371, 98700/EP15314/422; Henderson tel. 1428 to State Department, 7 October 1952, RG 59, 888.2553/10-752. See also Middleton tel. 783 to FO, 7 October 1952, FO 371, 98700/EP15314/421.

31. Acheson tel. to U.S. embassy, Tehran, 10 October 1952, *FRUS, 1952–1954*, vol. 10, pp. 488–90; Acheson tel. 845 to U.S. embassy, Tehran, 7 October 1952, RG 59, 888.2553/10-752; Franks tel. 1910 to FO, 9 October 1952, FO 371, 98700/EP15314/429.

32. A. D. M. Ross minute, 10 October 1952, FO 371, 98700/EP15314/431; FO tel. 4309 to British embassy, Washington, 11 October 1952, FO 371, 98700/EP15314/431; FO tel. 4331 to British embassy, Washington, 12 October 1952, FO 371, 98701/EP15314/435. See also Franks tel. 1929 to FO, 11 October 1952, FO 371, 98701/EP15314/435.

33. Franks tel. 1929 to FO, 11 October 1952, FO 371, 98701/EP15314/435; Acheson tel. 2593 to U.S. embassy, London, 12 October 1952, Truman Papers, PSF—General

File, box 159, folder: Cabinet—Secretary of State, Misc.; and Gifford tel. to State Department, 13 October 1952, *FRUS, 1952–1954*, vol. 10, pp. 493–94.

34. "Note from the British Government to the Persian Government, Rejecting the Persian Claims of 26 September and 7 October," 14 October 1952, Royal Institute of International Affairs, *Documents on International Affairs, 1952* (London: Oxford University Press, 1953), pp. 348–51.

35. Stutesman memorandum of conversation between Acheson and Saleh, 3 October 1952, Acheson Papers, box 68, folder: Memoranda of Conversations, October 1952; C.(52)341, "Persia: Internal Political Situation, Note by the Secretary of State for Foreign Affairs," 17 October 1952, CAB 129/55; Henderson tel. 1515 to State Department, 13 October 1953, RG 59, 788.00/10-1352.

36. Henderson tel. to State Department, 18 October 1952, *FRUS, 1952–1954*, vol. 10, pp. 498–99.

37. See Gifford tels. (2) to State Department, 20 October 1952, *FRUS, 1952–1954*, vol. 10, pp. 499–503; Ross memorandum, 21 October 1952, FO 371, 98702/EP15314/465; C.(52)354, "Persia: United States Ideas for a Settlement of the Oil Dispute: Memorandum by the Secretary of State for Foreign Affairs," 23 October 1952, CAB 129/56; and C.C.(52)89th Conclusions, 23 October 1952, CAB 128/25.

38. Unsigned "Notes for Talk with Mr. Nitze," 24 October 1952, FO 371, 98702/EP15314/470; C.(52)354, "Persia: United States Ideas for a Settlement of the Oil Dispute: Memorandum by the Secretary of State," 23 October 1952, CAB 129/56; FO tel. 4571 to British embassy, Washington, 25 October 1952, FO 371, 98702/EP15314/465.

39. See Middleton tel. 855 to FO, 22 October 1952, FO 371, 98621/EP1053/20.

40. Middleton tel. 829 to FO, 17 October 1952, FO 371, 98621/EP1053/4; Henderson tel. 1611 to State Department, 21 October 1952, RG 59, 788.00/10-2152.

41. Mossadeq to Middleton, 30 October 1952, Grady Papers, General File, box 3, folder: Iran—Post-Ambassador Correspondence; Rothnie minute, 4 November 1952, FO 371, 98621/EP1053/27.

42. Henderson tel. 1765 to State Department, 30 October 1952, RG 59, 641.88/10-3052.

43. Acheson to Lovett, 4 November 1952, *FRUS, 1952–1954*, vol. 10, pp. 510–13.

44. See Acheson tel. to U.S. embassy, Tehran, 10 October 1952, *FRUS, 1952–1954*, vol. 10, pp. 488–90.

45. Nitze memorandum of conversation, 8 October 1952, Acheson Papers, box 68, folder: Memoranda of Conversations, October 1952. For the antitrust case see also Burton I. Kaufman, *The Oil Cartel Case: A Documentary Study of Antitrust Activity During the Cold War Era* (Westport, Conn.: Greenwood, 1978).

46. See Mead to Senator Thomas C. Hennings Jr., 23 April 1952, Truman Papers, WHCF—Confidential File, box 18, folder: FTC pt. 1; FTC memorandum, "Some Constructive Results Which May be Expected to Come from the Publication of the Federal Trade Commission's International Oil Cartel Report," 30 April 1952, Truman Papers, WHCF—Confidential File, box 18, folder: FTC pt. 1; and Stephen J. Spingarn memorandum for the files, "Publication of the International Oil Cartel Report," 6 May 1952, Spingarn Papers, FTC File—Oil Report, box 47, folder: Attacks on Oil Report, Vol. 1, Petroleum Cartels.

47. Eakens (PED) memorandum for Brown, 24 March 1952, RG 59, 811.2553/3-2452; Special Estimate-28, "Consequences of the Future Revelation of the Contents of

Certain Government Documents," 6 May 1952, *FRUS, 1952–1954*, vol. 1, pp. 1272–74; Truman to James M. Mead (chairman, FTC), 5 June 1952, Spingarn Papers, FTC File— Oil Report, box 47, folder: Attack on Oil Report, Vol. 1, Petroleum Cartels.

48. Unsigned "Oil Cartel Investigation," [September 1952], Truman Papers, PSF— General File, box 132, folder: Oil.

49. See Nitze memorandum of conversation, 19 September 1952, *FRUS, 1952–1954*, vol. 1, pp. 182–85; and W. C. Armstrong memorandum for Truman w/enclosure, 13 November 1952, RG 59, Records of the Policy Planning Staff, Country and Area Files, box 12, folder: Strategic Materials—Oil.

50. Donald Fergusson to William Strang, 21 August 1952, FO 371, 99178/UES1536/ 35; FO tel. 3589 to British embassy, Washington, 28 August 1952, FO 371, 99178/ UES1536/46.

51. See Franks to Makins, 3 September 1952, FO 371, 99178/UES1536/57; Jeffrey C. Kitchen (Executive Secretariat) memorandum, 3 September 1952, *FRUS, 1952– 1954*, vol. 1, p. 1282; and C.(52)315, "International Oil Industry: Federal Grand Jury Proceedings in the United States of America: Memorandum by the Secretary of State for Foreign Affairs," 30 September 1952, CAB 129/55.

52. Dean G. Acheson, *Present at the Creation: My Years in the State Department* (New York: Norton, 1969), pp. 682, 684.

53. Acheson memorandum to Truman, "Decisions Necessary if We Are to Move Forward toward a Solution of the Iranian Dispute," 7 November 1952, *FRUS, 1952– 1954*, vol. 10, pp. 518–21.

54. Logan to Leishman (private secretary to the foreign secretary), with enclosed memorandum, "Resumption of the Flow of Oil from Persia after Acceptance by the Persian Government of the Joint United States/United Kingdom Proposals of 30th August 1952," 18 November 1952, FO 371, 98703/EP15314/488.

55. Acheson quoted in Evelyn Shuckburgh, *Descent to Suez: Diaries, 1951–1956* (London: Weidenfeld and Nicolson, 1986), p. 55; Jebb tel. 855 to FO, 21 November 1952, FO 371, 98703/EP15314/493; American delegation to the Seventh General Assembly memorandum, 20 November 1952, Acheson Papers, box 68, folder: Memoranda of Conversations; Acheson, *Present at the Creation*, p. 683.

56. NSC-136/1, "The Present Situation in Iran," 20 November 1952, *FRUS, 1952– 1954*, vol. 10, pp. 529–34.

57. Kitchen memorandum of conversations, 4 December 1952, RG 59, 888.2553/12- 452. See also Acheson tel. 3763 to U.S. embassy, London, 4 December 1952, RG 59, 888.2553/12-452; Acheson tel. 3950 to U.S. embassy, London, 11 December 1952, RG 59, 888.2553/12-1152; and Selwyn Lloyd to Bowker, with attached record of conversation, 17 December 1952, FO 371, 98668/EP1532/430.

58. Wilkinson memorandum, "Iran," 12 December 1952, FO 371, 98668/EP1532/ 431. See also the sources cited in note 57.

59. Memorandum of discussion at the 127th meeting of the National Security Council, 17 December 1952, *FRUS, 1952–1954*, vol. 1, pp. 1298–1304; NSC-138, "National Security Problems Concerning Free World Petroleum Demands and Potential Supplies," 8 December 1952, Truman Papers, PSF—NSC Meetings, box 219, folder: NSC Meeting #127, 17 December 1952.

60. See NSC-138/1, "National Security Problems Concerning Free World Petroleum Demands and Potential Supplies," 6 January 1953, Papers of the White House Office

(WHO), Office of the Special Adviser on National Security Affairs (OSANSA), NSC Series, Policy Papers Subseries, box 3, folder: NSC 138/1—Petroleum Program (1952–53) [International Oil Case], Dwight D. Eisenhower Library, Abilene, Kansas (hereafter WHO, OSANSA, with filing information); memorandum of discussion at the 128th meeting of the National Security Council, 9 January 1953, *FRUS, 1952–1954*, vol. 1, pp. 1338–44; editorial note, *FRUS, 1952–1954*, vol. 1, pp. 1344–45; and Truman to McGranery, 12 January 1953, *FRUS, 1952–1954*, vol. 9, p. 656.

61. Bowker et al. minutes with attached FO memorandum, "Persian Oil: Resumed Discussions with Mr. Nitze of the State Department," 29 November 1952, FO 371, 98703/EP15314/506. See also Gifford tel. 20 to State Department, 11 December 1952, *FRUS, 1952–1954*, vol. 10, pp. 546–48; FO tel. 1680 to British embassy, Paris, 13 December 1952, FO 371, 98704/EP15314/526; FO tel. 5300 to British embassy, Washington, 20 December 1952, FO 371, 98704/EP15314/534; Ross, "Notes for Cabinet Meeting," 22 December 1952, FO 371, 98704/EP15314/541; C.C.(52)107th Conclusions, 22 December 1952, CAB 128/25; and Gifford tel. 3529 to State Department, 24 December 1952, RG 59, 888.2553/12-2452.

62. See Melbourne dispatch 514, "Political Trends from Mossadeq's Return to the Effective Break in Relations with Great Britain," 3 January 1953, RG 59, 788.00/1-353; Fakhreddin Azimi, *Iran: The Crisis of Democracy, 1941–1953* (London: I. B. Tauris, 1989), pp. 298–99; and Zabih, *Mossadegh Era*, p. 83.

63. See N. H. Kirk (ED) memorandum for Turnage (OFD), "Iranian Financial Situation," 12 November 1952, RG 59, 888.2553AIOC/11-1252; Norden dispatch 478, "Petroleum Developments in Iran," 17 December 1952, RG 59, 888.2553/12-1752; Melbourne dispatch 514, "Political Trends from Mosadeq's Return to Power to the Effective Break in Relations with Great Britain," 3 January 1953, RG 59, 788.00/1-353; and Norden dispatch 555, "Quarterly Economic and Financial Review, Iran, Fourth Quarter, 1952," 17 January 1953, RG 59, 888.00/1-1753.

64. Logan memorandum, 13 November 1952, FO 371, 98666/EP1532/364.

65. Acheson tel. to U.S. embassy, London, 29 December 1952, *FRUS, 1952–1954*, vol. 10, pp. 558–61. See also Henderson tel. 2425 to State Department, 26 December 1952, RG 59, 888.2553/12-2652; Acheson tel. to U.S. embassy, London, 31 December 1952, *FRUS, 1952–1954*, vol. 10, p. 562; and Henderson tel. to State Department, 31 December 1952, *FRUS, 1952–1954*, vol. 10, pp. 565–69.

66. Henderson tel. to Department of State, 31 December 1952, *FRUS, 1952–1954*, vol. 10, pp. 565–69. See also the sources cited in note 65.

67. See Henderson tel. 2425 to State Department, 26 December 1952, RG 59, 888.2553/12-2652; Acheson tel. 1568 to U.S. embassy, Tehran, 29 December 1952, RG 59, 888.2553/12-2652; Acheson tel. to U.S. embassy, London, 29 December 1952, *FRUS, 1952–1954*, vol. 10, pp. 558–61; Acheson tel. to U.S. embassy, London, 30 December 1952, *FRUS, 1952–1954*, vol. 10, p. 562; Henderson tel. 2461 to State Department, 30 December 1952, RG 59, 888.2553/12-3052; Henderson tel. 2505 to State Department, 2 January 1953, RG 59, 888.2553/1-253; and Henderson tel. to State Department, 3 January 1953, *FRUS, 1952–1954*, vol. 10, pp. 577–80.

68. Gifford tel. to State Department, 6 January 1953, *FRUS, 1952–1954*, vol. 10, pp. 582–85; Gifford tel. to State Department, 8 January 1953, *FRUS, 1952–1954*, vol. 10, pp. 593–95. See also Gifford tel. to State Department, 1 January 1953, *FRUS, 1952–1954*, vol. 10, pp. 570–73; C.(53)6, "Persian Oil: Memorandum by the Secretary of

State for Foreign Affairs," 6 January 1953, CAB 129/58; C.C.(53)1st Conclusions, 6 January 1953, CAB 128/26 part 1; and Gifford tel. 3789 to State Department, 11 January 1953, RG 59, 888.2553/1-1153.

69. Gifford tel. 3645 to State Department, 4 January 1953, RG 59, 888.2553/1-453. See also Acheson tel. 4382 to U.S. embassy, London, 2 January 1953, RG 59, 888.2553/1-153; Henderson tel. 2504 to State Department, 2 January 1953, RG 59, 888.2553/1-253; Henderson tel. 2539 to State Department, 5 January 1953, RG 59, 888.2553/1-653; and Henderson tel. 2628 to State Department, 9 January 1953, RG 59, 888.2553/1-953.

70. Henderson tel. 2627 to State Department, 9 January 1953, RG 59, 888.2553/1-953; FO intel. 27 to British embassy, Baghdad, 17 January 1953, FO 371, 104610/EP1531/100.

71. Gifford tel. to State Department, 14 January 1953, *FRUS, 1952–1954*, vol. 10, pp. 617–20; Gifford tel. to State Department, 14 January 1953, *FRUS, 1952–1954*, vol. 10, pp. 611–15.

72. Henderson tel. 2727 to State Department, 16 January 1953, RG 59, 888.2553/1-1653; Henderson tel. 2741 to State Department, 16 January 1953, RG 59, 888.2553/1-1653. See also Henderson tel. to State Department, 17 January 1953, *FRUS, 1952–1954*, vol. 10, pp. 621–27; and Henderson tel. 2755 to State Department, 17 January 1953, RG 59, 888.2553/1-1753.

73. Henderson tel. to State Department, 17 January 1953, *FRUS, 1952–1954*, vol. 10, pp. 634–35. See also Henderson tels. (2) to State Department, 17 January 1953, *FRUS, 1952–1954*, vol. 10, pp. 627–33; Henderson tel. 2768 to State Department, 18 January 1953, RG 59, 888.2553/1-1853; and Henderson tel. 2775 to State Department, 18 January 1953, RG 59, 888.2553/1-1853.

74. Pierson Dixon (FO) memorandum, 19 January 1953, FO 371, 104610/EP15316/102. See also Acheson tel. to U.S. embassy, London, 18 January 1953, *FRUS, 1952–1954*, vol. 10, pp. 636–37; Gifford tels. (2) to State Department, *FRUS, 1952–1954*, vol. 10, pp. 638–42; and Gifford tel. 3956 to State Department, 19 January 1953, RG 59, 888.2553/1-1953.

75. Henderson tel. 2803 to State Department, 19 January 1953, RG 59, 888.2553/1-1953; Henderson tel. to State Department, 19 January 1953, *FRUS, 1952–1954*, vol. 10, pp. 642–47.

76. Azimi, *Iran*, p. 310–13; and Zabih, *Mossadegh Era*, pp. 85–87. For U.S. analysis see NIE-75/1, "Probable Developments in Iran through 1953," 9 January 1953, Truman Papers, PSF—Intelligence File, box 254, folder: Central Intelligence Reports, NIE 67–75.

7. The Triumph of Transatlantic Cooperation

1. See Henderson tel. 2814 to State Department, 21 January 1953, RG 59, 888.2553/1-2153; Gifford tel. 4039 to State Department, 22 January 1953, RG 59, 888.2553/1-2253; FO tel. 302 to British embassy, Washington, 23 January 1953, FO 371, 104610/EP1531/106; and Henderson tel. 2847 to State Department, 23 January 1953, RG 59, 888.2553/1-2353.

2. Henderson tel. 2847 to State Department, 23 January 1953, RG 59, 888.2553/1-2353; FO tel. 302 to British embassy, Washington, 23 January 1953, FO 371, 104610/EP1531/106; Makins (British ambassador, Washington) tel. 155 to FO, 26 January 1953, FO 371, 104610/EP1531/107; Holmes (London) tel. 4132 to State Depart-

ment, 27 January 1953, RG 59, 888.2553/1-2753; Makins tel. 184 to FO, 28 January 1953, FO 371, 104610/EP1531/117.

3. Dulles tel. to U.S. embassy, London, 26 January 1953, *Foreign Relations of the United States, 1952–1954*, vol. 10 (Washington, D.C.: Government Printing Office, 1978), pp. 647–51 (hereafter *FRUS*). See also Richards memorandum of conversation re "Department's Comments on British Draft Compensation Agreement," 27 January 1953, RG 59, 888.2553/1-2753; Makins tel. 172 to FO, 27 January 1953, FO 371, 104610/EP1531/114; and Henderson tel. 2929 to State Department, 29 January 1953, RG 59, 888.2553/1-2853.

4. Henderson tel. to State Department, 28 January 1953, *FRUS, 1952–1954*, vol. 10, pp. 651–55; Henderson tel. 3035 to State Department, 4 February 1953, RG 59, 888.2553/2-453; Henderson tel. 2943 to State Department, 29 January 1953, RG 59, 888.2553/1-2953; H. Freeman Matthews (acting secretary of state) tel. to U.S. embassy, London, 30 January 1953, *FRUS, 1952–1954*, vol. 10, pp. 656–59.

5. See the sources cited in note 4.

6. Makins tel. 225 to FO, 2 February 1953, FO 371, 104611/EP1531/136; Makins tel. 217 to FO, 1 February 1953, FO 371, 104611/EP1531/128. See also Henderson tel. 2948 to State Department, 30 January 1953, RG 59, 888.2553/1-3053; Pierson Dixon (FO) notes of conversation with Julius Holmes, 31 January 1953, FO 371, 104611/EP1531/144; FO tel. 457 to British embassy, Washington, 2 February 1953, FO 371, 104611/EP1531/128; and Ramsbotham memorandum, "Persian Oil," 3 February 1953, FO 371, 104611/EP1531/136.

7. Makins tel. 288 to FO, 10 February 1953, FO 371, 104612/EP1531/152; Holmes tel. 4373 to State Department, 7 February 1953, RG 59, 888.2553/2-743. See also Matthews (acting secretary of state) tel. 1996 to U.S. embassy, Tehran, 6 February 1953, RG 59, 888.2553/2-653; "U.K. Record of Meeting with Dulles and [Mutual Security Director Harold E.] Stassen," 9 February 1953, FO 371, 104612/EP1531/149; Dulles tel. to U.S. embassy, London, 10 February 1953, *FRUS, 1952–1954*, vol. 10, pp. 662–64; C.(53)66, "Persia: Note by the Secretary of State for Foreign Affairs," 17 February 1953, CAB 129/59; Dulles tel. to U.S. embassy, Tehran, 18 February 1953, *FRUS, 1952–1954*, vol. 10, pp. 668–69; and Makins tel. 345 to FO, 18 February 1953, FO 371, 104612/EP1531/158.

8. Henderson tel. to State Department, 20 February 1953, *FRUS, 1952–1954*, vol. 10, pp. 670–74. See also Henderson tel. 3296 to State Department, 20 February 1953, RG 59, 888.2553/2-2053.

9. Henderson tel. to State Department, 22 February 1953, *FRUS, 1952–1954*, vol. 10, pp. 674–77. See also Henderson tels. (2) to State Department, 23 and 24 February 1953, *FRUS, 1952–1954*, vol. 10, pp. 679—81; and Fakhreddin Azimi, *Iran: Crisis of Democracy, 1941–1953* (London: I. B. Tauris, 1989), pp. 313–15.

10. Anthony Eden, *The Memoirs of Anthony Eden: Full Circle* (Boston: Houghton Mifflin, 1960), p. 236.

11. See Mark J. Gasiorowski, *U.S. Foreign Policy and the Shah: Building a Client State in Iran* (Ithaca, N.Y.: Cornell University Press, 1991), pp. 73–74; and Kermit Roosevelt, *Countercoup: The Struggle for the Control of Iran*, paperback ed. (New York: McGraw-Hill, 1981), pp. 120–24.

12. For U.S. concerns about Iran's safety see "Extract from Record of Meeting at State Department," 6 March 1953, FO 371, 104613/EP1531/197; Dulles tel. to U.S.

embassy, London, 7 March 1953, *FRUS, 1952–1954*, vol. 10, pp. 702–703; Makins tel. 487 to FO, 7 March 1953, FO 371, 104613/EP1531/197; and Makins tel. 526 to FO, 9 March 1953, FO 371, 104613/EP1531/200.

13. See the sources cited in notes 11 and 12.

14. The shah's claims may be found in Mohammad Reza Shah Pahlavi, *Mission for My Country* (New York: McGraw-Hill, 1961). Mossadeq's version is contained in, among other sources, Azimi, *Iran*, pp. 315–16; Homa Katouzian, *Musaddiq and the Struggle for Power in Iran* (London: I. B. Tauris, 1990), pp. 171–72, 178–83; and Homa Katouzian, ed., *Musaddiq's Memoirs* (London: JEBHE, National Movement of Iran, 1988), pp. 273–78.

15. Mossadeq's report to the Majlis is found in Katouzian, *Musaddiq's Memoirs*, pp. 296–305. Reports from the U.S. embassy tell a slightly different story. See Henderson tels. (2) to State Department, 28 February 1953, *FRUS, 1952–1954*, vol. 10, pp. 685–89.

16. The fullest account of these charges is contained in Mossadeq's report to the Majlis. See Katouzian, *Musaddiq's Memoirs*, pp. 296–305. Later that spring, in a desperate effort to rescue his declining political fortunes, Mossadeq made the incident public by releasing his statement before the Majlis to the press on 6 April.

17. See Henderson tel. 3532 to State Department, 4 March 1953, RG 59, 888.2553/3-453.

18. See Katouzian, *Musaddiq and the Struggle*, p. 183; and Azimi, *Iran*, pp. 317–18. For U.S. assessments of Iran's political situation see memorandum prepared for the president in the Office of National Estimates, Central Intelligence Agency, "The Iranian Situation," 1 March 1953, *FRUS, 1952–1954*, vol. 10, pp. 689–91; Dulles tel. to U.S. embassy, Tehran, 2 March 1953, *FRUS, 1952–1954*, vol. 10, pp. 691–92; memorandum of discussion at the 135th meeting of the National Security Council, 4 March 1953, *FRUS, 1952–1954*, vol. 10, pp. 692–701; Henderson tel. 3654 to State Department, 11 March 1953, RG 59, 788.00/3-1153; and Henderson tel. 3688 to State Department, 14 March 1953, RG 59, 888.2553/3-1453.

19. Henderson tel. 3548 to State Department, 5 March 1953, RG 59, 888.2553/3-553; Henderson tel. 3688 to State Department, 14 March 1953, RG 59, 888.2553/3-1453. See also FO tel. 1088 to British embassy, Washington, 7 March 1953, FO 371, 104613/EP1531/211; Dulles tel. to U.S. embassy, Tehran, 13 March 1953, *FRUS, 1952–1954*, vol. 10, pp. 714–15; and Henderson tel. to State Department, 18 March 1953, *FRUS, 1952–1954*, vol. 10, pp. 716–19.

20. Henderson tel. 3732 to State Department, 17 March 1953, RG 59, 888.2553/3-1753; Nelson Aldrich (U.S. ambassador, London) tel. 5209 to State Department, 20 March 1953, RG 59, 888.2553/3-2053. See also Dixon minute, 9 April 1953, FO 371, 104615/EP1531/242; and Dixon memorandum, "Persian Oil: Future Policy," 14 April 1953, FO 371, 104615/EP1531/243.

21. Makins tel. 526 to FO, 9 March 1953, FO 371, 104613/EP1531/200. See also Ramsbotham minute, with enclosed draft letter to Makins, 2 April 1953, FO 371, 105165/UES1538/6; N. W. Tyson (State Department) memorandum, "Iran," 20 April 1953, RG 59, 888.2553/4-2053; and Gasiorowski, *U.S. Foreign Policy*, pp. 74–75.

22. Carr dispatch 933, "Monthly Economic Survey, Iran, April 1953," 12 May 1953, RG 59, 888.00/5-1253. See also J. H. Brook (Ministry of Fuel and Power) to Ramsbotham, with enclosed paper, "Memorandum on Possible Scope for Sale of

Persian Oil and Consequent Effects of Such Sales," 16 April 1953, FO 371, 105165/UES1538/12.

23. See Gasiorowski, *U.S. Foreign Policy*, pp. 73–75; Katouzian, *Musaddiq and the Struggle*, pp. 183–85; and Azimi, *Iran*, pp. 320–21.

24. Henderson tel. to State Department, 8 May 1953, *FRUS, 1952–1954*, vol. 10, pp. 726–27. See also Katouzian, *Musaddiq and the Struggle*, pp. 184–85; and Azimi, *Iran*, pp. 321–23.

25. Henderson tel. to State Department, 20 May 1953, *FRUS, 1952–1954*, vol. 10, pp. 727–28; A. D. M. Ross (FO) memorandum, 5 May 1953, FO 371, 104581/EP10345/10. See also Henderson tel. 4292 to State Department, 4 May 1953, RG 59, 611.88/5-453; and Henderson tel. to State Department, 25 May 1953, *FRUS, 1952–1954*, vol. 10, pp. 728–29.

26. Mossadeq to Eisenhower, 28 May 1953, Royal Institute of International Affairs, *Documents on International Affairs, 1953* (London: Oxford University Press, 1954), pp. 349–51. See also Henderson tel. 4579 to State Department, 31 May 1953, RG 59, 888.2553/5-3153; and Byroade memorandum for Dulles, "Letter from Dr. Mosadeq to President Eisenhower," 5 June 1953, *FRUS, 1952–1954*, vol. 10, p. 732.

27. Dulles tel. 3295 to U.S. embassy, Tehran, transmitting Eisenhower reply to Mossadeq, 30 June 1953, Ann Whitman File—International Series, box 29, folder: Iran, 1953 through 1959, Eisenhower Library.

28. Makins to Bowker, 25 June 1953, FO 371, 104616/EP1531/276. See also Henderson tel. 4579 to State Department, 31 May 1953, RG 59, 888.2553/5-3153; and Carr dispatch 1069, "Monthly Economic Survey: Iran, May 1953," 11 June 1953, RG 59, 888.00/6-1153.

29. Philby is quoted in Kuross A. Samii, *Involvement by Invitation: American Strategies of Containment in Iran* (University Park: Pennsylvania State University Press, 1987), p. 115.

30. See Roosevelt, *Countercoup*, pp. 120–22.

31. Henderson, quoted in Roosevelt, *Countercoup*, p. 18. See also NSC Planning Board report to the NSC, "Statement of Policy Proposed by the National Security Council on a National Petroleum Policy," 20 May 1953, *FRUS, 1952–1954*, vol. 1, pp. 963–67; discussion at 146th NSC meeting, 30 May 1953, Ann Whitman File—NSC Series, box 4, folder: 146 Meeting, May 27, 1953; James A. Bill, *Eagle and the Lion: The Tragedy of American-Iranian Relations* (New Haven, Conn.: Yale University Press, 1988), pp. 88–89; and Gasiorowski, *U.S. Foreign Policy*, pp. 74–75.

32. J. R. Colville memorandum, 1 July 1953, FO 371, 104581/EP10345/2.

33. See Azimi, *Iran*, pp. 323–24; Sepehr Zabih, *The Mossadegh Era: Roots of the Iranian Revolution* (Chicago: Lake View, 1982), p. 104; and Katouzian, *Musaddiq and the Struggle*, pp. 185–86.

34. Carr dispatch 1069, "Monthly Economic Survey, Iran, May 1953," 11 June 1953, RG 59, 888.00/6-1153; Mattison tel. to State Department, 13 July 1953, *FRUS, 1952–1954*, vol. 10, pp. 734–35; Parke (acting commercial chargé, U.S. embassy, Tehran) dispatch 104, "Monthly Economic Survey, Iran, July 1953," 14 August 1953, RG 59, 888.00/8-1453; and Azimi, *Iran*, p. 326.

35. Mossadeq quoted in Katouzian, *Musaddiq's Memoirs*, pp. 336. See also the editor's introduction to Katouzian, *Musaddiq's Memoirs*, pp. 65–67; and Katouzian, *Musaddiq and the Struggle*, pp. 186–87.

36. Mattison tels. (2) to State Department, 14 and 17 July 1953, *FRUS, 1952–1954*, vol. 10, pp. 735–37; Azimi, *Iran*, pp. 329–30; and Zabih, *Mossadegh Era*, pp. 110–11.

37. See Azimi, *Iran*, p. 330; and Zabih, *Mossadegh Era*, pp. 111–12.

38. Mossadeq, quoted in Zabih, *Mossadegh Era*, p. 113.

39. See Burton Y. Berry (U.S. ambassador to Iraq) tel. to State Department, 17 August 1953, *FRUS, 1952–1954*, vol. 10, pp. 746–48; Azimi, *Iran*, pp. 330–31; and Zabih, *Mossadegh Era*, pp. 112–13.

40. Mattison tel. to State Department, 17 July 1953, *FRUS, 1952–1954*, vol. 10, pp. 736–37; Henderson tel. to State Department, 10 March 1953, *FRUS, 1952–1954*, vol. 10, pp. 706–708; Mattison tel. to State Department, 12 August 1953, *FRUS, 1952–1954*, vol. 10, pp. 742–44; Mattison tel. to State Department, 25 July 1953, *FRUS, 1952–1954*, vol. 10, pp. 738–39; Berry tel. to State Department, 17 August 1953, *FRUS, 1952–1954*, vol. 10, pp. 746–48.

41. See Berry tel. to State Department, 17 August 1953, *FRUS, 1952–1954*, vol. 10, pp. 746–48; Gasiorowski, *U.S. Foreign Policy*, pp. 74–76; Samii, *Involvement by Invitation*, pp. 113–17; and Roosevelt, *Countercoup*, pp. 145–49, 155–57. For early U.S. efforts to sell Zahedi to the shah see Henderson tel. to State Department, 30 May 1953, *FRUS, 1952–1954*, vol. 10, pp. 730–32.

42. For detailed examinations of the coup see Gasiorowski, *U.S. Foreign Policy*, pp. 76–79; Roosevelt, *Countercoup*, pp. 169–99; Zabih, *Mossadegh Era*, pp. 116–26; Farhad Diba, *Mohammad Mossadegh: A Political Biography* (London: Croom Helm, 1986), pp. 184–92; Katouzian, *Musaddiq and the Struggle*, pp. 188–93; Samii, *Involvement by Invitation*, pp. 136–39; Bill, *Eagle and the Lion*, pp. 89–94; and H. W. Brands, *Inside the Cold War: Loy Henderson and the Rise of the American Empire, 1918–1961* (New York: Oxford University Press, 1991), pp. 283–89.

43. Eden, *Memoirs*, p. 237. For a more extensive discussion of the decisive U.S. role in the coup see Gasiorowski, *U.S. Foreign Policy*, pp. 79–81.

44. For subsequent operations see Gasiorowski, *U.S. Foreign Policy*, pp. 82–83.

8. The "Miraculous Second Chance"

1. Robert B. Parke (acting commercial attaché, Tehran) dispatch 162 to State Department, 12 September 1953, RG 59, 888.00/9-1253. See also memorandum of discussion at 160th meeting of the NSC, 27 August 1953, *Foreign Relations of the United States, 1952–1954*, vol. 10 (Washington, D.C.: Government Printing Office, 1978), pp. 771–75 (hereafter *FRUS*); and Tehran dispatch 435, "Iranian Political Developments from the Advent of the Zahedi Government to the Arrival of the British Diplomatic Mission (August 19–December 21, 1953)," 21 January 1954, RG 59, 788.00/1-2154.

2. Roy M. Melbourne (first secretary, U.S. embassy, Tehran) dispatch 187, "Aspects of the Political Environment of the Zahedi Government," 26 September 1953, RG 59, 788.00/9-2653. See also Henderson tel. to State Department, 27 August 1953, *FRUS, 1952–1954*, vol. 10, pp. 769–71; Homa Katouzian, *Musaddiq and the Struggle for Power in Iran* (London: I. B. Tauris, 1990), pp. 208–209; and Sepehr Zabih, *The Communist Movement in Iran* (Berkeley: University of California Press, 1966), pp. 208–10.

3. Henderson tel. to State Department, 27 August 1953, *FRUS, 1952–1954*, vol. 10, pp. 769–71. See also "U.S. Aid to Iran," 26 August 1953, U.S. Department of State

Bulletin 29 (14 September 1953): 349–50; and Henderson tel. to State Department, 31 August 1953, *FRUS, 1952–1954*, vol. 10, pp. 775–77.

4. See Henderson tel. to State Department, 31 August 1953, *FRUS, 1952–1954*, vol. 10, pp. 777–78; Dulles memorandum of conversation with British ambassador, 3 September 1953, RG 59, 611.41/9-353; and R. J. Bowker memorandum, 7 September 1953, FO 371, 104640/EP15316/15.

5. On the government's efforts to educate the Iranian people see C. T. Gandy (FO) "Note for Lord Salisbury's Meeting with the Press," 28 August 1953, FO 371, 104577/EP1024/4; Henderson tel. 520 to State Department, 29 August 1953, RG 59, 888.2553/8-2953; Bowker memorandum, 7 September 1953, FO 371, 104640/EP15316/15; Henderson tel. 820 to State Department, 2 October 1953, RG 59, 888.2553/10-253; John Stutesman memorandum of conversation, "Discussions Regarding the Iranian Oil Situation," 1 October 1953, RG 59, 888.2553/10-153; and Roger Allen minute, with attached memorandum by L. A. C. Fry, 28 November 1953, FO 371, 104643/EP15316/109.

6. See Melbourne dispatch 187, "Aspects of the Political Environment of the Zahedi Government," 26 September 1953, RG 59, 788.00/9-2653; Henderson tel. 1150 to State Department, 20 November 1953, RG 59, 788.13/11-2053; and Henderson tel. 1397 to State Department, 24 December 1953, RG 59, 788.00/12-2453.

7. See Aldrich (London) tel. 1407 to State Department, 2 October 1953, RG 59, 888.2553/10-253; Henderson tel. to State Department, 9 October 1953, *FRUS, 1952–1954*, vol. 10, pp. 810–13; Henderson dispatch 368, "Memorandum of Conversation Between Shah of Iran and Loy W. Henderson," 28 December 1953, RG 59, 788.00/12-2853; NSC-5402, "United States Policy Toward Iran," 2 January 1954, *FRUS, 1952–1954*, vol. 10, pp. 865–89; Henderson tel. to State Department, 18 January 1954, *FRUS, 1952–1954*, vol. 10, p. 899.

8. On Mossadeq's trial see Melbourne dispatch 281, "Color Background of the Dr. Mosadeq Treason Trial," 16 November 1953, RG 59, 788.00/11-1653; Melbourne dispatch 416, "Transmittal of Verdict Against Mosadeq and Riahi," 14 January 1954, RG 59, 788.13/1-1454; Melbourne dispatch 651, "Current Status of Mosadeq Case," 3 April 1954, RG 59, 788.13/4-354; Richard W. Cottam, *Nationalism in Iran*, 2d rev. ed. (Pittsburgh, Pa.: University of Pittsburgh Press, 1979), pp. 287–88; and Homa Katouzian, ed., *Musaddiq's Memoirs* (London: JEBHE, National Movement of Iran, 1988), pp. 73–77. Detailed coverage may be found in RG 59, file 788.13.

9. See Henderson tel. 781 to State Department, 29 September 1953, RG 59, 888.2553/9-2953; Henderson tel. 878 to State Department, 11 October 1953, RG 59, 888.2553/10-1153; Sir William Strang memorandum, 23 October 1953, FO 371, 104585/EP1051/33; Selwyn Lloyd memorandum, 15 November 1953, FO 371, 104586/EP1051/59; Stutesman memorandum of conversation with Iranian Ambassador Nasrollah Entezam and Byroade, 17 November 1953, RG 59, 641.88/11-1753; and Henderson tel. to State Department, 19 November 1953, *FRUS, 1952–1954*, vol. 10, pp. 838–39.

10. See Robert H. S. Eakens (chief, petroleum staff, Office of International Materials Policy) to Willis C. Armstrong (U.S. embassy, London), 23 October 1953, RG 59, 888.2553/10-2353; FO tel. 4450 to British embassy, Washington, 31 October 1953, FO 371, 104585/EP1051/40; Pierson Dixon memorandum, 3 November 1953, FO 371, 104586/EP1051/53; Allen, "Note for Secretary of State's Use in Cabinet," 30 November 1953, FO 371, 104587/EP1051/77. On the reestablishment of Anglo-Iranian diplomatic

relations see Aldrich tel. to State Department, 6 November 1953, *FRUS, 1952–1954*, vol. 10, pp. 824–25; Henderson tel. to State Department, 12 November 1953, *FRUS, 1952–1954*, vol. 10, pp. 829–31; Henderson tel. to State Department, 19 November 1953, *FRUS, 1952–1954*, vol. 10, pp. 838–39; Aldrich tels. (2) to State Department, 19 and 24 November 1953, *FRUS, 1952–1954*, vol. 10, pp. 842–44; and Henderson tel. to State Department, 3 December 1953, *FRUS, 1952–1954*, vol. 10, pp. 846–48.

11. Henderson tel. 1148 to State Department, 20 November 1953, RG 59, 641.88/11-2053. See also Henderson tel. to State Department, 9 October 1953, *FRUS, 1952–1954*, vol. 10, pp. 810–13; Henderson tel. 1085 to State Department, 11 November 1953, RG 59, 888.2553/11-1153; and Henderson tel. 1087 to State Department, 12 November 1953, RG 59, 888.2553/11-1253.

12. For government discussions see Henderson tel. 1195 to State Department, 28 November 1953, RG 59, 888.2553/11-2853; Henderson tel. 1198 to State Department, 28 November 1953, RG 59, 888.2553/11-2853; Henderson tel. 1223 to State Department, 2 December 1953, RG 59, 641.88/12-253; Henderson tel. to State Department, 3 December 1953, *FRUS, 1952–1954*, vol. 10, pp. 846–48; and "Communiqué Issued by the British and Persian Governments on the Resumption of Diplomatic Relations Between the Two Countries," 5 December 1953, Royal Institute of International Affairs, *Documents on International Affairs, 1953* (London: Oxford University Press, 1954), p. 356.

13. Henderson tel. 1256 to State Department, 5 December 1953, RG 59, 641.88/12-553. See also Henderson tel. to State Department, 3 December 1953, *FRUS, 1952–1954*, vol. 10, pp. 846–48; and FO Eastern Department memorandum, "Persia: Quarterly Political Report, October–December 1953," February 1954, FO 371, 109990/EP1018/1.

14. Wright dispatch 9 to FO, "Political Developments in Persia During the Last Six Months and the Outlook for the Near Future," 12 February 1954, PREM11/726. See also Stevens dispatch 16 to FO, 13 March 1954, FO 371, 110060/EP1534/49; Mark J. Gasiorowski, *U.S. Foreign Policy and the Shah: Building a Client State in Iran* (Ithaca, N.Y.: Cornell University Press, 1991), pp. 85–90; and Richard W. Cottam, *Iran and the United States: A Cold War Case Study* (Pittsburgh, Pa.: University of Pittsburgh Press, 1988), pp. 110–13.

15. See Roger Stevens (British ambassador to Iran) dispatch 27 to FO, 9 April 1954, FO 371, 109990/EP1018/2; and Cottam, *Iran and the United States*, pp. 110–13.

16. Dulles memorandum of telephone conversation with Secretary of the Treasury George Humphrey, 25 August 1953, Dulles Papers, Telephone Conversation Series, box 1, folder: Telephone Memoranda (Excepting to and from White House), July–Oct. 1953 (3), Eisenhower Library. See also Dulles tel. 612 to U.S. embassy, Tehran, 25 August 1953, RG 59, 888.2553/8-2553; Henderson tel. 567 to State Department, 3 September 1953, RG 59, 788.00/9-353; Dulles tel. to U.S. embassy, London, 8 September 1953, *FRUS, 1952–1954*, vol. 10, pp. 790–91; memorandum of discussion at the 162d meeting of the NSC, 17 September 1953, *FRUS, 1952–1954*, vol. 10, pp. 794–96.

17. Byroade memorandum for the secretary, "Iran," 25 August 1953, RG 59, 888.2553/8-2553; Byroade memorandum for Robert Bowie (director, Policy Planning Staff), "Iran," 21 August 1953, *FRUS, 1952–1954*, vol. 10, pp. 760–61; Henderson tel. 718 to State Department, 21 September 1953, RG 59, 641.88/9-2153.

18. Henderson tel. 718 to State Department, 21 September 1953, RG 59, 641.88/9-2153. See also Dulles tel. 612 to U.S. embassy, Tehran, 25 August 1953, RG 59,

888.2553/8-2553; Dulles tel. to U.S. embassy, London (with personal message from him to Lord Salisbury, "Dear Bobbety"), 8 September 1953, *FRUS, 1952–1954*, vol. 10, pp. 790–91; memorandum of discussion at 160th meeting of NSC, 27 August 1953, *FRUS, 1952–1954*, vol. 10, pp. 771–75; and Henderson tel. to State Department, 31 August 1953, *FRUS, 1952–1954*, vol. 10, pp. 777–78.

19. Gandy minute, 24 August 1953, FO 371, 104640/EP15316/10; Fry minute, "Persian Oil," 30 September 1953, FO 371, 104642/EP15316/46. See also Aldrich tel. 1267 to State Department, 24 September 1953, RG 59, 888.2553/9-2453.

20. FO record of meeting, 26 August 1953, FO 371, 104577/EP1024/4. See also Fry minute, "Persian Oil," 30 September 1953, FO 371, 104642/EP15316/46; and Makins tel. 2077 to FO, 1 October 1953, FO 371, 104641/EP15316/36.

21. FO tel. 3531 to British embassy, Washington, 10 September 1953, FO 371, 104640/EP15316/15. See also Belgrave minute, 26 August 1953, FO 371, 104640/EP15316/1; Aldrich (London) tel. 869 to State Department, 29 August 1953, RG 59, 888.2553/8-2953; Belgrave memorandum, "Persian Oil—Alternative Solutions," 22 September 1953, FO 371, 104641/EP15316/26; and Aldrich tel. 1267 to State Department, 24 September 1953, RG 59, 888.2553/9-2453.

22. Victor Butler (MFP) to Fry, with attached note to Maud, 19 October 1953, FO 371, 104642/EP14316/56; Dulles tel. to U.S. embassy, Tehran, 23 September 1953, *FRUS, 1952–1954*, vol. 10, pp. 802–804. See also Makins tel. 1962 to FO, 11 September 1953, FO 371, 104640/EP15316/17; Stutesman memorandum of conversation, "Discussions Regarding the Iranian Oil Problem," 25 September 1953, RG 59, 888.2553/9-2553; Makins tel. 2030 to FO, 25 September 1953, FO 371, 104641/EP15316/31; and Stutesman memorandum of conversation, "Discussions Regarding the Iranian Oil Problem," 26 September 1953, RG 59, 888.2553/9-2653.

23. Stutesman memorandum of conversation, "Discussions Regarding the Iranian Oil Problem," 26 September 1953, RG 59, 888.2553/9-2653. See also Dulles tel. to U.S. embassy, Tehran, 23 September 1953, *FRUS, 1952–1954*, vol. 10, pp. 802–804; Dulles tel. to U.S. embassy, Tehran, 29 September 1953, *FRUS, 1952–1954*, vol. 10, pp. 806–807; Makins tel. 2077 to FO, 1 October 1953, FO 371, 104641/EP15316/36; and Dulles tel. 1908 to U.S. embassy, London, 8 October 1953, RG 59, 888.2553/10-853.

24. Henderson tel. 970 to State Department, 24 October 1953, RG 59, 888.2553/10-2453; Henderson tel. 948 to State Department, 22 October 1953, RG 59, 888.2553/10-2253. See also Henderson tel. 949 to State Department, 22 October 1953, RG 59, 888.2553/10-2253; and Henderson tel. to State Department, 29 October 1953, *FRUS, 1952–1954*, vol. 10, pp. 815–19.

25. Henderson tel. to State Department, 29 October 1953, *FRUS, 1952–1954*, vol. 10, pp. 815–19; Henderson tel. to State Department, 2 November 1953, *FRUS, 1952–1954*, vol. 10, pp. 819–21; Henderson tel. 1020 to State Department, 2 November 1953, RG 59, 888.2553/11-253.

26. Butler to Fry, with attached note to Maud, 19 October 1953, FO 371, 104642/EP15316/56; Gass to Allen (FO), 20 October 1953, FO 371, 104642/EP15316/54; Gandy memorandum, "Forthcoming Discussions with Mr. Hoover: Note for Use by Sir Pierson Dixon at This Week's Meeting of the Persia Committee," 28 October 1953, FO 371, 104642/EP15316/64. See also Belgrave memorandum, 2 November 1953, FO 371, 104642/EP15316/73.

27. Aldrich tel. to State Department, 5 November 1953, *FRUS, 1952–1954*, vol. 10, p.

823; Aldrich tel. to State Department, 5 November 1953, *FRUS, 1952–1954*, vol. 10, pp. 821–22; Aldrich tel. to State Department, 7 November 1953, *FRUS, 1952–1954*, vol. 10, pp. 825–28; Fry memorandum, 5 November 1953, FO 371, 104642/EP15316/77.

28. See Dixon memorandum, 5 November 1953, FO 371, 104642/EP15316/78; Aldrich tel. to State Department, 6 November 1953, *FRUS, 1952–1954*, vol. 10, pp. 824–25; Allen minute, 12 November 1953, FO 371, 104643/EP15316/87; and FO tel. 3814 to British embassy, Washington, 19 November 1953, FO 371, 104643/EP15316/82.

29. For efforts to soften the blow of the British decision to reject the Iranian memorandum see Henderson tel. 1049 to State Department, 6 November 1953, RG 59, 888.2553/11-653; Aldrich tel. 2026 to State Department, 9 November 1953, RG 59, 888.2553/11-953; and Fry memorandum, 9 November 1953, FO 371, 104642/EP15316/74.

30. See Aldrich tel. to State Department, 6 November 1953, *FRUS, 1952–1954*, vol. 10, pp. 824–25; and Aldrich tel. to State Department, 14 November 1953, *FRUS, 1952–1954*, vol. 10, pp. 835–36.

31. Dulles (Hoover) tel. to U.S. embassy, London, 9 November 1953, *FRUS, 1952–1954*, vol. 10, pp. 828–29.

32. Ibid.

33. Herman Phleger (legal adviser, State Department) memorandum of conversation with Brownell, Assistant Attorney General Stanley Barnes, and Hoover, 12 November 1953, RG 59, 888.2553/11-1253. For Justice Department involvement with the Iranian problem see also Brownell to Robert Cutler (administrative assistant to the president), 6 October 1953, U.S. Congress, Senate, Committee on Foreign Affairs, Subcommittee on Multinational Corporations, *The International Petroleum Cartel, the Iranian Consortium, and U.S. National Security*, 93d Cong., 2d sess., 1975, Committee Print, p. 50; Leonard Emmerglick memorandum for the files, "Conference with State Department and Department of Defense Officials Concerning Middle East Oil," 15 October 1953, U.S. Congress, *International Petroleum Cartel*, pp. 54–55; Brownell to Cutler, 26 October 1953, Papers of the White House Office, Office of the Special Assistant for National Security Affairs (OSANSA), NSC Series, Briefing Notes Subseries, box 14, folder: Petroleum—Policies and Issues, 1953–1960 (1), Eisenhower Library; and Phleger memorandum of conversation, "Iranian Oil," 24 November 1953, RG 59, 888.2553/11-2453.

34. Aldrich tel. 2322 to State Department, 27 November 1953, RG 59, 888.2553/11-2753. See also Allen minute with enclosed memorandum by Fry, 28 November 1953, FO 371, 104643/EP15316/109; and Fry et al. minutes, 7 December 1953, FO 371, 104644/EP15316/120.

35. Aldrich tel. to State Department, 30 November 1953, *FRUS, 1952–1954*, vol. 10, pp. 844–46; Aldrich (Hoover) tel. to State Department, 5 December 1953, *FRUS, 1952–1954*, vol. 10, pp. 848–49. See also Aldrich tel. 2375 to State Department, 1 December 1953, RG 59, 888.2553/12-153; and Allen draft tel. to British delegation, Bermuda, 1 December 1953, FO 371, 104643/EP15316/108. For Fraser's invitation see FO tel. 51 to British delegation, United Nations, 3 December 1953, FO 371, 104644/EP15316/112.

36. Justice Department statement, 21 April 1953, Spingarn Papers, FTC File, Oil Report, box 48, folder: Oil Report—International Petroleum Cartel, Vol. 4, Truman Library. See also memorandum of discussion at 139th meeting of the NSC, 8 April 1953, *FRUS, 1952–1954*, vol. 1, pp. 1346–48; and Justice Department press release, 9

April 1953, Stephen J. Spingarn Papers, FTC File, Oil Report, box 48, folder: Oil Report—International Petroleum Cartel, Vol. 4.

37. Jernegan memorandum of conversation, "Consultation of American Oil Companies with AIOC Regarding Iranian Oil Problem," 5 December 1953, RG 59, 888.2553/12-553. See also Phleger memorandum, "Iranian Oil," 7 December 1953, RG 59, 888.2553/12-753; Aldrich (Hoover) tel. 2457 to Department of State, 7 December 1953, RG 59, 888.2553/12-753; Stutesman memorandum of conversation, "Request by Sir William Fraser for Early Discussions with Certain Major Oil Companies on the Iranian Problem," 8 December 1953, RG 59, 888.2553/12-853; Smith to Orville Harden (vice president, Standard Oil Company of New York), 8 December 1953, RG 59, 888.2553/12-953; and Phleger memorandum, "Iranian Oil," 8 December 1953, *FRUS, 1952–1954*, vol. 10, pp. 849–50.

38. W. Walton Butterworth (chargé d'affaires, U.S. embassy, London) tel. to State Department, 18 December 1953, *FRUS, 1952–1954*, vol. 10, pp. 852–54; Belgrave et al. minutes, 18 December 1953, FO 371, 104644/EP15316/128; Belgrave minute, 22 December 1953, FO 371, 110046/EP1531/2.

39. Fry minute, with draft dispatch to Wright, 14 December 1953, FO 371, 104587/EP1051/84; FO tel. 13 to British embassy, Tehran, 31 December 1953, FO 371, 104644/EP15316/127.

40. Wright to Allen, 31 December 1953, FO 371, 110046/EP1531/13; Henderson tel. 1477 to State Department, 6 January 1954, RG 59, 888.2553/1-654; Wright tel. 15 to FO, 6 January 1954, FO 371, 110059/EP1534/1; Wright tel. 15 to FO, 6 January 1954, FO 371, 110059/EP1534/1.

41. C.C.(54)2d Conclusions, 12 January 1954, CAB 128/27 part 1; C.C.(54)1st Conclusions, 7 January 1954, CAB 128/27 part 1; FO tel. 182 to British embassy, Washington, 13 January 1954, FO 371, 110046/EP1531/16; C.C.(54)4th Conclusions, 21 January 1954, CAB 128/27 part 1. See also FO record of meeting held on 1 January 1954 with attached paper, "A Consortium for Persian Oil," 5 January 1954, FO 371, 110046/EP1531/11; C.(54)3, "Persian Oil: Memorandum by the Secretary of State for Foreign Affairs," 5 January 1954, CAB 129/65; C.(54)12, "Persian Oil: Memorandum by the Secretary of State for Foreign Affairs," 11 January 1954, CAB 129/65; Butterworth (London) tel. 3038 to State Department, 18 January 1954, RG 59, 888.2553/1-1854; and Arthur L. Richards (GTI) memorandum of conversation with Harold Beeley (counselor, British embassy, Washington) and Hoover re "Iranian Oil Negotiations," 19 January 1954, *FRUS, 1952–1954*, vol. 10, pp. 899–901.

42. See memorandum of discussion at 178th meeting of the NSC, 30 December 1953, *FRUS, 1952–1954*, vol. 10, pp. 858–64; NSC-5402, "United States Policy toward Iran," 2 January 1954, *FRUS, 1952–1954*, vol. 10, pp. 865–89; and Cutler memorandum for Dulles, 4 January 1954, *FRUS, 1952–1954*, vol. 10, pp. 864–65.

43. Brownell to National Security Council, 20 January 1954, *FRUS, 1952–1954*, vol. 10, pp. 901–904; memorandum of discussion at 181st meeting of the NSC, 21 January 1954, *FRUS, 1952–1954*, vol. 10, pp. 907–11. See also Dulles tel. 3502 to U.S. embassy, London, 6 January 1954, RG 59, 888.2553/1-654; Phleger to Brownell, 8 January 1954, U.S. Congress, *International Petroleum Cartel*, pp. 60–61; Dulles memorandum, "Iranian Oil," 8 January 1954, Dulles Papers, General Correspondence Files, box 6, folder: Chronological—JFD January 1954 (3); Hoover memorandum of conversation, "Iranian Oil Problem," 12 January 1954, RG 59, 888.2553/1-1254; memorandum of

discussion at 180th meeting of the NSC, 14 January 1954, *FRUS, 1952–1954*, vol. 10, pp. 897–98; Hoover memorandum to Dulles, "National Security Action on Iranian Oil Settlement," 21 January 1954, *FRUS, 1952–1954*, vol. 10, p. 905; Hoover memorandum to Eisenhower, "Iranian Oil Situation," 21 January 1954, *FRUS, 1952–1954*, vol. 10, pp. 906–907; Smith to heads of major U.S. oil companies, 28 January 1954, RG 59, 888.2553/1-2854; David S. Painter, *Oil and the American Century: The Political Economy of U.S. Foreign Oil Policy, 1941–1954* (Baltimore: Johns Hopkins University Press, 1986), p. 195; and Burton I. Kaufman, *The Oil Cartel Case: A Documentary History of Antitrust Activity in the Cold War Era* (Westport, Conn.: Greenwood, 1978), p. 58.

44. See FO tel. 75 to British embassy, Tehran, 26 January 1954, FO 371, 110046/EP1531/35; Aldrich (Hoover) tel. to State Department, 28 January 1954, *FRUS, 1952–1954*, vol. 10, pp. 913–16; Belgrave memorandum, "Shares in the Consortium," 1 February 1954, FO 371, 110047/EP1531/64; P.O.(M)(54)1, "Formation of a Consortium for Persian Oil," 2 February 1954, PREM11/726; and Fry record of conversation between Basil Jackson (AIOC) and Sir Harold Caccia (FO), 4 February 1954, FO 371, 110047/EP1531/57.

45. P.O.(M)(54)1, "Formation of a Consortium for Persian Oil," 2 February 1954, FO 371, PREM11/726. See also the sources cited note 46.

46. See also FO tel. 5 to British embassy, Berlin (Eden), 28 January 1954, FO 371, 110047/EP1531/46; Belgrave memorandum, "Middle East Oil Committee—Persian Oil," 29 January 1954, FO 371, 110046/EP1531/41; Dixon memorandum, 3 February 1954, FO 371, 110047/EP1531/59; and P.O.(M)(54)1st meeting, minutes of Persia Committee meeting, 3 February 1954, PREM11/726.

47. The AIOC's invitation to the U.S. companies may be found in FO tel. 1 to British consulate, New York, 26 January 1954, FO 371, 110047/EP1531/45. For their response see Aldrich (Hoover) tel. to State Department, 26 January 1954, *FRUS, 1952–1954*, vol. 10, pp. 911–13; and Smith tel. 4250 to U.S. embassy, London, 17 February 1954, RG 59, 888.2553/2-1654.

48. Smith tel. to Dulles, 15 February 1954, *FRUS, 1952–1954*, vol. 10, pp. 923–24; Livingston Merchant (assistant secretary of state for European affairs) memorandum for Dulles, 16 February 1954, *FRUS, 1952–1954*, vol. 10, pp. 924–25; Eden tel. 223 to FO, 18 February 1954, FO 371, 110047/EP1531/74. See also Aldrich (Hoover) tel. to State Department, 5 February 1954, *FRUS, 1952–1954*, vol. 10, pp. 920–21; Caccia memorandum, 5 February 1954, FO 371, 110047/EP1531/73; Smith tel. to U.S. embassy, Tehran, 18 February 1954, *FRUS, 1952–1954*, vol. 10, p. 925; and FO tel. 714 to British embassy, Washington, 22 February 1954, FO 371, 110047/EP1531/77.

49. Smith tel. to U.S. embassy, London, 19 February 1954, *FRUS, 1952–1954*, vol. 10, pp. 926–28; Makins tel. 332 to FO, 25 February 1954, FO 371, 110047/EP1531/89; Aldrich (Hoover) tel. to State Department, 28 January 1954, *FRUS, 1952–1954*, vol. 10, pp. 913–15. See also Makins tel. 300 to FO, 19 February 1954, FO 371, 110047/EP1531/77; C.C.(54)10th Conclusions, 22 February 1954, CAB 128/27 part 1; Dulles tel. to U.S. embassy, London, 23 February 1954, *FRUS, 1952–1954*, vol. 10, pp. 930–31; Makins tel. 315 to FO, 23 February 1954, FO 371, 110047/EP1531/87; FO tel. 814 to British embassy, Washington, 2 March 1954, FO 371, 110048/EP1531/101; and Stutesman memorandum of conversation with Beeley, Byroade, and G. Hayden Raynor (BNA), "British Aide-Mémoire Regarding Composition of Oil Consortium," 3 March 1954, RG 59, 888.2553/3-354.

50. Smith tel. to U.S. embassy, London, 4 March 1954, *FRUS, 1952–1954*, vol. 10, pp. 940–41; Aldrich (Hoover) tel. to State Department, 30 March 1954, *FRUS, 1952–1954*, vol. 10, pp. 971–72. See also Olaf F. Sundt (petroleum attaché, U.S. embassy, Paris) to Eakens, with enclosure, 8 January 1954, RG 59, 888.2553/1-854; Makins tel. 315 to FO, 23 February 1954, FO 371, 110047/EP1531/87; Dulles (Hoover) tel. 4417 to U.S. embassy, London, 26 February 1954, RG 59, 888.2553/2-2654; FO tel. 814 to British embassy, Washington, 2 March 1954, FO 371, 110048/EP1531/101; and Makins tel. 385 to FO, 4 March 1954, FO 371, 110048/EP1531/102.

51. See Aldrich (Hoover) tel. 3948 to State Department, 13 March 1954, RG 59, 888.2553/3-1354; Butterworth (Hoover) tel. 3964 to State Department, 15 March 1954, RG 59, 888.2553/3-1554; Dulles tel. to U.S. embassy, London, 17 March 1954, *FRUS, 1952–1954*, vol. 10, pp. 949–50; and Aldrich (Hoover) tel. to State Department, 17 March 1954, *FRUS, 1952–1954*, vol. 10, pp. 950–53.

52. Aldrich (Hoover) tel. 3986 to State Department, 16 March 1954, RG 59, 888.2553/3-1654; Aldrich (Hoover) tel. to State Department, 17 March 1954, *FRUS, 1952–1954*, vol. 10, pp. 950–53. See also Aldrich (Hoover) tel. 3949 to State Department, 13 March 1954, RG 59, 888.2553/3-1354; and FO tel. 1111 to British embassy, Washington, 23 March 1954, FO 371, 110049/EP1531/138.

53. Aldrich (Hoover) tel. to State Department, 17 March 1954, *FRUS, 1952–1954*, vol. 10, pp. 950–53. See also Aldrich (Hoover) tel. 3949 to State Department, 13 March 1954, RG 59, 888.2553/3-1354; and FO memorandum, "Persian Oil: Negotiations between the Oil Companies," 15 March 1954, FO 371, 110048/EP1531/121.

54. Dulles tel. 4744 to U.S. embassy, London, 15 March 1954, RG 59, 888.2553/3-1554; Dulles telephone conversation with Wilson, 24 March 1954, Dulles Papers, Telephone Conversation Series, box 2, folder: Telephone Memoranda (Excepting to and from White House), March–April 1954 (2); Dulles telephone conversation with Secretary of the Treasury George M. Humphrey, 24 March 1954, Dulles Papers, Telephone Conversation Series, box 2, folder: Telephone Memoranda (Excepting to and from White House), March–April 1954 (2).

55. Dulles telephone conversation with Wilson, 17 March 1954, Dulles Papers, Telephone Conversation Series, box 2, folder: Telephone Memoranda (Excepting to and from White House), March–April 1954 (3); Dulles tel. to U.S. embassy, London, 17 March 1954, *FRUS, 1952–1954*, vol. 10, pp. 949–50; Makins tel. 448 to FO, 17 March 1954, FO 371, 110048/EP16531/129. See also Makins tel. 447 to FO, 17 March 1954, FO 371, 110048/EP1531/127.

56. Dulles telephone conversation with Wilson, 17 March 1954, Dulles Papers, Telephone Conversation Series, box 2, folder: Telephone Memoranda (Excepting to and from White House), March–April 1954 (3); Makins tel. 448 to FO, 17 March 1954, FO 371, 110048/EP1531/129; Max W. Bishop (OCB staff representative) memorandum for the record, "Meeting of the OCB Working Group on NSC 5402 (Iran), March 18, 1954," with attached Arthur L. Richards (chairman, OCB Working Group on NSC-5402) memorandum for the executive officer, OCB, "Recommendations for Action by OCB," 22 March 1954, Papers of the White House Office, National Security Council Staff, 1948–1961, OCB Central Files Series, box 42, folder: OCB 091.Iran (File #1) (3), Eisenhower Library.

57. Bishop memorandum for the record, "Meeting of the OCB Working Group on NSC 5402 (Iran), March 18, 1954," with attached Richards memorandum for the executive officer, OCB, "Recommendations for Action by OCB," 22 March 1954, Papers of

the White House Office, National Security Council Staff, 1948–1961, OCB Central Files Series, box 42, folder: OCB 091.Iran (File #1) (3).

58. C.C.(54)20th Conclusions, 17 March 1954, CAB 128/27 part 1. See also Aldrich (Hoover) tel. 4022 to State Department, 18 March 1954, RG 59, 888.2553/3-1854; Aldrich (Hoover) tel. 4046 to State Department, 19 March 1954, RG 59, 888.2553/3-1954; and C.C.(54)18th Conclusions, 15 March 1954, CAB 128/27 part 1.

59. Makins tel. 464 to FO, 19 March 1954, FO 371, 110048/EP1531/131; FO tel. 1024 to British embassy, Washington, 18 March 1954, FO 371, 110048/EP1531/131. See also FO tel. 1074 to British embassy, Washington, 20 March 1954, FO 371, 110049/EP1531/135.

60. FO tel. 1073 to British embassy, Washington, 20 March 1954, FO 371, 110049/EP1531/135; FO tel. 1076 to British embassy, Washington, 20 March 1954, FO 371, 110049/EP1531/135; FO tel. 1025 to British embassy, Washington, 18 March 1954, FO 371, 110048/EP1531/131.

61. Stevens tel. 212 to FO, 20 March 1954, FO 371, 110049/EP1531/132; Aldrich (Hoover) tel. to State Department, 18 March 1954, *FRUS, 1952–1954*, vol. 10, pp. 958–59. See also Aldrich (Hoover) tel. 4022 to State Department, 18 March 1954, RG 59, 888.2553/3-1854; Makins tel. 464 to FO, 19 March 1954, FO 371, 110048/EP1531/131; Henderson tel. to State Department, 20 March 1954, *FRUS, 1952–1954*, vol. 10, pp. 960–62; Dulles telephone conversation with Humphrey, 22 March 1954, Dulles Papers, Telephone Conversation Series, box 2, folder: Telephone Memoranda (Excepting to and from White House), March–April 1954 (3); FO tel. 1121 to British embassy, Washington, 23 March 1954, FO 371, 110049/EP1531/137; and Dulles tel. to U.S. embassy, London (Hoover), 22 March 1954, *FRUS, 1952–1954*, vol. 10, pp. 964–65.

62. Aldrich (Hoover) tel. to State Department, 25 March 1954, *FRUS, 1952–1954*, vol. 10, pp. 968–69. See also FO tel. 1121 to British embassy, Washington, 23 March 1954, FO 371, 110049/EP1531/137; FO tel. 1122 to British embassy, Washington, 23 March 1954, FO 371, 110049/EP1531/137; Jernegan memorandum of conversation with Beeley re "Further British Observations on Iranian Oil Negotiations," 24 March 1954, RG 59, 888.2553/3-2554; and Dulles tel. 4993 to U.S. embassy, London, 26 March 1954, RG 59, 888.2553/3-2654.

63. On these issues see Belgrave memorandum, "Middle East Oil Committee—Persian Oil," 29 January 1954, FO 371, 110046/EP1531/41; P.O.M.(54)1, "Formation of a Consortium for Persian Oil," 2 February 1954, PREM11/726; minutes of Persia Committee meeting, P.O.(M)(51)1st Meeting, 2 February 1954, PREM11/726; and Caccia to Evelyn Shuckburgh, 13 February 1954, FO 371, 110047/EP1531/66.

64. See unsigned note of meeting, 26 February 1954, T236/3900; Treasury record of meeting held on 2/24/54, 3 March 1954, T236/3900; and FO tel. 58 to British embassy, Tehran, 31 March 1954, FO 371, 110007/EP1111/10.

65. See Caccia to Shuckburgh, 13 February 1954, FO 371, 110047/EP1531/66.

66. See "Memorandum on Points on Which U.S. Oil Companies Have Agreed as Common Principles," 17 February 1954, FO 371, 110047/EP1531/84; and Henderson (Hoover) tel. 2134 to State Department, 15 April 1954, RG 59, 888.2553/4-1554.

67. FO tel. 262 to British embassy, Tehran, 20 March 1954, FO 371, 110007/EP1111/7; Dulles tel. 5230 to U.S. embassy, London, 23 March 1954, RG 59, 888.2553/3-2354. See also Aldrich tel. 3648 to State Department, 24 February 1954, RG 59, 888.2553/2-2454; FO tel. 263 to British embassy, Tehran, 20 March 1954, FO 371,

110007/EP1111/7; and Henderson tel. 1989 to State Department, 23 March 1954, RG 59, 888.2553/3-2354.

68. Memorandum of discussion at 199th meeting of NSC, 27 May 1954, *FRUS, 1952–1954*, vol. 10, pp. 1008–12. The formal creation of the consortium took place on 9 April 1954. The document may be found in "Memorandum of Understanding on 'Basis for the Settlement with Anglo-Iranian' Following Discussions Between Representatives of the Following Interests: Gulf Oil, Texas, California Standard, Jersey Standard, Socony Vacuum, C.F.P., Royal Dutch Shell, and Anglo-Iranian," 28 April 1954, PREM11/726.

69. Stevens tel. 316 to FO, 14 April 1954, FO 371, 110060/EP1534/58. See also Henderson (Hoover) tel. 2134 to State Department, 15 April 1954, RG 59, 888.2553/4-1554.

70. Fry to Beeley, 23 April 1954, FO 371, 110061/EP1534/74.

71. See Henderson (Hoover) tel. 2138 to State Department, 15 April 1954, RG 59, 888.2553/4-1554; Stevens tel. 339 to FO, 18 April 1954, FO 371, 110061/EP1534/66; and Stevens tel. 345 to FO, 19 April 1954, FO 371, 110061/EP1534/67.

72. See Iranian Foreign Ministry note to British Foreign Office, 15 April 1954, FO 371, 110061/EP1534/83; Henderson (Hoover) tel. 2135 to State Department, 15 April 1954, RG 59, 888.2553/4-1554; and Henderson tel. 2147 to State Department, 16 April 1954, RG 59, 888.2553/4-1654.

73. Fry to Beeley, 23 April 1954, FO 371, 110061/EP1534/74; Stevens tel. 367 to FO, 22 April 1954, FO 371, 110007/EP1111/24. See also Stevens tel. 343 to FO, 19 April 1954, FO 371, 110007/EP1111/23; Aldrich tel. 5217 to State Department, 20 May 1954, RG 59, 888.2553/5-2054; and Aldrich tel. 5443 to State Department, 1 June 1954, RG 59, 888.2553/6-154.

74. For American thinking during the payments negotiations see Smith (acting secretary of state) tel. 5552 to U.S. embassy, London, 18 April 1954, RG 59, 888.2553/4-1854; and Aldrich tel. 4912 to State Department, 5 May 1954, RG 59, 888.2553/5-554.

75. See Stevens tel. 381 to FO, 25 April 1954, FO 371, 110061/EP1534/85; Henderson tel. 2210 to State Department, 26 April 1954, RG 59, 888.2553/4-2654; Stevens tel. 407 to FO, 28 April 1954, FO 371, 110061/EP1534/85; Henderson (Hoover) tel. 2264 to State Department, 4 May 1954, RG 59, 888.2553/5-454; David Serpell (British treasury representative in Tehran) to William Armstrong, 5 May 1954, FO 371, 110062/EP1534/109; Stevens to Caccia, 5 May 1954, with enclosed Iranian memorandum, FO 371, 110062/EP1534/107; Henderson (Hoover) tel. to State Department, 8 May 1954, *FRUS, 1952–1954*, vol. 10, pp. 994–98; Iranian memorandum, 9 May 1954, FO 371, 110062/EP1534/113; Henderson (Hoover) tel. 2323 to State Department, 13 May 1954, RG 59, 888.2553/5-1354; Henderson tel. to State Department, 17 May 1954, *FRUS, 1952–1954*, vol. 10, pp. 999–1001; and unsigned "Note on Discussions Between the Government of Iran and the Consortium up to 11th May 1954," 19 May 1954, FO 371, 110064/EP1534/156.

76. See FO tel. 378 to British embassy, Tehran, 20 April 1954, FO 371, 110061/EP1534/67; Henderson tel. 2273 to State Department, 5 May 1954, RG 59, 888.2553/5-554; FO tel. 321 to British delegation to Geneva conference, 8 May 1954, FO 371, 110062/EP1534/102; Henderson (Hoover) tel. 2323 to State Department, 13 May 1954, RG 59, 888.2553/5-1354; and Aldrich tel. 5166 to State Department, 18 May 1954, RG 59, 888.2553/5-1854.

77. Dulles tel. to U.S. embassy, London, 24 May 1954, *FRUS, 1952–1954*, vol. 10, pp. 1007–1008; memorandum of discussion at 199th meeting of NSC, 27 May 1954, *FRUS, 1952–1954*, vol. 10, pp. 1008–12. See also Byroade memorandum to Murphy, 20 May 1954, with attached "Talking Paper for Meeting with Oil Company Principals, Friday, May 21," RG 59, 888.2553/5-2054; memorandum of conversation re "Iranian Oil Negotiations," 21 May 1954, RG 59, 888.2553/5-2154; and Richards memorandum for the OCB executive officer, 24 May 1954, Papers of the White House Office, OCB Central Files, box 42, folder: 091 Iran (File #1) (6).

78. Belgrave paper, "Persian Oil," 24 May 1954, with attached FO minutes, FO 371, 110080/EP15311/6. See also Victor Mallet minute re Belgrave memorandum of 5/24/54, 25 May 1954, FO 371, 110080/EP15311/7; and Denis Wright (British chargé d'affaires, Tehran), 2 June 1954, FO 371, 110173/UES1174/20.

79. Allen to Stevens, 1 May 1954, FO 371, 110061/EP1534/83. See also Henderson tel. 2277 to State Department, 6 May 1954, RG 59, 888.2553/5-654; Rountree (Hoover) tel. 2318 to State Department, 12 May 1954, RG 59, 888.2553/5-1254; Rountree (Hoover) tel. 2336 to State Department, 15 May 1954, RG 59, 888.2553/5-1554; and Fry memorandum, "Blockade of Persian Oil," 16 July 1954, FO 371, 110057/EP1533/117.

80. See Henderson (Hoover) tel. 2323 to State Department, 13 May 1954, RG 59, 888.2553/5-1354; Jernegan memorandum for Murphy, "Iranian Oil Consortium," 15 May 1954, RG 59, 888.2553/5-1554; Dulles tel. to U.S. embassy, London, 24 May 1954, *FRUS, 1952–1954*, vol. 10, pp. 1007–1008; Aldrich (Hoover) tel. to State Department, 7 June 1954, *FRUS, 1952–1954*, vol. 10, pp. 1025–26; Aldrich (Hoover) tel. 5616 to State Department, 9 June 1954, RG 59, 888.2553/6-954; and Aldrich (Hoover) tel. to State Department, 15 June 1954, *FRUS, 1952–1954*, vol. 10, pp. 1028–29. For the importance of the consortium's acceptance of an agency arrangement see Stevens dispatch 63 to FO, 13 August 1954, PREM11/726.

81. Dulles tel. 6507 to U.S. embassy, London, 2 June 1954, RG 59, 888.2553/6-254. See also Henderson tel. to State Department, 29 May 1954, *FRUS, 1952–1954*, vol. 10, pp. 1016–17; and John Stutesman (GTI) memorandum of conversation re "Iranian Oil Negotiations," 3 June 1954, RG 59, 888.2553/6-354.

82. Dulles tel. 2330 to U.S. embassy, Tehran, 28 May 1954, RG 59, 888.2553/5-2854; FO tel. 979 to British delegation to Geneva Conference (Eden), 9 June 1954, FO 371, 110064/EP1534/171. See also Stutesman memorandum of conversation re "Registration of Iranian Oil Operating Companies," 28 May 1954, RG 59, 888.2553/5-2854; C. A. E. Shuckburgh memorandum, "Persian Oil Negotiations: Nationality of the Holding [sic] Companies," 4 June 1954, FO 371, 110064/EP1534/172; Ivone Kirkpatrick minute to Eden, 5 June 1954, FO 371, 110064/EP1534/169; and minutes of Cabinet meeting, 9 June 1954, GEN 407/1st Meeting, CAB 130/102.

83. For discussions with Fraser see Shuckburgh memorandum, "Persian Oil Negotiations: Nationality of the Holding [sic] Companies," 4 June 1954, FO 371, 110064/EP1534/172; Shuckburgh memorandum, 8 June 1954, FO 371, 110064/EP1534/171; Belgrave minute, 12 June 1954, FO 371, 110065/EP1534/177; and Fry minute, 15 June 1954, FO 371, 110065/EP1534/179.

84. See Stevens tel. 647 to FO, 23 June 1954, FO 371, 110065/EP1534/189; Stevens tel. 648 to FO, 23 June 1954, FO 371, 110065/EP1534/186; consortium memorandum, "Notes on Organization, Nationality, and Functions of Companies," 23 June 1954, RG 59, 888.2553/6-2354; and Stevens tel. 673 to FO, 28 June 1954, FO 371,110065/EP1534/194.

85. Stevens dispatch 43 to FO, 1 July 1954, FO 371, 110066/EP1534/203; Henderson (Hoover) tel. to State Department, 6 July 1954, *FRUS, 1952–1954*, vol. 10, pp. 1038–39. See also consortium memorandum, "Notes on Organization, Nationality, and Functions of Companies," 23 June 1954, RG 59, 888.2553/6-2354; and Stevens to Sir William Fraser, 10 July 1954, FO 371, 110067/EP1534/215.

86. For these discussions see Henderson (Hoover) tel. to State Department, *FRUS, 1952–1954*, vol. 10, pp. 1033–35; Henderson (Hoover) tel. 89 to State Department, 13 July 1954, RG 59, 888.2553/7-1354; Snow (AIOC member of consortium team) to Fraser, 14 July 1954, FO 371, 110068/EP1534/229; Henderson tel. 167 to State Department, 23 July 1954, RG 59, 888.2553/7-2354; Stevens tel. 800 to FO, 25 July 1954, FO 371, 110068/EP1534/238; and Henderson (Hoover) tel. 217 to State Department, 29 July 1954, RG 59, 888.2553/7-2954.

87. See Henderson tel. 249 to State Department, 1 August 1954, RG 59, 888.2553/8-154; Painter, *Oil and the American Century*, p. 197; Fereidun Fesharaki, *Development of the Iranian Oil Industry: International and Domestic Aspects* (New York: Praeger, 1976), pp. 50–54; and Anthony Sampson, *The Seven Sisters: The Great Oil Companies and the World They Shaped* (New York: Viking, 1975), p. 131. The final agreement may be found in U.S. Congress, *International Petroleum Cartel*, pp. 95–116.

88. A. Samuel memorandum, "Persian Oil," 27 July 1954, FO 371, 110083/EP15315/50. See also Stevens tel. 675 to FO, 29 June 1954, FO 371, 110082/EP15315/22; Fraser to H. E. Snow (AIOC member of consortium team), 15 July 1954, FO 371, 110068/EP1531/229; FO tel. 797 to British embassy, Tehran, 28 July 1954, FO 371, 110083/EP15315/44; C.C.(54)55th Conclusions, 28 July 1954, CAB 128/27 part 2; FO tel. 808 to British embassy, Tehran, 30 July 1954, FO 371, 110083/EP15315/47; Henderson tel. to State Department, 31 July 1954, *FRUS, 1952–1954*, vol. 10, p. 1043; FO tel. 833 to British embassy, Tehran, 2 August 1954, FO 371, 110084/EP15315/56; and Henderson tels. (2) to State Department, 5 August 1954, *FRUS, 1952–1954*, vol. 10, pp. 1044–46.

89. See Sampson, *Seven Sisters*, pp. 131–32; Fesharaki, *Development of the Iranian Oil Industry*, pp. 54–55; and Amin Saikal, *The Rise and Fall of the Shah* (Princeton, N.J.: Princeton University Press, 1980), pp. 48–51.

90. On the shah's long-standing efforts to secure U.S. military aid see the documents in *FRUS, 1952–1954*, vol. 10, pp. 797–801, 805–806, 831–35, 850–52, 928–30, 933–39, 943–49, 954–58, 1008–12, 1023–24. See also Henderson tel. 2466 to State Department, 4 June 1954, RG 59, 888.2553/6-454; Henderson tel. 2499 to State Department, 9 June 1954, RG 59, 888.2553/6-954; C.C.(54)56th Conclusions, 29 July 1954, CAB 128/27 part 2; Henderson tel. 825 to State Department, 7 October 1954, RG 59, 888.2553/10-754; and Henderson tel. 945 to State Department, 24 October 1954, RG 59, 888.00/10-2454.

91. See Leonard J. Emmerglick (attorney, Anti-Trust Division, Department of Justice) memorandum to Stanley N. Barnes (assistant attorney general, Anti-Trust Division), 19 August 1954, U.S. Congress, *International Petroleum Cartel*, pp. 89–90; Kenneth Harris memorandum for Barnes, 15 September 1954, U.S. Congress, *International Petroleum Cartel*, p. 91; Emmerglick memorandum for Barnes, 15 September 1954, U.S. Congress, *International Petroleum Cartel*, pp. 92–93; Smith (acting secretary of state) tel. to U.S. embassy, Tehran, 15 September 1954, *FRUS, 1952–1954*, vol. 10, pp. 1049–50; Wilson memorandum to Bernard M. Shanley (special counsel to the

president), 15 October 1954, White House Central Files—Confidential File, Subject Series, box 34, folder: Iranian Oil Consortium, Eisenhower Library; and Smith tel. to U.S. embassy, Tehran, 17 September 1954, *FRUS, 1952–1954*, vol. 10, p. 1051.

92. See Kaufman, *Oil Cartel Case*, pp. 59–61; see pp. 64–114 for subsequent conduct of the watered-down suit.

93. See FO tel. 905 to British embassy, Tehran, 11 August 1954, FO 371, 110071/ EP1534/312; D. L. Stewart minute, 31 August 1954, FO 371, 110073/EP1534/354; Henderson tel. 532 to State Department, 1 September 1954, RG 59, 888.2553/9-154; Stevens tel. 1082 to FO, 2 September 1954, FO 371, 110073/EP1534/351; and Henderson tel. 678 to State Department, 20 September 1954, RG 59, 888.2553/9-2054.

94. Henderson tel. to State Department, 21 September 1954, *FRUS, 1952–1954*, vol. 10, pp. 1053–54; Stevens dispatch 75 to FO, 28 September 1954, FO 371, 110075/EP1534/388. See also Henderson tel. 606 to State Department, 14 September 1954, RG 59, 888.2553/9-1454; Henderson tel. 733 to State Department, 25 September 1954, RG 59, 888.2553/9-2554; Henderson tel. 735 to State Department, 25 September 1954, RG 59, 888.2553/9-2554; and Belgrave paper with attached memorandum, 15 December 1954, FO 371, 110080/EP15311/13.

95. Henderson tel. 762 to State Department, 29 September 1954, RG 59, 888.2553/ 9-2954.

96. Stevens tel. 1164 to FO, 7 October 1954, FO 371, 110075/EP1534/396. See also Henderson tel. 724 to State Department, 24 September 1954, RG 59, 888.2553/9-2454; Stevens tel. 1151 to FO, 3 October 1954, FO 371, 110075/EP1534/392; Henderson tel. 814 to State Department, 6 October 1954, RG 59, 888.2553/10-654; Henderson tel. 823 to State Department, 7 October 1954, RG 59, 888.2553/10-754; Butterworth (London) tel. 1801 to State Department, 8 October 1954, RG 59, 888.2553/10-854; and Henderson tel. 845 to State Department, 11 October 1954, RG 59, 888.2553/10-1154.

97. Henderson tel. 845 to State Department, 11 October 1954, RG 59, 888.2553/10-1154; Stevens tel. 66 to FO, 25 October 1954, FO 371, 109998/EP1051/34. See also Henderson tel. 866 to State Department, 14 October 1954, RG 59, 888.2553/10-1454; Rountree tel. 926 to State Department, 21 October 1954, RG 59, 888.2553/10-2154; Rountree tel. 962 to State Department, 28 October 1954, RG 59, 888.2553/10-2854; L. P. Elwell-Sutton, *Persian Oil: A Study in Power Politics* (London: Lawrence & Wishart, 1955), pp. 325–27; and Saikal, *Rise and Fall*, pp. 97–99. On Kashani see also Henderson dispatch 195, "Feeling of Some Iranians Against British and the Hope that the U.S. Will Follow an Independent Policy in Iran," 8 October 1954, RG 59, 641.88/10-854.

98. On economic assistance see Henderson tel. 2293 to State Department, 10 May 1954, RG 59, 888.2553/5-1054; Henderson tel. 145 to State Department, 20 July 1954, RG 59, 888.2553/7-2054; Smith tel. to U.S. embassy, Tehran, 13 October 1954, *FRUS, 1952–1954*, vol. 10, pp. 1057–59; and Dulles tel. 855 to U.S. embassy, Tehran, 29 October 1954, RG 59, 888.2553/10-2954.

99. On plans for post-oil settlement assistance see Jernegan memorandum to Bowie, "Proposed Program of Military Aid to Iran," 18 September 1954, *FRUS, 1952–1954*, vol. 10, pp. 1052–53; Dulles to Wilson, 8 November 1954, *FRUS, 1952–1954*, vol. 10, pp. 1063–66; and NSC-5402/1, "U.S. Policy toward Iran" (draft), 30 December 1954, Papers of the White House Office, OSANSA, NSC Series, Policy Papers Subseries, box 8, folder: NSC 5402—Iran [Private Oil Companies and Middle East Oil] (1).

100. See Jernegan memorandum to Dulles, "Visit of His Imperial Majesty Moham-mad Reza Pahlavi Shahinshah of Iran and Empress Soraya," 8 December 1954, *FRUS, 1952–1954,* vol. 10, pp. 1066–73; Dulles tel. to U.S. embassy, Tehran, 13 December 1954, *FRUS, 1952–1954,* vol. 10, pp. 1073–74; Hoover (undersecretary of state) memo-randum to Eisenhower, 21 December 1954, *FRUS, 1952–1954,* vol. 10, p. 1077; and NSC-5402/1, "U.S. Policy toward Iran" (draft), 30 December 1954, Papers of the White House Office, OSANSA, NSC Series, Policy Papers Subseries, box 8, folder: NSC 5402—Iran [Private Oil Companies and Middle East Oil] (1).

101. Henderson tel. 906 to State Department, 19 October 1954, RG 59, 888.2553/10-1954. See also OCB, working draft, "Progress Report on NSC-5402, 'United States Policy toward Iran,'" 28 September 1954, Papers of the White House Office, National Security Council Staff Papers, 1948–1961, OCB Central Files Series, box 43, folder: OCB 091.Iran (File #1) (9); OCB draft, "Progress Report on NSC-5402, 'United States Policy Toward Iran,'" 4 October 1954, Papers of the White House Office, National Security Council Staff Papers, 1948–1961, OCB Central Files Series, box 43, folder: OCB 091.Iran (File #2) (1); OCB, "Progress Report on NSC 5402, 'United States Policy Toward Iran,'" 13 October 1954, Papers of the White House Office, OSANSA, NSC Series, Policy Papers Subseries, box 8, folder: NSC 5402—Iran [Private Oil Companies and Middle East Oil] (1); and W. Park Armstrong Jr., memorandum for Eisenhower, "NIE-34–54: Probable Developments in Iran through 1955," 16 December 1954, RG 59, 788.00/12-1654.

102. On the Iranian-American client relationship see Gasiorowski, *Client State,* pp. 85–101.

9. The Anglo-Iranian Oil Crisis: An Appraisal

1. Eden, quoted in Wm. Roger Louis, "Musaddiq and the Dilemmas of British Impe-rialism," in James A. Bill and Wm. Roger Louis (eds.), *Musaddiq, Iranian Nationalism, and Oil* (Austin: University of Texas Press, 1988), p. 246.

2. For accounts that credit the U.S. majors with less influence see, for example, Irvine H. Anderson, *ARAMCO, the United States, and Saudi Arabia: A Study in the Dy-namics of Foreign Oil Policy, 1933–1950* (Princeton, N.J.: Princeton University Press, 1981); and David S. Painter, *Oil and the American Century: The Political Economy of U.S. Foreign Oil Policy, 1941–1954* (Baltimore: Johns Hopkins University Press, 1986).

3. Shepherd to Bowker, 22 May 1951, FO 371, 91542/EP1531/547.

4. Acheson memorandum for the president, "Luncheon Meeting with Prime Minister Mosadeq," 22 October 1951, Truman Papers, PSF—Subject File, box 180, folder: Iran—W. Averell Harriman.

5. Although previous accounts of the Anglo-Iranian oil crisis have noted Mossadeq's tendency to weep, they have not made much of how the prime minister's tears affected Anglo-American officials. See, for example, Daniel Yergin, *The Prize: The Epic Quest for Oil, Money, and Power* (New York: Simon & Schuster, 1991), chap. 23; and H. W. Brands, *Inside the Cold War: Loy Henderson and the Rise of the American Empire, 1918–1961* (New York: Oxford University Press, 1991), chap. 16.

6. Henderson tel. 3178 to State Department, 13 February 1953, RG 59, 888.2553/2-1353; Acheson memorandum for the president, "Luncheon Meeting with Prime Minis-

ter Mosadeq," 22 October 1951, Truman Papers, PSF—Subject File, box 180, folder: Iran—W. Averell Harriman.

7. Henderson tel. 2803 to State Department, 19 January 1953, RG 59, 888.2553/1-1953.

8. Ibid.

9. Ramsbotham to Logan, 20 August 1951, FO 371, 91580/EP1531/1391.

10. Good discussions of Mossadeq's "negative equilibrium" may be found in Farhad Diba, *Mohammed Mossadegh: A Political Biography* (London: Croom Helm, 1986), pp. 84–90; and Sepehr Zabih, *The Mossadegh Era: Roots of the Iranian Revolution* (Chicago: Lake View, 1982), chap. 6.

11. For an examination of how Indian neutrality evoked similar condemnations from U.S. officials see Andrew J. Rotter, "Gender Relations, Foreign Relations: The United States and South Asia, 1947–1964," *Journal of American History* 81 (September 1994): 535–36.

12. D. A. Logan, "Brief for the Minister of State for the meeting of the Cabinet on the 26th of September 1952," w/enclosed annex, "Persian Reply to Joint U.S./U.K. Offer," 25 September 1952, FO 371, 98700/EP15314/412; Ramsbotham minute, "Persia: Oil," 8 September 1952, FO 371, 98697/EP15314/332; Henderson tel. 422 to State Department, 28 July 1952, *Foreign Relations of the United States, 1952–1954*, vol. 10 (Washington, D.C.: Government Printing Office, 1978), p. 417 (hereafter *FRUS*); C.(52)275. "Political Developments in Persia: Note by the Secretary of State for Foreign Affairs," 5 August 1952, CAB 129/54.

13. Gifford tel. to State Department, 5 October 1951, *FRUS, 1952–1954*, vol. 10, p. 205.

14. Henderson tel. 377 to State Department, 24 July 1952, RG 59, 788.00/7-2452.

15. H. Freeman Matthews memorandum of conversation, 2 August 1951, Acheson Papers, box 66, folder: Memoranda of Conversations, Aug. 1951; C. Steel (Washington) tel. 2321 to FO, 23 February 1952, FO 371, 98707/EP15317/1.

16. FO tel. 1576 to British ambassador, United Nations, 10 October 1951, FO 371, 91606/EP1531/1988; Middleton tel. 189 to FO, 23 February 1952, FO 371, 98707/EP1531/1.

17. Andrew F. Westwood, "Politics of Distrust in Iran," *Annals of the American Academy of Political and Social Sciences* 358 (March 1965): 127. See also Sattareh Farman Farmaian, with Dona Munker, *Daughter of Persia: A Woman's Journey from Her Father's Harem Through the Islamic Revolution* (New York: Crown, 1992), p. 173. I am grateful to Sholeh Quinn for pointing me to the latter source.

18. For one recounting of this famous tale see Yergin, *The Prize*, p. 457.

19. See Carol Cohn, "Wars, Wimps, and Women: Talking Gender and Thinking War," in *Gendering War Talk*, ed. Miriam Cooke and Angela Woollacott (Princeton, N.J.: Princeton University, 1993), pp. 227–46; and Emily S. Rosenberg, "Gender," *Journal of American History* 77 (June 1990): 116–24.

20. George Middleton to A. D. M. Ross (Eastern Department, FO), 16 June 1952, FO 371, 98707/EP15317/8.

21. Henry A. Byroade (assistant secretary of state for Near Eastern, South Asian, and African affairs) memorandum to Robert Bowie (director, Policy Planning Staff), "Iran," 21 August 1953, *FRUS, 1952–1954*, vol. 10, p. 761.

22. "Man of the Year," *Time*, 7 January 1952, pp. 18–21. Other contenders for Man of the Year honors included Dwight Eisenhower, Douglas MacArthur, Winston Churchill, and John Foster Dulles.

23. For instability throughout the developing nations see Robert J. McMahon, "Eisenhower and Third World Nationalism: A Critique of the Revisionists," *Political Science Quarterly* 101 (October 1986): 453–73.

bibliography

Primary Sources

Private Manuscript Collections

Dwight D. Eisenhower Library, Abilene, Kans.

Herbert Brownell Oral History Interview
John Foster Dulles Papers
Dwight D. Eisenhower Papers (Ann Whitman File)
Dwight D. Eisenhower Pre-Presidential Records
Dwight D. Eisenhower Records as President
Andrew Goodpaster Oral History Interview
Loy Henderson Oral History Interview
C. D. Jackson Papers
Robert A. Lovett Oral History Interview
John J. McCloy Oral History Interview
National Security Council Staff Papers
Records of the White House Office of Special Assistant for National
    Security Affairs
Records of the White House Staff Secretary
Vernon Walters Oral History Interview

Harry S Truman Library, Independence, Mo.

Dean G. Acheson Oral History Interview
Dean G. Acheson Papers
George V. Allen Papers
Oscar L. Chapman Papers
Matthew Connelly Papers
John Foster Dulles Papers
Henry F. Grady Papers
Robert Eakens Oral History Interview
W. Averell Harriman Oral History Interview
Loy W. Henderson Oral History Interview
Robert A. Lovett Oral History Interview
George C. McGhee Oral History Interview
George C. McGhee Papers
Stephen J. Spingarn Oral History Interview
Stephen J. Spingarn Papers
Harry S Truman Papers

Seeley G. Mudd Library, Princeton University, Princeton, N.J.

Allen Welsh Dulles Papers
John Foster Dulles Oral History Collection
John Foster Dulles Papers

Government Archives

Great Britain

Public Record Office, Kew, England

Record Class CAB 21, Registered Files: Prime Minister's Briefs
Record Class CAB 125, Lord President of the Secretariat Files
Record Class CAB 128, Cabinet Minutes, Conclusions, and Memoranda
Record Class CAB 129, Cabinet Papers
Record Class CAB 130, Ad Hoc Committees: General and Miscellaneous Series
Record Class DEFE 4–5, Records of the Defence Committee
Record Class FO 371, Foreign Office General Political Papers
Record Class FO 800, Private Collections: Minutes and Officials
Record Class PREM 11, Papers of the Prime Minister's Office
Record Class T 171, Budget and Finance Bill Papers
Record Class T 225, Defence Policy and Material Division
Record Class T 229–238, Central Economic Planning Staff

United States

Library of Congress, Washington, D.C.

W. Averell Harriman Papers
Loy Henderson Papers

National Archives of the United States, Washington, D.C.

Record Group 48, Records of the Office of the Secretary of the Interior
Record Group 59, General Records of the Department of State
Record Group 218, Records of the Joint Chiefs of Staff
Record Group 330, Records of the Office of the Secretary of Defense

Washington National Records Center, Suitland, Md.

Record Group 84, Records of Foreign Service Posts of the Department of State

Published Government Documents

Great Britain

Parliament. *Parliamentary Debates*, 1948–1954
Foreign Office. *Foreign and State Papers*, 1948–1954
———. *Correspondence Between His Majesty's Government in the United Kingdom and the Persian Government, and Related Documents Concerning the Oil Industry in Persia, February 1951 to September 1951.* London: H. M. Stationery Office, 1951. (Cmnd. 8425).
———. *Correspondence Between Her Majesty's Government in the United Kingdom and the Iranian Government, and Related Documents Concerning the Joint Anglo-American Proposal for a Settlement of the Oil Dispute, August 1952 to October 1952.* London: H. M. Stationery Office, 1952. (Cmnd. 8677).

United States

Congress. House. Committee on Foreign Affairs. *Selected Executive Session Hearings of the Committee, 1951–1956*, vol. 16, *The Middle East, Africa, and Inter-American Affairs*. 82d Cong., 1st sess., 82d Cong., 2d sess., 83d Cong., 1st sess., 83d Cong., 2d sess., 84th Cong., 2d sess., 1980.
Congress. House. Committee on Foreign Relations. Subcommittee on Multinational Corporations. *Report on Multinational Corporations and U.S. Foreign Policy.* 93d Cong., 2d sess., 1975.
———. *Hearings, Multinational Corporations and U.S. Foreign Policy.* 93d. Cong., 2d. sess., 1975.

——. *Executive Session of the Senate Foreign Relations Committee*. 82d. Cong., 1st sess., 1976.

Congress. House. Committee on the Judiciary. Subcommittee on Antitrust. *Hearings, Current Antitrust Problems*. 84th Cong., 1st sess., 1955. Committee serial 3.

Congress. Senate. Committee on Banking and Currency. *Study of Export-Income Bank and World Bank*. 83d Cong., 2d sess., 1954.

Congress. Senate. Committee on Foreign Affairs. Subcommittee on Multinational Corporations. *The International Petroleum Cartel, the Iranian Consortium, and U.S. National Security*. 93d Cong., 2d sess., 1975. Committee Print.

——. *Multinational Petroleum Companies and Foreign Policy*. 93d Cong., 2d sess., 1975.

Congress. Senate. Committee on the Judiciary. Subcommittee on Antitrust and Monopoly. *Petroleum, the Antitrust Laws, and Government Policies*. 85th Cong., 1st sess., 1957.

——. *Hearings, International Aspects of Antitrust*. 89th Cong., 2d sess., 1966.

——. *Hearings on Governmental Intervention in the Market Mechanism, The Petroleum Industry*. 91st Cong., 1st sess., 1969.

Congress. Senate. Committee on Small Business. *The International Petroleum Cartel: Staff Report to the Federal Trade Commission*. 82d Cong., 2d sess., 1952. Committee Print 6.

Department of State. *Bulletin*. 1946–1954.

——. *Foreign Relations of the United States, 1946–1954*. Washington, D.C.: Government Printing Office.

Memoirs, Collected Documents, Contemporary Accounts, and Studies by Participants

Acheson, Dean G. *Present at the Creation: My Years in the State Department*. New York: Norton, 1969.

Alexander, Yonah and Allan Nanes, eds. *The United States and Iran: A Documentary History*. Frederick, Md.: University Publications of America, 1980.

Attlee, C. R. *As It Happened*. New York: Viking, 1954.

Branyan, Robert L. and Lawrence H. Larsen, eds. *The Eisenhower Administration, 1953–1961: A Documentary History*. New York: Random House, 1971.

Brown, Bruce K. *Oil Men in Washington: An Informal Account of the Organization and Activities of the Petroleum Administration for Defense During the Korean War, 1950–1952*. Evanil Press, 1965.

Eden, Anthony. *Full Circle: The Memoirs of Anthony Eden*. Boston: Houghton Mifflin, 1960.

Eisenhower, Dwight D. *Mandate for Change: White House Years, 1953–1961*. Garden City, N.Y.: Doubleday, 1963.

Farman Farmaian, Sattareh, with Dona Munker. *Daughter of Persia: A Woman's Journey from Her Father's Harem Through the Islamic Revolution*. New York: Crown, 1992.

Ferrell, Robert H., ed. *The Eisenhower Diaries*. New York: Norton, 1981.

Ford, Alan W. *The Anglo-Iranian Oil Dispute of 1951–1952: A Study of the Role of Law in the Relations of States*. Berkeley: University of California, 1954.

International Court of Justice. *Pleadings, Oral Arguments, Documents: Anglo-Iranian Oil Case (United Kingdom v. Iran)*. The Hague: International Court of Justice, 1952.

International Labour Office. *Labour Conditions in the Oil Industry in Iran*. Geneva: International Labour Office, 1950.

Iranian Embassy. *Some Documents on the Nationalization of the Oil Industry in Iran*. Washington, D.C.: Iranian Embassy, 1951.

Katouzian, Homa, ed. *Musaddiq's Memoirs*. London: JEBHE, National Movement of Iran, 1988.

Kemp, Norman. *Abadan: A First-Hand Account of the Persian Oil Crisis*. London: Wingate, 1953.

Macmillan, Harold. *Tides of Fortune: 1945–1955*. New York: Harper & Row, 1969.

McGhee, George. *Envoy to the Middle World: Adventures in Diplomacy*. New York: Harper & Row, 1983.

Morrison, Herbert. *Herbert Morrison: An Autobiography*. London: Oldhams, 1960.

Overseas Consultants. *Report on the Seven-Year Development Plan Organization of the Imperial Government of Iran*, 5 vols. New York: Overseas Consultants, 1949.

Pahlavi, Mohammed Reza Shah. *Mission for My Country*. New York: McGraw-Hill, 1961.

Roosevelt, Kermit. *Countercoup: The Struggle for the Control of Iran*. New York: McGraw-Hill, 1979.

Schuckburgh, Evelyn. *Descent to Suez: Diaries, 1951–56*. London: Weidenfeld and Nicolson, 1986.

Shinwell, Emanuel. *I've Lived Through It All*. London: Victor Gollancz, 1973.

Truman, Harry S. *Memoirs: Years of Trial and Hope, 1946–53*. Garden City, N.Y.: Doubleday, 1956.

Walters, Vernon A. *Silent Missions*. Garden City, N.Y.: Doubleday, 1978.

Williams, Francis. *A Prime Minister Remembers: The War and Postwar Memoirs of The Rt. Hon. Earl Attlee*. London: Heinemann, 1961.

Williams, Philip M., ed. *The Diary of Hugh Gaitskell, 1945–1956*. London: Jonathan Cape, 1983.

Woodhouse, C. M. *Something Ventured*. London: Granada, 1982.

Secondary Sources

Articles

Atyeo, Henry C. "Political Developments in Iran, 1952–1954," *Middle Eastern Affairs* 5 (1955): 249–59.

Bayne, E. A. "Crisis of Confidence in Iran," *Foreign Affairs* 31 (1953): 278–90.

Beck, Peter J. "The Anglo-Persian Oil Dispute of 1932–33," *Journal of Contemporary History* 9 (October 1974): 123–51.

Brands, H. W. "The Cairo-Tehran Connection in Anglo-American Rivalry in the

Middle East, 1951–1953," *International History Review* 11 (August 1989): 434–56.

Bullard, Reader. "Behind the Oil Dispute in Iran: A British View," *Foreign Affairs* 31 (April 1953): 461–71.

Carey, Jane Perry Clark. "Iran and Control of Its Oil Resources," *Political Science Quarterly* 89 (March 1974): 147–74.

Chandler, Geoffrey. "The Innocence of Oil Companies," *Foreign Policy* 27 (1977): 52–71.

"Chronology," *Middle Eastern Affairs* (January 1952): 29–30.

Clawson, Patrick and Cyrus Sassanpour. "Adjustment to a Foreign Exchange Shock: Iran, 1951–1953," *International Journal of Middle East Studies* 19 (February 1987): 1–22.

Cottam, Richard W. "The United States, Iran, and the Cold War," *Iranian Studies* 3 (Winter 1970): 3–33.

Efimenco, N. Marbury. "An Experiment with Civilian Dictatorship in Iran: The Case of Mohammed Mossadegh," *Journal of Politics* 17 (May 1953): 390–406.

Ferguson, Thomas. "From Normalcy to New Deal: Industrial Structure, Party Competition, and American Public Policy in the Great Depression," *International Organization* 38 (Winter 1984): 41–94.

Firoozi, Fereydoon. "The United States Economic Interest in Iran," *International Studies* 15 (1976): 29–43.

Griffith, Robert. "Dwight D. Eisenhower and the Corporate Commonwealth," *American Historical Review* 87 (February 1982): 87–122.

Harbutt, Fraser J. "American Challenge, Soviet Response: The Beginning of the Cold War, February–March 1946," *Political Science Quarterly* 96 (Winter 1981–1982): 623–39.

Harter, John J. "Mr. Foreign Service on Mossadegh and Wristonization: An Interview with Loy W. Henderson," *Foreign Service Journal* 57 (November 1980): 16–20.

Hess, Gary R. "The Iranian Crisis of 1945–1946 and the Cold War," *Political Science Quarterly* 89 (March 1974): 117–46.

Hogan, Michael J. "Informal Entente: Public Policy and Private Management in Anglo-American Petroleum Affairs," *Business History Review* 48 (Summer 1974): 187–205.

Katzenstein, Peter J. "International and Domestic Structures: Foreign Economic Policies of Advanced Industrial States," *International Organization* 30 (Winter 1976): 1–45.

———. "Conclusion: Domestic Structures and Strategies of Foreign Economic Policy," *International Organization* 31 (Autumn 1977): 879–920.

———. "Introduction: Domestic and International Forces and Strategies of Foreign Economic Policy," *International Organization* 31 (Autumn 1977): 587–606.

Kaufman, Burton I. "Mideast Multinational Oil, U.S. Foreign Policy, and Antitrust: The 1950s," *Journal of American History* 63 (March 1977): 937–59.

———. "Oil and Antitrust: The Oil Cartel Case and the Cold War," *Business History Review* 51 (Spring 1977): 35–56.

Leffler, Melvyn P. "The American Conception of National Security and the Origins of the Cold War," *American Historical Review* 89 (April 1984): 346–81.

Lockhart, Laurence. "The Causes of the Anglo-Persian Dispute," *Journal of the Royal Central Asian Society* 40 (June 1953): 134–50.

McFarland, Stephen L. "A Peripheral View of the Origins of the Cold War: The Crisis in Iran, 1941–1947," *Diplomatic History* 4 (Fall 1980): 333–51.

Mark, Eduard M. "Allied Relations in Iran, 1941–1947: The Origins of a Cold War Crisis," *Wisconsin Magazine of History* 59 (Autumn 1975): 51–63.

McMahon, Robert J. "Eisenhower and Third World Nationalism: A Critique of the Revisionists," *Political Science Quarterly* 101 (October 1986): 453–73.

Melbourne, Roy M. "America and Iran in Perspective: 1953 and 1980," *Foreign Service Journal* 57 (April 1980): 10–17.

Pfau, Richard A. "Avoiding the Cold War: The United States and the Iranian Oil Crisis, 1944," *Essays in History* 18 (1974): 104–14.

———. "Containment in Iran, 1946: The Shift to an Active Policy," *Diplomatic History* 1 (Fall 1977): 359–72.

Ricks, Thomas M. "U.S. Military Missions to Iran, 1943–1978: The Political Economy of Military Assistance," *Iranian Studies* 12 (Summer–Autumn 1979): 163–93.

Rotter, Andrew J. "Gender Relations, Foreign Relations: The United States and South Asia, 1947–1964," *Journal of American History* 81 (September 1994): 518–42.

Shwadran, Benjamin. "The Anglo-Iranian Oil Dispute, 1948–1953," *Middle Eastern Affairs* 5 (1954): 193–231.

Sinclair, Angus. "Iranian Oil," *Middle Eastern Affairs* 2 (1951): 213–24.

Taylor, Graham D. "Debate in the United States over the Control of International Cartels, 1942–1950," *International History Review* 3 (July 1981): 385–98.

Walden, Jerrold L. "The International Petroleum Cartel in Iran—Private Power and the Public Interest," *Journal of Public Law* 11 (Spring 1962): 64–121.

Westwood, Andrew F. "Politics of Distrust in Iran," *Annals of the American Academy of Political and Social Sciences* 358 (March 1965): 123–35.

Books

Abrahamian, Evrand. *Iran Between Two Revolutions*. Princeton, N.J.: Princeton University Press, 1982.

Abrams, Rudy. *Spanning the Century: The Life of W. Averell Harriman, 1891–1986*. New York: Morrow, 1992.

Afshar, Haleh. *Iran: A Revolution in Turmoil*. London: Macmillan, 1985.

Amuzegar, Jahangir. *Iran: An Economic Profile*. Washington, D.C.: Middle East Institute, 1977.

Arjomand, Said Amir. *The Turban for the Crown: The Islamic Revolution in Iran*. New York: Oxford University Press, 1988.

Ambrose, Stephen E. *Eisenhower: The President*. New York: Simon & Schuster, 1984.

Ambrose, Stephen E., with Richard H. Immerman. *Ike's Spies: Eisenhower and the Espionage Establishment*. Garden City, N.Y.: Doubleday, 1981.

Amirsadeghi, Hossein, ed. *Twentieth-Century Iran*. London: Heinemann, 1977.

Amuzegar, Jahangir. *Technical Assistance in Theory and Practice: The Case of Iran.* New York: Praeger, 1966.

Anderson, Irvine H. *ARAMCO, the United States, and Saudi Arabia: A Study in the Dynamics of Foreign Oil Policy, 1933–1950.* Princeton, N.J.: Princeton University Press, 1981.

Anderson, J. R. L. *East of Suez: A Study of Britain's Greatest Trading Enterprise.* London: Hodder & Stoughton, 1969.

Anderson, Robert O. *Fundamentals of the Petroleum Industry.* Norman: University of Oklahoma Press, 1984.

Avery, Peter. *Modern Iran.* New York: Praeger, 1965.

Azimi, Fakhreddin. *Iran: The Crisis of Democracy.* London: I. B. Tauris, 1989.

Bamberg, J. H. *The History of the British Petroleum Company,* vol. 2: *The Anglo-Iranian Years, 1928–1954.* Cambridge, England: Cambridge University Press, 1994.

Baram, Phillip J. *The Department of State and the Middle East, 1919–1945.* Philadelphia: University of Pennsylvania Press, 1978.

Barnet, Richard. *Intervention and Revolution: America's Confrontation with Insurgent Movements Around the World.* New York: World Publishing, 1968.

Behrman, James. *Some Patterns in the Rise of Multinational Enterprise.* Chapel Hill: University of North Carolina Press, 1969.

Beloff, Nora. *Transit of Britain: A Report on Britain's Changing Role in the Postwar World.* London: Collins, 1973.

Betancourt, Rómulo. *Venezuela: Oil and Politics.* Boston: Houghton Mifflin, 1979.

Bill, James A. *The Politics of Iran: Groups, Classes, and Modernization.* Columbus, Ohio: Merrill, 1972.

———. *The Eagle and the Lion: The Tragedy of Iranian-American Relations.* New Haven, Conn.: Yale University Press, 1988.

Bill, James A. and Wm. Roger Louis, eds. *Iranian Nationalism, Musaddiq, and Oil.* Austin: University of Texas Press, 1988.

Blair, John M. *Economic Concentration: Structure, Behavior, and Public Policy.* New York: Harcourt, Brace, Jovanovich, 1972.

———. *The Control of Oil.* New York: Pantheon, 1976.

Brands, H. W. *Inside the Cold War: Loy Henderson and the Rise of the American Empire, 1918–1961.* New York: Oxford University Press, 1991.

Bullock, Alan. *Ernest Bevin, Foreign Secretary, 1945–1951.* New York: Norton, 1983.

Butler, D. E. *The British General Election of 1951.* London: Macmillan, 1952.

Calvocoressi, Peter. *The British Experience, 1945–1975.* London: Bodley Head, 1978.

Chehabi, H. E. *Iranian Politics and Religious Modernism: The Liberation Movement of Iran Under the Shah and Khomeini.* Ithaca, N.Y.: Cornell University Press, 1990.

Chester, Edward W. *United States Oil Policy and Diplomacy: A Twentieth-Century Overview.* Westport, Conn.: Greenwood, 1983.

Chubin, Shahram and Sepehr Zabih. *The Foreign Relations of Iran: A Developing State in a Zone of Great Power Conflict.* Berkeley: University of California Press, 1974.

Coronel, Gustavo. *The Nationalization of the Venezuelan Oil Industry: From Technocratic Success to Political Failure*. Lexington, Mass.: Heath, 1983.

Cottam, Richard W. *Nationalism in Iran*. Pittsburgh, Pa.: University of Pittsburgh Press, 1979.

——. *Iran and the United States: A Cold War Case Study*. Pittsburgh, Pa.: University of Pittsburgh Press, 1988.

Darby, Phillip. *British Defense Policy East of Suez, 1947–1968*. New York: Oxford University Press, 1973.

Diba, Farhad. *Mohammad Mossadegh: A Political Biography*. London: Croom Helm, 1986.

Divine, Robert A. *Eisenhower and the Cold War*. New York: Oxford University Press, 1981.

Donoughue, Bernard and G. W. Jones. *Herbert Morrison: Portrait of a Politician*. London: Weidenfeld and Nicolonson, 1973.

Donovan, John C. *The Cold-Warriors: A Policy-Making Elite*. Lexington, Mass.: Heath, 1974.

Donovan, Robert A. *Conflict and Crisis: The Presidency of Harry S Truman, 1945–1948*. New York: Norton, 1977.

——. *Tumultuous Years: The Presidency of Harry S Truman, 1948–1953*. New York: Norton, 1982.

Eatwell, Roger. *The 1945–1951 Labour Governments*. London: Batsford Academic, 1979.

Edmonds, Robin. *Setting the Mould: The United States and Britain, 1945–1950*. Oxford, England: Clarendon, 1986.

Elm, Mostafa. *Oil, Power, and Principle: Iran's Oil Nationalization and Its Aftermath*. Syracuse, N.Y.: Syracuse University Press, 1992.

Elwell-Sutton, L. P. *Persian Oil: A Study in Power Politics*. London: Lawrence & Wishart, 1955.

Engler, Robert. *The Politics of Oil: Private Power and Democratic Directions*. Chicago: University of Chicago Press, 1961.

Epstein, Leon D. *British Politics in the Suez Crisis*. Urbana: University of Illinois Press, 1964.

Erickson, Edward W. and Leonard Waverman, eds. *The Energy Question: An International Failure of Policy*. Toronto: University of Toronto Press, 1974.

Eveland, Wilbur. *Ropes of Sand: America's Failure in the Middle East*. New York: Norton, 1980.

Fatemi, Faramarz S. *The U.S.S.R. in Iran: The Background History of Russian and American Conflict in Iran and Its Effect on Iranian Nationalism and the Fall of the Shah*. South Brunswick, N.J.: A. S. Barnes, 1980.

Fatemi, Nassrollah S. *Oil Diplomacy, Powderkeg in Iran*. New York: Whittier, 1954.

——. *While the United States Slept*. New York: Cornwall, 1982.

Ferrier, Ronald W. *The History of the British Petroleum Company*, vol. 1: *The Developing Years, 1901–1932*. New York: Cambridge University Press, 1982.

Fesharaki, Fereidun. *Development of the Iranian Oil Industry: International and Domestic Aspects*. New York: Praeger, 1976.

Finnie, David H. *Desert Enterprise: The Middle East Oil Industry in its Local Environment*. Cambridge, Mass.: Harvard University Press, 1958.

Fischer, Michael M. J. *Iran: From Religious Dispute to Revolution*. Cambridge, Mass.: Harvard University Press, 1980.

Fitzsimons, Matthew A. *The Foreign Policy of the British Labour Government, 1945–1951*. Notre Dame, Ind.: University of Notre Dame Press, 1953.

———. *Empire by Treaty: Britain and the Middle East in the Twentieth Century*. Notre Dame, Ind.: University of Notre Dame Press, 1964.

Frye, Richard N. and Lewis V. Thomas. *The United States and Turkey and Iran*. Cambridge, Mass.: Harvard University Press, 1952.

Fugate, Wilbur Lindsay. *Foreign Commerce and the Antitrust Laws*, 3d ed. Boston: Little, Brown, 1982.

Gasiorowski, Mark J. *U.S. Foreign Policy and the Shah: Building a Client State in Iran*. Ithaca, N.Y.: Cornell University Press, 1991.

Ghods, M. Reza. *Iran in the Twentieth Century: A Political History*. Boulder, Colo.: Lynne Rienner, 1989.

Ghosh, Sunil Kanti. *The Anglo-Iranian Oil Dispute: A Study of the Problems of Nationalization of Foreign Investment and Their Impact on International Law*. Calcutta, India: Firma K. L. Mukhopadhjay, 1960.

Goode, James F. *The United States and Iran, 1946–51: The Diplomacy of Neglect*. New York: St. Martin's, 1989.

Gordon, Michael R. *Conflict and Consensus in Labour's Foreign Policy, 1914–1967*. Stanford, Calif.: Stanford University Press, 1969.

Greene, William N. *Strategies of the Major Oil Companies*. Ann Arbor, Mich.: UMI Research Press, 1985.

Hamilton, Charles W. *Americans in the Middle East*. Houston, Texas: Gulf Publishing, 1962.

Harbutt, Fraser J. *The Iron Curtain: Churchill, America, and the Origins of the Cold War*. New York: Oxford University Press, 1986.

Harris, Kenneth. *Attlee*. London: Weidenfield & Nicolson, 1982.

Harris, Nigel. *Competition and the Corporate Society: British Conservatives, the State, and Industry, 1945–1964*. London: Methuen, 1972.

Hartshorn, Jack E. *Politics and World Oil Economies: An Account of the International Oil Industry in Its Political Environment*. New York: Praeger, 1962.

Hathaway, Robert M. *Ambiguous Partnership: Britain and America, 1941–1947*. New York: Columbia University Press, 1981.

Hoffman, John D. *The Conservative Party in Opposition, 1945–1951*. London: MacGibbon & Kee, 1964.

Hoskins, Halford L. *Middle East Oil in United States Foreign Policy*. Washington, D.C.: 1950.

———. *The Middle East: Problem Area in World Politics*. New York: Macmillan, 1957.

Jacoby, Neil H. *Multinational Oil: A Study of Industrial Dynamics*. New York: Macmillan, 1974.

James, Robert Rhodes. *Anthony Eden*. New York: McGraw-Hill, 1987.

Jeffreys-Jones, Rhodri. *The CIA and American Democracy*. New Haven, Conn.: Yale University Press, 1989.

Jones, Geoffrey. *The State and the Emergence of the British Oil Industry*. London: Macmillan, 1981.

Katouzian, Homa. *The Political Economy of Modern Iran: Despotism and Pseudo-Modernism, 1926–1979*. New York: New York University Press, 1981.

———. *Musaddiq and the Struggle for Power in Iran*. London: I. B. Tauris, 1990.

Kaufman, Burton I. *The Oil Cartel Case: A Documentary History of Antitrust Activity in the Cold War Era*. Westport, Conn.: Greenwood, 1978.

———. *Trade and Aid: Eisenhower's Foreign Economic Policy, 1953–1961*. Baltimore: Johns Hopkins University Press, 1982.

Keddie, Nikki R, ed. *Roots of Revolution: An Interpretive History of Modern Iran*. New Haven, Conn.: Yale University Press, 1981.

———. *Religion and Politics in Iran*. New Haven, Conn.: Yale University Press, 1983.

Keddie, Nikki R. and Mark J. Gasiorowski, eds. *Neither East Nor West: Iran, the Soviet Union, and the United States*. New Haven, Conn.: Yale University Press, 1990.

Krasner, Stephen D. *Defending the National Interest: Raw Materials Investments and U.S. Foreign Policy*. Princeton, N.J.: Princeton University Press, 1978.

Krueger, Robert. *The United States and International Oil: A Report for the Federal Energy Administration*. New York: Praeger, 1975.

Kuniholm, Bruce R. *The Origins of the Cold War in the Near East: Great Power Conflict and Diplomacy in Iran, Turkey, and Greece*. Princeton, N.J.: Princeton University Press, 1980.

Kwitny, Jonathan. *Endless Enemies: The Making of an Unfriendly World*. New York: Congdon and Weed, 1984.

Lambton, Ann K. S. *Landlord and Peasant in Persia*. Oxford, England: Oxford University Press, 1953.

Lapping, Brian. *End of Empire*. New York: St. Martin's, 1985.

Leeman, Wayne A. *The Price of Middle East Oil: An Essay in Political Economy*. Ithaca, N.Y.: Cornell University Press, 1962.

Lenczowski, George. *Russia and the West in Iran, 1918–1948: A Study in Big Power Rivalry*. New York: Greenwood, 1968.

Lenczowski, George, ed. *Iran Under the Pahlavis*. Stanford, Calif.: Hoover Institution Press, 1982.

Levy, Walter J. *Oil Strategy and Politics, 1941–1981*. Boulder, Colo.: Westview, 1982.

Longhurst, Henry. *Adventure in Oil: The Story of British Petroleum*. London: Sidgwick and Jackson, 1959.

Longrigg, Stephen H. *Oil in the Middle East: Its Discovery and Development*, 3d ed. London: Oxford University Press, 1968.

Looney, Robert E. *Economic Origins of the Iranian Revolution*. New York: Pergamon, 1982.

Louis, Wm. Roger. *Imperialism at Bay: The United States and the Decolonization of the British Empire, 1941–1945*. New York: Oxford University Press, 1977.

———. *The British Empire in the Middle East, 1945–1951: Arab Nationalism, the United States, and Postwar Imperialism*. New York: Oxford University Press, 1984.

Louis, Wm. Roger and Hedley Bull, eds. *The "Special Relationship": Anglo-American Relations, 1945–1950*. Oxford, England: Clarendon, 1986.

Lytle, Mark H. *The Origins of the Iranian-American Alliance, 1941–1953*. New York: Holmes & Maier, 1987.

McBeth, B. S. *British Oil Policy, 1919–1939*. London: Frank Cass, 1986.

McDonald, Ian S., ed. *Anglo-American Relations Since the Second World War*. New York: St. Martin's, 1974.

McLellan, David S. *Dean Acheson: The State Department Years*. New York: Dodd, Mead, 1976.

Mason, Edward S. and Robert E. Asher, eds. *The World Bank Since Bretton Woods*. Washington, D.C.: Brookings Institution Press, 1973.

Mikdashi, Zuhayr. *A Financial Analysis of Middle Eastern Oil Concessions, 1901–65*. New York: Praeger, 1966.

Mikesell, Raymond F., et al. *Foreign Investment in the Petroleum and Mineral Industries: Case Studies of Investor-Host Country Relations*. Baltimore: Johns Hopkins University Press, 1971.

Miller, Aaron David. *Search for Security: Saudi Arabian Oil and American Foreign Policy, 1939–1949*. Chapel Hill: University of North Carolina Press, 1980.

Milward, Alan S. *The Reconstruction of Western Europe, 1945–1951*. Berkeley: University of California Press, 1984.

Moaddel, Mansoor. *Class, Politics, and Ideology in the Iranian Revolution*. New York: Columbia University Press, 1993.

Monroe, Elizabeth. *Britain's Moment in the Middle East, 1914–1971*, rev. ed. Baltimore: Johns Hopkins University Press, 1981.

Morgan, Kenneth O. *Labour in Power, 1945–1951*. Oxford, England: Clarendon, 1984.

Mosley, Leonard. *Power Play: The Tumultuous World of Middle East Oil, 1890–1973*. London: Weidenfeld and Nicolson, 1973.

Mottahedeh, Roy. *The Mantle of the Prophet: Religion and Politics in Iran*. New York: Simon & Schuster, 1985.

Nash, Gerald D. *United States Oil Policy, 1890–1964: Business and Government in Twentieth Century America*. Pittsburgh, Pa.: University of Pittsburgh Press, 1968.

Northedge, F. S. *Descent from Power: British Foreign Policy, 1945–1973*. London: Allen & Unwin, 1974.

Odell, Peter R. *Oil and World Power*, 7th ed. Middlesex, England: Penguin, 1983.

Ovendale, Ritchie, ed. *The Foreign Policy of the British Labour Governments, 1945–1951*. Leicester, England: Leicester University Press, 1984.

Painter, David S. *Oil and the American Century: The Political Economy of U.S. Foreign Oil Policy, 1941–1954*. Baltimore: Johns Hopkins University Press, 1986.

Parsa, Misagh. *Social Origins of the Iranian Revolution*. New Brunswick, N.J.: Rutgers University Press, 1989.

Penrose, Edith J. *The Large International Firm in Developing Countries: The International Petroleum Industry*. London: Allen & Unwin, 1968.

———. *The Growth of Firms, Middle East Oil, and Other Essays*. London: Frank Cass, 1971.

Rabe, Stephen G. *The Road to OPEC: United States Relations with Venezuela, 1919–1976*. Austin: University of Texas Press, 1982.

Ramazani, Rouhollah K. *Iran's Foreign Policy, 1941–1973: A Study of Foreign Policy in Modernizing Nations.* Charlottesville: University of Virginia Press, 1975.

Rand, Christopher T. *Making Democracy Safe for Oil: Oilmen and the Islamic East.* Boston: Little, Brown, 1975.

Randall, Stephen J. *United States Foreign Oil Policy, 1919–1948: For Profits and Security.* Kingston, Ontario, Canada: McGill-Queen's University Press, 1985.

Rothwell, Victor. *Britain and the Cold War, 1941–1947.* London: Jonathan Cape, 1982.

Rowland, John and Basil Cadman. *Ambassador for Oil: The Life of John, First Baron Cadman.* London: H. Jenkins, 1960.

Rubin, Barry M. *Paved with Good Intentions: The American Experience and Iran.* New York: Oxford University Press, 1980.

Said, Edward W. *Orientalism.* New York: Vintage, 1978.

———. *Culture and Imperialism.* New York: Vintage, 1993.

Saikal, Amin. *The Rise and Fall of the Shah.* Princeton, N.J.: Princeton University Press, 1980.

Samii, Kuross A. *Involvement by Invitation: American Strategies of Containment in Iran.* University Park: Pennsylvania State University Press, 1987.

Sampson, Anthony. *The Seven Sisters: The Great Oil Companies and the World They Shaped.* New York: Viking, 1975.

Schurr, Sam H. and Paul Homan. *Middle Eastern Oil and the Western World: Prospects and Problems.* New York: American Elsevier, 1971.

Seldon, Anthony. *Churchill's Indian Summer: The Conservative Government, 1951–1955.* London: Hodder & Stoughton, 1981.

Shawcross, William. *The Shah's Last Ride: The Fate of an Ally.* New York: Simon & Schuster, 1988.

Shwadran, Benjamin. *The Middle East, Oil, and the Great Powers.* New York: Wiley, 1973.

Sheehan, Michael K. *Iran: The Impact of United States Interests and Policies, 1941–1954.* New York: Gaus, 1968.

Sick, Gary. *All Fall Down: America's Tragic Encounter with Iran.* New York: Viking Penguin, 1986.

Sobel, Robert. *The Age of Giant Corporations: A Macroeconomic History of American Business, 1914–1970.* Westport, Conn.: Greenwood, 1970.

Stempel, John D. *Inside the Iranian Revolution.* Bloomington: Indiana University Press, 1981.

Stocking, George W. *Middle East Oil: A Study in Political and Economic Controversy.* Nashville, Tenn.: Vanderbilt University Press, 1970.

Stoff, Michael B. *Oil, War, and American Security: The Search for a National Policy on Foreign Oil, 1941–1947.* New Haven, Conn.: Yale University Press, 1980.

Supple, Barry, ed. *Essays in British Business History.* New York: Clarendon, 1972.

Taheri, Amir. *Nest of Spies: America's Journey to Disaster in Iran.* London: Hutchinson, 1988.

Tugwell, Franklin. *The Politics of Oil in Venezuela.* Stanford, Calif.: Stanford University Press, 1958.

Tully, Andrew. *CIA: The Inside Story.* New York: William Morrow, 1962.

Vernon, Raymond. *Sovereignty at Bay: The Multinational Spread of U.S. Foreign Enterprises*. New York: Basic Books, 1971.

Verrier, Anthony. *Through the Looking Glass: British Foreign Policy in an Age of Illusions*. London: Jonathan Cape, 1983.

Wilkins, Mira. *The Maturing of Multinational Enterprise: American Business Abroad, 1914–1970*. Cambridge, Mass.: Harvard University Press, 1974.

Williams, Philip M. *Hugh Gaitskell: A Political Biography*. London: Jonathan Cape, 1979.

Williamson, Harold F., et al. *The American Petroleum Industry: The Age of Energy, 1899–1959*. Evanston, Ill.: Northwestern University Press, 1963.

Wright, Denis. *The Persians Amongst the English: Episodes in Anglo-Persian History*. London: I. B. Tauris, 1985.

Yergin, Daniel. *The Prize: The Epic Quest for Oil, Money, and Power*. New York: Simon & Schuster, 1991.

Zabih, Sepehr. *The Communist Movement in Iran*. Berkeley: University of California Press, 1966.

——. *The Mossadegh Era: Roots of the Iranian Revolution*. Chicago: Lake View, 1982.

Zonis, Marvin. *The Political Elite of Iran*. Princeton, N.J.: Princeton University Press, 1971.